OXFORD TEXTBOOKS IN LINGUISTICS

MW01259207

Compositional Semantics

OXFORD TEXTBOOKS IN LINGUISTICS

PUBLISHED

Compositional Semantics
An Introduction to the Syntax/Semantics
Interface
by Pauline Jacobson

The Grammar of Words
An Introduction to Linguistic Morphology
Third edition
by Geert Booij

A Practical Introduction to Phonetics
Second edition
by J. C. Catford

Meaning in Language
An Introduction to Semantics and
Pragmatics
Third edition
by Alan Cruse

Natural Language Syntax
by Peter W. Culicover

Principles and Parameters
An Introduction to Syntactic Theory
by Peter W. Culicover

A Semantic Approach to English Grammar
by R. M. W. Dixon

Semantic Analysis
A Practical Introduction
by Cliff Goddard

Pragmatics
by Yan Huang

The History of Languages
An Introduction
by Tore Janson

Diachronic Syntax
by Ian Roberts

Cognitive Grammar
An Introduction
by John R. Taylor

Linguistic Categorization
Third edition
by John R. Taylor

IN PREPARATION

The Lexicon
An Introduction
by Elisabetta Ježek

Functional Discourse Analysis
by Evelien Keizer

Semantics and Pragmatics
Meaning in Language and Discourse
Second edition
by Kasia M. Jaszczolt

Translation
Theory and Practice
by Kirsten Malmkjaer

Linguistic Typology
Theory, Method, Data
by Jae Jung Song

Compositional Semantics

An Introduction to the Syntax/Semantics Interface

Pauline Jacobson

OXFORD

UNIVERSITY PRESS

OXFORD

UNIVERSITY PRESS

Great Clarendon Street, Oxford, OX2 6DP,
United Kingdom

Oxford University Press is a department of the University of Oxford.
It furthers the University's objective of excellence in research, scholarship,
and education by publishing worldwide. Oxford is a registered trade mark of
Oxford University Press in the UK and in certain other countries

© Pauline Jacobson 2014

The moral rights of the author have been asserted

First Edition published in 2014

Impression: 1

All rights reserved. No part of this publication may be reproduced, stored in
a retrieval system, or transmitted, in any form or by any means, without the
prior permission in writing of Oxford University Press, or as expressly permitted
by law, by licence, or under terms agreed with the appropriate reprographics
rights organization. Enquiries concerning reproduction outside the scope of the
above should be sent to the Rights Department, Oxford University Press, at the
address above

You must not circulate this work in any other form
and you must impose this same condition on any acquirer

Published in the United States of America by Oxford University Press
198 Madison Avenue, New York, NY 10016, United States of America

British Library Cataloguing in Publication Data
Data available

Library of Congress Control Number: 2013957565

ISBN 978–0–19–967714–6 (Hbk.)
978–0–19–967715–3 (Pbk.)

Printed and bound by
CPI Group (UK) Ltd, Croydon CR0 4YY

Links to third party websites are provided by Oxford in good faith and
for information only. Oxford disclaims any responsibility for the materials
contained in any third party website referenced in this work.

To the memory of my parents,
Florence and Nathan Jacobson (Florie and Jake)

Contents

Sections and exercises marked with * are more advanced and/or less central (and on some occasions intended as open-ended speculation). These may be skipped with little or no consequence for later sections.

Part IV: Further Topics

Acknowledgments

This book began life as a series of handouts for my Formal Semantics course in 1998. The handouts grew and were revised over the years until I realized they were trying to become a book. I owe my greatest debt to the students in these classes. I never would have undertaken to write this book were it not for the enthusiasm and insight of my students who have always made teaching Formal Semantics just plain fun. I am also indebted to three scholars whose work has influenced my thinking in ways sometimes obvious and sometimes subtle. The influence of Barbara Partee will be obvious throughout this book. To David Dowty, I owe an understanding of how to think "semantically," and my thinking about Categorial Grammar and its elegance as a theory of the syntax/semantics interface owes much to the work of Emmon Bach. The way of thinking that I learned directly or indirectly from these three semanticists has shaped in various ways the point of view taken in this book, and the way the material is put together.

Oxford University Press provided me with three detailed and extraordinarily helpful referee reports. Probably none of the referees will be satisfied with all of my decisions, but hopefully each will find ways in which their thoughtful comments have greatly improved the manuscript. I thank also Chris Kennedy both for very helpful comments on the manuscript and for "dry-running" parts of it in his courses.

I owe a huge debt to Peter Klecha, who did a heroic job of going through the manuscript in detail—working through all of the exercises to make sure they were doable (indeed sometimes they weren't), to make sure they were not presupposing material not yet introduced (indeed, sometimes they were), and to make sure the formalism was consistent (indeed, sometimes it wasn't). I have been amazed at Peet's ability to see just what a student new to the material could or could not be expected to do, and at his astute reading of the material which saved me from some embarrassing mistakes. I am also extremely indebted to Jackson Golden, who has done a fantastic job in helping to put together the bibliography, and to Christopher Mescher for help in compiling the index. I thank NSF for funding on my grant BCS 0646081; although this is a textbook it also contains much of my own research which was funded under the grant.

Finally, I thank Michael Rosen, for always encouraging this project, for putting up with its writing over the last two years, and for everything else.

Foreword: On Using this Book

Each instructor will no doubt find her or his own most useful path through this book (or parts of it), but some suggestions might be helpful. The book obviously contains more material than can realistically be covered in a single semester's introductory formal semantics course. In teaching this material myself in introductory formal semantics courses (with a mix of graduate students and advanced undergraduates) I have found that I can teach most of the material through Part III plus Chapter 16 and a brief foray into one other of additional topics in Part IV, although I do not go through the material in the full detail given here. (One reason for writing such a book is so that students can get more detail on their own.) Hence, an instructor might choose to do (most of) Chapters 1–15, and one or two additional chapters in Part IV. One plan for this is to spend about three to four weeks on the material through Chapter 5, one week on Chapters 6 and 7 combined, and then approximately one chapter a week for the rest (Chapter 12 could take less than a week and Chapter 15 probably more). Depending on the students' background, another reasonable semester's goal might instead be to work in detail through Part II and then approach some of the material in Part III. The material would also probably work as the full text for a two-quarter or one-year semantics course (perhaps supplemented at the end with some readings from original sources), and the later material can be the basis of a more advanced course, supplemented with readings from the literature. I hope that the book might also be used by students already familiar with basic formal semantics but not familiar with the viewpoint of Direct Compositionality (or not familiar with Categorial Grammar); such a student can systematically work through the material from what would be for them a new point of view. This could easily be part of a second-semester or second-year semantics course.

There are some choice points in the order in which to read the material. I myself always teach Chapter 16 (on Negative Polarity Items) right after Chapter 10. This is because once students have learned about generalized quantifiers, they have the tools to approach the domain of Negative Polarity Items. I feel it is an especially satisfying reward—after working through much technical apparatus—to apply the apparatus to a domain that is rich and so beautifully illustrates the relevance of the formal tools to the distribution of items that are entirely natural and conversational. So right after Chapter 10 there is a fork point: one can either go on to Chapter 11 or digress and read Chapter 16. I have set it up so that neither chapter (nor subsequent ones) presupposes the other except in occasional minor ways. Chapter 16 could also be read between Parts II and III. Moreover, the chapters in Part IV can be read in any order.

The decision to include two theoretical points of view—the Direct Compositional view and a view that instead uses Logical Form—poses some difficulties. While I would love to have written the book purely from the point of view of Direct Compositionality, I feel it would be doing students a disservice to not be able to read and appreciate the rich body of work that uses the notion of a Logical Form. My solution, then, was to illustrate these two different viewpoints side by side with respect to a key body of data (relative clauses, quantifiers in object positions, scopes, and binding). But this could be confusing for a student new to this material, so I have set it up in such a way that a student can—on a first pass—work through the relevant chapters carefully from just one of the points of view, and later go back to work through the other. In general, the material on the other point of view will need to be skimmed as it will sometimes contain empirical data of relevance to the discussion, but the technical details can be postponed.

Another difficult decision centered on the material on binding. As is pointed out in the text, I give two versions of pronominal binding: a fairly standard one that makes use of Logical Form and variables, and one making no use of variables in the semantics set within the Direct Compositional framework. (This is based in part although not exclusively on my own work on variable-free semantics.) But this makes it appear as if Direct Compositionality is crucially tied in with a variable-free semantics. It is not, and in an earlier draft (as well as in the way I have often taught this material) I also exposit an intermediate position: one which is Direct Compositional but does make use of variables. In the end, I decided that to develop three approaches to a single domain was bound to be just too much for an introductory book. With some regret, then, I decided it was prudent to remove the discussion of the intermediate position. Still, I feel it is worthwhile to be able to access this material—both for the sake of historical accuracy (it was a well-developed position) and to understand that the issue of whether or not to have variables is to some extent independent of the issue of Direct Compositionality. For those who are not fans of the variable-free approach, I don't want to leave the impression that if variable-free semantics is wrong, so is Direct Compositionality: there is a very good Direct Compositional semantics of pronouns using variables. So in order to allow access to a discussion of that intermediate position, I have made it available on the textbook website, which is <http://sites.clps.brown.edu/compositional.sem>.

One further decision that some have found unusual is to delay the formal introduction of the lambda calculus until Chapter 9 which is the end of Part I. There is a reason for this. I want to stress that this is just a convenient notation for writing model-theoretic objects, and not some level of representation that is a crucial part of the theory. (For example, lambda conversion is not intended as a rule of grammar, but just as a way to convert one way of writing a model-theoretic object into another way of writing it.) To stress the difference between the notation and the actual meanings of expressions, I have always found it helpful to try to use ordinary prose in naming model-theoretic objects wherever possible, even when this prose leads to cumbersome descriptions like "the set of all sets that contain the dog-set as a subset." Eventually, of course, English prose gets too cumbersome (and is not sufficiently unambiguous) and we need a better notation (hence the lambda calculus). But I find that insisting on prose whenever possible alongside with a clearer notation is helpful—not only for understanding that notation is just that, but also to get a better intuition about fancy objects like sets of sets or functions from sets of sets to truth values. However, an instructor who prefers to make use of the lambda calculus earlier can move Chapter 9; it could have been placed after Chapter 6.

For the student with no prior background in elementary set theory, I have included an appendix to Chapter 1 that contains all of the basic notions of set theory, ordered pairs, relations, and functions that are necessary for the later material. There is quite a bit of material there, and so I would recommend that a student with no relevant background just read the discussion of sets first, and then come back to subsequent notions as they appear in the text. It is often easiest to absorb this material when one has a reason to do so, and when it is in the context of the fuller semantic theory for which it is being pressed into service.

A word about the sections and exercises marked with an asterisk. These are more advanced and any of them truly can be skipped (especially on a first pass through the material). They are intended to provide greater coverage and depth for the ambitious and curious student, and the starred exercises can be quite challenging. Some—especially toward the end—are actually open-ended; I hope that a few might even spawn some interesting research topics for students. In any case, the starred exercises are there to be enjoyed and not to be frustrating, so I would recommend picking and choosing wisely according to a student's level of interest and ambition. I do hope that some of these will be fun.

Finally, as noted above, there is a website for this book at <http://sites.clps. brown.edu/compositional.sem>. It contains the supplementary material on binding and will be updated from time to time with other supplementary material, along with errata as they are discovered.

PART I

Foundational Concepts:
Building a Fragment

1

Introduction

1.1. Goals

This book stems from a belief that linguistic semantics is a beautiful field, that the tools used to study formal semantics have yielded a rich body of results about fascinating and subtle data, that the field continues to produce exciting new insights at an impressive rate,[1] and that there are simple and

---

[1] Readers wishing a taste of many of the ongoing developments in formal semantics and in the syntax/semantics interface might want to look at the journals *Linguistics and Philosophy* (Springer), *Natural Language Semantics* (Springer), *Journal of Semantics* (Oxford University Press), and *Semantics and Pragmatics* (online journal, available at <http://semprag.org/>), among many other journals. Regular conferences at which cutting-edge research is presented include the annual Semantics and Linguistic Theory (SALT) conference, Sinn und Bedeutung (also annual), the biannual Amsterdam Colloquium for Language, Logic, and Information, and Semantics of Underrepresented Languages of the Americas, as well as most of the more general regular linguistics conferences. Of course, most of the work in these venues will not be accessible to a student just learning formal semantics, but it is hoped that this book will give a large part of the necessary background for following at least some of this research. In any case, a glance at the list of papers in

elegant tools to model how the syntax and semantics of a natural language work together. We begin with a very elementary "fragment" of English and proceed to expand it further and further—adding tools as needed but aiming to keep the basic machinery relatively simple. The goal of proceeding in this way is to account for a domain of data which is sufficiently rich as to show the excitement of studying formal semantics and its interaction with syntax. We note one limitation from the outset: this book concentrates entirely on the analysis of English. The project of modeling the semantics and the syntax/semantics interaction of any single language already provides such a rich set of results that one can hopefully find this limitation justified for an introductory book like this. In fact, the results that have been gleaned from a detailed modeling of one language have in recent years allowed the field to expand so as to provide a wealth of analyses of other languages.[2] This book hopes to give the foundation to approach that literature.

1.1.1. Compositional semantics and (some of) the goals of semantic theory

One of the most striking and fundamental properties of language—any language—is that speakers have the ability to produce *and understand* an unlimited number of expressions that they have never produced or heard before (indeed many of these will have never before been uttered by anyone). This simple point is stressed in just about every introductory linguistics textbook, often phrased this way: "A speaker of a language is able to recognize as well-formed an unlimited number of expressions that s/he has never heard before." Examples that demonstrate this are easy to construct. One can, for instance, note the existence of expressions like those in (1):

any of these venues can give the reader a taste of the richness of the domain of inquiry within linguistic semantics.

  [2] Much cross-linguistic semantic work can be found in the journals and conference proceedings cited in footnote 1. An early edited volume on this is Bach et al.'s *Quantification in Natural Languages.* There is now also an annual conference Semantics of Underrepresented Languages of the Americas with published conference proceedings. And many of the specialized conferences on individual languages and language families regularly include work on semantics.

(1) a. the tallest linguistics major
 b. the tallest linguistics major who is graduating in December
 c. the tallest linguistics major who is graduating in December who is enrolled in formal semantics
 d. the tallest linguistics major who is graduating in December who is enrolled in formal semantics who took phonology last semester...

One can keep forming longer and longer expressions like this by adding new relative clauses (each of the phrases that begin with *who* here is what is commonly known as a *relative clause*). But while this is often put in terms of a speaker's ability to recognize that these are well-formed, that is surely only part of the story. Even more interesting (at least to a semanticist) is the fact that speakers know how to *interpret* these expressions. The rule system that speakers have unconsciously learned is hardly just a system to determine whether a given string of words is an expression of the language in question (here English); language would be quite useless if it were just a collection of meaningless strings.

And so, in modeling what a speaker of English "knows" (in an unconscious sense, of course) about her/his language we want to predict how it is that s/he can understand expressions like those in (1) no matter how many relative clauses they contain. Thus speakers obviously have as part of their knowledge a finite set of basic items—call these the *words* and call the collection of the basic items *the lexicon*. (Here and for most of this text we ignore the distinction between words and morphemes.) Since the lexicon is finite, the meanings of the basic items can be learned on a case-by-case basis. But this obviously cannot be the case for the larger expressions: there has to be some systematic set of principles that speakers have that allows them to understand their meanings on the basis of the meanings of the smaller parts (ultimately the words) that make them up. This is the system which is called the *compositional semantics*—and one of the jobs of a theory of the semantics (of any language) is to model the rules and/or principles which allow speakers to understand an unlimited number of expressions. This book is primarily about just this.

Let's look a bit more at the expressions in (1). When a speaker utters any of these expressions—perhaps as part of a fuller sentence like in (2)—the act of uttering these expressions takes place in a fuller discourse context, and we understand them relative to facts about that context:

(2) We need to make sure to order academic regalia which is long enough to fit the tallest linguistics major (who is graduating in December (who...))

The role of context will be discussed more formally at various points in the text, but the informal notion of a speech or discourse context is clear enough. So suppose we are using the expressions in (1) in a context in which it is obvious that we are concerned with the students at Brown University. Given this (or any other context), we can see that any speaker of English immediately knows some interesting facts about these expressions—facts which our model of the compositional semantics needs to account for. Take for instance (1a). It refers to some unique individual.[3] The hearer may well not know who exactly that is—in fact the speaker might not either (as is clear in a context like (2)). But both parties assume that there is a particular individual (and only one) referred to by each of these expressions. And there are many other inferences that can be drawn from these. For example, we immediately know that if the individual described by (1a) is Nora, then either she's also the individual described by (1b) or else she is not graduating in December. Moreover, if Nora is not the person picked out by (1b) then whoever that person is, s/he must be shorter than Nora. Similarly, with each successively longer phrase we either refer to the same person, or to one who is shorter. Suppose that Zorba is the person described by (1b). We know that he is shorter than Nora, and also know that if he is not the person described by (1c) then he is not enrolled in formal semantics. And whoever the (1c) person is—let's say Otto—Otto must be shorter than Zorba. The addition of each successive relative clause either keeps the referent constant or allows shorter and shorter people to "rise to the top." This kind of knowledge is automatic and immediate, and it is the job of a model of the compositional semantics to explicitly account for inferences like this.

We won't give a serious account of any of this at this point, but can hint at one possible account. Suppose that an expression like *linguistics major* refers to some set of individuals. (Readers not familiar with basic notions of set theory should consult the Appendix to this chapter.) When this set is put together with *the tallest* (pretend that *the tallest* is a single word here), the entire expression ends up referring to the tallest member of that set. Nothing

---

[3] In reality there could conceivably be two individuals of exactly the same height. But use of the expressions in (1) does seem to assume that there is a unique referent for these. This is sometimes called a *presupposition*; these are rather odd expressions if the speaker knows that there are two individuals with exactly the same height (in that case the speaker might have said *the two tallest linguistics majors*).

surprising so far. But what is more interesting is what happens with the addition of further relative clauses. It seems plausible that something like *who is graduating in December* also refers to a set (obviously, the set of December graduates). The above facts will make sense if the compositional semantics first combines the two sets (the set of linguistics majors and the set of December graduates) and *intersects* them to give a new set. (The *intersection* of two sets is all things that are in both sets; again see the Appendix.) So (1b) ends up picking out the tallest member of that set. It is now possible to demonstrate that the system correctly predicts that if the referent of (1b) is not Nora, it can only be because she is not graduating in December. For if Nora is taller than anyone in the linguistics major set (call that L) then she is taller than anyone in the intersection of L with the December graduates (call that D). After all, everyone who is in that intersection of L and D is also in L. So if Nora is not the referent of (1b) it can only be that she's not in the intersection of D and L, and since she's in L (by assumption) it follows that she can't be in D. It also follows that if (1b) refers to Zorba, he must be shorter than Nora. By the definition of intersection, if Zorba is in the intersection of D and L he is in L, but we already know that Nora is taller than everyone else in L. All of this is very simple logic that we—the linguists—can work out in the form of an informal proof as above. It could also be worked more formally if one were so inclined. Pedantic though it may seem, it shows that our compositional procedure (which involves intersecting two sets) can be used to correctly model inferences that speakers of English effortlessly make.

Moreover, the appeal here is that this is perfectly general and extends no matter how many new relative clauses are added. Take (1c). The semantics set-up above extends immediately to this. The new relative clause in (1c) is *who is enrolled in formal semantics*. This picks out yet another set—and so this now intersects with the set that we already formed for (1b). The fact that the referent of (1c) can either be Zorba or someone shorter than Zorba follows by the same logic shown above; the reader can work out the details. And the procedure can be repeated over and over no matter how many relative clauses are introduced.

1.1. Because this example is just meant to illustrate the notion of a *compositional semantics*, we have made some assumptions about the order in which the semantics put things together without justifying them. Suppose that rather than the way it was set up here, the meanings of the two relative clauses (1c) first combined, and then that combined with *linguistics major*. Would that make any difference to the basic semantic compositional picture that we have set up here? Would the procedure extend correctly to (1d)?

1.1.2. Direct Compositionality—and its role in this text

This book has a rather ambitious set of goals. On the one hand, I intend this to be a stand-alone text for anyone wishing to have an introduction to formal semantics, compositional semantics, or what is commonly known as *the syntax/semantics interface*. In other words, we will be asking (as in the above example) what a compositional semantics might look like: how can we model the tools available (again, of course, unconsciously) to speakers of a language that allow them to compute meanings of larger expressions from the meanings of the smaller ones that make them up. What are the formal ways in which meanings combine? And what are the types of objects that we need in order to model that? (For example, the discussion above shows that some simple tools of set theory can be useful.)

But while most semanticists agree that (in general) the meaning of a larger expression is built in some systematic way from the meanings of the parts that make it up, just exactly how the syntactic system of a language and the compositional semantics work together is a matter of considerable controversy, and is one of the central questions addressed in this book. And so this book takes one particular point of view on this: the point of view known as *Direct Compositionality*. This view was explored perhaps most notably in Montague (1970) and was either generally accepted or at least taken as a serious desideratum in much of the work in linguistic formal semantics throughout the 1970s and 1980s (particularly work in what was then known as the Montague Grammar program). It was also taken as the foundation for semantics in syntactic theories such as Generalized Phrase Structure Grammar (Gazdar, Klein, Pullum, and Sag 1985), and is assumed in a large body within current grammatical theories that go under the rubric of Categorial Grammar, Type-Logical Grammar, and other related theories.

To elucidate, a fairly uncontroversial claim is that the grammar of any natural language is a system of rules (or principles, if one prefers) that define the set of well-formed expressions of the language (i.e., the syntax) and a set of rules (or principles) pairing these with meanings (i.e., the semantics). The hypothesis of Direct Compositionality is a simple one: the two systems work in tandem. Each expression that is proven well-formed in the syntax is assigned a meaning by the semantics, and the syntactic rules or principles which prove an expression as well-formed are paired with the semantics which assign the expression a meaning. (An interesting consequence of this view is that every well-formed syntactic expression does have a meaning.[4]) It is not only the case that every well-formed *sentence* has a meaning, but also each local expression ("constituent") within the sentence that the syntax defines as well-formed has a meaning. Of course putting it this way is arguably not much more than just a slogan: the empirical content of this depends in part on just how the syntax works and what one takes to be a *meaning*. This will be filled in as we proceed. It might also seem at first glance that the hypothesis of Direct Compositionality is a fairly trivial one. But in fact it is not always immediately obvious how to give a Direct Compositional analysis. Even the example in 1.1.1 is a case in point. If the syntax and semantics work together, then the analysis given above leads to the conclusion that *in the syntax* a relative clause like *who is graduating in December* combines with *linguistics major* rather than with *the tallest linguistics major*. But this very question regarding the syntax of relative clauses has been debated in the literature since the 1960s, and many researchers have claimed that the syntactic constituent structure of *the tallest linguistics major who is graduating next year* is not the structure that was used above for the semantic analysis. We will actually revisit this particular question in later chapters (see, e.g., section 13.2). So one of the goals of this book will be to see what it takes to give Direct Compositional analyses of a variety of constructions.

While the material in this book is generally exposited from the Direct Compositional point of view (along with discussion of the challenges to this hypothesis), the book is also intended to be a perfectly reasonable

---

[4] Of course one of the earliest arguments in Generative Grammar *for* divorcing the syntax from the semantics (and thus a putative argument *against* Direct Compositionality) is based on the claim that there are well-formed expressions that don't have any meaning (Chomsky 1957). This is addressed in section 7.1.

stand-alone textbook for any formal semantics course. Thus it is suitable for any linguistics student or linguist wanting a ground-up introduction to formal semantics, and for a philosophy or logic student wanting a background in formal semantics within linguistics. In the service of being a stand-alone text in modern formal semantic theory, the book will, where relevant, also develop the mechanics of at least one fairly standard non-Direct Compositional theory of the syntax/semantics interface. This is done especially in Part III (Chapters 13–15) where some phenomena are discussed from both direct and non-Direct Compositional points of view. There are several reasons for expositing parallel Direct and non-Direct Compositional accounts of some domains. One is to enable readers to approach the wide range of literature written from either point of view. Second, this allows for a serious comparison of two different approaches. Third, learning more than one set of details for the analysis of any construction allows for a deeper understanding of the basic generalizations and results—generalizations which often transcend the particulars of one theoretical implementation. Finally, a student who has already learned formal semantics from a non-Direct Compositional point of view can hopefully also profit from this book by seeing an interesting fragment of English explicitly analyzed from the Direct Compositional point of view.

1.2. A brief note on the history of semantics within modern linguistic theory

The subfield of semantics as a core field in modern linguistic theory is relatively recent and is one of the fastest growing subfields.[5] Early work within the general enterprise of generative grammar had little to say about semantics. To be sure, by the end of about the 1960s and the early 1970s there was considerable discussion as to how the syntax and the semantics interacted; such discussion was mostly framed in terms of a debate between *Generative Semantics* (see, e.g., McCawley 1971; Lakoff 1971) and *Interpretive Semantics* (see Chomsky 1970; Jackendoff 1972). We will not discuss the content of that debate here, but much of the work framed within these

---

[5] A much more extensive and authoritative history of the development of formal semantics within modern linguistic theory can be found in Partee (forthcoming).

two competing points of view did not incorporate a systematic view of the semantics itself. Of course, the linguistics literature during that period contained many seminal observations about semantic notions such as scope, negation, and "binding," but these were generally not embedded within a full-blown theory of semantics designed to capture semantic notions like entailment and truth conditions (see Chapter 2), although they easily could have been embedded into such a theory. The fact that semantics was not taken a subfield in and of itself during this period comes—at least in part— from Noam Chomsky's emphasis on syntax during the early development of generative grammar. Chomsky (1957) explicitly rejects the notion that semantics is relevant in the construction of grammars, and this notion persisted for quite some time.

It is probably fair to say that modern formal semantics as a subfield within linguistic theory began in the early to mid-1970s with the cross-fertilization of linguistic theory and philosophy of language (including semantics) sparked by Barbara Partee, Richmond Thomason, David Lewis, and others. Partee's work was a particularly influential bridge between linguistics and philosophy as she had originally been a student of Chomsky's at MIT and always had a strong interest in the connections between language and logic, and hence in topics like quantifiers, negation, etc. As an assistant professor at UCLA, she became acquainted with the seminal work of Richard Montague, a philosopher and logician who (among his many other contributions within philosophy and logic) had a major interest in modeling the semantics (and the syntax/semantics interaction) of natural language (although Montague himself dealt only with English). In fact, the program of Direct Compositionality is advocated in his work (see especially Montague 1970). We will have more to say about his specific contributions as this book proceeds; for now, we note that one of the appeals of his work from the point of view of a linguist was his notion that the semantic composition of natural language reflects and respects its syntax. Partee saw the relevance of Montague's work to linguistic theory and wrote a series of papers aimed at synthesizing some of the insights from Montague's work with results within Transformational Grammar (see, for example, Partee 1973). At the same time, the appearance of Lewis (1970), Stalnaker and Thomason (1973), and other work in the philosophy of language also helped launch modern formal semantics and cement its connection to linguistic theory. Such work within philosophy as well as Partee's early group of students (both at UCLA and later at the University of Massachusetts) continued the tradition, broadening the domain of inquiry and results. From there was born the enterprise known as Montague grammar[6] which eventually gave rise to the more general subfield of formal semantics. Montague himself died in 1971,[7] and the field of formal semantics evolved in many ways quite different from the original work in Montague grammar. Nonetheless, many of the basic tools of linguistic formal semantics as it is developed to this day stem from some of this early work cited above. Since the late 1970s the field has blossomed, and is now within linguistics generally considered as one of the core areas along with at least phonology and syntax.

1.3. The notion of a "fragment" and its use in this text

Inspired by the work of Montague in papers such as Montague (1973), much work in formal semantics within the 1970s and 1980s took it as axiomatic that a goal was to formulate fully explicit grammars (in both syntactic and semantic detail) of the fragment of the language one is concerned with (English in most such work). The term "fragment" got extended to mean not only the portion of the language being modeled, but also the portion of the grammar being proposed as an explicit account of the facts. The strategy of writing fragments (of grammars) has the advantage of giving an explicit theory which makes testable predictions, and of making theory and/or proposal comparison easier.

Unfortunately, the goal of formulating fully explicit fragments went out of style during the last two decades or so. This is in part due to the fact that linguistic theories often promised that many of the particular details did not need to be stated as they would fall out from very general principles. It is certainly reasonable to hope that this is ultimately true, but the relevant principles often go unstated or are stated only rather vaguely, making it extremely difficult to really compare proposals and/or evaluate theories and theoretical claims. Having rules and principles be as general as possible is, of course, highly desirable. But this does not mean that they should not be

---

[6] An excellent introduction to the general program of Montague semantics and an explication especially of Montague (1973) can be found in Dowty, Wall, and Peters (1981).

[7] Montague was murdered on March 7, 1971. No arrest was ever made in conjunction with the murder.

formulated explicitly—only that more mileage will be gotten out of explicit formulations.

The present text is therefore committed to trying to revive the notion of explicit fragment construction. We cannot promise to give every detail of the domain of English syntax and semantics we are trying to model. Some parts will be left tentative, some stated informally, and some simply omitted. Nonetheless, the goal is to give a reasonable amount of an explicit fragment. We will therefore periodically take stock by summarizing the fragment constructed so far, and a full summary is provided at the end of Part III.

*1.4. An intriguing puzzle

This introductory chapter concludes with an illustration of a puzzle, a solution to which is proposed in section 15.6. However, the goal here is not to champion any one particular solution, and readers may safely skip this section and return to the data only in section 15.6. But we include this in the introductory remarks for the reader who wants a preview of just what kinds of complex and subtle data a theory of syntax and semantics ultimately hopes to account for. To fully appreciate the particular puzzle here, one should keep the following in mind. The contrasts are quite real; the judgments have been checked with many speakers over the years by myself and many others. Yet—like other subtle facts in syntax, phonology, and semantics—these are not generalizations which we have ever been consciously taught nor even generalizations that most of us are even aware of until we see them in a linguistics course (or book). What, then, is there about our unconscious knowledge of the grammatical system that predicts these judgments? This is the sort of puzzle that theories of semantics and its interaction with syntax ultimately seek to solve.

So, consider what we will call the *A-B-C party scenario*. I go to a small party consisting of only myself and three married couples: Alice and Abe, Betty and Bert, and Cathy and Carl. I learn that Alice and Abe met each other only a few years ago, and similarly for Cathy and Carl. But interestingly, I also find out that Betty and Bert have been sweethearts since childhood. I like Betty a lot, and spend a good part of the evening talking to her. The next day, you ask me how I enjoyed the party and if there was anyone that I especially enjoyed meeting. I certainly can answer with (3):

(3)   Oh yes, I especially enjoyed talking to Betty.

But now suppose that I can't remember Betty's name, although I do remember that her husband's name is Bert. I can answer with either (4a) or (4b):

(4)   a. Oh yes, I especially enjoyed talking to—oh, I can't remember her name— you know, the woman who is married to Bert.
      b. Oh yes, I especially enjoyed talking to—oh, I can't remember her name— you know, the wife of Bert.

((4b) would sound more natural if we substituted *Bert's wife* for *the wife of Bert*; this will not impact on the ultimate point and the exposition is simplified using (4b).)

Now, let us tweak the scenario slightly and assume that I am one of those people who just doesn't remember names very well. As a result, I remember neither Betty's name nor Bert's name, although I do remember the interesting fact that they are the only couple at the party who have been sweethearts since childhood. As an answer to your question, (5) would be quite natural:

(5)   Oh yes, I especially enjoyed talking to—oh, I can't remember her name—you know, the woman who is married to her childhood sweetheart.

But what is striking is that I can't answer with (6):

(6)   *Oh yes, I especially enjoyed talking to—oh I can't remember her name—you know, the wife of her childhood sweetheart.

(We are taking liberties with the * notation here. This is generally used in works in syntax to indicate something that is ill-formed. (6) in fact is fine, just not on the intended reading; and we will continue to notate a sentence with an asterisk in front of it when we mean "bad on a particular reading" provided that it is clear what the intended reading is.) It should be noted that some speakers find the contrast rather subtle but there is general agreement that (6) is stranger than (5).

All of these examples contain various extra material (the parentheticals, etc.) which are there to make them sound natural and conversational. But as we proceed it will be convenient to strip away the parts that are irrelevant to figuring out the semantics, so we can recast (6) as (7)—also impossible as an answer to the question and in this context:

(7)   *I especially enjoyed talking to the wife of her childhood sweetheart.

Of course, (7) is a perfectly good sentence, but it cannot be used in our party scenario as a way to identify Betty.

Since some readers do find the contrast subtle, two points are worth noting. First, one should resist the temptation to recast (7) in one's mind as *I especially enjoyed talking to the one who's the wife of her childhood sweetheart* or *I especially enjoyed talking to the woman who's the wife of her childhood sweetheart*. That would be cheating; the point is not to find a closely related way to say the same thing but to notice that the actual way in (7) contrasts with *I especially enjoyed talking to the woman who is married to her childhood sweetheart* (and contrasts with the above variants too). As to why these variants are good, we return to that shortly. Moreover, while the contrasts above may be subtle for some speakers, there is a related mystery where the facts dramatically pop out. Thus take (8) in the same scenario, where the only people at issue are Alice, Betty, and Cathy:

(8)   Betty is the only woman who is married to her childhood sweetheart.

This can be making two different claims. The obvious one in this scenario is that Cathy is not married to Cathy's childhood sweetheart, and Alice is not married to Alice's childhood sweetheart. The other is the "non-polygamous" reading: it asserts that Bert (or whoever Betty's husband might be) has only one wife. Since we (generally) assume that people have just one wife, this reading (given standard assumptions) is not the first one that someone would think of since it is less likely to be conveying any interesting information. But despite the fact that the non-polygamous reading is the less obvious one for (8), it is the only reading (or at least the one that pops out first) for (9):

(9)   Betty is the only wife of her childhood sweetheart.

Why should that be? We'll put (8) and (9) aside for the moment, and return to the simpler case of (7).

So the mystery is why (7) is bad as a way to identify Betty. This is especially puzzling in that both (4b) and (5) are perfectly good—or, to give their stripped-down versions, (10) and (11) are both fine. Each one differs minimally from our bad case, yet neither of these two has any problem.

(10)   I especially enjoyed talking to the woman who is married to her childhood sweetheart.

(11)   I especially enjoyed talking to the wife of Bert.

So surely there is nothing incoherent or wrong with the meaning that (7) is trying convey, for (10) is just a slightly different form and conveys exactly this meaning. Hence the puzzle has something to do with the mapping between syntax and semantics: why one is a good way to package the relevant information while the other is not.

We can informally recast the puzzle in the following way. Compare the two expressions *the woman who is married to Bert* and *the wife of Bert*. (Following a long tradition within linguistics, we will refer to these as NPs, which comes from "noun phrases." They are also in much modern literature referred to as DPs, for "determiner phrases," but we stick to the more traditional terminology in this text.)[8] Both of these can correspond to meanings that we can (roughly and informally) represent as (12):

(12)   the x: x is a woman and x is married to Bert

But while the object NP in (10) can be represented as in (11), the object NP in (7) cannot:

(13)   the x: x is a woman and x is married to x's childhood sweetheart

The basic phenomenon here was discussed in, among others, Jacobson (1977) (where it was called *Langendoen's constraint*), Chomsky (1981 under the rubric of *i-within-i condition*), and many since. As there seems to be nothing wrong with the meaning, we can assume that the phenomenon in question has something to do with the way the syntax and semantics interact.

Notice that we have given a kind of formula (and one that uses a "variable" *x*) to represent the meanings in question, but for now we should think of these simply as placeholders to bring out the intuition. After all, recasting *her* in the above examples as *x* doesn't really immediately give us the tools for computing the meanings of the expression: we have traded a

---

[8] In theories which use the term DP, the NP is used instead to refer to material after the Determiner; e.g., *mother of Romeo* in an expression like *the mother of Romeo*. Here we will be calling this simply N (i.e., a "noun") and allowing terms like N to refer both to simple material consisting of just one word and to complex material. This is discussed further in Chapter 6. We are aware that this will initially cause some confusion to a reader who is used to using "NP" to mean a noun and its complement, but it is well worth becoming fluent in both sets of terminologies. The terminology here is the traditional one found in large amounts of literature not only in syntax and semantics but in neighboring fields like psycholinguistics, philosophy, cognitive science, etc.

pronoun *her* for a variable x. But this accomplishes little until we have a way to think about what a variable like x means. (Indeed this is explored in detail in Chapters 9 and 15, including developing an alternative view that does not make use of variables in the semantics.) We thus caution that formulas like (12) and (13) are best seen simply as informal and helpful ways to bring out the intended meanings. Similarly, one often sees indices used in the literature as a way to bring this out; one will find discussions using the notation in (14) and (15) to make the point, where the indexation in (14) indicates a good possible reading for the NP while (15) cannot be understood in the intended way:

(14)   the woman$_i$ who$_i$ is married to her$_i$ childhood sweetheart

(15)   *the wife$_i$ of her$_i$ childhood sweetheart

Much work in grammatical theory actually assumes that NPs and pronouns come with (obviously silent) indices in the syntax; here we will be using indices from time to time simply as a way to notate intended readings without any commitment to their being actual pieces of grammatical machinery.

Before leaving this (for now), there's one other interesting point to notice. However we ultimately state the principle, the claim is that an NP like *the wife of her childhood sweetheart* cannot correspond to the meaning shown earlier in (13):

(13)   the x: x is a woman and x is married to x's childhood sweetheart

But one might think that this is not really correct, since it is in fact just fine to use (16) as a way to identify Betty:

(16)   I especially enjoyed meeting the woman who is the wife of her childhood sweetheart.

This point was made earlier; many speakers on reading (7) tend to recast it in their minds as (16). Similarly, (17) is impeccable on the understanding where *her* is Betty:

(17)   Betty is the wife of her childhood sweetheart.

But a close reflection reveals that this does not threaten the generalization. Again, using indices or variables simply as a convenient way to elucidate the point, it is easy to see in (17) that *her* need not be "coindexed with" (or "correspond to the same variable as") *wife* but rather it just refers directly to *Betty*. That is, we can represent it as in (18a) using indices, or as in (18b) using the more spelled-out formula (though still quite informal).

(18)   a. Betty$_j$ is [$_{NP}$ the wife$_i$ of her$_j$ childhood sweetheart].
       b. Betty, y [y = the x: x is a woman and x is married to y's childhood sweetheart]

Since we are asserting identity between Betty and the person married to Betty's childhood sweetheart, it of course follows that Betty is married to Betty's childhood sweetheart and so the full sentence (16) will end up with the relevant meaning.[9] But the claim that the object NP itself (*the wife of her childhood sweetheart*) does have the meaning represented in (12) is not threatened. The same point holds for (17), whose meaning can be represented as (19a) or (19b).

(19)   a. the woman$_j$ who$_j$ is the wife$_i$ of her$_j$ childhood sweetheart
       b. the y: y is a woman and y = the x: x is a woman and x is married to y's childhood sweetheart

Is there a way to confirm that this is the right sort of explanation for these apparent counterexamples? Indeed there is, and it centers on the contrast between (8) and (9) which was discussed earlier. We leave it to the interested reader in the exercise to play with this and get a sense of why (8) is ambiguous and (9) is not. Having completed that, one should be able to see how it is that this gives support for the explanation offered above as to why (17) does not threaten the claim that *the wife of her childhood sweetheart* cannot correspond to the meaning shown informally in (12).

---

*1.2. Work out—using the informal representations either with indices or the representations with variables—why it is that (7) is ambiguous and (8) is not. Of course you will need to think a bit about how to treat *only*, but nothing very complex is required. You can be perfectly informal in your treatment of *only*, but you should be able to get a feel for why these two differ.

---

[9] This general observation—although for a slightly different case—was made in Postal (1970) who distinguished between "presuppposed" coreference and "asserted" coreference. Here the fact that *Betty* and *the wife of her childhood sweetheart* end up "referring" to the same individual is exactly what the sentence is asserting.

As noted at the outset of this section, the goal here is just to provide a mystery to whet the reader's appetite; the tools needed to provide a hypothesis as to the explanation of the mystery will be developed later.

1.5. Appendix: Sets and Functions

1.5.1. Sets, members, and subsets

Since the notions of sets and of functions are crucial throughout this book, some formal definitions and discussion are provided here for readers not entirely familiar with these notions. We begin with the notion of a *set*. A set is simply any collection of objects (it can have a finite number of objects, an infinite number, or none at all). For example, we can talk about the set of positive integers less than 10; sets can be notated by listing the members and enclosing the list in curly brackets: {1,2,3,4,5,6,7,8,9}. The order in which they are listed makes no difference; a set is just a collection of things without any order. So if we were to write {2,5,3,4,9,7,8,1,6}, this names the same set. Each integer in this set is called a *member* or an *element* of the set. If we were to name this set A, then the notation $4 \in A$ means that 4 is a member (or element) of A. Something either is or is not in a set; it makes no sense to say it occurs twice (or more) in the set. Note also that a set can have a single member; this is called a *singleton set*. Thus {4} is the set with only one member; this set is distinct from 4 itself. (4 is a member of {4}.)

   A set can have an infinite number of members; the set of positive integers for example is infinite. Obviously this can't be named by listing the members. One can in this case specify the set by a recursive procedure. Call the set I, then one can specify I by two statements: (a) (what is known as the base step): $1 \in I$, and (b) (the recursion step) if $n \in I$ then $n+1 \in I$. (It is understood when one lists things this way that nothing else is in I.) One will also often see a notation which describes rather than lists the members. For example, we can write the following set, call it B: {x|x is a New England state}. This names a finite set, and so we could also give B in list form as follows: {Maine, New Hampshire, Vermont, Massachusetts, Rhode Island, Connecticut}. These two are just different notations for naming the same set. This can also be used, of course, for infinite sets. Take, for example, the set {x|x is an integer and x > 9}. This names the set of integers greater than 9. And, a set can have no members. There is only one such set; its name is *the null set* or *the empty set*, and is generally written as ∅. Of course, there are other ways one can describe the null set. For example, the set of integers each of which is greater than 9 and less than 10 is the empty set. The *cardinality* of some set refers to the number of elements in that set; the notation |B| means the cardinality of B. Hence, given our set B above, |B| is six.

Take some set A. Then a *subset* of A is any set all of whose members are also in A. Suppose, for example, we begin with a set C which is {1,2,3}. Then {1,2} is a subset of C, as is {1,3} and so forth. The notation for the subset relation is ⊆. The full definition of subset is as follows: B ⊆ A if and only if every member of B is a member of A. From this it follows that every set is a subset of itself (so for the set C above, one of its subsets is the set {1,2,3}). It is, however, sometimes convenient to refer to those subsets distinct from the original set; in that case we can talk about a *proper subset* of some set. The symbol for this is ⊂, so B ⊂ A if and only if B ⊆ A and B ≠ A. Since the definition of subset says that B is a subset of A if and only if everything that is in B is also in A, it follows that if nothing is in B then B is a subset of A. thus the null set is a subset of every other set. Sets themselves can have sets as members, and so one can talk about the set of all subsets of a set A. This is called the *power set* of A, written as $\mathscr{P}$(A). For example, given the set C above, $\mathscr{P}$(A) = {∅, {1}, {2}, {3}, {1,2}, {1,3}, {2,3}, {1,2,3}}.

---

*1.3. If a set A has n members, then the number of subsets of A is 2^n. Try to see why this is true. *Hint:* for every member x of some set A, then for each subset B of A, x is either in B or is not in B.

1.4. How many members does the following set have: {∅}?

*1.5. What is $\mathscr{P}$(∅)?

We will also have occasion to talk about the reverse of the subset relation—i.e., the *superset* relation. A is a superset of B if and only if B is a subset of A. The notation for this is A ⊇ B. Once again this is defined in such a way that every set is a superset of itself; a superset of B which is not identical to B is called a *proper superset*, and the notation for this is ⊃.

1.5.2. Union, intersection, and complement

Take any two sets A and B. Then there is a set C which consists of everything that is in A and everything that is in B. This is called the *union* of A and B, and is written A ∪ B. For example, if A is {1,2,3} and B is {2,4,6} then A ∪ B is {1,2,3,4,6}. Moreover, for any two sets A and B the *intersection* of A and B is the set of all things that are in both A and B. This is written A ∩ B. So, for example, in the case directly above, the intersection of A and B is {2}. Or, if we were to intersect the set of integers which can be evenly divided by 2 (the set of even integers) with the set of integers which can be evenly divided by 3, we end up with the set of integers that can be evenly divided by 6.

1.6.   a. For any two sets A and B such that A ⊆ B, what set is A ∪ B?
   b. For any two sets A and B such that A ⊆ B, what set is A ∩ B?

One final useful notion here is the *complement* of a set. The complement of some set A is the set of all things which are not in A (this is sometimes notated as A′). Usually one talks about this notion with respect to some larger domain. Strictly speaking, the complement of {1,2,3} would include not only all integers greater than 3 but also all sorts of other numbers (like 1/3), the sun, my dog Kiana, and the kitchen sink. Rarely are we interested in that sort of set; so in practice when one talks about "the complement of some set A" this is generally with respect to some larger set B of which A is a subset. Then the complement of A refers to all things in B that are not in A (this is notated as B-A). For example, when restricting the discussion to the set of positive integers, the complement of {1,2,3} is the set of all integers greater than 3.

1.5.3. Ordered pairs, relations, equivalence relations, and partitions

Sets are unordered collections of objects. But it is quite useful (as will become very apparent as this book proceeds) to be able to talk about pairs of objects that are ordered in some way. An *ordered pair* is just that:

it is two objects with some ordering between them. If the two objects are a and b, then (a,b) is an ordered pair; (b,a) is a different ordered pair. An ordered pair need not contain distinct items: (a,a) is an ordered pair. In applying this to actual natural relations that exist in the world we are generally interested in *sets of ordered pairs*. (One can generalize this notion to ordered triples and so forth; an *ordered n-tuple* means an ordered list of n items.)

This notion is easiest to grasp with some concrete examples. Take again the set {1,2,3}, and take the relation "is greater than." Then this can be seen as a set of ordered pairs; if we are restricting this to items from our little 1-2-3 set, this would be the set {(2,1), (3,1), (3,2)}. Now suppose we instead take the following set of ordered pairs: {(2,1), (3,1), (3,2), (1,1), (2,2), (3,3)}. Then (restricting this again to our 1-2-3 set) we have now actually listed the relation "is greater than or equal to." Or, take the set {(1,1), (2,2), (3,3)}. That is the relation "is equal to" (defined for the set of integers {1,2,3}).

In other words, what we are calling a *relation* is just some set of ordered pairs. In the example above, both the first and second member of each ordered pair was drawn from the same set (the set {1,2,3}). But this is not necessary; we can have a set of ordered pairs each of whose first member is drawn from some set A and the second member from some set B where A and B are different (they can, but need not, have some of the same members). For example, the relation "is the capital of" is a relation between cities and states; it can be expressed as a set of ordered pairs of the general form {(Providence, Rhode Island), (Boston, Massachusetts), (Springfield, Illinois), (Pierre, South Dakota),...} (the...here is a shorthand for the remaining 46 pairs).

Take two sets A and B (they could be the same set or different). Then A x B refers to the set of all ordered pairs whose first member is in A and whose second member is in B. (This is also called the *Cartesian product* of A and B.) As in the case above, it is helpful to give the intuition of this by coming up with some concrete example. Suppose we take as our set A some group of professors — say, Professor Magoo, Professor Carberry, and Professor Glazie. Call that set P (for shorthand, let's call its members m, c, and g, so P is the set {m,c,g}). Now suppose we have a set S which consists of three students who we will just indicate as x, y, and z (so S = {x,y,z}). Then P x S = {(m,x}, (m,y), (m,z), (c,x), (c,y), (c,z), (g,x), (g,y), (g,z)}. Suppose that Magoo wrote a letter of recommendation for all three students, Carberry wrote one for only y, and Glazie wrote one for y and z. Then the relation "wrote a recommendation for" is a subset of P x S, and is the set of ordered pairs {(m,x}, (m,y), (m,z), (c,y), (g,y), (g,z)}.

More generally, we define a *relation* (between members of A and B) as any subset of A x B. There are some special and interesting properties that can be defined when the two sets are the same. That is, we are now looking at subsets of A x A. Consider a relation R (some subset of A x A) which is such that for all x in A, (x,x) is in R. Such a relation is called a *reflexive* relation. (These need not be the only kinds of pairs to be in R for R to be reflexive; other pairs can be in there too.) For example, if talking about the set of integers again, the relation "is greater than or equal to" is reflexive; for all numbers n, (n,n) is in the set of ordered pairs described by that relation. A relation R is called *irreflexive* if for all x in A, (x,x) is *not* in R. Further, consider any two members x and y (both members of A). Then if it's the case that for all x and y if (x,y) is in R then (y,x) is also in R, the relation is called *symmetric.* Imagine, for example, a lovely world with no unrequited love. Then *is in love with* is symmetric in that world. If our set were {m, c, g, and p}, then if the pair (m,c) were in our relation R (i.e., "is in love with") the fact that R is symmetric means that (c,m) is also in R. (Notice that our definition neither requires (c,c) to be in R nor excludes that; either is possible.) Or, to look at a relation which is symmetric by definition: consider the relation *is a sibling of*. (While *is a sibling of* is symmetric, *is a sister of* is not. Why not?) One final useful definition is a *transitive relation*. A transitive relation R is one for which for every x, y, and z, if (x,y) is in R and (y,z) is in R, then (x,z) is in R. (The relation "is greater than" is transitive, as is the relation "is greater than or equal to").

Any relation R which is reflexive, transitive, and symmetric is called an *equivalence relation*. As an example of such a relation, consider the set of students (call it S) at an elementary school that services grades 1 through 6. Then "is in the same grade as" is an equivalence relation in S x S. (While it is unusual to use the phrase "in the same grade as" when referring to the same person it seems false to say *Johnny is not in the same grade as himself* so we can see that this relation is reflexive.) It is also obvious that it is symmetric and transitive. Note that this—and any other equivalence relation—divides up the original set (here, S) into a group of non-overlapping subsets. The set of these subsets is called a *partition*. Thus, a *partition* of any set S is a set of subsets of S such that for each distinct subset A and B, A ∩ B = ∅, and the union of all the subsets is S. To show that any equivalence relation induces such a partition, take any x in S and define S_x as {y|(y,x) is in R}. Since R is reflexive, we know that x is in S_x (and hence we know that S_x is guaranteed not to be empty). Moreover, the fact that R is reflexive means that each member of S is guaranteed to be in at least one such subset, so we know that the union of all of these is S. We can further show that for any two such subsets S_a and S_b, they either have no members in common (i.e., they have a null intersection) or they are the same. Thus, take any c which is in both S_a and S_b. By definition, this means that (c,a) is in R and (c,b) is in R. By the fact that R is transitive and symmetric, it follows that (a,b) and (b,a) are in R (the reader can work through the necessary steps). But then, for all x such that (x,a) is in R, (x,b) is also in R. To show this note again that R is transitive. If (x,a) is in R and (a,b) is in R then (x,b) is also in R. Hence given the initial premise that there is a non-empty intersection between S_a and S_b, it follows that everything in S_a is in S_b. That everything in S_b is also in S_a follows in the same way, and so the two are the same set. Each subset in a partition is called a *cell* in that partition.

In the example above, the cells correspond to the different grades. (There don't have to be six cells—it could be that one of the grades has no student in it. But there can be no more than six; recall that by definition a cell can't be empty.) Just as any equivalence relation induces a partition, given any partition one can give an equivalence relation that corresponds to any partition; this is the relation that holds between any two a and b in S such that a and b are in the same cell in the partition.

1.5.4. Functions

A function takes every member of some set A and assigns it a value from a set B (B could be the same set as A, but need not be). This can also be formalized using the notion of a set of ordered pairs. Thus, consider two sets A and B (which again could be the same but need not be). Then, a (total) function from A to B is any set of ordered pairs (i.e., any subset of A x B) such that for each a in A, there is one and only one ordered pair with a as first member. Thus if we think of the function f as assigning to each a in A some values in B, note that the criterion above ensures that each member of A is indeed assigned a value, and is assigned a unique value. A is referred to as the *domain* of the function, and B is referred to as the *co-domain*. For any function f and any a in the domain of f, we write f(a) to indicate the value that f assigns to a. (To use other common terminology, f(a) means the result that one gets by applying the function f to a.) There is no restriction that each member of B must appear as second member of some ordered pair; the term *range* of the function f is the set of all b in B such that there is some a such that f(a) = b. Note that these definitions are such that the range of a function is a subset of the co-domain. In practice (at least in works within linguistics) the terms "range" and "co-domain" are often not distinguished.

As noted above, there is no restriction that each member of B appear as second member of an ordered pair. Nor is there a restriction that it appear only once. If each member of B is used as a value only once (that is, for each b in B, there is a unique a such that f(a) = b) then B obviously can be no smaller than a. It can have more members, or it can be the same size. If the latter is the case, then it also follows that for every b in B, there is some a such that f(a) = b. When both conditions above hold (i.e., for each b in B, there is one and only one a such that f(a) = b, we say that there is a *one-to-one correspondence* between A and B. Note that for any function f which is a one-to-one correspondence, there is a corresponding function f^1 which is just the reverse: it is a function mapping each member of B to a member of A such that for all a in A and b in B, if f(a) = b then $f^1(b)$ = a.[10]

We will have some occasion to talk about the notion of a *partial function*. A partial function is one where not every member of A is actually assigned a value by f; f is *undefined* for some subset of A. (Of course any partial function f is also a total function with a smaller domain.) We can illustrate this by returning to our earlier example of ordered pairs of US cities and states, where the first member of each ordered pair is the capital of the second. This is a *partial function* from the set of US cities to states (not every US city is a capital). We can reverse it, and have each state as the first member of the ordered pair and the second as its capital (this function could be expressed in prose as *has as its capital*). This is now a total function from

---

[10] Incidentally, the notion of the availability of a one-to-one correspondence can be used to define what it means for two sets to have the same cardinality. Obviously for two finite sets it is clear what it means to have the same cardinality, since we can count the members. But consider the case of infinite sets. Take the following two sets: A = the set of positive integers {1,2,3,...} and B = the set of positive even integers {2,4,6,...}. Both are infinite. Surprisingly (when one first hears this) they are also of the same cardinality, because one can establish a one-to-one correspondence between them (each member of A is paired with a member of B by multiplying by 2: we will never run out of members in B).

the set of states (every state does have a capital) to the set of US cities. But it is not a one-to-one correspondence for the same reason that our original relation is not a total function; there are many cities without the honor of being a capital.

Occasionally in this text it will be useful to list out some actual functions—that is, to name every member in the domain and name what the function at issue maps that member to. There are a variety of ways one could do this. To illustrate, take a domain of four children {Zacky, Yonnie, Shelley, and Baba} (call that set C) and four men {Abe, Bert, Carl, David} (call that set M). Suppose there is a function f from C to M which maps each child to their father. Assume that Abe is the father of Zacky and Yonnie, Bert is the father of Shelley, and David is the father of Baba. Then one can write this information out in various ways. One would be to simply give the set of ordered pairs: {(Zacky, Abe), (Yonnie, Abe), (Shelley, Bert), (Baba, David)}. Usually this notation, however, is not terribly easy to read. We could also write this out in either of the ways shown in (20):

(20)   a.   f(Zacky) = Abe   b.   Zacky → Abe
            f(Yonnie) = Abe   Yonnie → Abe
            f(Shelley) = Bert   Shelley → Bert
            f(Baba) = David   Baba → David

Or, sometimes it is more convenient to list out the domain on the left and the co-domain on the right and connect them with arrows as in (21):

(21)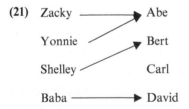

Which notation is chosen makes no difference; the choice should be dictated by clarity.

2

Semantic foundations

2.1. Model-theoretic semantics

The primary focus of this book is the syntax/semantics interface—that is, how the syntax and semantics work so that sentences (and other well-formed linguistic expressions) are paired with a meaning. But of course this task is impossible without some idea of what meaning is. Can we talk about meaning without relegating it to the realm of the mysterious, or leaving it solely to folks who work on cognition to deal with? The answer (of course) is yes—there is a rich tradition within linguistics and the philosophy of language for modeling linguistic meaning.

In some early work within linguistic theory—especially in the 1960s—meaning was taken to be just a symbolic representation (call it a Logical Form, or LF). While it remains an open question as to whether such representations play an actual role in the way the grammar pairs expressions with meanings, this book (along with much other modern work in formal semantics) assumes that meaning is not just some string of symbols, but rather some actual object out there in the world. Call this a *model-theoretic object*. (More precisely, we are taking meaning to be an object which forms part of a model which is an abstract representation of the world: hence the term *model theory*.) Of course, we need some way to name these objects, and so throughout we will use strings of symbols as ways to name them. But the point is that the grammar maps each linguistic expression into something beyond just a symbolic representation. Otherwise—as so aptly pointed out by David Lewis (1970)—we are simply mapping one language (say, English) into another (what Lewis termed "Markerese"). Yet language is used to convey facts about the world; we draw inferences about the world from what we hear and we gain information about what is true and what is not. So semantics must be a system mapping a linguistic expression to something in the world.

But what exactly is meant by model-theoretic objects? These can in fact be quite abstract. Still, they are the "stuff" that is out there in the universe— something constructed out of actual bits of the universe (or, at least, the ontology of the universe as given by language). This would include things like individuals, times, possibilities, and perhaps others; just what are the basic objects that we need is an open question and is part of what semantic theory addresses. The strategy here will be to use a fairly sparse set of primitive objects, and construct more complex objects out of these. Let us, then, begin by setting up two basic building blocks which are foundational in much of the work in linguistic formal semantics.

2.2. Truth conditions

A common adage in semantics is: "To know the meaning of a (declarative) sentence is to know what it would take to make it true." We can use this adage as a first step in constructing the building blocks for meanings: a fundamental fact about declarative sentences is that they are either true or false[1] (and since we use language to communicate information about the world, a listener will in general assume that a sentence they have just heard

---

[1] Henceforth we use the term "sentence" to mean a declarative sentence. There is actually no reason to consider questions to be of the same category as declarative sentences even though they also are traditionally referred to as "sentences." Questions have a different external distribution from declarative sentences (for example, *wonder* can occur only with a question as its complement, not an ordinary sentence, while the reverse is true for *believe*); they have a different kind of meaning, and they have a different internal structure. Whether imperatives and declaratives should be considered the same category is a bit less clear (they are more similar), but we will not deal with those here either.

is true, and uses that fact to enrich their knowledge of the world). Thus (1) is true and (2) is false:

(1)   Barack Obama moved into the White House on Jan. 20, 2009.

(2)   John McCain moved into the White House on Jan. 20, 2009.

Hence, one basic notion used for the construction of meanings is a truth value—for now assume that there are just two such values: true and false. (More on this directly.) The claim that truth values are a fundamental part of meaning is also motivated by noting that—as shown by the examples above—speakers have intuitions about truth, given certain facts about the world, just like they do about acceptability. And these judgments can be used to test the adequacy of particular theories of meaning. Following standard practice, we use 1 for true and 0 for false. Thus the set of truth values {1,0} and we will also refer to this set as t. Let us use [[α]] to mean the semantic value (i.e., the meaning) of a linguistic expression α. Then (temporarily) we can say that [[*Barack Obama moved into the White House on Jan. 20, 2009*]] = 1.

Some worries should immediately spring to mind. The most obvious is that something seems amiss in calling the *meaning* of (1) "true" even if we are willing to accept the fact that it is true. We will enrich the toolbox directly to take care of that. But there are other objections: does it really make sense to say that all declarative sentences are true or false? Clearly not—for some sentences the truth value depends on who is speaking (and on when the sentence is spoken). Take (3):

(3)   I am President of the United States.

This is true if spoken by Barack Obama in 2011, but not if spoken by John McCain and not true if spoken by Barack Obama in 2006. So this has no truth value in and of itself. Nonetheless once certain parameters are fixed (time of utterance and speaker) it is either true or false. So we might want to think of the meaning of (3) as a *function* into {1,0}—it does yield a truth value but only once we fix certain parameters. But it seems inescapable that a declarative sentence is telling us something about the world, and so truth values are certainly one fundamental piece.

In fact, there are many parameters that need to be set in order to derive a truth value. Certain words like *I*, *you*, *here*, *now*, etc. quite obviously have the property that their value depends on when, where, and by whom these are spoken (these are called *indexicals*). There are also more subtle cases—such as (4) and (5)—where truth seems to depend on what is at issue in the discourse context in which these are uttered:

(4)   Magic Johnson is tall.

(5)   Every student got an A on their formal semantics midterm.

(4) might be true if we are comparing Magic Johnson to the general population (Magic Johnson is a former basketball player for the Los Angeles Lakers) but perhaps not true if we are comparing him to the set of basketball players. The context of utterance usually makes it clear what is the relevant comparison class. (5) may be true if we are restricting the interpretation of *students* to those students in my formal semantics class in 2011, but not if we mean every student in the world, or even every student at Brown or every student who has ever taken formal semantics from me. We return to cases like these in (among other places) sections 8.4, 10.6, and 17.4.

2.1. In what ways do the following sentences also show a dependency on context of utterance? (Some may show this in more than one way.)

 (i) The dog did not get a walk today.
 (ii) Samantha hasn't eaten yet.
 (iii) All of the ex-presidents of the US gathered at the State of the Union address.

So far, we have two reasons that it is oversimplified to say that the meaning of a sentence is true or false: (a) even once we do determine the truth value of a sentence we surely don't want to call that "meaning," and (b) often the truth value can't be determined until we know the context of utterance. Two further worries have to do with the fact that (c) there are vague sentences where some have the intuition that the truth value is something in between 1 and 0, and (d) some sentences (even once we fix the context of utterance) seem to be neither true nor false (nor anything in between).

As to (d), these are cases which have generally gone under the rubric of *presupposition failure*. The classic example from Russell (1905) is (6); another example would be (7) said of someone who never went to an aerobics class:

(6)   The present King of France is bald.

(7)   He stopped going to aerobics class.

Surely (6) is not true, but do we want to say it is false?[2] For the most part, we will make the expository simplification of assuming all sentences are true or false, although we will return to the issue of presupposition from time to time.

   This still leaves the issue of vagueness. For example, even once we do fix the comparison class at issue in a sentence like (4) there remains some vagueness: is a 6 foot 9 inch basketball player tall for a basketball player? If so, exactly where does one draw the line between tall and not tall? There is a rich literature on the problem of modeling vagueness and some have attempted to model it using intermediate truth values (where a sentence can have any value between 1 and 0). Like many other domains, we can set this aside in this introductory text (but for a nice discussion aimed at introductory students, see Chierchia and McConnell-Ginet 1990: chapter 8). For the present purposes, take all declarative sentences (once fixed to a context) to have just one of two truth values: 1 or 0.

2.3. Possible worlds

2.3.1. Introducing the notion

The one important observation that we will not set aside is the first problem noted above: it hardly makes sense to think of the *meaning* of a sentence like (1) as true. There are plenty of reasons to find this absurd. First, we can know the meaning of a sentence without having the slightest idea of whether it is true or false: I know the meaning of (8) but have no idea of its truth value:

(8)   The tallest man alive anywhere on January 1, 2010 had pomegranate juice for breakfast.

---

[2] Russell (1905) answered this question "yes"; under his analysis (6) is false. Strawson (1950) argued "no" and introduced the notion of presupposition by which a sentence like (6) is neither true nor false.

And surely we do not want all true sentences to have the same meaning (ditto for all false sentences). In fact if this were all there is to meaning we would be able to express only two things: "1" or "0." Obviously a rather strange notion of what we do with language! But let us return to the adage: "To know the meaning of a sentence is to know what it would take to make the sentence true." Thus enters the notion of a set of *possibilities*, otherwise known as a set of *possible worlds*.[3] This gives us just the tool we need: to know the meaning of a sentence is to know what the world would have to be like to make it true: i.e. the meaning of a declarative sentence, then, is a function from ways the world could be (possible worlds) to {1,0}. (Readers not familiar with the notion of a function should consult the appendix to Chapter 1.)

This makes good sense. We can know the meaning of a sentence without knowing its truth value not because of our lack of linguistic knowledge but precisely because we don't know what is the actual world in which we live. But if we did—if we were omniscient—then for every sentence we would of course know whether it is true or false. Moreover, think of what it means for one's information to grow as we communicate. As we hear a sentence (and if we also assume that the speaker is speaking truthfully) we narrow down the space of possible worlds that we could be in; all worlds mapped to 0 by the relevant sentence are eliminated. This also provides a nice way to capture the notion of an *entailment*. (9), for example, entails (10) (Mitka is the name of the author's former dog):

(9)   Mitka killed the bird that had been trapped on the porch.

(10)   The bird that had been trapped on the porch died.

Hence, we can say that a sentence S_1 *entails* S_2 if and only if every world mapped to true by S_1 is mapped to true by S_2. Put differently (but equivalently), the set of worlds in which (9) is true is a subset of worlds in which

---

[3] The terminology of "possible worlds" often causes people to cringe—it brings with it some unfortunate terminological baggage. While there may be deep philosophical questions that ultimately need to be addressed here, one can go quite far without worrying too much about the *real* status of "alternate possible worlds." Surely we do talk about other ways the world might be (see the discussion below). And surely there are many facts about the actual world that we do not know, hence think of a possible world as a way the world might be compatible with our knowledge state.

(10) is true. (The reverse of course does not hold; (10) can be true because a different dog killed the unfortunate bird, or because it died of a broken heart.) Similarly, we can call two sentences *synonymous* if and only if they entail each other—i.e., they have exactly the same truth conditions.[4]

As soon as one begins to talk about possible worlds and truth conditions, an interesting question arises. Consider a sentence that is necessarily true— that is, one which seems to be true no matter how the world happens to be and hence true in all possible worlds. If the meaning of a sentence is a function from worlds to values, then all necessarily true sentences have the same meaning. But do we want to say that all necessarily true sentences really have the same meaning? (Similarly for all sentences that are necessarily false.) These are thorny issues. But some of the discomfort posed by modeling the meaning of a sentence as a function from possible worlds to the set t can perhaps be allayed by taking a rather charitable view of what it means to be a possible world. Consider the (often cited) case of mathematical facts. Such facts are what they are—they are not really contingent facts about the world (the world could not change in such a way as to make them false). Yet there is a strong intuition that (11a) and (11b) do not have the same meaning:

(11)   a. The largest prime number less than 1000 is 997.
       b. The largest prime number less than 2000 is 1999.

---

[4] Many find this an unsatisfying definition of "synonymy" since two sentences can have the same truth conditions but a variety of subtle differences such as differences in when they are appropriately used, what they draw attention to, etc. Consider active–passive pairs:

(i)   a. Mitka killed the bird that had been trapped on the porch.
      b. The bird that had been trapped on the porch was killed by Mitka.

One can imagine a variety of situations in which it would be appropriate to utter (ia). For example, if I come home at the end of the day and ask my husband what Mitka did during the day, (ia) would be a reasonable answer. It is also a reasonable answer to the question of why the porch appears to be full of feathers. But while (ib) is reasonable in this second scenario, it is an odd answer to the question of what Mitka did during the day. These kinds of differences often go under the rubric of *information structure*. Ultimately, then, one might well want a much finer-grained notion of synonymy that includes not only the truth conditions of a sentence but other factors as well. But this is simply a matter of terminology: here we elect to use the term synonymy in this rather coarse-grained way (referring to having the same truth conditions). One could substitute in "mutual entailment" if one prefers.

Arguably, though, this is because the set of possible worlds includes more than just the mathematically possible worlds; rather, it includes all worlds which we can conceive of. Until writing out (11a) and consulting a number theorist I had no idea whether it was true or not: surely the space of epistemically possible worlds (worlds compatible with my knowledge state) includes worlds in which (11a) is true and worlds in which it is false. Similarly for (11b). Indeed, the truths of mathematical statements are subject to discovery (and ditto for truths that hold via physical laws of the universe) and so there's no real reason to restrict the notion of possible worlds to those in which those laws hold. (If one prefers, we should perhaps rename these as *imaginable worlds*—but we stick here to the term *possible worlds* out of convention.) Thus at least some of these concerns can be allayed in this way.

This still leaves the case of sentences known as *tautologies* (true by logic and/or by definition) such as the pair in (12). No amount of imagination would make these false (someone who thinks they are false presumably just does not know the meaning of *or*) and so the theory says they have the same meaning:

(12) a. Henry had breakfast yesterday or Henry didn't have breakfast yesterday.
b. Sally climbed Mt Washington or Sally didn't climb Mt Washington.

We will simply agree to live with this problem (if it is really is one). Perhaps literally these two do have the same meaning. As will be discussed at points throughout this text, there is a distinction between the literal meaning of sentences and other things that they might be used to convey (the latter being the domain of *pragmatics*). It is not unreasonable to think that the pair in (12) have the same meaning but could be used for different purposes. A full-blown theory of pragmatics should be able to predict that while both sentences are always true, they can indirectly convey different information and hence be used in different circumstances. So the notion that the meaning of a sentence is a function from possible worlds (broadly construed) to truth values does not seem fundamentally threatened by these cases.

Incidentally given the meaning of a sentence as a function from worlds to the set $\{1,0\}$, the notion of a *partial function* can be used to model presupposition failure. Hence a common account of the fact that *The present King of France is bald* seems somehow just nonsensical in our world is to suppose that it assigns neither true nor false to this world. The meaning of this sentence is thus a function from worlds (and times) to truth values, but a partial one—undefined for this world. Whether this is the right way to think about presupposition is a topic that we leave open in this work, although we will be confronting the issue(s) from time to time.

2.3.2. Characteristic function of a set

Take any function f from some domain D into the set t (i.e., the set $\{1,0\}$). Then consider that subset of D consisting of all and only the members of D that are mapped to 1 by f; call it D'. Then we can say that D' is the set *characterized by* f. (Note that D' can be $\emptyset$.) Similarly, if we have a set D' which is a subset of D, then we can construct the function f that maps every member of D' to 1 and every member of D not in D' to 0. f is called the *characteristic function* of the set D'. Note that for any function f into $\{1,0\}$ we can recover the set D'. Note moreover that for any D' a subset of D and any D, we can uniquely recover the total function f that maps all members of D' to 1 and everything else to 0. In this way we can go back and forth between talking about certain functions (those whose domain is $\{1,0\}$) and the sets that they characterize.

This is useful in thinking about the meaning of sentences. We have taken the meaning of a sentence to be a function from worlds to $\{1,0\}$ but one can equivalently take it to be a *set of possible worlds* (namely, all worlds mapped to 1 by the relevant function). It is useful to be able to go back and forth between these two conceptions. Note that the function is uniquely recoverable from the set only under the assumption that every sentence is indeed assigned 1 or 0 in every world. Thus if we treat presupposition failure as best modeled by allowing partial functions—a sentence which is true in some worlds, false in others, and assigned no value in yet other worlds—then there is no way to uniquely recover the relevant function from the set of worlds mapped to true. (Those not in the set might have been mapped to 0 or might have been given no value.) However, as long as the function is total (thus all worlds are assigned 1 or 0 by the relevant function) it can be uniquely recovered. The reverse holds in either case: one can always construct the set characterized by a function f whose co-domain is $\{1,0\}$: that set is the set assigned 1.

2.2. Consider the function f whose domain is the set of New England states and co-domain is {1,0} which is as follows: f(Maine) = 0, f(New Hampshire) = 1, f(Vermont) = 1, f(Massachusetts) = 1, f(Rhode Island) = 0, f(Connecticut) =1. Show the set it characterizes.

2.3. Now consider the case of partial functions from the set of New England states to {1,0}. That is, we are considering functions which map each state into either 1, 0, or where the function can be undefined for some states (some states will be mapped into neither value). Consider the set {Maine, Vermont, Rhode Island}. List out all of the possible functions (partial or total) which characterize this set. (For readers unfamiliar with American geography, the remaining New England states are as given above—they are New Hampshire, Massachusetts, and Connecticut.) See Appendix to Chapter 1 for ways to write out functions.

2.3.3. Notation and terminology

Recall that t is the set {1,0} (i.e., the set of truth values). We will use w to mean the set of worlds. We will use the notation <a,b> to mean the set of all functions whose domain is the set a and co-domain is the set b.[5] Thus <w,t> is the set of functions from worlds to truth values. We will speak of the *semantic type* of a syntactic category such as a "sentence" (S) as being <w,t>; this means that every expression of this category has as its meaning some member of <w,t>. (Thus <a,b> itself means the set of all functions from a to b; the terminology "of type <a,b>" means that an expression has as its meaning a member of <a,b>.)

Take any expression whose meaning is a function from possible worlds to something else. (So far we have seen this just for the case of sentences.) We call that function the *intension* of the expression. Thus the intension of an expression is its actual meaning, not its value in some particular world.

---

[5] This is very slightly different from the way this notation is used in some other works in semantics (in particular this differs slightly from its use in Montague 1973 which is how it was introduced into linguistic semantics). However, the differences are inconsequential for the purposes here.

When talking about the value of some expression α at some particular world, we will use the term *extension of* α *at a world w*. Most often we are concerned with its value in the actual world, and in such cases we will simply refer to the *extension* of the expression.

2.3.4. Talking about worlds

Possible worlds have been added to the basic toolbox as a way to capture the fact that the meaning of a sentence is not simply 1 or 0, but rather can be thought of as a function from worlds to truth values. But there is a second reason for incorporating possible worlds into the theory, which is that natural language contains all sorts of expressions and constructions which actually make reference to worlds other than the actual one. Put differently, there are words whose meanings crucially combine with the *intensions* of sentences (or other expressions).

A rather striking example of how language allows us to talk about possible worlds is the case of *counterfactual conditionals*. These are sentences of the form *If S₁ then S₂,* where there are special forms of the verbs (or auxiliaries) in these sentences (in particular, the *then-* clause often contains the auxiliary *would*). Consider (13):

(13) If the US Supreme Court had not stopped the Florida recount in 2000, nuclear power plants would no longer be in use in the US.

Some relevant background: the outcome of the 2000 US Presidential election (between Al Gore and George W. Bush) hinged on a few hundred votes in Florida. Although Bush was initially declared the winner of Florida (and hence of the US election), Gore asked for a recount of the votes in key precincts. There was a complex series of court decisions, leading up to the Florida Supreme Court ruling in favor of Gore's request. Bush then took this to the US Supreme Court. While the recount was in process (and hence no one knows for sure what the outcome would have been), the US Supreme Court halted the recount, and subsequently ruled that it should not proceed. Bush therefore remained the victor in Florida and hence won the US presidency. An additional bit of relevant background is that Al Gore is very opposed to the use of nuclear power.

Given this, it is easy to understand (13), and to understand the reasoning leading a speaker to say this. What is interesting about such sentences is that we can argue about whether they are true or false but we can never really know, as we are arguing about a chain of events in another possible world. A reasonable approximation of the truth *conditions* of a counterfactual conditional sentence of the form *If S_1 then S_2* is that it is true if in the closest world to ours where S_1 is true S_2 is also true. "Closest" means the world just like ours where we make minimal changes. In other words, we look at a world in which the *if*-clause (known as the *antecedent*) is true and where nothing else changes except those facts that follow from the truth of the antecedent. (Usually these are uttered in a situation where the antecedent clause is not true in the real world and hence the closest world is not our world, but this is not necessary; the closest world in question could be the actual one.[6]) Of course in those cases where the relevant other world is not ours, we are not omniscient; we can't just jump over to another possible world. And this is exactly why we argue about the truth of counterfactual conditionals: we don't really know what the facts are in our relevant alternate reality. In fact, (13) is interesting because we don't even know for sure whether Gore would have won the election had the Supreme Court not stopped the recount. People argue about this (different newspapers tried to do counts, and came up with different results), so we actually don't even know the truth value of a simpler sentence like *If the Supreme Court had not stopped the Florida recount, Gore would have become President*. But we do know what these sentences all mean: we know what it would take to make them true.

Notice, incidentally, that we have restricted the semantics to looking only at the *closest* world in which the antecedent is true (the world most like ours where we change as little as possible). It would be incorrect to posit, for example, that the consequent must be true in *all* worlds in which the

---

[6] An illustration of the fact that the construction does not require the antecedent to be false in the actual world is the following "detective" scenario (modified from discussion in Anderson 1951): A great detective is analyzing the scene of a murder in which there are bloody footprints of a size 12 shoe, an empty vial of an extremely rare poison available only in Saskatchewan, and a note clearly scribbled with a magenta felt-tip marker. Our detective reports his thinking as follows. "Let's see now. If Mr Magoo had committed this murder he would have left bloody footprints from a size 12 shoe. If he had committed the murder he would have purchased his poison in Saskatchewan. And if Mr Magoo had committed the murder he would have left a note with his favorite magenta felt-tip marker. I therefore conclude that Mr Magoo is indeed our murderer."

antecedent is true. For surely there is a possible world in which the recount proceeded, Gore did get more votes, was assassinated his second day in office, and where his successor Lieberman had no qualms about nuclear power. Or for that matter, one cannot doubt the existence of a *possible* world (quite remote) in which the majority of votes in Florida had actually been cast for Patrick Buchanan or even Mickey Mouse.

The interesting point here, then, is that while we cannot really determine the truth *value* of (13), it does indeed have truth *conditions* (otherwise there would be nothing to argue about), and we can rather precisely state the truth conditions—if not the truth value—using the notion of possible worlds. Our ignorance, as always, comes from the fact that we are not omniscient: we do not have access to the full set of facts in our world nor to the full structure of other possible worlds. Thus in order to give a semantics for *if...then*, the theory needs access to possible worlds.

In fact, one does not even need to consider constructions with such exotic syntax to see that we reason and talk about alternative possibilities in everyday language. Even the semantics of the verb form called the *progressive* (as in *I am writing a book*) arguably requires access to possible worlds. (The discussion below—although not the particular example—is based on the analysis in Dowty 1979.)

Consider the following (silly but wonderfully illustrative) two scenarios.

Scenario 1: Mr Peepers lives alone and spends a lot of time watching the activity in his street out his window. A turtle who he has named Myrtle lives in a nearby pond, but every morning Ms Goodheart who lives across the street from Mr Peepers places food on the curb (across the street from Mr Peepers) for Myrtle. And so every morning at the same time, Myrtle slowly ambles across the street, gets to the curb on the other side, eats her food, and slowly ambles back. One fateful day, Myrtle gets exactly a third of the way across the street, and a large truck comes and hits her and Myrtle dies. Mr Peepers is reporting this, and can quite naturally say:

(14) Poor Myrtle the Turtle was crossing the street when she got hit by a truck and died.

Scenario 2: Exactly the same, except that in this case Ms Goodheart always puts the food right in the middle of the street. Of course this means that every day, Myrtle goes just halfway across the street, has her breakfast, and then returns. But the rest is the same, and so on the fateful day, Myrtle gets exactly a third of the way across the street, and a large truck comes and hits her and Myrtle dies.

Can Mr Peepers report Scenario 2 with (14)? The judgment here is quite robust: no. Yet—in terms of the event that would be described by (14)—the two scenarios contain *exactly identical events!* What is the difference? It is clear that in Scenario 1 we expect that Myrtle would have crossed the street had she not been hit by the truck. (Notice the use of the counterfactual conditional in reporting this.) In other words, the semantics of the progressive is appealing to another possible world in which the truck had not killed Myrtle. (Dowty calls the relevant other possible world the "inertial" continuation of our world: the world that would have materialized had nothing extraordinary intervened.) So even ordinary everyday constructions like the progressive require reference to possible worlds to fully flesh out their truth conditions.[7]

---

[7] One might dispute the claim above that exactly the same events happened in the two scenarios: in Scenario 1 Myrtle had the intention to go to the other side of the street and in Scenario 2 she did not. So one might argue that the difference does not come from the different possible worlds which are the inertial continuations, but rather is located in the intentions of the subject of a progressive verb.

However, one can repeat the scenario (albeit not as colorfully) with subjects that denote non-sentient beings. *Scenario 1:* A bowler named Jack always throws his bowling ball exactly the same way, and it always lands in the gutter. On the day in question, I watch him play a game—he throws his ball in the usual way, it goes on the usual path. But just as it is five inches from the gutter, a very heavy overhead light falls from the ceiling of the bowling alley and smashes the ball. I can report this as (i):

(i) Jack's ball was rolling into the gutter when an overhead light fell on it and destroyed it.

Now we modify the scenario much as we did with Myrtle. *Scenario 2:* Again, Jack always throws the ball in exactly the same way, and he throws it in exactly the same way as in the first scenario. However, the bowling alley is also home to a small genie who magically appears every time that the ball is three inches from the gutter, corrects its course, and Jack gets a strike every time. (I have resorted to the genie here to make sure that the ball itself is thrown in exactly the same way in the two scenarios. There is no hidden torque on it in Scenario 2; the change in outcome is due neither to the ball nor to Jack, and until the genie appears the events in the two scenarios are exactly identical.) Once again the light falls on the ball when it is five inches from the gutter. Here again (i) is not a good report of Scenario 2.

2.4. Times

It is not enough to think of the meaning of sentences as functions from ways the world might be to truth values. Their truth is also time-dependent. As noted earlier, (3) is true when uttered by Barack Obama in 2010 but not in 2006. Similarly, consider an ordinary past-tense sentence:

(15)   George W. Bush was president of the US for 8 years.

This is true now, but when uttered in 1998 it was not true. So the value of a sentence is not only a function from worlds but also times to truth values.

The relation between worlds and times is a tricky one. For the present purposes it will work well to think of the set of times and the set of worlds as completely separate sets. Notice that we can easily talk about "now" in other possible worlds:

(16)   If I weren't here now, I'd be outside enjoying the beautiful weather.

It seems that here we are importing the "now" time to another possible world—which is most easily made sense of if we treat the worlds and the times as independent sets.

Thus the full meaning or *intension* of a sentence is a function from worlds and times to truth values, and since the two are independent we can think of it as a function from world–time pairs to truth values. (And its *extension* is the value of this function taken at some particular world and some particular time.) We will use i to represent the set of times. Whenever it is convenient to ignore the worlds but not the times, we will speak as if the value of a sentence is something in the set <i,t>. When it is convenient to ignore the times but not the worlds, we will speak of it as having a meaning of type <w,t>. In reality, though, it is a function from both: and the standard terminology is to use s to name the set of world–time pairs; thus the semantic type of a sentence is <s,t>. As is the case with worlds, there are many linguistic expressions whose meanings crucially combine with time-dependent objects (the past-tense morpheme is one). We explore this briefly in the final chapter. The strategy in this book will be, for the most part, to give an *extensional* semantics (ignoring both worlds and times) as one can get quite far in considering the syntax/semantics interface by looking only at constructions in which intensions don't interact with the syntax. However, the final chapter is concerned with the fact that some expressions are crucially sensitive to intensions, and considers the implications of this to further issues concerning the syntax/semantics interface.

3

Compositionality, Direct Compositionality, and the syntax/semantics interface

As noted in the preceding chapter, the program of semantics often takes as its point of departure the adage "To know the meaning of a (declarative) sentence is to know what it would take to make it true." There is a second foundational adage: "The meaning of the whole is computed in some predictable way from the meaning of its parts." This is also often known as *Frege's principle* or *the principle of compositionality*. Taken in its broadest sense, this is fairly weak: obviously speakers of a language know the basic units (words, or more accurately, morphemes) and know some system to combine these into larger meaningful expressions. Surely at least most of language has to be compositional, or there would be no way to systematically combine units into larger meaningful expressions which have never been uttered (or heard) before.[1] In other words, we can see the grammar of a natural language as a specification of the set of well-formed expressions of the language, combined with rules which map each well-formed expression

---

[1] But there is a question about whether everything is compositional. Idioms are a classic case of items that at least appear to be non-compositional.

into a meaning (that is, some object built out of our model-theoretic toolbox, which so far consists only of truth values, worlds, and times).

But while it is generally accepted that the meanings of larger expressions are computed in some predictable way from the meanings of smaller ones, what is not so clear is just what that predictable way is and how complex it is. A very simple and elegant view on this is as follows. The syntax consists of statements that predict the existence of well-formed expressions on the basis of the existence of other well-formed expressions. At the base of this is the lexicon; the list of basic units (for our purposes, words). The semantics works in tandem with the syntax: each syntactic rule which predicts the existence of some well-formed expression (as output) is paired with a semantic rule which gives the meaning of the output expression in terms of the meaning(s) of the input expressions. This is what we mean by **Direct Compositionality**, and is the point of view that will mainly be pursued in this book.

3.1. Building a fragment: First steps

Every expression of a language, including the basic expressions (the words), can be seen as a triple of <[sound], syntactic category, [[meaning]]>. Borrowing notation from phonology, we enclose the sound part in square brackets (although we simply use English orthography rather than phonetic transcription), and the meaning part is enclosed in double square brackets [[. . .]]. A rule is thus something which takes one or more triples as input and yields a triple as output. A reader who is used to thinking of the syntax as consisting not of a number of very specific "rules" (such as phrase structure rules) but a set of much more general rules (or "principles") such as the X-bar schemata need not worry: Chapter 6 will give the rules in far more general form.[2] Since we will often be adopting rules which are temporary and will later be revised, simplified, or generalized, any rule not part of the

---

[2] A certain amount of modern linguistics has eschewed the term "rule" on the grounds that the grammar hopefully does not consist of a list of a large number of "rules" rather than having the apparatus stated in much more general format. Nonetheless, most agree that the grammar contains statements that predict the set of well-formed expressions and assign them a meaning, and here the term "rule" is being used in the most general sense here to simply mean these statements. We will

final fragment will be notated as TR (followed by a number). (Rules which do remain in the ultimate fragment are simply labeled with R.)

Assume that the set of syntactic categories includes S which we use to mean a sentence.[3] We continue here to assume that all Ss have as their truth value 1 or 0 (i.e., none are undefined in some worlds). Moreover, for now let us go back to ignoring the world (and time) parameters, and give a purely extensional semantics. Then we begin with the following:

TR-1.   If α is an expression of the form <[α], S, [[α]]> and β is an expression of the form <[β], S, [[β]]>, then there is an expression γ of the form <[α-and-β], S, 1 if and only if [[α]] = 1 and [[β]] = 1>. (Hereafter we use the standard *iff* to abbreviate "if and only if.")

There are a variety of other ways this rule could be written. For example, we could write the syntax as a *(context-free) phrase structure rule* and pair this with a semantic part. This notation was used in much of the literature within Generalized Phrase Structure Grammar (GPSG) (Gazdar, Klein, Pullum, and Sag 1985):

TR-1'. $S_1 \rightarrow S_2$ and S_3; $[[S_1]] = 1$ iff $[[S_2]] = 1$ and $[[S_3]] = 1$.

A phrase structure rule by itself, then, is a rule which gives the phonological and syntactic part of a rule such as TR-1 but not the semantics. When supplemented with the semantics—as in TR-1'—this is just TR-1 in a different format. Note also that TR-1' uses subscripts in the syntactic part of the rule, but these are not actually meant as a part of the syntactic category.[4] These are needed just to state the semantics; this is avoided in the notational system in TR-1.

indeed be moving towards a view of grammar which contains just a few rather general statements to this effect, but there is no reason not to call these rules.

[3] In some current theories of syntax (Minimalism and some of its predecessors) this category is instead called TP (*Tense Phrase*) and in slightly earlier versions of that theory it is called IP (*Inflectional Phrase*). As with the label NP, we are using the terminology standard in many other theories and in many other related disciplines; readers familiar with the terms TP or IP instead can make the appropriate translation.

[4] A *context-free phrase structure rule* specifies the well-formedness of an expression of some grammatical category X in terms of concatenations of strings of other expressions in the language. These other expressions are described either listed on a case-by-case basis (like *and* above) or are described by their grammatical category. The set of grammatical categories is finite, and it does not include things like S_1 etc.

To forestall one objection: one should not be misled by the fact that the word "and" is used in the semantic part to give a meaning for English sentences containing *and*. The word "and" in the first part of the triple in TR-1 is the English word [ænd] where English is the *object language*—the language whose syntax and semantics is being modeled. But we need a language in which to describe the grammar, and we have chosen English for that purpose as well. So here English is also being used as the *metalanguage*. The confusion that arises by using English as the metalanguage to model English as the object language would go away if we were using English to, e.g., model the grammar of Swahili—or if we wrote the semantics for English using some sort of purely symbolic notation (whose meaning had been agreed on). There are other ways to alleviate the potential confusion; we could just as well have written the semantic part of the rule by means of what is known as a truth table. This is illustrated below where we rewrite the semantic part of TR-1 by listing the possible combinations of values for each of the α and β followed by the value that this gives for the string $[\alpha\text{-and-}\beta]$:

(1) | $[[\alpha]]$ | $[[\beta]]$ | $[[\alpha\text{-and-}\beta]]$ |
|---|---|---|
| 1 | 1 | 1 |
| 1 | 0 | 0 |
| 0 | 1 | 0 |
| 0 | 0 | 0 |

From now on we use the format in TR-1 as our official notation, although at times will use phrase structure rule format or other notational systems as convenient. Incidentally, TR-1 introduces *and* directly as part of the rule rather than treating it as an item in the lexicon with a grammatical category. This is known as treating it *syncategorematically*. This decision to treat *and* not as a lexical item but rather as only something introduced by a rule is not essential (and is almost certainly incorrect), and will be revised later.

The rule for *or* is analogous (here we will highlight the lack of need to use the English word "or" in stating the semantics).

(Of course we could posit such a category, as long as there are a finite number of them, but that is not the intent in the rule above.) In the rule above, the idea is that the syntactic rule is just S → S and S. The reason that the subscripts are there in the rule is because the semantics needs to refer to them. Note that this is just an artifact of this particular notational system; the rule in TR-1 doesn't use any subscripts in the syntax.

TR-2.   If α is an expression of the form <[α], S, [[α]]> and β is an expression of the form <[β], S, [[β]]>, then there is an expression γ of the form <[α-or-β], S, 0 iff [[α]] = 0 and [[β]] = 0 >.

3.2. Implicatures vs truth conditions

Before continuing with the fragment, a digression is in order about the meaning of *or*. (More extensive discussion is found in section 10.4.) According to the semantics in TR-2, the sentence in (2) is true if Carol skydives and doesn't bungee jump, if she bungee jumps and doesn't skydive, and also if she does both.

(2)   Carol will go sky dive on her vacation, or she will go bungee jumping on her vacation.

This is what is known as *inclusive or*: both sentences can be true. But is that result correct? One might at first think not—there surely is a strong temptation to read (1) as saying she will do one or the other but not both. On the basis of this it is tempting to think that English *or* actually has as its meaning what is known as *exclusive or*—either conjunct could be true but not both. If that were correct then of course TR-2 needs revision.

But we can show that English *or* is actually inclusive. Although we often take sentences like (2) to convey that both events will not happen, this is not a part of its actual truth conditions. Note first that if I say (2) to you and it turns out that Carol goes completely wild and does both, you can hardly accuse me of lying. And it is easy to construct cases where there is no exclusive *or* suggestion and where things would not make sense if the meaning of *or* were "one or the other but not both." So, take a linguistics department which is very strict about enforcing prerequisites. There is a course called Phonetics and Phonology II (Phon/Phon II). The course brochure contains the language in (3):

(3)   Students may not enroll in any course unless they have had the prerequisite(s). You will be allowed to enroll in Phon/Phon II if and only if you have taken Phonology I or you have taken Phonetics I.

Suppose you are a student in love with all of phonetics and phonology, so of course you have taken both Phonetics I and Phonology I. You now go to enroll in Phon/Phon II. Surely you would be shocked if the Registrar told you could not enroll in this course. Anyone reading this course brochure would certainly come to the conclusion that someone who had both courses is eligible for the more advanced one. But if *or* meant "one or the other but not both" then that is exactly what (3) would be saying.[5]

Of course there is still one other possibility: that *or* is ambiguous and that (2) uses "exclusive *or*" and (3) uses "inclusive *or*." But if it were ambiguous, then each of these sentences should be too—it should be possible to read (3) in such a way that the Registrar would be entitled to block you from enrolling. But (3) has no such understanding; the Registrar simply could not legitimately come back to you and say "Oh, sorry you misunderstood. You've taken both Phonetics I and Phonology I; so you do not fit the eligibility requirement for enrollment in Phon/Phon II."[6]

---

[5] This point is amusingly illustrated by the following true story. An Ivy League institution which will remain nameless has a teaching center as a resource for graduate students to hone their teaching skills, and gives a certificate to any student who completes a program that includes a series of workshops and other activities (including a "micro-teaching" session). In February of 2011, students in the program received the following e-mail:

Attendance in Workshop #5 is MANDATORY if you belong in any of the following categories:
a. You haven't completed workshop #5, or
b. You haven't completed the Micro-Teaching requirement, or
c. You haven't completed workshop #5 AND you haven't completed the Micro-Teaching requirement.

Of course anyone reading this would be completely amused and wonder why on earth (c) was included here. Surely, no one who had both not completed the workshop and not completed the Micro-Teaching requirement would really think that they were exempt. The fact that we react to this e-mail as being a silly instance of bureaucratic language confirms the point.

[6] The argument is not quite complete, because one might still think that *or* is ambiguous, but that the reason the exclusive interpretation does not emerge is simply because it would be strange in this situation. Our knowledge of how prerequisites work makes this a highly unlikely interpretation in this scenario. But we can tweak the scenario to make the "exclusive" interpretation one that *might* make sense, but is still absent. Suppose that the linguistics department is also very unhappy with students taking courses that overlap too much with what they already know. And suppose that Phon/Phon II overlaps in some ways with Phonetics I and in some ways with Phonology II. In other words, the department is concerned not only about underqualified students, but also overqualified ones. Yet even in this situation, you would be genuinely outraged if the Registrar blocked your enrolment in the course.

Thus while an example like (2) often carries with it the suggestion that only one of the two conjuncts is true, this is just a suggestion and is what is known as an *implicature* rather than being part of the truth conditions. Sometimes the exclusive implicature is quite natural, as in (2), and sometimes it disappears, as in (3). In fact, when embedded under *if* (as in (3)) the exclusive suggestion associated with *or* systematically disappears. Ultimately one would hope for a single, stable meaning, where other principles can predict when the exclusive *or* implicature arises and when it doesn't. Indeed, by assigning it the inclusive semantics in TR-2 combined with a theory of language use (pragmatics), this can be done. (Many readers will be familiar with this under the rubric of *scalar implicature*.) This is the subject of sections 10.4 and 16.6.

3.3. Folding in worlds (and times)

TR-1 and TR-2 are obviously inadequate in that they are given purely *extensionally*: they both ignore the fact that the value of a sentence is not 1 or 0 but a function of type $<w,t>$ (or really $<s,t>$). For convenience, this book generally gives the rules in purely extensional fashion, but this is always just for expository simplification. We can easily write these rules in a more adequate fashion. Thus let us rewrite TR-1 as what we will call INT-TR-1 (INT here for intensional) as follows (actually this includes just the world argument and not the time; the full intensional version would replace "w" with "s" (a world–time pair):

INT-TR-1.   If α is an expression of the form $<[\alpha], S, [[\alpha]]>$ and β is an expression of the form $<[\beta], S, [[\beta]]>$, then there is an expression γ of the form $<[\alpha\text{-and-}\beta], S$, for any world w, $[[\gamma]](w) = 1$ iff $[[\alpha]](w) = 1$ and $[[\beta]](w) = 1>$.

Very often the world argument is given as a superscript, so one can rewrite the semantic part of this rule as given below:

$[[\gamma]]^w = 1$ iff $[[\alpha]]^w = 1$ and $[[\beta]]^w = 1$

Indeed, if the intent were to keep out both the underqualified and the overqualified student, the brochure would have to be revised to say "if you have taken Phonology I or you have taken Phonetics I and you have not taken both." So even in a scenario designed to bring out the "exclusive *or*" interpretation, it is not there.

One will commonly find this notation in the literature (and this will be used from time to time in this book). Notice that $[[\alpha]]^w$ means exactly the same thing as $[[\alpha]](w)$ –the superscript notation has an implicit "for all worlds w" at the beginning of the whole rule. One should keep in mind that nothing (other than taste and expository ease) hinges on the choice of notation. The grammar is a system that proves expressions well-formed and assigns each expression a model-theoretic interpretation; the notation that one chooses to express the model-theoretic object being assigned is of no theoretical consequence.

3.1. Rewrite the intensional version of TR-2 (i.e., INT-TR-2) using both of the notations for dealing with the world argument shown above.

3.2. For any function f that characterizes a set, let us use the notation f_S to mean the set characterized by f. Now recall that we can think of the value of a sentence as a function of type <w,t> (a function from worlds to truth values) or—equivalently—as a set of worlds; the set mapped to 1 by the function. Thinking in set terms, what does *and* do? (That is, what operation on sets does it correspond to?) What about *or*? Using the notation suggested just above, write out the semantics for INT-TR-1 in set terms. Do the same for INT-TR-2.

3.4. Negation: A first pass

Readers familiar with first-order logic (or simple propositional logic) will recognize that the syntax and semantics of English sketched so far looks a bit like the syntax of simple logical languages in which two propositions p and q may be connected with $\wedge$ ("and") and $\vee$ ("or"). A third operator that one might be used to seeing from elementary logic is a negation operator which is prefixed in front of a proposition. (Thus, in the development of an elementary propositional logic, there is a rule saying that if p is a well-formed formula then so is ~p. The truth value of ~p is the reverse of that of p.)

If we try to model English directly using the tools from first-order logic in this way, we immediately reach a challenge for the Direct Compositional program. For a sentence like (4b) is the negation of (4a): if the first is true the second is false and vice versa:

(4)   a. Olympia Snowe voted for Bill 1838 (the only time it came up for a vote).
   b. Olympia Snowe didn't vote for Bill 1838 (the only time it came up for a vote).

Yet the syntax of English is completely different from the syntax of propositional logic. *Not* is not prefixed at the beginning of a sentence. It is not even prefixed at the beginning of a verb phrase. It generally shows up as a clitic on an auxiliary (as in *didn't* above, where it is a suffix attached to *did*.) Semantically, though, it seems reasonable to think of it as negating the entire sentence in which it sits.

There are two choices for resolving this apparent mismatch between the syntax and the semantics. One is to reject the Direct Compositional hypothesis. A common solution here is to imagine that actual English syntax is mapped into another level (called Logical Form, or LF) and that the grammar proceeds containing a rule or series of rules that map (4) into something like (5) (or perhaps something even more abstract), and that the compositional semantics interprets (5):

(5)   not [Olympia Snowe voted for Bill 1838 (the only time it came up for a vote)]

Then *not* here can be given the interpretation exactly like the symbol ~ is in logic. The second possibility is to conclude that it is a mistake to try to copy logic in giving a meaning for English *n't*—its meaning might have something to do with "~" but perhaps it is a more complex packaging of negation. This is the strategy that we will ultimately aim for; it allows for a much simpler conception of the grammar.

Temporarily, though, we take a third tack: which is to postpone incorporating into our fragment the natural way to do negation in English, and instead pretend that English has a single word *it-is-not-the-case-that* which can be prefixed to a sentence to negate it. Hence we enrich our fragment with TR-3 and its intensional counterpart INT-TR-3:

TR-3.   If a is an expression of the form $<[a], S, [[a]]>$ then there is an expression β of the form $<[it\text{-}is\text{-}not\text{-}the\text{-}case\text{-}that\text{-}a], S, 1$ iff $[[a]] = 0>$.

INT-TR-3. If α is an expression of the form $<[\alpha], S, [[\alpha]]>$ then there is an expression β of the form $<[\text{it-is-not-the-case-that-}\alpha], S, [[\beta]]$ is a function from worlds to truth values such that for any w, $[[\beta]](w) = 1$ iff $[[\alpha]](w) = 0>$.

(or, using the shorthand, the semantic part would read $[[\beta]]^w = 1$ iff $[[\alpha]]^w = 0$).

For truth in advertising, while the final fragment will be closer to actual English, it will still not be a complete account of English *n't*, simply because space precludes an account of the English auxiliary system. But TR-3 will be improved upon.

3.3. As in Exercise 3.2, rewrite this in set terms. What is the operation on sets that corresponds to negation?

4

Expanding the fragment: Syntactic categories and semantic types

4.1. Noun phrases

English has a variety of expressions like *the woman who is jogging down Blackstone Boulevard, the most disobedient puppy in Alexandra's puppy class, the house on the southeast of Chace Ave. and Hope St.*, etc. We will take it as given that these are all of the same grammatical category and will refer to them as NPs (see Chapter 1, n. 8). Let us assume that all expressions of the same syntactic category correspond to the same type (very broadly speaking) of semantic object. This assumption was already made for the case of S; we took each S to have a meaning of type $\langle s,t \rangle$, i.e., a function from world–time pairs to truth values. Recall that our basic semantic toolbox so far consists of the set of truth values, worlds, and times. But none of these are obvious candidates for NP meanings. What, then, is the type of thing that NPs have as their semantic values?

For the NPs illustrated above the answer seems simple: add to the toolbox a set of individuals, and assume that each NP picks out an individual. The notation e will denote the set of individuals; hence the value of an NP is some member of e. Of course, one immediately observes that this has a problem analogous to the problem of saying that the value of a sentence is a truth value. After all, the individual picked out by *the most disobedient puppy in Alexandra's puppy class* is entirely contingent on how the world happens to be: it could have been the puppy Mitka but it could instead have been the puppy Brunhilde. Besides, this can also depend on when this is uttered—the referent of the puppy-NP will change from year to year. Moreover, one can know the meaning of an NP without knowing who it picks out: I know what it means to say *the tallest man in the world on Jan. 1, 2011* but I have no idea who this is. So the solution is also analogous to the situation with sentences: the *intension* (the actual meaning) of an NP is a function from worlds and times to individuals—that is, some function in <s,e>. Note that this says that if one knows the meaning of an NP *and knows everything there is to know about the actual world and time*, one can indeed pick out the relevant individual. But we are not omniscient, so we know the meaning (the intension) without necessarily knowing the extension. Our toolbox for constructing meanings now consists of the set of worlds (w), the set of times (i) (we continue to use s for the set of world–time pairs), the set of truth values (t), and the set of individuals (e). Incidentally, one might wonder whether the individuals are separate from the worlds: does it make sense to talk about an individual independent of the world in which it is located? As for the case of times, we will here treat the set of individuals as separate from the set of worlds and the evidence for this is quite similar (we can march an individual from world to world using a counterfactual conditional). We return to this shortly.

The claim that NPs pick out (in any given world and time) an individual has some interesting consequences. First, this means we need to think of "individual" rather broadly; the domain of individuals needs to include quite abstract things like those things picked out by the NPs *the idea that the earth is flat*, *the desire to leave*, etc. Moreover, in addition to our normal individuals like you, me, and my dog we have plural individuals (*the dogs*). We will not deal with these here, save to say that they can be treated as a special kind of individual (Link 1983). Finally, there is a class of expressions traditionally called NPs which really do seem to resist being treated as individuals: these are "NPs" with quantificational determiners like *every dog, no dog, few dogs*, and so forth. These will simply be excluded from the fragment for now. They form the basis of some of the most interesting and rich work in semantics, and will be the subject of Chapter 10.

Consider now the case of names like *Mitka, Barack Obama*, etc. Traditional grammar tells us that these are "nouns" (they are considered "proper nouns" as opposed to "common nouns" like *dog, table, stream*, but both are called nouns). But in fact names (in English) have nothing in common syntactically, morphologically, or semantically with common nouns. Unlike ordinary common nouns, they do not take plural morphology. They do not occur with determiners like *the*.[1] And, as we will see below, while NPs denote individuals, common nouns surely do not (*the hungry dog* picks out an individual, but *dog* does not). On the other hand, names have exactly the same syntactic distribution as do ordinary NPs; the name *Mitka* can occur in all the same syntactic environments as an NP like *the disobedient husky*. Moreover, names and NPs are similar semantically: clearly a name picks out an individual, just like more a complex NP containing *the*. Given that names have the same syntactic distribution and the same semantic type as NPs in general, the conclusion is obvious: they are NPs. Our fragment will treat these as listed in the lexicon as NPs. Incidentally, we will also for now take complex NPs such as *the disobedient husky, the first man on the moon*, and so forth to just be listed in the fragment as single items; the internal structure of these is the subject of Chapter 8.

Note that this departs from a traditional view that a category label like NP (noun *phrase*) is an appropriate label only for expressions containing more than one word. Along with this traditional view goes the idea that single words must have as their category one of what is traditionally called the "basic parts of speech"—noun, verb, adjective, preposition, determiner (or article), adverb, and perhaps a few others. (These are the "parts of

---

[1] There are examples where proper nouns occur with determiners, as in (i) and (ii):

(i) The Berrymans are coming over to dinner tonight.

(ii) Every Dmitri in the semantics class might be a bit annoyed at the use of the name *Mitka* in so many example sentences.

But we can analyze these as cases where a proper noun shifts its class and is used as an ordinary common noun. English is very free with shifting items from one category to another (along with a meaning change). It should, however, be noted that a number of semanticists have explored a different view of proper names according to which *Mitka* instead means something like "the one who is named Mitka."

speech" that still form the subject of colorful posters decorating elementary school walls, along with such odd definitions as "a verb is an action word" and "an adjective describes a pronoun.") The traditional parts of speech are not entirely fiction—the notion that at least some of these categories are appropriate labels for a class of words is based on *morphological commonalities*. "Nouns," for example, can (generally) combine with the suffix /z/ to form plurals; "verbs" combine with (among others) the suffix *-ing*, "adjectives" can (generally) combine with *-er* to form comparatives, etc. Thus the grammar may well need access to the notion of a class of "nouns," "verbs," and "adjectives" for the purposes of the morphology. But even granted that, we have already seen that proper nouns do not show noun-like morphology. There is no reason then not to call them NPs. The category name is arbitrary; it could as well be 342, D, or Butternutsquash; a category is just the name for a group of expressions with the same syntactic distribution and semantic type. (Under the Categorial Grammar syntax developed in Chapter 6 it turns out that many category labels are not actually arbitrary since the names themselves encode distributional information. But there will be a set of basic category names, including NP, which remain arbitrary.) Incidentally, there are plurals (like *dogs*) and mass nouns (like *water*), which can function both as nouns (they can occur with the determiner *the* to give an NP) or as NPs as in *Dogs make good pets*, *Water is plentiful on this island*. When they are NPs they have some similarity to proper names: they name "kinds" of objects. (For much more detailed discussion, see Carlson 1980 among others.)

Still, there does seem to be one difference between a name such as *Barack Obama* and an NP like *the president of the US in 2011*. As discussed above, the referent of the latter depends on how the world happens to be. One can imagine worlds in which things had worked out differently and this NP picked out John McCain, or more distant worlds in which this picked out Dennis Kucinich. One can even imagine yet more distant worlds in which it picked out the lead dog of the winning Iditarod team (just imagine a massive change in the political system, a revision in the duties of the president, and a bit of dog worship). But the referent of a proper name like *Barack Obama* is stable; change the world all you want, let in a bit of dog worship and a massive change in the political system, and the referent of this NP remains the same. One can even change some rather fundamental properties—assume that Barack Obama not only is not president but happens to have been born in Kenya, moved to France, and became a master sommelier. The referent remains the same—just many things about him are changed.[2]

The account of this proposed by Kripke (1980) is to treat names as *rigid designators*. This simply means that a name does indeed denote a function from worlds to individuals, but the relevant function maps every world to the same individual. Any function which assigns the same value to everything in its domain is called a *constant function*. Note that this hinges on the assumption made earlier: that the domain of individuals is not world-dependent—the set of individuals is independent of the worlds.[3] Odd though this may seem at first glance, we can use the tool of counterfactual conditionals to give plausibility both to the claim that the same individual can march around from world to world, and for the claim that proper names are rigid designators. Consider the following sentences:

(1) If Barack Obama had been born in Kenya, he would not have been eligible to be president of the US.

(2) If Barack Obama had grown up in France, he would have become a master sommelier.

The semantics in Chapter 2 for counterfactual conditionals leads to the conclusion that there is some individual—call that individual o—whose properties can vary from world to world but is nonetheless a single individual. Moreover, the name *Barack Obama* picks out o in our world, where he is President of the US in 2013 and was born in Hawaii, and continues to pick

---

[2] Notice that we can change large facts about a person—even their birthplace—as we move them from world to world while still considering them the same person. Lest one think that a person's birthplace is a necessary fact about them—rather than a contingent fact—consider the claims of the "Birthers." These are a group of people who have continually insisted that Barack Obama was actually born in Kenya (and hence ineligible to be president of the US). Notice that while this group insists on a world in which the Barack Obama individual was born somewhere else, they never once disputed that Barack Obama is Barack Obama. The dispute kept the individual constant, and simply centered on a world (not the actual one) in which that same individual had a different birthplace from his actual one (which is Hawaii).

[3] One might wonder how could this be, since it is a contingent fact as to who is born, and therefore who is "actual" in any given world. We can, however, assume that there is an equivocation here about the word "existence." Let us imagine some very abstract notion of "existence" which holds for all individuals who are present in any world. And of course one can also wonder about the proper account of fictional individuals like *Santa Claus*. These worries are all beyond the present scope.

out o in the world in (1) in which o was born in Kenya, and in the world in (2) in which o grew up in France.

While difficult, one can even change more basic facts about the individuals. My dog Mitka happens to be a Siberian husky, but I could meaningfully assert (3a) and even (3b):

(3)   a. If Mitka had been a Labrador Retriever, I would have been able to let him off leash.
b. If Mitka had been a wolf, his fear of thunder would not have let him survive.

Again these sentences make sense if we can take the individual rigidly referred to by *Mitka*, locate him in a different world, and change his properties, while still tracking that it is the same individual. We will thus adopt Kripke's semantics for these. This allows us to account for the observations above, while keeping their semantic type the same as that of other NPs: functions of type <s,e>. They just happen to be constant functions.

---

*4.1. The verb *think* takes as its object (or complement) a sentence as in *Chris thought that the earth was flat*. This verb is a good example of something which crucially combines with *intensions*. The object of Chris's thoughts is not just a truth value 1 or 0, but a set of worlds (all worlds compatible with what he believes). If one wishes to simplify, one can think of this as simply a single world—for the purposes of this question it makes no difference.

Notice that there is an interesting ambiguity in a sentence like the following:

(i)   Bill thinks that the mayor of Providence will win the marinara sauce competition.

See if you can detect what the ambiguity is and describe—perfectly informally—how one might account for the ambiguity. (Do note that this exercise is *not* looking for a formal account, as the tools for that are developed only in Chapter 19. The hope is that the informal intuition might be accessible.) Keep in mind that phrases like *the mayor of Providence* are functions from worlds to individuals; this is crucial. Assume further that in putting the whole semantics together, some actual world is "plugged in" as the argument of the function so that this NP ends up denoting an individual, but the individual can vary from world to world. Incidentally, this phrase is also time-dependent (it actually denotes a

(cont.)

> function of type <s,e>) but this fact can and should be ignored here; keep the time constant.
>
> Now notice that (ii) does not display the same type of ambiguity:
>
> (ii) Bill thought that Buddy Cianci would win the marinara sauce competition.
>
> Comment on why this is not surprising. (A historical note: Buddy Cianci is not the mayor of Providence at the time of writing this book. But he was, and indeed he did make award-winning marinara sauce.)

Before leaving this, we can also note that some NPs fail to refer to anyone in the actual world, giving rise to the classic notion of presupposition failure. The time-honored example (from Russell 1905) is *the (present) King of France*. As mentioned earlier, this book contains no in-depth discussion of presupposition, but we can note that one account is to treat the meaning of such NPs as partial functions from worlds to individuals, undefined for this world.

4.2. Intransitive verbs/verb phrases

The toolbox so far contains as basic building blocks a set of worlds, a set of times, a set of truth values, and a set of individuals. While there is controversy as to whether other primitives (e.g., events) are necessary, one can get surprisingly far using only these sets and constructing other semantic objects using sets and functions built out of these. As a first step, consider the case of sentences with intransitive verbs. First a small bit of housekeeping. Sentences with simple intransitive verbs in English can contain the verbs in the past tense, as in:

(4) The president coughed.

(5) Mitka howled.

But we are ignoring the semantics of the past tense (as we wish to ignore times), and so in using examples of this type it should be kept in mind that the semantics is incomplete. Note, incidentally, that we could not give a fuller account by recasting into the syntactic form which is called the *simple present*, as in (6) and (7), for the semantics of these is even more complex:

(6) The president coughs.

(7) Mitka howls.

Sentences with "eventive" verbs (*coughs*, *runs*, *howls*) in the tense which is called simple present in English actually do not make a statement about an event holding true at the moment of utterance. For example, (6) does not entail that the president is coughing at this moment, but that this happens from time to time with some regularity. These are called *habitual* statements. So we will refrain from using these sentences, and stick to past-tense cases.

We begin with the syntax. We will refer to the category of intransitive verbs as V_I, and will at this point assume that English contains the two phrase structure rules in (8):

(8) a. S $\rightarrow$ NP VP   b. VP $\rightarrow$ V_I

Of course, a different possibility would be to adopt only the rule in (8a) and simply think of *cough*, *howl*, and so forth as lexical VPs. After all, it was shown above that single words could be lexical NPs, and it would make sense to take the same solution here. But in the present case the situation is more complex, for here transitive verbs (*like*, *kill*, etc.), ditransitive verbs (*give*, *put*, etc.), and intransitive verbs (and many other things that are traditionally call ed "verbs") *do* have common properties. They are the class that takes past-tense morphology, the *-ing* suffix, etc. In other words, the morphology treats them as a single class, giving some basis for the traditional notion that these form a single "part of speech." For now, then, let us stick with tradition and call these all verbs (using a subscript feature as above in order to distinguish their syntactic distribution—and, shortly, their semantic type) which leads us to adopt the two rules in (8). All of this will be modified in Chapter 6 when we turn to Categorial Grammar.

The simplest semantics to associate with the rule (8b) is one which says that meaning of the VP is the same as the meaning of the V_1. Put in the official notation then, (8b) can be recast as follows:

TR-4. If a is an expression of the form $<[a], V_I, [[a]]>$, then there is an expression β of the form $<[a], VP, [[a]]>$.

The remaining challenge is to determine the type of meaning for the intransitive verb (and hence the VP) itself. This can easily be done without introducing any new primitives into the basic set: let these pick out (in a world and at a time) a *set* of individuals.

At first, this seems odd. But first, note that—as with NPs and Ss—there is a distinction between the *intension* of an intransitive verb and its *extension*. The intension is a function from worlds (and times) to sets; it is only the extension that is a set. Indeed, if you knew everything about the world (and time) that you were living in, and you knew the meaning of the word *cough*, you could determine the set of coughers. So intransitive verbs have meanings of type $<s,<e,t>>$. To make this a bit more intuitive, we digress briefly to talk about word meaning. Modeling the meaning of intransitive verbs as functions into sets of individuals gives some nice tools for talking about the relationship between the meanings of different words that clearly have certain semantic properties in common.

4.3. A brief look at lexical semantics

Thus while this book is primarily about compositional semantics—how the meanings of smaller expressions (including individual words) combine to give the meanings of larger expressions—that project itself is obviously intimately tied up with *lexical semantics*, i.e., the project of determining the meanings of the basic units (the words). And the tools developed so far are quite useful for lexical semantics as well as compositional semantics. Consider, for example, the fact that (9) entails (10) and that this is clearly a fact about the meanings of *dance* and *move*:

(9) Sabrina danced.

(10) Sabrina moved.

If we stick to the idea that the extension of any intransitive verb is a set of individuals, there is a simple way to express the relation between these two verbs. One part of the meaning of [[dance]] is that for every individual in the set it picks out, that individual is also in the [[move]] set. Put differently, the extension of [[dance]] at any world is a subset of [[move]] (in that world). (Of course [[dance]] is richer than just this, so the full lexical entry will say more.)

   This also provides tools for the meanings of certain words which are often thought of as being decomposable into other bits of meanings. To illustrate, we turn from intransitive verbs to nouns. As will be discussed more fully in Chapter 8, nouns also plausibly have as their meanings world- and time-dependent sets of individuals. Some noun meanings lend themselves to a combination of other concepts. A famous example (see, e.g., Katz and Fodor 1963) is *bachelor*, which in early work on lexical semantics within generative grammar was treated as being composed of a few primitive concepts. Oversimplifying somewhat, we can reconstruct this idea by saying that [[bachelor]] is a function from worlds and times to sets of individuals such that for any world w and time i [[bachelor]] at w and i is the set: $\{x|x \in$ [[male]] (at i and in w) and $x \in$ [[adult]] (at i and w) and $x \notin$ [[married]] (at i and w)}. This recapitulates—in model-theoretic terms—the early "lexical decomposition" analysis of this in terms of primitive concepts. Of course the above needs refining, but we have the tools to make the necessary refinements. For a bachelor is not any unmarried male adult, but one who has never been married. Thus we can revise the above by requiring that for each x in the [[bachelor]] set at world w and time i, there is no time i' prior to and including i at which $x \in$ [[married]].

4.2. The situation is even more interesting: possible worlds also appear to be necessary to give a full treatment of even a simple word like *bachelor* which is often trotted out in lexical semantics courses to illustrate how words decompose into other concepts. Thus most speakers have the intuition that a Catholic priest is not felicitously referred to as a *bachelor*, nor is a gay man in a state which does not recognize same-sex marriage.

   (i)   How can the use of possible worlds provide a way to capture these intuitions?

   (ii) Having done (i), does this also us to eliminate any other part of the above definition? Note too that we did not put [[human]] in the definition above although this might have struck the reader as a missing ingredient. But given (i), do we need it?

Moral: A speaker's ability to use perfectly ordinary words like *bachelor* involves counterfactual reasoning.

4.4. Back to the compositional semantics

With this much, we can now formulate the semantics for the rule in (8a). Recasting into the official notation yields TR-5 (given extensionally):

TR-5.   If α is an expression of the form <[α], NP, [[α]]> and β is an expression of the form <[β], VP, [[β]]>, then there is an expression γ of the form <[α-β], S, 1 if [[α]] ϵ [[β]], and 0 otherwise>.

Notice that TR-5 as formulated above leaves no room for treating certain kinds of presupposition failure as a case of a sentence being neither true nor false. In other words, for the sake of discussion take *stop-smoking* as a single intransitive verb. It is sometimes assumed that when predicated of someone who never smoked the result is neither 1 nor 0 but is simply undefined. The semantics above provides no way to accommodate for this view; every sentence of the form *NP stopped smoking* will be either true or false. We remedy this directly below.

> **4.3.** Give the intensional version of TR-5.

TR-5 is based on treating the meaning of an intransitive verb as (relative to a world and time) a set of individuals. But as shown in Chapter 2, any set can be recast as the characteristic function of that set. Thus an intransitive verb like *cough* or *howl* can instead be taken as picking out (in any world and time) a function from individuals to truth values. Using e to mean the set of all individuals, this then picks out a function of type <e,t> (so its full meaning is a function of type <s,<e,t>>). Using functions rather than sets has two potential advantages. First, it provides a more general tool for modeling meanings, as will be clear later. Second, it is a richer notion than the set version because potentially there could be *partial functions* (in this case, a function defined only for a subset of the domain of individuals). If these do exist, one can always recover a set of individuals from a (possibly partial) function of type <e,t>: the relevant set is the set mapped to true by the function. But one cannot recover the function from the set (if something is not in the set, it could be that it is assigned 0 by the function, or it could be that it is simply not in the domain of the function). For the most part this book will make little use of partial functions, but will leave open the possibility of using it for presupposition failure. Under this technique [[stop-smoking]] maps an individual to true (at a time i) if that individual smoked at a time earlier than i and does not smoke at i; false (at time i) if that individual smoked at a time earlier than i and also smokes at i, and undefined otherwise.

Having made this revision on the semantic types, we revise TR-5 as follows (given extensionally here):

TR-5'. If there is an expression a of the form $<[a]$, NP, $[[a]]>$ and an expression β of the form $<[\beta]$, VP, $[[\beta]]>$, then there is an expression of the form $<[a\text{-}\beta]$, S, $[[\beta]]$ ($[[a]]$)$>$.

If there are partial functions and if $[[a]]$ is not in the domain of $[[\beta]]$ then we have undefinedness (and hence the result is undefined at the world and time in question); otherwise the VP-function applies to the individual in question and yields either 1 or 0.

4.4. Give TR-5' in its intensional form.

4.5. Illustrating the syntactic/semantic composition

Let us illustrate the workings of the fragment that has been developed so far (along with a suitable lexicon). Consider (11).

(11)   The disobedient husky escaped and the obedient husky slept.

We assume the lexical items *escaped*, *slept*, etc. of category V_1 with meanings of type $<s,<e,t>>$; and *the-disobedient-husky* and *the-obedient-husky* of category NP with meanings of type $<s,e>$. Extensionally, a V_1 denotes a function in $<e,t>$ and an NP denotes some member of e. If we actually knew all the facts about the world in question, we could show out the actual extensions of each of these at that world. By way of illustration, imagine a "universe" with four individuals $\{a,b,c,d\}$. Further, imagine a world w_1, whereby $[[\text{the-disobedient-husky}]](w_1) = a$ and $[[\text{the-obedient-husky}]]$ $(w_1) = c$. Assume further that $[[\text{escaped}]](w_1)$ is the function mapping a and c to 1 and b and d to 0 (thus it characterizes the set $\{a,c\}$, while $[[\text{slept}]](w_1)$ maps b to 1 and a, c, and d to 0 (thus it characterizes the set $\{b\}$). We can now use the notation in (12) as one way to illustrate how it is that the grammar proves (11) as well-formed and puts together its meaning.

In the semantic part, we are showing *only* the extension of each expression at w_1. We give each expression as a triple of phonology, category, meaning (actually, extension). For visual ease we will omit the brackets < ... > around each triple, and we will omit the brackets [...] and [[...]] around the sound and meaning parts respectively.

(12)   the-disobedient-husky; NP; a
escaped; V_I; a → 1, b → 0, c → 1, d → 0
                these two lines just show the information that is in the lexicon
escaped; VP; a → 1, b → 0, c → 1, d → 0 (by TR-4)
the-disobedient-husky escaped; S; 1 (by TR-5′)
the-obedient-husky; NP; c
slept; V_I; a → 0, b → 1, c → 0, d → 0 (these two lines again given by the lexicon)
slept; VP; a → 0, b → 1, c → 0, d → 0 (by TR-4)
the-obedient-husky slept; S; 0 (by TR-5′)
the-disobedient-husky escaped and the-obedient-husky slept; S; 0 (by TR-1)

There are many other ways one could illustrate this. Since we generally do not have all the facts of some actual world at our disposal, we could write the semantic composition more generally. For example, the semantic part of the fourth line can be rewritten as follows: $[[\text{escape}]]^w([[\text{the-disobedient-husky}]]^w)$. Remember that formulas like this contain a hidden clause at the beginning: so this says that for all worlds w, the value of this expression is the value [[escaped]] at w applied to the value of [[the-disobedient-husky]] at w. Thus one can show part of the composition as in (13):

(13)   the-disobedient-husky; NP; [[the-disobedient-husky]] w
escaped; V_I; $[[\text{escaped}]]^w$
escaped; VP; $[[\text{escaped}]]^w$ (by TR-4)
the-disobedient-husky escaped; S; $[[\text{escaped}]]^w$ $([[\text{the-disobedient-husky}]]^w$ (by INT-TR-5′)

In fact, in general we will illustrate the semantics this way (since we could not list the actual function which corresponds to, e.g. [[escaped]]). Among other difficulties in doing that, we would have to list this out for every possible world. But it is sometimes useful to pick a world and demonstrate the composition extensionally as in (12) as a reminder that the semantics is not computing formulas, but actual model-theoretic objects. Formulas—as in (13)—are just what we humans need in order to write out those objects. It is also generally not necessary to put in each rule that licenses the next line;

this is useful only when it serves some clarificational purpose. The literature contains other methods for visually displaying the syntax and semantics at work. Often this is shown as an annotated tree. A traditional tree shows just the phonological part—what precedes what—and the categories of each expression, but not the meanings). One could then "decorate" each node label with the semantics.

4.5. Consider the following model of a tiny universe. We will be concerned with just one world and one time, so we can consider everything extensionally. Our universe has four individuals {a,b,c,d}. At the world in question, [[howl]] maps a and c to 1, b and d to 0. [[cough]] maps b to 1 and all other individuals to 0. [[Balto]] picks out a; [[the hungry dog]] picks out d. Show the full syntactic and semantic composition for

(i) Balto howled and the hungry dog coughed.

In this case, the task is to show the actual extension of each expression at the world in question; thus use (12) as the model for showing this.

4.6. To make things interesting, and to give a flavor for intensionality, let us add in another world. World 1 (which we will label as w_1) will be exactly the world set up in Exercise 4.5. World 2 (labeled w_2) is as follows: [[Balto]] still picks out a (of course, since it is a rigid designator); [[the hungry dog]] picks out c; [[is-howling]] maps all four individuals to 0; and [[is-coughing]] maps a, c, and d to 1 and b to 0. Now show the syntactic and semantic composition where at each step you should show the full function from each of the two worlds to its value, and show how this is computed step by step.

5

Transitive verbs: Resolving an apparent syntax/semantics mismatch

This chapter is somewhat didactic—for a reason. The immediate goal is to discover the semantic type of transitive verbs, which could be done in a few pages. But we will instead go down a lengthy and winding path (which will turn out to be fruitless). This involves setting up a somewhat naive "Straw Man," whose hypothesis requires giving up Direct Compositionality and then leads to greater and greater complications. After Straw Man has taken enough twists and turns, we abandon that path, and turn to a simple Direct Compositional solution. In one sense the lengths to which Straw Man goes is a bit silly, for in reality most work in modern semantics does not take the Straw Man position. The ultimate solution arrived at in this chapter is fairly standard (even in non-Direct Compositional theories).[1] But this is precisely what makes this domain an important one. For here the Direct Compositional solution turns out to be

---

[1] An exception to this is work done under the rubric of *Neo-Davidsonian event semantics*; see, e.g., Parsons (1990).

reasonably obvious with some fairly simple tools that allow the semantics to be set up in such a way as to respect the syntax. Perhaps, then, this basic strategy extends to other domains; perhaps slightly more subtle tools can be pressed into service in other cases that appear to challenge Direct Compositionality.

5.1. First pass: Straw Man's solution

Consider sentences with transitive verbs like those in (1):

(1)   a. Juliet loves Romeo.
      b. The pig chased the wolf.
      c. Lee kissed Sandy.

(Once again t eventive verbs like *chase* and *kiss* are put into the past tense to avoid the habitual reading that emerges with present-tense morphology.) What kind of meaning should be assigned to *kiss*, which is often thought of as a relation between individuals? Straw Man consults an elementary logic book, in which sentences like (1c) are translated into a formula of first-order predicate logic and are represented as in (2):[2]

(2)   K(l,s)

Recall that an intransitive verb has as its value a (world/time-dependent) function of type $<e,t>$. If asked how to construe (2) as a way to name a model-theoretic object, a reasonable answer is to take l and s in the formula above to denote individuals, and to take [[K]] to be a function whose domain is the set of all ordered pairs of individuals and whose co-domain is the set of truth values. In other words, (l,s) picks out an ordered pair of two individuals, and [[K]] is a function mapping such a pair to true or false. In set terms, [[K]] characterizes a *set of ordered pairs of individuals*.

Straw Man applies this to the semantic composition of English, and concludes that English [[kiss]] is like [[K]]: a function from the set of ordered pairs of individuals to t. (Recall that the set of all ordered pairs whose first member is in set A and second is in set B is represented as A x B.) Thus the

---

[2] While we will show that this is not a good way to represent the semantic composition of English, the point here is *not* to criticize the use of such formulas in a logic textbook: most work using formulae like this does not claim to be modeling the grammar of natural language. The goal of the logician is quite different (to provide a way to represent valid reasoning systems).

type of meaning for a transitive verb would be $<e \times e,t>$ (or, more accurately, $<s,<e \times e,t>>$). Incidentally, one need not have taken a logic class to come up with the hypothesis that transitive verbs take ordered pairs as their arguments. We often speak of *kiss* as denoting a (two-place) relation between two individuals. But recall that the formal notion of a (two-place) relation is a set of ordered pairs (and of course any set can be recast as the characteristic function of that set, which gives the type above).[3] It is also common parlance to say that the verb applies to a pair of a "kisser" and "kissee," or to an "agent" and a "theme," and this also leads naturally to the hypothesis that the type for transitive verbs is as above. There is, in fact, nothing wrong with this informal terminology; the central question of this chapter is whether the type above is the right way to formally model the informal intuition.

Let us call the syntactic category of a transitive verb V_2. Then the semantic type assumed above leads us to posit FR-1. (Fictional rules that will quickly be discarded will be notated as FR.) To minimize notational collision, an ordered pair whose first member is a and second is b will (non-standardly) be notated as {a,b} (with boldface curly brackets to distinguish from ordinary curly brackets which are used for sets). This notation is not ideal, but unfortunately all of the other types of bracket are used elsewhere in our formalism (the standard representation of an ordered pair is (a,b), but parentheses are also used to indicate the argument of a function). FR-1 is given extensionally here; the interested reader can supply the intensional version:

FR-1   If there is an expression α of the form $<[\alpha]$, NP, $[[\alpha]]>$, an expression β of the form $<[\beta]$, NP, $[[\beta]]>$ and an expression γ of the form $<[\gamma]$, V_T, $[[\gamma]]>$ then there is an expression δ of the form $<[\alpha$-γ-$\beta]$, S, $[[\gamma]](\{[[\alpha]], [[\beta]]\})>$.

Since the meaning of the transitive verb combines with the meanings of its subject and object simultaneously in the semantics (i.e., by applying to an ordered pair) the syntax also directly combines the two NPs with the transitive verb.

But wait, says the syntactician. We learn from our introductory syntax texts that this cannot be the right syntax. The phrase structure rule embodied in FR-1 is S → NP V_2 NP, but we know (or at least we think) that *loves Juliet* in (1a) is a constituent and similarly for *kissed Sandy* in (1c). Moreover, we know (or at least we think) that these expressions are of exactly

---

[3] A two-place relation means a set of ordered pairs. There are also three-place relations which are sets of ordered triples, and more generally one can speak of *ordered n-tuples*.

the same category as expressions consisting of only single intransitive verbs—i.e., they are VPs. It is actually worth occasionally reminding oneself of the arguments that lead to this conclusion; we mention just one here. Expressions like *kissed Sandy, watered the plants,* or *fed the pig* can conjoin with each other, and can also conjoin with simple intransitive verbs:[4]

(3) a. Lee watered the plants and fed the pig.
     b. Lee watered the plants and meditated.
     c. Lee meditated and fed the pig.

If transitive verbs were introduced in the syntax in the flat way given in FR-1, we would need three additional syntactic rules for these:

(4) a. S → NP V_T NP and V_T NP
     b. S → NP V_T NP and V_I
     c. S → NP V_I and V_T NP

But this would still not be enough for these conjunctions can be iterated:

(5) a. Lee fed the pig and chased the wolf and meditated.
     b. Lee fed the pig and meditated and watered the plants and studied.

Additional rules would thus be needed, but since one can iterate these indefinitely, no amount of new rules will be enough. Positing a category VP solves all of this: simply add a syntactic rule of the form in (6), and assume the two VP rules in (7):

(6) VP → VP and VP

(7) a. VP → V_I
     b. VP → V_T NP

Note that the remarks above concerning *and* extend also to *or* as in (8), and so we also add the rule in (9):

(8) a. Lee milked the cow or fed the pig.
     b. Lee milked the cow or meditated.

(9) VP → VP or VP

---

[4] There are actually many versions of generative grammar—including earliest Transformational Grammar—in which it is assumed that all verbs must have a subject (at least at some level) in the syntax. This would invalidate the argument below. For *fed the pig* in (3a) for example would at some level have a deleted or silent subject and be a full sentence; and all conjunction would actually involve S conjunction. We will not consider these here, but see the discussion in section 5.3.

Ultimately, there are many refinements one could make to (6) and (9), but these formulations are fine for now as we turn back to the semantics.

All is well as far as the syntax is concerned, but since the goal is a theory of syntax *and* semantics it is striking to notice that the rules above give only the syntactic side. What would be the semantics that goes along with (7b)? Well, if we continue with the Straw Man hypothesis (i.e., [[kiss]] is a function that takes as its argument some ordered pair) there can be none. The reason is simple: V_2 is not of the right type to combine with just the one individual denoted by the object NP. And since there is no semantics for (7b), it also does not make sense to ask about the semantics associated with (6) and (9); there is none.

5.2. Abandoning Direct Compositionality

Straw Man is stubborn and does not wish to give up on the idea that [[kiss]] is a function whose domain is e x e. But he has learned his syntax well and is happy enough with the syntactic rules above. Thus he decides to abandon the hypothesis of Direct Compositionality. He will leave the syntax of (7) alone, and adopt a different model of grammar from the one we have been assuming so far. Before developing this, a word about the role of trees. Probably a bit surprisingly for a linguist, there has so far not been a single tree drawn in this book. This is because we have simply stated the rules, and the rules so far make no reference to trees. Consider a complex sentence like, for example, *Mitka howled and Porky grunted*. (Porky made his debut in semantics in Lewis 1970.) One can of course draw a tree for this, but the tree is just a representation of the steps in a proof of the well-formedness of the sentence. Suppose that the rules combining expressions do nothing more than put such expressions next to each other: this is known as *concatenation* (this assumption will be subject to greater scrutiny in 5.5). Put differently, the syntactic portion of the rules are just those that could be written as a context-free phrase structure grammar (see Chapter 3, n. 4).[5] Under this

---

[5] It is well known that ultimately a theory of grammar will need to include rules beyond just context-free phrase structure rules (which only concatenate expressions). While the jury may remain out for the case of English, considerable debate about this point during the 1980s (especially within the theory of Generalized Phrase Structure Grammar) showed that additional devices beyond context-free phrase structure grammars will be needed for other languages. But just how much "extra" is needed remains open. See section 5.5 for discussion of these points.

view, the grammar never needs to refer to trees as it never refers to the internal structure of some expression. A tree is always just a way to represent the proof of the well-formedness of some expression, and given the Direct Compositional hypothesis, it is also a representation of the steps in the semantic composition. Under Direct Compositionality, then, combined with a rather impoverished view of the set of syntactic operations, a tree is a convenient representation for the linguist but it is not something that the grammar itself "sees."

But of course much work in syntax and semantics assumes that the grammar does have access to the trees, and the view of semantics to which we are about to turn also makes this assumption. Thus in order for Straw Man to both adopt (7b) in the syntax and at the same time maintain that [[kiss]] is a function of type <exe,t> (or the intensional counterpart), the syntax and semantics must be pulled apart. The syntax not only proves strings well-formed but keeps track of the steps used so that in the end it is a proof of the well-formedness *of a tree*. Moreover, it "feeds" into the semantics as a separate system: a system which provides interpretations for trees. Hence we adopt the syntactic rules in (7), and add a semantic rule interpreting a tree as in FR-2. (The notation here is inspired by the notation developed in Heim and Kratzer 1998, although they do not use it for this case as they adopt the same solution for transitive verbs as is developed later in this chapter.)

FR-2

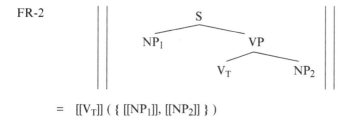

= $[[V_T]] (\{ [[NP_1]], [[NP_2]] \})$

(This is given extensionally; it is easy enough to fold in intensionality.) If this move is made, the entire fragment would be revised; each syntactic/semantic rule pair developed up to this point will be stripped of its semantic part. However, in all of the cases we have discussed so far the necessary revisions are straightforward; the revisions are left to the reader in the following exercise.

> **5.1.** Take the rules in the fragment so far (this means only those rules labeled TR). For each one, assume that they give just the syntactic and phonological part (they could be stated as phrase structure rules or they could be stated in the notation used here). Assume further that for each such rule there is a separate semantic rule whose input is a tree. Then state each of these semantic rules, using FR-2 as a model for the statement of the semantic rules. You should note that FR-2 differs from the other rules you will be constructing in that all of those rules have as their input a *local tree*—that is, only a mother node and one or more daughter nodes—while FR-2 (by necessity) refers to a bigger chunk of tree— mother, daughter, and granddaughters.

The Direct Compositional strategy vs "syntax feeds semantics" strategy is discussed in Chapter 7, but for now we can note that the syntax feeds semantics strategy for this particular case comes at a cost. In the case of a sentence like *Lee kissed Sandy*, the fact that *kissed Sandy* has no meaning was remedied by the adoption of FR-2. But then, how does the semantics work for the case of conjoined VPs (i.e., cases where VPs are connected by *and* or *or*)? Recall that Straw Man posits the syntactic conjunction rule in (7). Now consider the syntactic structure in (10):

(10)

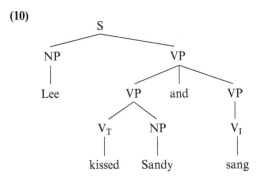

Do the rules in Straw Man's grammar provide an interpretation for this sentence? The answer is no: there is no rule to interpret either the topmost VP here nor the entire S. FR-2 is not relevant; it interprets only Ss of the form [$_S$ NP [$_{VP}$ V$_T$ NP]], and none of the rules that you will have formulated in your answer to Exercise 5.1 will help either. So there would need to be an additional rule to interpret this tree.

> **5.2.** Formulate the relevant rule (remembering to keep in mind the types that Straw Man is assuming).

But of course even adding the rule asked for in Exercise 5.2 does not complete the task. For the additional rules for (10) will do nothing for cases like those in (5), which have (as one possibility) the shape in (11):

(11)

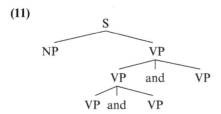

Due to the recursive nature of the *and*-rule, Straw Man could never finish stating the semantic rules. This is completely parallel to the reasoning as to why the syntax needs a VP constituent: the same reasoning leads to the conclusion that we need to find a meaning for each VP, which will be done in section 5.4.

5.3. Hidden S conjunction?

But first, Straw Man makes one final attempt to save his hypothesis. And this is to posit that the semantics actually does not interpret structures with VP conjunction. Rather, at the level at which these are interpreted, these are actually the conjunction of two sentences. This is actually not a straw man; this view has been taken in one form or another in many theories of grammar, and has been implemented in various ways. For example, in early Transformational Grammar it was assumed that there were no phrase structure rules like that in (6) and (9). Sentences like (3) were actually at an underlying level (deep structure) instances of S conjunction, with a transformational rule called Conjunction Reduction which mapped trees of the form in (12) to those in (13), provided that NP_1 was identical to NP_2 (see, e.g., Jacobs and Rosenbaum 1968):

(12) $\Rightarrow$ **(13)**

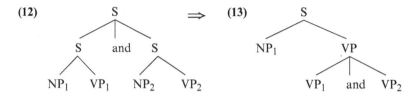

(The rule can be generalized to extend to the case of *or*.) Additionally, it was assumed that the input to the semantic interpretation was the deep structure, and so the semantics would be assigning a meaning to structures of the sort shown in (12) and not to (13). Since we already have semantics for S conjunction, there would be no need to worry about interpretation for the case of VP conjunction. Hence for a sentence like *Romeo kissed Lee and watered the plants* we don't need to worry about giving a meaning for *kissed Lee*. The semantics would separately interpret the two sentences *Romeo kissed Lee* and *Romeo watered the plants* (along with the rule interpreting the conjunction of the two). FR-2 will do the job. (One might notice that under this view of conjoined sentences, the argument given earlier for a VP constituent has been undermined, but we will not pursue the consequences of this.) A variant on this strategy is to view the picture in reverse. That is, assume that the phrase structure rules do give something like (13) directly, but this is mapped to (12) (as its "Logical Form"). The semantics operates so as to compositionally interpret that level. Again FR-2 (combined with the other rules suitably reformulated in tree terms, as in Exercise 5.1) will now be adequate.

But the hidden S conjunction strategy also comes at a cost. First and foremost the syntax has again been complicated, no matter which variant is chosen. Either variant posits an additional level of representation and hence needs a set of explicit rules to map one level to the other. There is also an empirical difficulty centering on sentences whose subjects contain quantifiers. Consider the pairs in (14) and (15). In each pair the first involves conjunction or disjunction of just bare VPs, and the second is the corresponding conjoined Ss with (syntactically) identical subjects:

(14) a. Some pig chased the wolf and grunted.
  b. Some pig chased the wolf and some pig grunted.

(15) a. Every pig chased the wolf or grunted.
  b. Every pig chased the wolf or every pig grunted.

The meaning of (14b) is weaker than (14a); in the former the chaser and grunter must be the same. In (14b) the chaser and grunter could happen to be the same, but they need not be.[6] Hence (14a) entails (14b) but not vice versa. The reverse situation holds in the *every* case. Here (15a) is weaker— the most salient reading for (15a) is each pig did one or the other of these things, but they need not have all been in agreement as to which act to perform. (15b) has the stronger requirement that they all did the same thing. Incidentally, it is true that (15a) also (at least marginally) has a second reading which is the same as (15b); this is best brought out by the continuation in (16):

(16)   Every pig chased the wolf or grunted—but I can't remember which.

Nonetheless, the most salient reading of (15a) is clearly the weaker one and is true in situations in which (15b) is not. (The second reading is accounted for in Chapter 11; its existence does not affect the point at hand here.)

Consider a theory in which the Logical Form in (12) is related to the surface form in (13) and where the requirement for this is that the two NP subjects in the two clauses in (12) must be identical. Then, of course, we get the wrong prediction. In the cases above, the (a) sentences should have the same meaning as the (b) sentences. As noted above, there is a secondary reading of (15a) which is synonymous with (15b) but this is of little consolation since the correct theory needs to also pair (15a) with its primary meaning. To be sure, there are ways to solve these problems with more complex Logical Forms and additional conditions on the rules effecting the mapping to (or from) Logical Forms.[7] But the methods involved require yet further rules. Perhaps it is time to abandon Straw Man's path.

---

[6] It might appear at first glance that (14b) requires the wolf-chasing pig and the grunting pig to be different pigs. But closer inspection reveals that this is just an *implicature* (see section 3.2) and not part of the truth conditions. If a speaker knew that a single pig did both, they would more likely have used (14a)—hence the conclusion on hearing (14b) that different pigs are involved. But this can't really be part of the truth conditions. For if I hear a grunting pig and have no idea who it is and at the same time have some other indirect evidence about there being a wolf-chasing pig, I can certainly say (14b) with no commitment one way or the other as to whether it is the same pig. (And if it turns out to be the same pig, I have not said anything false.)

[7] Readers familiar with the "Quantifier Raising" solution to quantified NPs (see section 14.2) might think that one automatically gets the right meanings of the (b) sentences once one combines Quantifier Raising with the rule that produces the two-sentence LF. But it is not automatic, for a principle is needed to ensure that the two processes happen in the right order. We leave it to the interested reader to verify this.

5.4. Back to the drawing board: Curry'ed functions

5.4.1. Recasting the meaning of transitive verbs

The complications above are all the result of Straw Man's insistence that the meaning of a transitive verb is a function from ordered pairs to truth values. The problem is that this makes semantic composition look very different from the syntax, for the semantics treats the composition as "flat" while the syntax does not. But there is a simple way to recast things so that the semantics respects the syntax. The technique to be used here relies on the observation that any function whose domain is a set of ordered n-tuples (in this case, ordered pairs) can be mapped to a function that takes the arguments one at a time. The observation that this can be done for any such function is due originally to Schönfinkel (1924) and later H. B. Curry (see, e.g., Curry and Feys 1958). Although Schönfinkel's work is earlier, this is generally known as *Currying* a function (although see Heim and Kratzer 1998 who do use the historically more accurate term *Schönfinkelization*).

In the case at hand, we begin with the original [[K]] (a function from e x e to t) and recast this as a function which takes one individual and returns a function of type <e,t>. This can be done without loss of information—this is just repackaging the meaning. Thus [[kiss]] is a function of type <e,<e,t>>. Note that there are actually two different ways that one can recast the initial logician's [[K]] (which maps an ordered pair {x,y} to true just in case in the world in question x does kiss y). One way is to create a new function such that for any x and y such that [[K]]({x,y}) is true, [[kissed]](x)(y) is true. In other words, the "kisser" is the first argument of the new function, and the "kissee" is the second. The other mapping does just the reverse: for any x and y such that [[K]]({x,y}) is true, then [[kissed]](y)(x) is true.

It turns out that the second strategy is the correct one, given the assumption that meanings are packaged in such a way as to reflect the syntactic composition. Our new function combines with the meaning of the *syntactic direct object* first, because this is what happens in the syntax. It combines next with the subject. This is often confusing when first encountered because of the left-to-right order in which we write things: in a sentence like *Lee kissed Sandy*, the semantic composition will be [[kissed]] ([[Sandy]]) ([[Lee]]). (The other meaning can be thought of as the meaning of *was-kissed-by*).

To illustrate in greater detail, suppose that the universe consists of three individuals, a, b, and c. We will, moreover, be considering just one world w_1. To use English to describe the facts of the world, let it be the case that a kisses b and c, b kisses c, and c kisses a and c. Then the function [[kiss]] in w_1 is as follows:

(17)

$$a \to \left\{ \begin{array}{l} a \to 0 \\ b \to 0 \\ c \to 1 \end{array} \right\}$$

$$b \to \left\{ \begin{array}{l} a \to 1 \\ b \to 0 \\ c \to 0 \end{array} \right\}$$

$$c \to \left\{ \begin{array}{l} a \to 1 \\ b \to 1 \\ c \to 1 \end{array} \right\}$$

In order to get any mileage out of this, we also need to make explicit what was implicit in the discussion above—i.e., the syntactic and semantic combinatory rule for combining transitive verbs with their objects:

TR-6.   If α is an expression of the form $<[\alpha], V_T, [[\alpha]]>$ and β is an expression of the form $<[\beta], NP, [[\beta]]>$ then there is an expression γ of the form $<[\alpha\text{-}\beta], VP, [[\alpha]]([[\beta]])>$.

Hence consider the composition of *Lee kissed Sandy*. Assume that [[Lee]] (in all worlds) is a and [[Sandy]] is b. Then *kissed Sandy* has a meaning; it is the function shown in (17) applied to the argument b, so it is that function of type $<e,t>$ which maps a to 1 and b and c to 0. In set terms, *kissed Sandy* characterizes the set of Sandy-kissers (which in this case is the singleton set {a}). Then this VP combines with its subject by the syntactic and semantic rule TR-5′, and the resulting semantics is 1, as we would expect.

5.3. The picture above in (17) is the extension of [[kiss]] in a world that we have labeled w_1. Now take a different world w_2 in which the facts are that a kisses a, b, and c, b kisses no one, and c kisses only c. (Ignore the obvious lack of pragmatic plausibility here!)

(cont.)

First, show the extension of [[kiss]] at w_2 where this again will be shown as a Curry'ed function of the same basic structure as (17). Then show the full syntactic and semantic composition of *Sandy kissed Lee*, where at each step you will be showing the meaning of each expression as a function from worlds to some other object. (You already have [[kiss]]; it is a function mapping w_1 to the object shown above in (17) and mapping w_2 to the new object that you will have constructed.) The two NPs are listed in the lexicon and each is a constant function from worlds to individuals as given above. So your task is to show how the syntax and the semantics put this all together step by step. Do this using (12) in Chapter 4 as the model.

Does this strategy introduce undue complexity into the modeling of meanings? Not at all. We have simply taken [[kiss]] to be a function whose *co-domain* itself is a function. The general approach of the kind of model-theoretic semantics being assumed here is to have a small set of primitive model-theoretic objects (worlds, times, truth values, and individuals) and take other kinds of meanings to be constructed from these using the notion of functions.[8] There is no reason to be surprised to find that certain expressions denote functions which themselves have functions as their co-domain (or, for that matter, as their domain; see Chapter 10). In fact, such objects are already in the system. In the fully intensional semantics, the meaning of an intransitive verb, for example, is a function of type $<s,<e,t>>$.

Incidentally, one finds different notations for the semantic composition of a sentence like *Lee kissed Sandy*, even among researchers who agree that [[kiss]] is the Curry'ed function of type $<e,<e,t>>$ (combining first with the individual denoted by the object). Given the world above, the composition is most accurately represented as [[kiss]](b)(a). However, one sometimes finds more reader-friendly notation when the actual step-by-step composition doesn't matter, and so one might see something like [[kiss]](a,b), which looks like it is going back to the hypothesis that [[kiss]] takes

---

[8] There are debates as to whether others are needed—see especially the work in event semantics (e.g., Parsons 1990) which takes events as primitives. But these will suffice for what we will be considering in this book.

an ordered pair as argument. But generally this is intended simply as a way to make things easier to read; this is called the relational notation. It's ultimately helpful to get used to going back and forth between the two notations.

*5.4.2. Currying more generally

The above illustrates the technique of Currying to a function that has as its domain a set of ordered pairs, but this is quite general. For any function f which takes an ordered n-tuple as its argument to give some result x, there is a corresponding function f' which takes a single argument, and returns as value a function g from an n-1 tuple to x. This can apply recursively, until we have a function that takes its arguments one at a time.

Generalizing the remarks above, concerning the fact that there are different ways to Curry a function like [[K]], there are many ways to effect the mapping from f to the one-place function f', depending on which position of the n-tuple is peeled off (A one-place function is one which takes just a single argument, not an ordered tuple). Call f'^{-i} the function that peels off the ith position of the n-tuple. Then there is a unique way to map f to f'^{-i} (and vice versa). Notice that the relationship between the naive meaning of *kiss* (a function taking ordered pairs of kissers and kissees) and our hypothesized actual meaning of English *kiss* is such that [[kiss]] is $[[K^{-2}]]$ since we took the second member of the ordered pair to be the first argument of [[kiss]]. This is crucial: this was done to model the way in which the syntax works, as the syntax first combines *kiss* with its object and then with its subject (and, simply because it is traditional, we took "naive-kiss" to map a pair {a,b} to true just in case a kisses b).

---

*5.4. Take a set A with two members {a,b}, a set B with two members {c,d}, a set C with two members {e,f}, and a set D with three members {1,2,3}. Consider a function f whose domain is the set of ordered triples in A x B x C and whose co-domain is D. (In other words, it takes each triple that can be composed by taking a member of A, a member of B, and a member of C and maps each such triple into some member of D.) The actual function is as follows:

(*cont.*)

{a,c,e} → 1
{a,c,f} → 1
{a,d,e} → 3
{a,d,f} → 2
{b,c,e} → 1
{b,c,f} → 3
{b,d,e} → 2
{b,d,f} → 3

Convert this to the corresponding Curry'ed function of type <C,<B, <A,D>>>.

5.4.3. Solving Straw Man's problems

Let us consider whether this strategy solves the problems encountered by Straw Man. First, as seen above, a VP such as *kissed Sandy* now has a meaning. And, having Curry'ed the transitive verb, this VP has a meaning of exactly the same type as the meaning of a VP with only an intransitive verb. Both are world/time-dependent functions of type $<e,t>$ (put differently, they characterize sets of individuals). Because of this, we also now have a simple way to give the semantics for conjoined VPs without having to assume that these really involve hidden S conjunction. For expository simplicity, we ignore the possibility of allowing the denotation of a VP to be a partial function from the domain of individuals, and so assume that each VP maps each individual into either true or false.[9] Consider the phrase structure rule in (6) which introduces VPs conjoined with *and*. (Keep in mind that this will eventually be generalized to allow coordination of all categories.) Up until now we have in our fragment only a semantics for *and* that conjoins sentences (TR-1), but the discussion in 5.1 led to the conclusion that there is VP conjunction as well. Direct Compositionality requires a semantics to go with (6), and we are now in a position to see what this

---

[9] As noted several times, a possible way to model presupposition failure is to use partial functions. To use an example we have seen before, we might ultimately want to treat the presupposition in a predicate *stopped smoking* by saying that it is undefined (at a world/time pair) for all individuals who never smoked. If this is correct, the rule for conjunction given below will need refinement.

semantics is. Thinking in set terms, the contribution of *and* is simply intersection. (Ultimately one would hope for single *and* for sentences, VPs, and other expressions; this is accomplished in Chapter 12.) In other words, consider a sentence like a slight variant of (3c) *Lee meditated and fed Porky*. The intuition is easiest to get in set (rather than function) terms. Since [[feed]] is of type <e,<e,t>>, it combines with [[Porky]] (some individual) to give the characteristic function of the set of individuals who fed Porky. [[meditated]] also characterizes some set. These two sets can intersect; and the result is the set of individuals in both the pig-feeding set and the meditating set. This is exactly right; when this combines with Lee, the sentence says that Lee is in this set—i.e., the set which is the intersection of the meditators and Porky-feeders. By the definition of intersection, it follows that Lee is in each set. Notice, then, that with ordinary individual-denoting subjects (like *Lee*) the truth conditions for the case of conjoined VPs are the same as the truth conditions for the case of conjoined sentences, as in *Lee fed Porky and Lee meditated*. But this follows from the semantics that intersects the two VP meanings, and so the correct truth conditions are arrived at without having to pretend that there are really two sentences.

To formalize the rule for conjoined VPs, note first that since we are not considering the case of partial functions here we can safely go back and forth from talking about sets of individuals to the corresponding characteristic function of this set and vice versa. Given a function f of type <x,t> (for any set x) we have introduced the notation f_S to indicate that subset of x mapped to 1 by f. Now take any set z which is a subset of some set x. We now introduce the notation z_F to indicate the function of type <x,t> that characterizes z (i.e., the function mapping all members of z to 1 and all other members of x to 0). Using these notational devices, we can state the VP conjunction rule (extensionally):

TR-7.   If α is an expression of the form <[α], VP, [[α]]> and β is an expression of the form <[β], VP, [[β]]>, then there is an expression γ of the form <[α-and-β], VP, ([[α]]$_S$ ∩ [[β]]$_S$)$_F$>.

Thus the meaning of the conjoined VP is the function characterizing the intersection of the two sets characterized by the daughter VPs. The rule introducing *or* is similar, where here the relevant semantics is set union:

TR-8.   If α is an expression of the form <[α], VP, [[α]]> and β is an expression of the form <[β], VP, [[β]]>, then there is an expression γ of the form <[α-or-β], VP, ([[α]]$_S$ ∪ [[β]]$_S$)$_F$>.

5.5. Take a universe with three individuals {a,b,c}. Take a world w_1 such that [[kiss]](w_1) is as shown in (17) above. Assume further the following: [[Juliet]](w_1) = a and [[Romeo]](w_1) = c. Moreover [[sleepwalk]](w_1) is the following function:

a $\rightarrow$ 0, b $\rightarrow$ 1, c $\rightarrow$ 1.

Take the sentences in (i) and (ii):

(i) Juliet sleepwalked and kissed Romeo.
(ii) Romeo kissed Juliet or sleepwalked.

Show the full syntactic and semantic composition of this sentence extensionally with respect to w_1. In other words, show the value of each expression at w_1 which the syntax proves well-formed. (Use the model in (12) in Chapter 4 for how to display this.) For all of the VPs, show these both as sets and as the functions which characterize those sets. What is crucial is to see why the sentence doesn't need to be converted into two separate sentences in order to arrive at the correct semantics for the whole; showing out the extension of each of the well-formed VPs in set terms helps to elucidate that point.

This account will eventually be refined in several ways. First, *and* and *or* will ultimately be listed in the lexicon (so they themselves have a meaning) and will be members of a single syntactic category. Second, there appears to be evidence that both *and* and *or* actually take their arguments one at a time such that the structure of, for example, *walks and chews gum* is actually [walks[and[chews gum]]] (see, e.g., Munn 1993). Note that this means that [[and]] is (thinking in set terms) the Curry'ed version of the intersection operator. (The interested reader can use prose to state just exactly what this function is.) Both of these desiderata are accomplished in the revision in the next chapter. And finally, as noted above, conjunctions like *and* and *or* are cross-categorial: for any two expressions [α] and [β] of the same category X, there is also an expression of the form [α-and-β]. The complex expression itself is of category X; we know this because it has the same distribution as any other expression of category X. Ultimately then a single *and* and a single *or* should be listed in the lexicon which serves to conjoin expressions of any category. A full generalization is given in Chapter 12 (and section 13.4.4.2

contains yet another way to accomplish the generalization). But for the moment we will not collapse S conjunction (TR-1) with VP conjunction (TR-7). Note, though, that while the semantics for VP conjunction and for S conjunction look at first blush to be completely different, they have something in common. Recall that the value of an S is a function characterizing a set of worlds; the fully intensional version of the *and*-rule in the case of S conjunction also intersects these sets.

5.6. In light of the remarks above, it is tempting to try to collapse the two conjunction rules as follows:

FR-3   If there is an expression α of the form <[α], X, [[α]]> and an expression β of the form <[β], X, [[β]]> then there is an expression γ of the form <[α-and-β], X, ([[α]]$_S$ ∩ [[β]]$_S$)$_F$>, for X ranging over S and NP>.

Aside from the fact that ultimately we want to allow in conjunction of other categories besides just VP and S, there is a "cheat" embodied in FR-3. Why is it cheating to try to collapse the case of VP conjunction and S conjunction in the way done in FR-3?

Straw Man's final problem was that his conjecture that VP conjunction was secretly S conjunction gave (without additional complexities) the wrong meanings for sentences like (14a) and (15a) where the subjects are quantified:

(14)   a. Some pig chased the wolf and grunted.

(15)   a. Every pig chased the wolf or grunted.

Under the two-sentence analysis of these, these should have the same meaning as the corresponding sentences where the subject is repeated, and yet they do not. But we cannot truly boast that the Curry'ed transitive verb solution solves all of Straw Man's problems until it is shown that this problem is avoided here. In fact, we are not yet in a position to do that: but this is only because the meaning of NPs with quantifiers has not yet been discussed. We postpone this until Chapter 10. It turns out that armed with a meaning for expressions like *every man*, etc., the meaning (or at least preferred meaning) of (14a) and of (15a) is exactly as predicted. (It will also be shown that the secondary meanings can be derived.) At this point we can only say "stay tuned."

*5.5. A note on three-place verbs

English has many verbs that occur with two constituents within the verb phrase, as in *gave the new toy to Mitka*, which consist of the sequence V-NP-PP (we will call the verb V_3 here). There are also cases of verbs which take sequences of two NPs such as another version of *give*: *gave Mitka the new toy*. (The relationship between the two versions of *give* is much discussed in the generative grammar literature; here we focus only on the version that takes an NP and PP, but see also Exercise 9.10.) And some verbs take NPs and sentential-like expressions (which we will call CP) as in *told Chicken Little that the sky is falling* and so forth.

Here we focus on the V-NP-PP verbs such as *give*. Before going further we need to say something about the meaning of *to Mitka*. Assume that *to* functions much like a case marker and contributes nothing to the meaning, so that *to Mitka* means the same as *Mitka*. Returning to the full VP *gave the new toy to Mitka*, there are four logical possibilities for how this is put together in the syntax (indeed, all four possibilities have been suggested):

1. The VP is "flat": in phrase structure rule terms there is a rule of the form:
   VP → V_3 NP PP (see, e.g., Gazdar, Klein, Pullum, and Sag 1985).
2. The NP and PP actually form some sort of constituent; call it Z and there are two rules:
   VP → V_3 Z and Z → NP PP (see Kayne 1984).
3. *give* and *the new toy* form a constituent which then combines with a PP (as does the simple verb *dash*). The new rules would thus be something like:
   VP → V_4 PP and V_4 → V_3 NP.
   This means that *give* and *the new toy* combine to give a complex verb of the same category as things like *dash*; *gave the new toy* then combines with the PP *to Mitka* and the result is a VP (see, e.g., Dowty 1988).
4. The last possibility is one which requires additional apparatus in the syntax, as the syntax involves more than just concatenating expressions. This would be to assume that *give* actually first combines with *to Mitka* and the resulting expression then combines with *the new toy*. Versions of this (either for this case or for related cases) are proposed in Chomsky (1957) (for a VP like *consider George a fool*), and explored in much

subsequent Categorial Grammar literature (Bach 1979, 1980, Dowty 1982, and others), within GPSG by Jacobson (1987), and then again in Government and Binding theory in Larson (1988).

The basic idea of the proposals in 4 above is that *gave to Mitka* in the expression *give the toy to Mitka* is a *discontinuous constituent*. There are two broad classes of ways to implement this intuition. One makes use of two levels of representation in the grammar, and posits a movement rule to break up the constituent. This in turn has two possible implementations. (i) The basic structure is as in (18i) and *to Mitka* moves to the right as shown there, or (ii) the basic structure is as in (18ii) and *give* preposes (we suppress details of the actual proposals, and we arbitrarily adopt the label C for the expression that is the discontinuous constituent).

(18)

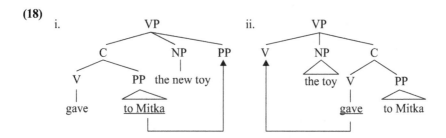

Chomsky (1957) proposed a version of (i) (although for a different set of cases), and Larson (1988) proposes a version of (ii).

A rather different way to implement the basic intuition is put forth in Bach (1979, 1980). This relies on the observation that the existence of discontinuous constituents does not inevitably lead to the conclusion that there is more than one level of representation. Rather, the syntactic rules combining two expressions might perform operations other than just putting one (or more) expressions next to each other. Perhaps there are also cases where one expression is infixed into another.[10] (Note that

---

[10] A common misconception is that the existence of "discontinuous constituents" requires more than one level of representation because a sentence must be represented as a tree, and trees do not admit of discontinuous constituents. If the grammar contained an infixation operation, the representation of the sentence would involve an object with crossing branches—not a tree. But the underlying assumption—that trees are sacred objects—makes little sense; a tree may or may not

morphological processes include infixation.) Bach dubbed the process in syntax as *Wrap*, and proposed that *give* first combines with *to Mitka* to form a complex transitive verb *give to Mitka*. Further, any complex transitive verb combining with its object (here, *the new toy)* does so by "wrapping" around its object. Bach's particular formulation of the operation referred to word boundaries: Wrap places one expression after the first *word* of the other. Wrap operations have been formalized in other ways as well. For example, Pollard (1984) suggests that the grammar refers not just to unanalyzed strings but *headed* strings. Each string has a distinguished head, and Wrap places the infix after the head of the other expression (or, in some languages, before the head of the other expression). If there are Wrap operations, the remarks made earlier regarding the role of structure in grammar are not quite correct: the grammar must keep track of just enough structure within an expression as to specify the infixation point. But none of the Wrap proposals requires the grammar to refer to structures as rich as full trees. We will formalize a variant of Pollard's proposal in Chapter 6.

This fourth solution is the most complex in terms of the syntax: it requires a Wrap operation (or a movement rule). Nonetheless, there seems to be some evidence for it (see section 15.4.2). To the extent that we deal in this book with three-place verbs, the Wrap solution is what we will (tentatively) adopt. (Note that this is compatible with the general architecture assumed here while the movement solution is not.) And even though the evidence for Wrap in the case of English is not entirely conclusive, there is independent evidence that grammars containing only the equivalent of context-free phrase structure rules will not be enough for other languages (see n. 5 and, e.g., Shieber 1985). Wrap operations have

be the appropriate representation as that depends entirely on what we discover is the correct rule system. (A tree is a sensible representation of how the rules work in a context-free phrase structure grammar; it is not a sensible representation in other systems.) Notice that if there are multiple levels of representation then it is also the case that a tree is not the appropriate representation for a sentence. Rather, a *sequence* of trees is. There is no particular reason to prefer a sequence of trees to some other kind of object. The important point is that *representations* represent the rule system(s); the task is to discover the kinds of rules employed by natural language.

been shown to be useful in the analysis of some of the key cases that lead to this conclusion.[11]

In any case, the main interest here is in how the semantics works. Given the hypothesis of Direct Compositionality, each of the four logically possible analyses of three-place verbs sketched earlier leads to a slightly different way to flesh out the semantics associated with the syntax. Here we consider only the possibilities labeled (3) and (4) above. While we have seen that (4) is syntactically more complex, (3) and (4) are equally straightforward in terms of the semantics. Either way, the idea is that—once again—the verb in the syntax is combining with its arguments one at a time. And since both of these are individuals, the resulting verb is of type $<e,<e,<e,t>>>$. The meanings would be different depending on whether we adopted (3) or (4). If (3) is correct, [[give]] as a function maps an individual which serves as the gift to a function taking the recipient to a function from givers to 1 or 0. If (4) is correct, the recipient is the first argument, the gift is the second argument, and the giver is the last argument in.

---

*5.7.   (i) If (1) were correct, what might be its associated semantics?

(ii) One way to give a semantics that goes along with (2) would be similar to the way you (hopefully) constructed for (i). Make this explicit.

---

[11] One such example is the analysis of "cross-serial dependencies" in Dutch given in Pollard (1984). The key phenomenon was discussed in Huybregts (1976). To illustrate the basic phenomenon, we use subordinate clauses (because Dutch, like most other Germanic languages, always has the main verb in second position in main clauses, which complicates the situation). Thus we find embedded sentences in Dutch like the following:

(i)   ...dat   Jan   Piet   Marie   Cecilia   zag   helpen   laten   zwemmen
      that   Jan   Piet   Marie   Cecilia   saw   help   make   Swim
      "that Jan saw Piet help Marie make Cecilia swim"

This consists of a series of NPs and a series of verbs, and the "subject" of the nth verb in the verb chain is the nth NP in the NP chain. (This is not an isolated example but a systematic phenomenon.) While a set of context-free phrase structure rules could literally give the relevant string set it cannot give it in a way which—assuming a Direct Compositional view—will give a sensible semantics. Pollard (1984) showed that supplementing concatenation rules with Wrap can account for this.

6

Categorial Grammar

While the goal of this book is not to develop a detailed theory of syntax, a work on the syntax/semantics interface obviously needs to be rooted in some theory of syntax, even if only for expository purposes. We thus now develop (one version of) the theory of Categorial Grammar, albeit in a somewhat rudimentary fashion.[1] The reason for adopting Categorial Grammar is that it provides an elegant account of how the syntax and semantics work together. However, one should bear in mind that most of the remarks in the rest of this book on the syntax/semantics interface could be imported

---

[1] Categorial Grammar actually predates other versions of generative grammar, and was first developed in Ajdukiewicz (1935). Montague (1973) adopted a version of Categorial Grammar as his syntax for much the same reason as we are using it here: it provides a transparent fit between the syntax and the semantics. There are a number of different versions of Categorial Grammar. See, for example, Steedman (1987, 1996) which has often gone under the name Combinatory Categorial Grammar (the basic version adopted in this text is quite close to although not identical with this). Much recent work in the general framework has gone under the rubric of "Type Logical Grammar"; see Carpenter (1998) for an introduction.

into other theories as well, with of course some modification. Indeed some of the proposals in this book are based on ones originally developed within the theory of Generalized Phrase Structure Grammar (Gazdar, Klein, Pullum, and Sag 1985) (which adopted the semantics of Montague 1973). Head-Driven Phrase Structure Grammar (HPSG) (see, e.g., Pollard and Sag 1994) incorporates a rather different theory of semantics, but nonetheless maintains essentially the same architecture as the one here for the syntax/ semantics interface. And while Government–Binding Theory and Minimalism both have very different views of the organization of the grammar, many of the basic insights to be discussed later regarding the semantics carry over to or even were developed within these theories. As we do not wish the main body of results reported in this book to be locked into a single theory of syntax, the reader familiar with other theories is strongly encouraged to translate the results into the terminology of those theories from time to time where possible.

6.1. Basics

A fundamental premise of Categorial Grammar (hereafter, CG) is that a syntactic category label is an expression of its distribution. The grammar contains a small set of primitive categories and defines other categories from these. Let us take the primitives to be S, NP, N, PP, and CP.[2] The fact that some of these (NP, PP) are of the form "XP" (standardly used to mean X-*phrase*) while others (S, N) are not is arbitrary and is just a bow to tradition: there is no distinction between categories which typically contain only one lexical item and those which typically contain more. Indeed this was noted already in section 4.1. There, complex expressions like *the disobedient husky* were treated as being of the same category (NP) as simple names like *Mitka*.

In addition to the primitive categories, we recursively define additional categories as follows:

(1) If A is a category and B is a category, then A/B is a category (this category is pronounced as "A slash B").

---

[2] CP is the name for the category of expressions like *that Mitka howled* in a fuller sentence like *Sabrina thinks that Mitka howled.* Thus this is distinct here from S (it is an S combined with *that*), although we will assume that *that Mitka howled* has a meaning of type <s,t>, just as does S.

The intuition behind labeling some expression with the category A/B (for some A and some B) is that such an expression combines with an expression of category B to give an expression of category A. In other words, the name of a category encodes what it syntactically combines with (as a sister) and the category of the resulting (mother) expression.

Obviously missing from the above list of primitives is the category "VP." This is because any expression of this category can be recast as something which combines with an NP to give an S;[3] the traditional "VP" is thus renamed as S/NP. We will, however, often use the label VP as a convenient abbreviation for S/NP. Consider then the case of transitive verbs such as *kiss*, *love*, *chase*, etc. Each of these combines with an NP to give a VP, and so each is of category (S/NP)/NP. A verb like *dash*, on the other hand, which takes a PP complement within the VP (*The frightened fox dashed into a hole*) is of category (S/NP)/PP. In other words, the complement that a verb takes within the VP is encoded into its category. What about intransitive verbs such as *sing*, *walk*, etc.? We now officially adopt the view that the grammar does not distinguish between complex phrasal expressions and expressions that have the same distribution but happen to consist of just a single lexical item.[4] Since *walk* has exactly the same distribution as the complex expression *chew gum* and the same type of meaning (as was demonstrated at great length in the preceding chapter) a simple intransitive verb like *walk* is also of category S/NP. The astute reader will notice that we have suddenly glossed

---

[3] In fact a variety of other constituents besides NPs can serve as subjects in English. This includes "CPs" (sentences introduced by *that*) as in *That Sarah was the nominee was extremely surprising*, and infinitive VPs as in *To ski while being pulled by a dog is tremendous fun*. Arguably verbs do not impose any idiosyncratic restrictions on the category of their subject in English: unlike in object position the category with which they occur seems to be predictable purely semantically. (See Grimshaw 1982 for discussion.) It may well be then that a "VP" should really be defined as S/X for X a variable over a set of categories, but we will not pursue this here.

[4] There is one situation in which English grammar seems to be sensitive to whether an expression has more than one word in it. Simple adjectives (like *red*) occur prenominally, but complex adjectives (*happy that Bill left*) occur only postnominally when they modify nouns. Of course this means that the two do not have exactly the same distribution so they could be given a different category. But in all other respects they are the same, so we will not take that route. We leave it open as to how exactly the grammar refers to this difference; see section 8.4 for a treatment of adjectival nominal modifiers.

over an observation made earlier: the traditional notion of "verb" is motivated by morphological considerations. As things are set up so far, *kiss* and
walk have nothing in common: one is of category S/NP and the other of
category (S/NP)/NP. But these items are treated alike by the morphology:
they all take past-tense morphology, they can take the suffix *-ing*, and so
forth. This will be addressed shortly.

Thus the intuition is that (like in many other theories), the combinatory
rules can be stated in a very general form. Most of the information about
what kinds of complements an item can combine with has to be listed in any
case as part of the lexical entry. Given that, the rest should follow from some
very general rule schemata. This is much like the idea in, for example, classic
X-bar theory but the particular rule schemata will be quite different from
those adopted in X-bar theory. (Readers unfamiliar with X-bar theory can
consult an introductory syntax text for discussion, but it will play no role in
this text.)

As noted above, the basic idea is that if something is of category A/B, it
can combine with an expression of category B to give an A. This however is
not quite enough: the category so far does not specify whether the
B expression goes to the left or to the right of the A/B expression (or, in
light of the remarks in section 5.5, possibly as an infix). We thus elaborate
the categories in such a way that they encode that as well. Using a notation
not entirely standard in Categorial Grammar, an expression of category
$A/_R B$ is something which combines with a B to its right to give an expression
of category A, and $A/_L B$ takes the B to its left.[5] (Cases involving Wrap—if
they exist—are dealt with in the fragment summary at the end of this
chapter.) The recursive definition of categories is then expanded as follows:

---

[5] There are two other common notational systems for this which unfortunately
collide. In one system (cf., Lambek 1958 and much work in Type Logical Grammar)
A/B means something which takes a B to its right to give an A, while B\A is
something which takes a B to its left to give an A. In Steedman (1987, 1996) and
related work A/B continues to mean something that takes a B to its right to give an
A, while A\B is something which takes a B to its left to give A. Thus the two systems
collide on the meaning of X\Y: in one the result is X and in the other the result is Y. It
is because of this potential confusion that we adopt the subscripts. Subscripts are
also convenient if the grammar turns out to include a Wrap operation; a "Wrapper"
can be notated as $A/_W B$. (This is what is known in morphology as a circumfix, as in
the German morpheme *ge...en* indicating past participle. Something which is an
infix would be an $A/_I B$.)

(2)   If A is a category and B is a category, then $A/_R B$ is a category and $A/_L B$ is a category.

The intuition behind these categories has already been discussed, but technically all we have in our grammar so far is a list of lexical items and categories. Thus the grammar also includes two general rule schemas, which replace rules TR-5′ and TR-6 in the earlier fragment (for now, the semantics is not spelled out: "..." is used as a placeholder). We will label these rules as R-1a and R-1b. Lest it appear that we are cheating by counting this as one rule when there really are two, later discussion (section 6.5) will collapse them into a single rule.

R-1a (partial):   If α is an expression of the form <[α], $A/_R B$, [[α]]> and β is an expression of the form <[β], B, [[β]]> then there is an expression γ of the form <[α-β], A, ... >.

R-1b (partial):   If α is an expression of the form <[α], $A/_L B$, [[α]]> and β is an expression of the form <[β], B, [[β]]> then there is an expression γ of the form <[β-α], A, ... >.

At this point these two rules replace only two rules in the fragment constructed earlier, and so there is no sense in which these rules are more general. But that is obviously only because the fragment so far is rather small: there will be many other applications of the rules R-1a and R-1b.

Speaking informally for the moment, there is a sense in which an expression with a category of the form $A/_L B$ is a function from strings to strings. (This will be formalized in 6.5.) Thus *sings* maps *Madonna* to *Madonna sings*. Similar remarks hold for right-slash categories. Hence, when an A/B combines with a B we refer to the former as the function and the latter as the argument. Unfortunately the syntactic notation reverses the domain and co-domain from the semantic notation; A/B takes an expression of category B and returns one of category A, while <a,b> is a function taking something from domain a and returning a value in co-domain b. This confusion is an unfortunate accident of history which simply takes some getting used to.

6.2. Syntax/semantics correspondence

What about filling in the semantics? For the two instances of the schemas that we know of (combining VPs with subjects and transitive verbs with objects) the semantics involves applying a function to an argument. In order to state this generally, the correspondence between syntactic categories and semantic types needs to be made explicit. Each primitive syntactic category corresponds to some semantic type, i.e., all expressions of some primitive syntactic category have as their meanings some member of the same set. The extensional type of S is t—in other words, the value of any S is a member of {1,0}. Its intensional type is <s,t>. The extensional type of NP is e (its intensional type <s,e>). We also see that S/NP is of type <e,t> (intension: <s,<e,t>>) and (S/NP)/NP of type <e,<e,t>> (intensional type: <s,<e,<e,t>>>). Assume then the following correspondence between syntactic category and semantic type: for an expression of category A/B, its extension is a function from the extensional type of B to the extensional type of A. (There is a caveat: some expressions are functions from intensions not extensions; this is the subject of Chapter 19.) This correspondence holds regardless of the directional feature on the slash. Note incidentally that while this assumes that all expressions of a given syntactic category have meanings of the same types, the reverse does not hold. Thus $A/_L B$ and $A/_R B$ are syntactically different categories, but have the same type of meaning. Put differently, word order has no reflex in the semantics and is purely a syntactic phenomenon. And Chapter 8 discusses two other syntactic categories besides S/NP whose meaning is of type <e,t>. The set of syntactic categories, then, is richer than the set of semantic types.

Having made explicit the correspondence between syntactic categories and semantic types, it is now obvious how to fill in the "..." part in the above rules. We give the full rules extensionally, and we will refer to R-1a as **r-app** and R-2a as **l-app**:

R-1a: If α is an expression of the form <[α], $A/_R B$, [[α]]> and β is an expression of the form <[β], B, [[β]]> then there is an expression γ of the form <[α-β], A, [[α]]([[β]])>.

R-1b: If α is an expression of the form <[α], $A/_L B$, [[α]]> and β is an expression of the form <[β], B, [[β]]> then there is an expression γ of the form <[β-α], A, [[α]]([[β]])>.

6.1. Give INT-R-1a, using the model for stating this shown in section 3.3.

6.3. Refinements

There are some aspects of this system that might strike a reader familiar with syntactic theory as objectionable, but these objections are easily addressed. First, we don't want to conclude that every intransitive verb is listed in the lexicon of English as having category $S/_L NP$, where the directional feature (L) is stipulated on a case-by-case basis. For it is a perfectly general fact about English syntax that subjects (which can be defined here as the last argument in forming an S) go to the left. Similarly for the right slash: all transitive verbs take their objects to the right and this should not be listed lexical item by lexical item. And the generalization is even broader: verbs in English that occur with a single complement within the VP take it to the right regardless of the category of that complement. In fact, most instances of expressions of category A/B—provided that A is not just the simple category S—combine with things to the right. Prepositions, for example, are of category PP/NP and they take the NP to the right; *the* is listed as NP/N and it takes the noun to the right, etc. In many syntactic theories, all of these facts are subsumed under the observation that English is a *head-first* language. (Verbs are thus seen as the head of the VP; determiners as head of the NP (often called DP for just that reason), prepositions as the head of the PP, etc.)

While the version of CG developed here has no formal notion of head,[6] the basic generalizations that go under the rubric of "head first" are easily accounted for. Note that there is a rough correspondence between the standard notion of head and the notion here of a function. Thus an expression α which is of category A/B can (roughly) be thought of as the head of an expression formed by combining it with a β of category B. To the extent that in general heads precede their complements, the generalization in CG can be recast as the observation that slashes in English are generally marked with a R-feature. An exception, of course, is the slash in S/NP (or S/X for other categories which can appear as subject).[7]

---

[6] Such a notion could be added in if need be, though it will play no role in this text except possibly for the formulation of Wrap operations (see section 5.5).

[7] In standard X-Bar theory, the fact that subjects precede VPs is accounted for by not treating the VP as a "head" but rather treating the subject with a separate label: "Specifier." There is no corresponding notion of a Specifier in (at least this version of) CG.

Assume, then, that a lexical item is listed in the lexicon with an under-specified category, and that there are general rules adding further information to the category. We will use the term *lexeme* to refer to that which is listed in the lexicon. Thus the directional feature is not listed on a case-by-case basis on individual lexemes: *kiss* is just listed in the lexicon (S/NP)/NP. But only a more fully specified version (with a slash directional feature) can actually combine with another expression. Hence the two rules in (3) apply in English, where X and Y are variables over any category. These are displayed informally but the intent should be clear (the notation ...(S/X)... means any occurrence of this material; this might be contained within a more complex category):

(3)   a. ...(S/X)...   b. ...(X/Y)....

If (b) applies after (a) the effect will be that a right slash is the default. (Thus a rule like this applies only to slashes not already marked with a directional feature.)

We add one additional directional rule. While modifiers have fairly free placement in English, a rough rule of thumb is that they occur to the right of what they modify. *Modifier* can be given a technical definition in CG: anything of category X/X is a modifier. Hence to the rules above can be added (c), which also applies before the (default) right-slash rule above (the order of application of (a) and (c) is not relevant):

   c. ...(X/X)...

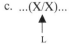

A second point to address is the fact that—despite the earlier observations about the morphological commonality of "verbs"—we seem to have no such notion at our disposal. Similar remarks would ultimately hold for nouns and adjectives. While ordinary intransitive nouns are of category N, nouns that take PP complements (including *relational nouns* like *aunt* which will be discussed in Chapter 8) are presumably of category N/PP. While beyond the scope of the semantic treatment here, there are also nouns that take CP complements (*belief that the world is round*) and hence presumably of category N/CP. Yet nouns like this all have a morphological commonality (they all can have plurals). Indeed—as noted in Chapter 4—the traditional parts of speech are motivated by morphological considerations. But there is no problem here: it is perfectly easy to recover the traditional notions in terms of the ultimate *result* category. A *verb* is something whose ultimate result category is S (this will be slightly refined in section 8.1). A *noun* is something whose ultimate result category is N. Morphological processes are presumably sensitive to classes defined in this way.

*6.4. Some further observations about syntax: Case marking and agreement

Once one starts thinking of a syntactic category A/B as the information that "my sister will be a B and my mother an A," there are other interesting consequences for syntax. As in most other theories of syntax, we can refine the basic categories given above to actually be feature bundles (let S, for example, be one feature in the bundle). Gender, number, case, and so forth are additional features on these labels. In CG, phenomena like case marking, agreement, and so forth are naturally handled as *selection* for elaborated categories (rather than as a process transferring features onto actual linguistic material). For example, *walks* is presumably S/NP[SING] while *walk* is S/NP[PLUR].[8] Presumably there is a single entry in the lexicon which is not specified for singular or plural, and morphological rules apply to the lexeme WALK of category S/NP and map this to [walk] of category S/NP[PLUR] and [walks] of category S/NP[SING]. There is also a semantic effect of this process. It was briefly noted in Chapter 4 that plurals can be thought of as individuals of a special type, and so the meaning of WALK is a function defined for the full set of individuals (both singular and plural). The mapping of this to the more fully specified version S/NP[SING] would remove the plural individuals from the domain of this function (and the reverse for the plural version).

Similarly, case marking is really case selection. Take a language with robust case marking but where the case marking is quite predictable—

---

[8] One might well want a more sophisticated theory of features where a feature is a name and a value, and so there could be a single feature named NUM whose possible values in English are SING/PLUR. In languages with a singular/dual/plural distinction, the NUM feature has three possible values. See Gazdar, Klein, Pullum, and Sag (1985) for a well-worked-out theory of features along these lines.

suppose for example all subjects are nominative and all objects accusative. Then all the transitive verbs in the language are actually of category (S/NP [NOM])/NP[ACC]. As for the case of English word order, one would not want to conclude that this information is listed in the lexicon on a case-by-case basis. Hence, let the verbs be listed in underspecified form, with the following two rules to add the case features to the NP slots:

(4)   a. ...(S/NP)...   b. ...(S/NP)/NP

$$\uparrow \qquad\qquad\qquad \uparrow$$

NOM   ACC

Even more interesting is the situation in a language like German in which the bulk of the verbs assign a predictable case to their objects (hence this is called *syntactic case*) while a small number assign a different case. For example, the verb *helfen* "help" assigns dative case, and it is generally assumed that this is a lexically idiosyncratic fact which must be learned by German speakers on a case-by-case basis (this is thus often called *lexical case*). On the other hand, speakers do not need to learn a list of verbs assigning accusative case, for that is the default. Here we assume that German contains the two rules in (4), but that *helfen* is listed in the lexicon as (S/NP)/NP[DAT]. As was the situation with the directional features, case features are assigned only to slots not already specified for a case feature. Hence they can add but never change the case feature on a slot. Thus phenomena like predictable (syntactic) case vs idiosyncratic (lexical) case are easy to handle.

---

*6.2. The remarks above show how one might ensure that NPs with the appropriate case markings appear in the correct position, but there remains the question of ensuring that the correct internal structure of an NP with a certain case marking. In some languages the actual case marking shows up in the morphology of the noun, in some it shows up in the determiner, and in some both.

Consider the case of an imaginary language in which the noun shows the case marking. We will call this language English', and imagine then that an NP in subject position which translates as English *the dog* is, in English', *the dog-us*. In object position the NP would be *the dog-um*. Assume (following, e.g., Gazdar, Klein, Pullum, and Sag 1985) a system as noted above where Case features can be analyzed as a feature name

(cont.)

and a feature value: the name is CASE and the possible values are NOM and ACC. Then we take *dog-us* to be N[CASE:NOM] and *dog-um* to be N[CASE:ACC].

Give the category for *the* in English'. You may need to make up some notational conventions, or you may be able to borrow one from phonology. The interested reader might also formulate the category of the suffixes *-um* and *-us.*

*6.3. Consider the case of a language (like German) where the case marking shows up in the particular form of the Determiner. Thus (mixing up German and English) let our imaginary language be English" which has NPs of the form *dem dog* in subject position and *den dog* in object position. Give the categories for *dem* and *dem.*

6.5. Further generalizing the rules

At the moment, R-1a and R-1b are—despite the numbering—two separate rules. But their semantics is exactly the same, suggesting that there should be a way to capture that generalization. Of course, there are only two rules at issue, and so it is not quite so obvious on the basis of just these two that any major generalization is being missed, but if there are similar additional rules such the Wrap process briefly discussed in section 5.5 there would be yet another case of an A/B combining with a B with the same semantics.

There are two conceivable resolutions (which are actually not mutually exclusive). The first is what is known as *type-driven interpretation*, which was put forth in, among others, Klein and Sag (1985), who were also working within a Direct Compositional framework. While their theory of syntax was different than that taken here, their basic solution carries over directly. Thus they proposed that each individual rule (schema) is not listed in the grammar with the semantic part, but that the semantic part can be filled in with the following principle (their terminology is slightly different):

(5) For any rule (schema) which allows an expression α whose meaning is a function in <a,b> to occur with an expression β whose meaning is a member of set a, the semantics is $[[\alpha]]([[\beta]])$.

The intuition, then, is that there are general principles in the grammar putting things together in the way suggested by the types, and so the semantics could be pulled out of what is listed as part of the particular rules. (The type-driven idea has also been borrowed—with modification—into a large body of work in a non-Direct Compositional framework in which the trees are the input to the semantics. The idea under this view is that semantic composition of each node in the tree is predictable from the type of its daughters. See Heim and Kratzer 1998 for one implementation.)

But it is not clear that type-driven principles (of the sort envisaged by Klein and Sag) are ever needed given the generality of rules in Categorial Grammar. The other option here is to collapse R-1a and R-1b (and if there is a Wrap rule it would collapse with these as well). This is the strategy that will be adopted here, which is why the two rules were numbered as 1a and 1b.

In order to collapse these, we first formalize the notion introduced informally earlier: that syntactic categories correspond to functions from strings to strings. While the necessary formalization might at this point seem like a lot of trouble to go to just to collapse these two rules, it actually has significant other benefits which will emerge in later chapters. Hence, each category of the form $A/_X B$ (where X is either L or R) corresponds to a function. The category itself is the name of a set of expressions, but it corresponds to some function which takes two strings (one at a time) and returns a third. We will notate the corresponding function as $F_{A/B}$, and define them as follows:

(6)   **a.** $F_{A/_R B}([\alpha])([\beta]) = [\alpha\text{-}\beta]$ **b.** $F_{A/_L B}([\alpha])([\beta]) = [\beta\text{-}\alpha]$

We can now state a single R-1 (call it **app**):

R-1.   If α is an expression of the form $<[\alpha], A/B, [[\alpha]]>$ and β is an expression of the form $<[\beta], B, [[\beta]]>$ then there is an expression γ of the form $<F_{CAT(\alpha)}([\alpha])([\beta]);$ A; $[[\alpha]]([[\beta]])>$ (where CAT(α) means the category of α).

For example, take the expression *sings* which is of category $S/_L NP$. The function which corresponds to this category is one which applies to the string *sings* and then yields a function which applies to *Madonna* to give *Madonna sings*. So the fact that *Madonna* goes to the left of *sings* when they combine is a result of the fact that R-1 says that the string resulting from the combination of *Madonna* with *sings* is the value of the function $F_{A/_L B}$ when applied to the string *sings* and then to *Madonna*. For expository convenience, we will often continue to refer to R-1a and R-1b separately.

6.6. *and, or,* negation, and case-marking prepositions

Before summarizing the new fragment, we are ready to make some modifications regarding *and* and *or*. In the fragment developed earlier, these words were not listed in the lexicon but were introduced syncategorematically. Moreover, both *and* and *or* were introduced by rules which were limited to just VP and S conjunction, but it is well known that any two expressions of the same category can combine (with either *and* or *or*) to give an expression of that category. That is, the resulting expression has exactly the same syntactic distribution as does each of the daughters.[9] Each of the italicized expressions below illustrates this point:

(7) a. The candidates spoke *to the moderator and to the audience.*
    b. Sam *cooked and ate* lentils for supper.
    c. A *friend and colleague* of mine was just named Dean of the Faculty.

So conjunction (and disjunction) should be generalized to be cross-categorial.

Moreover, in order to list *and* and *or* in the lexicon and to do so without introducing any new rules, we can assume that they combine with their arguments one at a time. In other words, both are of category (X/X)/X, for

---

[9] One might ask whether coordination involves *only* the combining of two expressions of the same category or whether there are other cases of coordination. There is a large literature on this question, and many have concluded that there are other kinds of coordination. For one thing, there appear to be cases where categories apparently of different types conjoin, as in (i). Second, there are cases of so-called Non-Constituent Coordination (including what is sometimes known as Right-Node Raising) as in (ii):

(i)   Linda is a bank teller and proud of it.
(ii) a. Mary loves and John hates model-theoretic semantics.
      b. Captain Jack served bananafish yesterday and lobster today.

But it will be shown in section 13.4.2 that within Categorial Grammar cases like (ii) of so-called "non-constituent conjunction" reduce to ordinary constituent conjunction (Dowty 1988). The cases in (i) are also not threatening to the generalization that all and only like constituents may conjoin with a more sophisticated notion of categories. This will not be pursued in this book, but the interested reader can consult Bayer (1996) for a CG treatment of these. A quick preview: this incorporates the notion of "union" categories and "intersection" categories. If categories name sets of strings, this becomes quite natural. See also Morrill (1994).

X a variable over categories. The claim that expressions like *Mitka and Kolya* do combine with their arguments one at a time actually has some motivation; see, e.g., Munn (1993).

6.4. Given the word order rules spelled out in (3a–c), what would be the directional features on each of these slashes? Show exactly how the grammar (in the syntax) thus derives expressions like *fed the pig and meditated* (ignoring, of course, the presence of the past-tense morphology). It is worth noting that—given certain assumptions shared in both Government–Binding theory (and its descendants) and in some versions of CG—there actually is evidence that the slash directionality features given here are correct. See Munn (1993) for the point phased in GB terms, and Jacobson (1999) for a similar observation within the framework here.

We are, however, not yet in the position to give a fully general meaning for *and* and for *or* (partly for the reason hopefully discovered in Exercise 5.6, and also because there are cases where *and* and *or* connect expressions that don't denote sets, such as transitive verbs). But we do know that whatever the general meaning of *and* is, it has the effect of intersection for the case where it conjoins VPs. In this case, then, its meaning is the Curry'ed version of the intersection operator. So assume that the general meaning is such that whenever two set-denoting expressions are conjoined, the result is (Curry'ed) intersection. For now, then, we just write a complicated meaning for the lexical entry which says this. This meaning is spelled out in the fragment at the end of this chapter, and all of this is cleaned up in Chapter 12.

Note too that so far all of the other lexical items have as their meanings functions from worlds and times to extensions. Items like *and* and *or* seem different: these do not appear to have values that are in any way world- (or time-)dependent. Given two VPs combined with *and*, whatever world we are in is such that the result (in set terms) is the intersection of the extension of those VPs. That the value of [[and]] is not world-dependent can be demonstrated as follows. Consider the sentence *The senior senator from Nebraska coughed and sneezed.* Imagine two worlds w_1 and w_2 such that this sentence is true at w_1 and false at w_2. Then either *the senior senator from Nebraska* has a different referent in those two worlds, the set of coughers is different, or the set of sneezers is different. If Nebraska's politics remain unchanged and the coughers and sneezers do too, this must have the same value at both worlds. This would not follow if [[and]] was world(/time)-dependent.

But this is no different than the situation that we saw for proper names which (at least arguably) have a constant extension regardless of the world. Thus one way to keep the semantic combinatorics uniform, is to assume [[and]] and [[or]] are indeed functions from worlds to (roughly) Curry'ed intersection, but are constant functions. In fact, this is true in general for what are traditionally thought of as closed-class items.[10] As we will see, prepositions, *the*, *be*, etc. also do not vary in their extensions from world to world. We will thus treat all of these as constant functions from worlds. Since these do not vary, we will from now on simply write their meaning extensionally. (The correlation between closed- vs open-class items and constant vs non-constant functions is not perfect, since the values of names are also (arguably) constant functions, but these are surely open-class items.) To a reader who feels that there is something rather clumsy and artificial about giving prepositions, *and*, etc. intensional meanings whose extensions are always constant across worlds, a possible modification of this will be very briefly explored in section 19.2.

We can also now give a somewhat more adequate treatment of English negation. Recall that the only kind of negation in the earlier fragment is introduced by TR-3, which appends *it-is-not-the-case-that* in front of a sentence and reverses its truth value. In reality, English negation generally involves either the word *not* after the first auxiliary, or *n't* as a clitic on the first auxiliary. But since a treatment of the English auxiliary system is beyond the scope of this book, we cannot here provide a fully accurate account of English negation. Still, we can do quite a bit better by pretending

---

[10] For readers not familiar with this terminology: *closed-class* items are those whose syntactic category contains a limited number of items and does not easily admit of new such items (e.g., prepositions, determiners, conjunctions), while *open-class* items are those in the traditional categories like noun, verb, adjective, to which new items can be added with no difficulty (new nouns, verbs, and adjectives are coined daily). The former category is also sometimes called "function words." We make no commitment here to this distinction having any real theoretical significance since the difference in terms of ability for new items to be added is really a matter of degree and not of kind. Still, it is interesting to note that this traditional distinction does correlate roughly with the semantic distinction of having constant vs non-constant values across worlds (and/or times).

that *didn't/doesn't* are unanalyzed units which combine with VPs.[11] This word, then, is of category $VP/_R VP^{12}$ and its meaning—in set terms—is set complementation. Hence [[didn't dance]] is the function characterizing the set of individuals in the complement of the set characterized by [[dance]]. In function terms, [[didn't]] takes some function [[VP]] of type <e,t>, and maps to 1 everything that [[VP]] maps to 0 and vice versa.[13]

One final housekeeping detail concerns the case of so-called case-marking prepositions, as in *give the toy to Mitka*. We are leaving three-place verbs somewhat in limbo in the official fragment. But regardless of how these are treated, it is clear that *to* functions much like a case marker. That is, one cannot list the verb *give* just as selecting for an NP and a PP within the VP; it specifically selects for a PP with *to* as the preposition. A verb like *talk* also selects for a PP with *to*, as in *talk to the principal*. There are a few other

---

[11] There are cases where negation occurs with other kinds of expressions, as in *Not everyone left*. But unlike the case of *and* and *or*, *not* is not fully cross-categorial. Thus (1a) is not good, although we do get things like *not Mitka* in (ib):

(i)   a. *Not Mitka ate the rawhide.

    b. Kolya but not Mitka ate the rawhide.

The full range of English negation is rather complex, and so we confine ourselves to VP negation and introduce it by the single word *didn't*.

[12] For convenience, we have built the feature R into the lexical specification here to make sure that this overrides the general rule in (3c) according to which items of category X/X (i.e., modifiers) take their arguments to the left. In fact all auxiliaries might appear at first glance to need this kind of lexical stipulation, since they are all of category VP/VP but all take their VP complements to the right. But actually, the fact that auxiliaries (including *didn't*) take their complements to the right is unsurprising, for strictly speaking they are actually not of the simple category VP/VP. Each auxiliary specifies a particular morphological form for the item it combines with. *be*, for example, is something roughly like VP/VP[PROG] and so forth. Thus the actual directional feature on *didn't* will be specified by the general word order rules in the predictable way.

[13] As usual, we ignore the possibility that some VPs denote partial functions on the domain of individuals; the usual assumption is that if some individual is not in the domain of [[VP]] then it is also not in the domain of [[didn't VP]]. In other words, if an individual is not assigned a truth value by [[VP]] then [[didn't VP]] also assigns no-value to that individual. In fact, a standard test for presupposition is that it "survives" negation, meaning exactly what is said above: if [[Bill]] is assigned no truth value by [[stop smoking]] because Bill never smoked, then [[Bill]] is also assigned no value by [[didn't stop smoking]].

prepositions in English which appear in places where they are not interchangeable with any other preposition. This includes *of* in *mother of Romeo*
(see section 8.5), *on* in cases like *rely on the weather*, and *by* in *(was) chased
by the wild boar*.

Syntactically, then, we need to mark the PP as a particular kind of
PP. Borrowing a convention from Gazdar, Klein, Pullum, and Sag (1985)
we will add a feature on such PPs, and—since there is nothing interesting
about the choice of name of this feature—will make it mnemonic by using
the name of the preposition as the feature. (Thus, *give* selects an NP and also
a PP[TO].) The preposition *to* has the category PP[TO]/NP. What about the
meaning of *to*, *of*, etc.? (We exclude the actual directional and/or locative
uses of *to*.) In section 5.5 it was speculated that *to Mitka* means the same as
Mitka. This means that the semantic type of the relevant PPs is type e.[14] One
might then determine that *to* is literally meaningless. But if so, we would
need to add a new combinatory rule to the fragment to account for the
semantic part of combining *to* with an NP. Thus instead of adding a new
rule, it is perfectly straightforward to give *to* a real meaning: let it denote the
identity function on individuals. Its semantic type is thus <e,e> (exactly as
one would expect, given its syntactic category), and it takes an individual as
argument and returns the same individual. That is the extensional meaning
of *to* (and the other case-marking preposition); in light of the remarks above
its full meaning is a constant function from worlds to the identity function.

6.7. Summary: The fragment so far

Here and henceforth we list the open-class and the closed-class items separately. Because we are not dealing with lexical semantics, there is in general

---

[14] The semantics of PPs is one place where one might question the wisdom of
assuming that all items of the same syntactic category have the same type of
meaning. Cases like the ones at hand where the preposition is a case marker appear
to be of type e. But PPs also occur both as noun and as VP modifiers, and even can
occur with a few verbs that explicitly subcategorize for "adverbs" as in examples like
word the letter carefully/word the letter in a careful manner (Bresnan and Grimshaw
1978). On the other hand, it may simply be a mistake to think that all of what we call
"PPs" are of the same syntactic category: their distribution does wildly differ.

little to say about the meaning of the open-class items. For these, then, we list only their syntactic category and not their meaning.

Lexicon:
Open-class items:
 NPs include: *Mitka, Balto, Barack Obama, the-disobedient-husky, the-pig,* . . .
 S/NP: *walk, talk,* . . .
 (S/NP)/NP: *kiss, likes, feeds,* . . .
 (S/NP)/PP[TO]: *talk, speak,* . . .
 (S/NP)/CP; *believe, think,* . . .

Closed-class items:
 (X/X)/X: *and, or*
  [[and]]
   if X is of type <a,t> (for any type a) [[and]] = Curry'ed intersection
   if X = S, [[and]] is the following function:

$$\left\{ \begin{array}{l} 1 \rightarrow \left\{ \begin{array}{l} 1 \rightarrow 1 \\ 0 \rightarrow 0 \end{array} \right\} \\ 0 \rightarrow \left\{ \begin{array}{l} 1 \rightarrow 0 \\ 0 \rightarrow 0 \end{array} \right\} \end{array} \right\}$$

  [[or]]: is left as an exercise
 VP/$_R$VP: *didn't*; [[didn't]] takes a function that characterizes a set S, and returns
   the function characterizing the complement of S
 PP[TO]/NP: *to*; [[to]] = identity function on individuals
 CP/S; *that*; [[that]] = identity function on propositions

Word order rules:

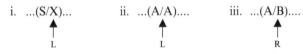

   i. ...(S/X)...   ii. ...(A/A)....   iii. ...(A/B)....
          ↑   ↑   ↑
          L   L   R

   where (i) and (ii) must apply before (iii)

Combinatory rule:
Definition of functions corresponding to categories of the form A/B:

   a. F$_{A/_R B}$ ([α])([β]) = [α-β]   b. F$_{A/_L B}$ ([α])([β]) = [β-α]

R-1 (app):
 If α is an expression of the form <[α], A/B, [[α]]> and β is an expression of the form
  <[β], B, [[β]]> then there is an expression γ of the form <A/B$_F$([α])([β]), A,
  [[α]]([[β]])>.

For expository convenience, we often break this into the two separate rules below:

R-1a: If α is an expression of the form $<[\alpha], A/_R B, [[\alpha]]>$ and β is an expression of the form $<[\beta], B, [[\beta]]>$ then there is an expression γ of the form $<[\alpha\text{-}\beta], A, [[\alpha]]([[\beta]]>$. (call this **r-app**)

R-1b: If α is an expression of the form $<[\alpha], A/_L B, [[\alpha]]>$ and β is an expression of the form $<[\beta], B, [[\beta]]>$ then there is an expression γ of the form $<[\beta\text{-}\alpha], A, [[\alpha]]([[\beta]]>$. (call this **l-app**)

Possible extension for three-place verbs:

A. If the Wrap analysis is incorrect, simply add to the lexicon items of category ((S/NP)/PP[TO])/NP: give, donate, ...

B. If Wrap is correct:

Lexicon:
((S/NP)/NP)/PP[TO]: give, donate, ...
Word order rules:

Add: ((S/NP)/NP)/X

W

Note: X here ranges over any category. One could also allow it to range over any category including nothing; then ordinary transitive verbs would also be marked with a wrap slash. Presumably, though, the effect of wrap in that case would just be vacuous.

Formalizing the Wrap operation:

a. Assume that each expression of the language is a string with an infixation point. We write such a string as [x|y].

b. Assume that each lexical item in English is a string of the form [x|]. (This is actually needed only for a small set of items, but we will give it in full generality here.)

c. Adopt a convention by which the infixation point in a new expression is inherited from the function. This can be done by refining the above definitions of the functions corresponding to syntactic categories as follows:

Definition of functions corresponding to categories of the form A/B:

Let α be some expression whose string is [x|y]. Then:

a. $F_{A/_R B}([\alpha])([\beta]) = [x|y\text{-}\beta]$ b. $F_{A/_L B}([\alpha])([\beta]) = [\beta\text{-}x|y]$

d. Define a function appropriate for $A/_W B$ as follows. Let α be some expression whose string is [x|y]. Then: $F_{A/_W B}([\alpha])([\beta]) = [x|\beta y]$

7

The autonomy of syntax?

As noted in the Introduction, this book will at times consider alternatives to the Direct Compositional architecture both to elucidate comparison and to familiarize the reader with alternative theories. Much of that discussion is featured in Part III. Here, however, we pursue a narrower goal: to defend Direct Compositionality against some challenges that one finds in the literature. Before proceeding, it is important to tease apart two questions which are sometimes conflated. The first (which is the subject of this chapter) is the question of whether the syntax and semantics proceed "in tandem" (as assumed in this text), or whether instead the syntax computes (i.e., proves well-formed) representations where these representations are the input to the compositional semantics. Those representations themselves could just be direct representations of the actual pronounced sentences, or could be more abstract representations such as Logical Forms. While the term *autonomous syntax* has been used in a variety of ways throughout the history of modern linguistic theory, we use it here *only* to refer to the view that the syntax computes representations which are "sent" to the semantics. The second question is whether what is interpreted—either by a direct compositional interpretation or via the autonomous syntax approach—is the actual pronounced sentence or a more abstract level of LF.

All four combinations of answers to these two questions are possible. The approach in this text combines Direct Compositional interpretation with the claim that the syntax directly builds—and the semantics interprets in tandem—the actual pronounced sentence. At the other end of the spectrum is what has come to be a standard view both within Government–Binding (GB) theory and some subsequent work in Minimalism. This is that the syntax computes representations via a sufficiently rich procedure that there is one representation for the pronounced sentence (i.e., "surface structure"), and a distinct LF which inputs the compositional semantics. In Government–Binding theory, the hypothesis is that surface structures are mapped into LFs by a series of rules. Variants of this have been explored especially within recent work under the rubric of Minimalism, but these differences are not relevant for discussions in this book. In either tradition (GB or Minimalism) it is a Logical Form which is assigned the model-theoretic interpretation, and in both views, the syntactic system which proves well-formed sentences and pairs them with LFs does not work in tandem with the model-theoretic semantic interpretation. So these views maintain LF and also maintain autonomous syntax (as defined here).

But there are other logically possible combinations regarding the organization of the grammar. For example, one can imagine a Direct Compositional syntax and semantics which builds LFs and simultaneously interprets them, followed by additional syntactic rules mapping those LFs to surface forms. This is similar to (although not exactly identical to) the architecture assumed under the theory of Generative Semantics which was explored in the 1960s and 1970s. Thus this view has in common with the GB/Minimalism view that there is a distinct level of LF, but it does not entirely divorce the syntactic computation (of LF) from the semantics, and so does not fit the definition of an autonomous syntax at issue here. The question of whether LF is needed is addressed throughout Part III of this book; the goal here is just to answer some classic arguments for the autonomy of syntax.

7.1. Good syntax—bad semantics

The most famous argument for the autonomy of syntax comes from the earliest days of Generative Grammar, when Chomsky (1957) constructed the by now legendary sentence *Colorless green ideas sleep furiously* as evidence that there can be syntactically well-formed but meaningless strings. But there is no clear sense in which the syntax-autonomous model(s) being discussed here and the Direct Compositional view actually handle such cases in any significantly different fashion. In the first place, it is probably not true that a sentence like this really has no meaning—it just has a rather silly meaning. The reality of this kind of example is that each of the pieces fits together in such a way that the combination either involves a presupposition violation and/or results in something which is massively uninformative. We can illustrate with just the combination of *ideas* (which is a plural noun but here functions as an NP) and *sleep*, so we can simplify the point with respect to the sentence *Ideas sleep*. Given the lexical meaning of *sleep*, it either is always necessarily false to say that [[ideas]] sleep, or else that [[sleep]] is undefined for [[ideas]]. So, for example, it could be [[sleep]] is a partial function of type <e,t>, where [[ideas]] is not in its domain in any world. Then the value of [[ideas sleep]] is undefined for every world w. Or, it could be that [[sleep]] is a total function, always mapping [[ideas]] to 0. Either way, the sentence is uninformative. Thus having the syntax and semantics work together has no problem accounting for the fact that the syntax allows these two words to combine, but the semantics predicts that they will feel like nonsense.

It is especially striking that the autonomous syntax view would say nothing different. For the words can of course be put together in the syntax, and if syntactic representations are sent to the semantics, the same basic story would have to be told. Each word has a meaning, and the grammar has to contain rules (possibly quite general ones) whose input includes structures of the form [$_S$ NP VP]. These are needed for things like *Sheep graze*. And so *Ideas sleep* fits that description; each word has a meaning, and so divorcing the syntactic and the semantic computation leads to no different result from the result given above. Either [[sleep]] is undefined in all worlds for [[ideas]] or it yields 0 in all worlds. Hence there is no clear sense in which autonomous syntax has any advantage over Direct Compositionality for cases like this; indeed both succeed in predicting that the syntax is fine but that the meaning could not be informative.

A related but slightly different case centers on "Jabberwocky" examples: cases of material put together from words which obey English phonotactics, look like they have an obvious syntactic category (due both to their distribution and their morphology), but also "have no meaning." The most famous Jabberwocky example comes from Lewis Carroll's Jabberwocky poem itself, which begins *'Twas brillig, and the slithy toves did gyre and gimble in the wabe* and was designed to be nonsense. Yet clearly it is syntactically well-formed (*did* is capitalized in the original because of the line breaks). For the sake of argument, suppose that *brillig*, *slithy*, *toves*, etc.

are truly meaningless; i.e., that a listener would have absolutely no idea of
what these mean, and therefore no idea of what each sentence in the entire
poem means. Nothing about Direct Compositionality precludes the existence of a word with phonology, syntactic category, and no meaning: we
simply would need to add in a principle that when such a word combines
with additional stuff the result also has no meaning. Note again that this is
no different under autonomous syntax. These are made-up words, but
words they are (otherwise there is no way that the syntax can put them
together). And since any theory takes words to usually be triples of sound,
category, and meaning, these have to be words with only the first two parts.
Hence again, there is no substantive difference between the theories that
leads to any conclusion concerning the organization of the grammar.

   In fact, though, it is not at all clear that this is the right way (under either
theory) to think about such examples. For language users are sufficiently
hungry to view language as an object with meaning that listeners make
guesses about the meanings of these novel words, and come up with some (at
least vague and general) meaning for the whole sentence. They do have
some idea of what this sentence is about. And, strikingly, a speaker of
English would certainly say that the above sentence is not synonymous
with *'Twas not brillig, and the slithy toves did not gyre nor gimble in the
wabe.* But this judgment would be a complete category error if the sentence
were literally meaningless. (Incidentally, one can construct the same argument for the *colorless green ideas* case.) Speakers can also conclude that the
Jabberwocky sentence entails *There were slithy toves that gyred and gimbled
in the wabe.* Again, this robust judgment about entailment would make no
sense if the Jabberwocky sentence literally had no meaning. For an English
speaker who knows absolutely no Mandarin, a sentence of Mandarin is
truly meaningless (and is not part of English) and the speaker will have no
judgments about synonymy and entailments. Presumably, then, even
though *slithy* is not part of a speakers' lexicon, s/he will add in this word
(perhaps temporarily), making an extension of English, and will make a
guess at its meaning. Thus unlike the Mandarin sentence, a Jabberwocky
sentence is English (or English-extended) and has some sort of meaning.
What examples like this do show is that we can sometimes use distributional
and morphological cues to guess the syntactic category of an item more
easily than its meaning (different listeners will come up with different
meanings for *toves* but everyone agrees that this is a plural noun), but this
does not bear on the question of the Direct Compositional architecture.

7.2. Bad syntax—good semantics

The flip side of the argument above is that there are cases which are syntactically ill-formed but perfectly interpretable. Such examples are easy to construct: they can involve agreement mismatches as in (1a), the wrong case marking as in (1b), or even category selection violations as found in (1c). (The interest in (1c) is that *dislike*—unlike *like*—has the surprising property that it cannot occur with bare infinitive VP complements but only with NPs, including gerundive NPs. Note then that (1c) becomes fine if we substitute *like* for *dislike*.[1])

(1) a. *The men is singing. / *The man are singing.
     b. *Him is singing.
     c. *I dislike to lose at poker. (vs I dislike losing at poker.)

Yet there is no problem understanding these sentences. If the semantics is divorced from the syntax and very general semantic principles are stated to interpret syntactic representations, then these principles could conceivably apply even in cases where the syntactic representation is ill-formed. This, for example, could be accomplished by translating the type-driven idea stated in Chapter 6 in the terms of Klein and Sag (1985) into principles for the interpretation of trees; see Heim and Kratzer (1998) for just such an implementation.

But a closer reflection of the situation shows that both Direct Compositionality and autonomous syntax once again have essentially the same account of these. Consider how these are interpreted under the autonomous syntax view. The hypothesis put forward in the above paragraph is that the rules can apply even where the syntactic representation is ill-formed. But *what* syntactic representation? In order for the interpretive procedure to work under autonomous syntax, there has to be some syntactic representation to input the semantics—even if it is a defective one. So an autonomous syntactician must conclude that speakers have access to a kind of secondary grammar which contains (fairly minimal) deviances from the actual rules of English. Otherwise we would have no idea *what* defective representation is inputting the semantics, and no way to account for the fact that (1c), for example, is not understood as "I am hungry." In some cases the secondary

[1] A related set of examples (although not this case) is discussed in Grimshaw (1982).

grammar would involve slightly altering a lexical entry: in the "Englishish" grammar that assigns a representation to (1c) the subcategorization restrictions of *dislike* are slightly altered. In (1a) the morphology is slightly different; *is* is the form of *be* taking plural subjects. Such representations are then allowed by an Englishish grammar and can input the interpretive rules since the latter are stated quite generally.

But once one allows for the possibility that listeners can understand (1) because they have access to a grammar for Englishish, then the autonomous syntax view has no advantage over the Direct Compositional view: the exact same story holds under Direct Compositionality. Once again, (1a) is constructed by slipping *dislike* from its English category that allows only for an NP complement in the VP to its Englishish category that allows an infinitive VP as complement.[2] Arguably the two items have the same meaning (so no meaning revision is required). But even if they don't, it is not particularly difficult to imagine how a listener might slightly alter the meaning of *dislike* (analogous to *like*). Either theory (autonomous syntax or Direct Compositionality) would need to say exactly the same thing about the meaning of the Englishish *dislike*. Under Direct Compositionality, Englishish *is* would once again be the form of *be* that wants a plural subject. In sum, to account for the interpretation of ill-formed material both theories need to endow the listener with the ability to slightly tweak English into Englishish—a skill which speakers surely do have.

7.1. Sometimes the term "autonomous syntax" is used to mean that not everything about the syntax can be inferred just from the semantics. This claim is compatible with and indeed endorsed in the program discussed in this text; syntax does not reduce to semantics. Discuss the ways in which the Categorial Grammar and more generally the Direct Compositional view elucidated so far endorses this claim.

---

[2] In many theories complements like *to lose at poker* are not VPs but sentences with hidden silent subjects. But this debate does not bear on the question at hand.

8

Adjectives, nouns, determiners, and more

8.1. Predicative adjectives

The fragment so far does not include predicative adjectives such as those in (1) (we return in 8.4 to prenominal adjectives as in *the disobedient husky*):

(1)   a. Mitka is disobedient.
      b. Kolya is affectionate.

Of course *is disobedient* and *is affectionate* are VPs and so presumably have (extensional) meanings of type <e,t>. But what is the semantic type of the adjective itself, and what is the contribution of *is*? Note too that expressions that combine with *is* to form VPs can be complex adjectives, as in *fond of thunderstorms, eager to wash the dishes*, etc. For the moment we confine the discussion to single-word adjectives. A reasonable assumption is that *disobedient, affectionate*, etc. themselves denote sets and so—like intransitive verbs—are of type <e,t> (their intensional type of course is <s,<e,t>>).

This means that simple adjectives and intransitive verbs have the same semantic type, but have a different syntax (adjectives generally occur with *be*, do not show verbal morphology, and similarly do not themselves encode tense). But while intransitive verbs and adjectives have the same basic type of meaning, it does not follow that what is lexicalized as an adjective and what is lexicalized as an intransitive verb is totally arbitrary; there are some rather broad tendencies (holding for English at least) differentiating the two classes. The most obvious is that many adjectives express what are known as gradable properties: one can be happy, disobedient, affectionate, and even fond of thunderstorms to different degrees. This is an aspect of adjective meaning that we will not discuss here; see, among many others, Kennedy (2007). Another difference (keeping in mind that these are only tendencies) is that adjectives often denote sets whose membership is more stable over time than run-of-the-mill intransitive verbs. In other words, they tend to denote predicates which are true of an individual for a relatively long length of time; this is tantamount to saying that the set of individuals in, e.g., [[disobedient]] will be more stable from moment to moment than the set of individuals in, e.g., [[howl]].

What about the syntax of adjectives? Because these are of type $<e,t>$ one might expect them to occur with NPs to give something of type t. Indeed this expectation is borne out: they occur with subjects in certain environments as, for example, the complement of *prefer*:

(2)   I would prefer Mitka (a bit more) obedient.

Phrases like *Mitka (a bit more) obedient* also combine with *with* to give sentential adverbial clauses:

(3)   With Mitka (a bit more) obedient, he might manage to graduate puppy class.

Such cases have gone under the rubric *small clause* (Stowell 1981, 1983). The intuition behind this terminology is that expressions like *Mitka (a bit more) obedient* are somewhat like sentences. They are, however, not quite the same as normal Ss for they never occur as root clauses which means they do not stand alone. In fact, they occur in a rather limited set of environments. But while they do have a different distribution from ordinary Ss, they also have something in common with Ss. For just as VPs take the NP with which they combine to their left, so do adjectives when giving a small clause. This suggests that perhaps what we are calling small clauses can be thought of as a feature bundle which has something in common with S but also has some difference. Let us add in two features [A] or [V] on S categories. Ordinary "VPs" are thus S[V]/NP while phrases like *obedient* or *proud of Mary* are S[A]/NP. For convenience, we will often refer to an expression of category S[A]/NP as an AP, which is exactly analogous to our shorthand use of the term VP. It should be noted that items of category S[V] generally contain additional features to account for their distribution. For example, an intransitive verb like *ran* (or *runs*) is not just an S[V]/NP but must contain an additional feature; assume it is actually S[V,Tense]/NP (for V and Tense two separate features). This is needed because only Ss of the form S[V,Tense] occur as root clauses. In fact, verbs occur with a variety of morphological features and VPs such as *chose the best candidate, choosing the best candidate,* and *chosen the best candidate* all occur in different environments. In particular, each occurs with a different auxiliary. All of these distributional facts can be accounted for with suitable use of features on the result S category.

We can now refine the definition of a verb which was given earlier and was needed for morphological purposes. Presumably a basic lexeme like HOWL is listed in the lexicon in its bare and underspecified form S[V]/NP, and morphological rules will map this to more fully specified forms (*howls, howling, howled*, etc.). Adjectives undergo their own morphological processes (e.g., addition of the comparative suffix *-er*). So a "verb"—for the purposes of the morphology—is anything whose ultimate result category is S[V] and an "adjective" is anything whose category is S[A]. We will henceforth omit the V and A features whenever not crucial for the discussion. But it is still the case that no matter how many and which complements a verb takes in order to give a VP, one can give a common definition of this class in terms of the ultimate result. The same is true of adjectives; *fond* is of category S[A]/PP while *tall* is just S[A], but they have the same result category and thus have morphological commonalities. In other words, the traditional parts of speech are reconstructed in terms of the ultimate result category of each lexeme.

The next task is to discover the category of *be* and its meaning. The first is simple: it is (S/NP)/AP, or—in more detail—it is (S[V]/NP)/AP. (*Be* does have a broader distribution than just this, but this will do for present purposes.) As to its meaning, we give it extensionally since (like the case of case-marking prepositions) its extension does not vary with worlds. Ignoring the contribution of tense or other contributions of morphology in the actual inflected forms, *be* contributes nothing—*obedient* and *is obedient* are the same set. This is quite similar to the situation with case-marking prepositions. Hence [[be]] is the identity function on properties (i.e., functions of type $\langle e,t \rangle$); it takes any such property P and returns P.

8.1. Take a "universe" with the three individuals {a,b,c,d} and a world w_1 in which [[Kolya]] at w_1 (and at all worlds) is b, and [[disobedient]]$_S$ at w_1 is {a,c}. Show the syntactic and semantic composition for:

i. Kolya is disobedient.

8.2. We have given a general syntactic category for *and* which allows us to compute things like *Kolya is obedient and affectionate.* However, in terms of its meaning, we have seen instances only of what it means when it combines two VPs or two Ss. Continuing to postpone the question of just how to state the meaning of *and* in a fully general way, what is its semantics when two adjectives are combined as in the case above?

8.3. What type of meaning does *fond* have, and what is its category?

This leaves us the question of how to treat adjectives when they occur prenominally, as in *the disobedient husky*. But first we turn to nouns and *the*.

8.2. Nouns ("common nouns")

What about the type of meaning (and category) of ordinary common nouns such as *dog, cat, table*, etc.? While NPs (*the dog, Balto*) denote individuals, obviously this is not the right type of meaning for nouns. In fact—as was the case for VPs and APs—it makes sense to think of nouns as denoting (world/time-dependent) sets of individuals. So, for example, [[dog]] is (at a given world and time) some set of individuals. A noun like *dog* denotes a relatively stable set across times (individuals who are dogs rarely jump out of that set into the enchanted frog set). The extension of other nouns such as [[student]] is more time-dependent. And interestingly what are sometimes called the *basic-level* nouns tend to denote mutually exclusive sets: a dog is not a cat, and a chair is not a table. But this of course is not true for all nouns, certainly [[professor]]$_S$ and [[assassin]]$_S$ can have a non-empty intersection.

There is an interesting and somewhat surprising fact about ordinary nouns. This is that—unlike VPs and APs—nouns never occur with subjects, even in the environments that support small clauses. Thus we do not get things like (4) and (5), all of which have been constructed to be pragmatically plausible. To bring this out, (4a) and (5a) have been surrounded with some context; the contexts for the (b) sentences seem rather obvious:[1]

(4)   a. Context: Jim thinks that linguists are people who know lots of languages, and so when he finds out that his daughter Nora is majoring in linguistics he says:

Oh good. *With Nora linguist, she'll be able to travel everywhere and speak the language.

   b. *With his new puppy husky, he's going to have to build a 6-foot fence around his yard.

(5)   a. Context: Same as in (4a), but Jim is disappointed as Nora switches her major to geology, and says:

*I would really prefer Nora linguist. (or *I would really prefer Nora linguistics major.)

   b. *I would really prefer his new puppy labrador retriever.

What this suggests, then, is that—in terms of the syntax—there is just a primitive category N which includes *dog, cat, table, linguist*, etc. Thus, despite the fact that these denote functions of type $\langle e,t \rangle$, their corresponding syntax is not something of category S/NP as we might expect. Nothing in the basic framework that has been outlined in Chapter 6 requires this; the only requirement is that every expression of category A/B has as its extension a function from (the extension of) B-type meanings to (the extension of) A-type meanings. The reverse is not required (although is admittedly somewhat surprising to find).

---

[1] There is a class of apparent exceptions to this claim; there are nouns such as *president, mayor, queen*, etc. which do appear here:

(i)   a. With Michelle president of the US, the EPA will quickly be dismantled.

   b. He would prefer Hillary president.

But these are actually only apparent counterexamples: it is well known that this class of "nouns" can also serve as NPs without determiners. They also occur as predicate NPs with *be*:

(ii)   Sabrina is president of Atlantis/mayor of Providence/queen of Middle Earth.

This shift from nouns to full NPs (without determiners) is restricted to a small set of nouns; they must denote sets which are (possibly because of cultural and/or political conventions) singletons. We will not give an analysis of these bare singular noun NPs here; the interested reader should be able to supply such an analysis by the end of this chapter.

8.3. *the*

The fragment at this point will include only the single determiner *the.* We leave quantificational determiners such as *every, some, most,* etc. until Chapter 10; indeed the analysis of expressions like *every cat* and *most students* is one of the most striking achievements in Montague (1973) and will be taken up in due course. For now, the goal is just to give a semantics for *the*.

Clearly *the* is of category NP/N and so we can infer that [[the]] maps a set to an individual. Thus *the dog* denotes some individual but *dog* denotes (the characteristic function of) a set; and so the (extensional) type of *the* must be $<<e,t>,e>$. But what is its exact meaning: how does it systematically map a set (or, a function) to an individual? There is no question that when *the* combines with a singleton set (i.e., a function that maps one and only one individual to 1) the individual that it returns is the single member of the set. Consider *the most disobedient husky.* Here [[most disobedient husky]]—in virtue of being a superlative—already denotes a singleton set, and *the* happily combines with this to yield the single member of that set. (In function terms, [[most disobedient husky]] maps only one individual to 1, and that individual is the value of [[the most disobedient husky]].)

But what is the (extensional) value of *the planet that was made of green cheese* if indeed there is no such planet, or *the beautiful dog* if there is more than one? The answer to this given by Russell (1905) is that *the* has a rather complex meaning such that a sentence like (6) asserts the existence, the uniqueness, and the baldness of the present King of France, and hence is simply false in our world and time:

(6)   The King of France is bald.

A sentence like (7) would also be false if uttered in 1379 in view of the fact that there were two popes at that time—even if indeed both were bald:

(7)   The pope of the Roman Catholic church is bald.

Strawson (1950) argued instead that both the existence and the uniqueness part are presuppositions. Thus one might conclude (7) is true for a world/ time pair with one and only one King if he is bald; false for a world/time pair with one and only one King and he is not bald, and undefined for all other world/time pairs.

To decide just how to resolve this controversy, we begin with the observation that the uniqueness requirement clearly has a rather different status from the existence requirement. We are happy to utter sentences in which uniqueness is violated and do so all the time—as long as it is clear to the listener what is being referred to. There are two senators from Rhode Island, but if Sheldon Whitehouse (one of them in 2013) raises his hand to be recognized by Joe Biden (the presiding officer of the senate in 2013), there is nothing odd about Biden saying "The Chair recognizes the senator from Rhode Island." Arguably, then, "uniqueness" means that [[the]] combines with some set and returns the single (or the most) contextually salient member of that set.[2] Thus it might be that the meaning of [[the]] is a function from speech contexts to (ignoring worlds and times) a function of type $<<e,t>,e>$. Chapter 2 noted other instances of words which require access to the speech context (in particular, "indexicals" like *I, you*, etc.). The reason (7) seems deviant is that it needs a richer context to select one of the popes; if such a context were supplied there would be nothing deviant about (7). To formally build the contribution of speech contexts into the semantics at this point is too lengthy a project, and so will not be attempted here. A different approach to narrowing down the set accessed by *the* is discussed later under the rubric of *domain restriction*; see especially section 17.4.

But this still leaves the question of how to treat the existence requirement: i.e., should the theory predict, with Russell, that (6) is false in our world and time or, with Strawson, that it is undefined? Little in this book hinges on the decision, but when needed we will take the position that [[the King of France]] at a world w and a time i has no value (i.e., is undefined) if there is no King of France. We will also assume that if the value of some expression is undefined at w and i then every expression in which it is embedded also has no value at w and i.[3] Hence if [[the King of France]] is undefined at our world and time, then [[the King of France is bald]] is also undefined.

---

[2] Section 17.4 contains further remarks of relevance, related to the observations made in section 2.2. Recall that it was pointed out there that even sentences like *Every student got an A* does not mean every student in the world, but only those from some salient subset. The situation with *the* is similar: when Susan says "The dog escaped" there is a contextually salient subset of dogs which is a singleton.

[3] This is a huge oversimplification as will be obvious by a casual glance at the literature on "presupposition projection." Interested readers can consult Levinson (1983) for an introduction.

8.4. Prenominal adjectives and unary rules

8.4.1. An additional binary rule?

Section 8.1 dealt with predicative adjectives like *tall*. But what are traditionally called "adjectives" also occur prenominally as noun modifiers (and they can iterate):

(8)   the disobedient husky; the intelligent seal; the intelligent obedient friendly elephant

In fact, there is a striking (near) generalization: any single word AP that can appear predicatively can also appear prenominally.[4] The situation is even more general: any AP—even when complex—can appear as a noun modifier. But the complex ones (*eager to win the primary, happy that the economy did so badly*) occur postnominally.[5] This is exemplified by NPs like the subjects in (9):

(9)   a. The candidate eager to win the primary said something very stupid.
       b. The candidate happy that the economy did so badly will pretend to be unhappy.

There are two broad classes of analyses for these cases. The first adds a new binary combinatory rule. Rather than spell it out in the official notation, we give first the syntax (and phonology) part as a phrase structure rule. We state this here as technically two rules, but a more sophisticated treatment could collapse them:

(10)   a. N → AP N (where AP consists of a single word)
       b. N → N AP (where AP consists of more than one rule)

What is the associated semantics? It cannot be functional application: the types are not right. Rather, a sensible semantics is intersection; *red book* is

---

[4] There is a small class of exceptions. One is the adjective *content* (see Pope 1971). Most of the others themselves form a class in that they all begin with the same bound morpheme: *awake, asleep, adrift, afloat, aghast*, etc.

[5] The discussion here and the rules formulated later oversimplify the situation a bit. There are single-word adjectives that can appear both pre- and postnominally where the different positions actually have different semantic effects. See, e.g., Bolinger (1967).

the set characterizing everything that is both red and is a book. Thus, continuing to use the space-saving notation, we write the full rule as follows:

TR-9. $N_1 \rightarrow$ AP(single word) N_2 or N_2 AP(complex); $[[N_1]]^w = [[AP]]^w \cap [[N_2]]^w$

Incidentally this has been phrased in Direct Compositional terms, but this general type of solution is common in autonomous syntax views as well. Some principle(s) of syntax will allow AP to be a sister to N (where single word adjectives occur on the left), and some principle(s) will take the trees licensed by this rule and interpret them by intersection. See, e.g., Heim and Kratzer (1998) for a version of this.

8.4.2. Interlude: Unary rules ("type shift" rules; morphological rules)

There is a second way to account for the noun modification cases of APs. This is to adopt a rule which maps any AP into something of category N/N with no phonological effect. To flesh this out, we digress to talk about the more general notion of a unary rule, a concept which is often found in the literature under the rubric of a *type shift* rule. Hence, recall that a linguistic expression is a triple of <sound, category, meaning> and the rules (or rule schemata, or principles) in the grammar take *one or more triple* as input and return a triple as output. The fragment so far contains only binary rules: rules whose input is two expressions. But there is no reason not to expect unary rules—i.e., rules whose input is a single expression. Moreover, it is quite possible that sometimes the output expression will be identical in one or more of the pieces of the triple to the input expression.

Such rules are actually common in discussions of morphology, although not necessarily phrased in these terms. But note that (at least some) morphological rules can be thought of as unary rules. They take as input a single triple (which happens to be just one word or possibly what we are calling a lexeme), and yield as output a word with a phonology which may or may not be different from that of the input, a syntactic category which may or may not be different from that of the input, and a meaning which usually is (though presumably need not always be) different from that of the input.[6]

---

[6] The typical discussion of morphological processes in introductory linguistics textbooks often conflates these three aspects of a morphological rule. For example,

While the output syntactic category can be the same as the input (as can be the phonology) usually there is at least some fine-grained difference, as for example the case of mapping singular nouns (or lexemes unspecified for number) to plural nouns. Consider for example reduplication in the Philippine language Ilokano (data from Hayes and Abad 1989). Noun plurals are formed by what Hayes and Abad refer to as "heavy reduduplication," meaning that the first consonant (if there is one), the next vowel, and the next consonant of the noun stem are reduplicated, as in [kaldíŋ] (goat)—[kalkaldíŋ] (goats); [púsa] (cat)—[puspúsa] (cats); and so forth. (For those familiar with phonology, this means that the first *heavy syllable* is reduplicated.) Pursuing the idea that lexemes are underspecified, this can be cast as a rule whose input is any triple with a phonology, a syntactic category—presumably N with no number feature—and a meaning of type <e,t>, whose domain is the set of both singular and plural individuals. The output has the new phonology described above, a new category which is N[PLURAL] and the semantics is the function whose domain is only plural individuals. Of special interest is also the fact that there are also morphological processes that do not change the phonology (these are sometimes called *zero derivation* in traditional works on morphology) but do change category and meaning. There is no reason not to assume the existence of unary rules like this whose inputs are larger expressions than just single words. The ones of relevance for the present purposes are those which (like zero derivation in morphology) have no effect on the phonology.

Before returning to the case of adjectives, it is worth making two terminological points. First, those rules that map single words into single words are sometimes referred to in the literature as *lexical rules*. We avoid that terminology here, and reserve the term *lexicon* for that which is listed. Hence, whenever there is a productive rule mapping one term to another,

one often finds a list of morphological processes which includes things like "reduplication," "suffixation," "(noun) incorporation," and "compounding." The first two are descriptions of what the phonology does. Noun incorporation generally refers to both the syntactic and semantic effect of a process (the phonological process is simply the concatenation of two morphemes), and "compounding" usually refers to a syntactic process (whose semantic reflex differs from case to case). This kind of taxonomy obscures the fact that every morphological process can be seen as a mapping from a triple to a triple.

the term *lexical rule* is an oxymoron—a form is either given by a rule or it is listed in the lexicon. Second, it is also the case that in much of the semantics literature, unary rules with no phonological consequences are often referred to as *type shift* rules. This too is a term that will be avoided here. For one thing, this terminology suggests rules whose output differs from the input only in meaning and semantic type and not also in syntactic category. Given the premises of Categorial Grammar as adopted here, any time an expression α is mapped to an expression β with a different type of meaning, β will also have to differ in syntactic category from α. Moreover, there is also nothing precluding a case where the output differs in meaning without differing in type. The morphological rule prefixing *un-* to certain adjectives is a case in point: *unhappy* obviously means something quite different from *happy* but there is no reason to believe that the two differ in type or in category. Type shift rules are thus just a special case of rules whose output differs in meaning from the input, but have no privileged status here.[7]

Finally, note that any unary rule which does not change the phonology can always be recast using what is often known as an *empty operator* which, in the terms here, would be a lexical item with a syntactic category and a meaning but no phonology. Given any unary rule which takes an expression α of the form <[α], X, [[α]]> and returns an expression of the form <[α], Y, f([[α]])> where f is the semantic operation performed by the rule, one can repackage this as a lexical item β of the form <[Φ], Y/X, f>, where β combines with α to give the result. (This is of course phrased in CG terms but can be implemented in any other theory.) There is little, if any, reason to choose between the unary rule and the silent lexical item approach; they

---

[7] We also note that we will eschew a slogan common in some literature to the effect that "an item may type-shift only as a last resort." This slogan makes sense only under the autonomous syntax view whereby a syntactic representation is computed and fed to the semantics. Under that conception, the "last resort" idea is that the rules of the grammar work in such a way as to only combine the basic meaning of two sisters to give the value of the mother. However, in a case where there are two sisters whose types are such that there is no rule allowing these meanings to combine, there could be a rule allowing one to map to a different type (and thus a different meaning). Under the architecture of the grammar proposed here the "type-shift as a last resort" slogan makes no sense. But even under the autonomous syntax view this slogan is potentially quite misleading; it suggests that the grammar has needs or goals, which of course it does not.

ultimately may just be different metaphors for the same thing.[8] In this text
we will adopt the phonologically inert unary rule solution, but should one
prefer the silent lexical item approach, readers are free to recast all of the
unary rules in that way. Here the term *unary rule* can be seen as a cover term
for a class of solutions that include unary rules or silent lexical items.

8.4.3. Back to adjectives

With this apparatus, it is easy to recast the new binary combinatory rule
from section 8.4.1. The rule is as follows, and will be referred to as **mod**:

R-2. For any expression α of the form $<[\alpha], AP, [[\alpha]]>$ there is an expression β of
the form $<[\alpha], N/N, [[\beta]]>$, where $[[\beta]]$ is a function (of type $<<e,t>,<e,t>>$)
which takes a function f and returns the function that characterizes the
intersection of f_S with $[[\alpha]]_S>$.
If $[\alpha]$ consists of a single word then the result is $N/_R N$.

Note that R-2 covers the case of both complex APs and single-word APs,
and builds in the exceptionality of the single-word case. Those new items not
covered by the last clause in R-2 will automatically be marked as $N/_L N$ by
the general word order rules. The semantic part is stated awkwardly—a
consequence of trying to phrase complex model-theoretic objects purely in
prose. The next chapter remedies this. (One might notice that operation that
maps the meaning of the input expression to the meaning of the output
expression is essentially Curry'ed intersection.)

[8] There is a tendency in some modern linguistic theories to favor theories which
keep the rules as simple as possible and put all "clutter" into the lexicon, and one
sometimes sees this used as an argument for the silent operator approach (it is, after
all, a lexical item, albeit a quiet one). But since the two solutions are arguably
equivalent, the preference for a silent lexical item over a unary rule seems irrational.
Pursuing this further, one sometimes sees claims to the effect that relegating all cross-
linguistic variation and irregularity to the lexicon helps explain how acquisition can
take place. But there is no obvious reason to believe that this hypothesis makes
language acquisition any less mysterious (at least not if there are silent items).
Invoking a silent lexical item goes no further towards explaining how a child could
learn the relevant phenomenon than does invoking a unary rule, for the learner
has no more direct access to a silent lexical item than to a phonologically inert
unary rule.

By way of example, take a universe with five individuals {a,b,c,d,e}, and a world such that the lexical item *disobedient* (of category AP) has as its extension the function mapping a,d, and e to 1 and b and c to 0. [[husky]] at the world in question maps a and b to 1 and the others to 0; [[lab]] maps c, d, and e to 1 and the others to 0. The derivation of *disobedient husky*, showing how the extensions are computed, is shown in (11); we use the label "disobedient$_1$" to indicate the version of that phonological form listed in the lexicon, and "disobedient$_2$" to be the homophonous form derived by R-2. Recall the notational conventions whereby for some set S, S_f is the function characterizing that set, and for a function f, f_S is the set characterized by f. (S_f can be computed from S only if there are no partial functions; in our example here there are none.)

(11)   disobedient$_1$, AP, function characterizing {a,d, e}   listed in lexicon
disobedient$_2$, N/$_L$N, [[husky]] → {a}$_{F}$;, [[lab]] →{d,e}$_F$ by **mod**
disobedient$_2$ husky, N, {a}$_F$ by **l-app**

The important step to understand here is the mapping from the meaning of *disobedient$_1$* to the meaning of *disobedient$_2$*. Put completely in set terms, the latter takes any set, and returns the intersection of that set with the set (characterized by) [[disobedient$_1$]].

---

*8.4. Recast **mod** using the silent lexical item approach.

Is there any reason to prefer the unary rule (or silent lexical item) solution over the binary rule solution given in 8.4.1? Each adds a rule, so neither is obviously simpler. Moreover, while the rule in R-2 accounts for both the case of single-word prenominal APs and complex post-nominal ones, we cannot really claim victory for R-2 on that basis because we simply did not explore ways to make the appropriate generalization for TR-9. There is, however, a difference between the two solutions. The unary rule solution composes material like *disobedient husky* in two stages and thereby predicts the existence of a new expression *disobedient$_2$* (in this case of category N/$_L$N). If there turns out to be some evidence that this is an expression of the language, there would be evidence for the unary rule R-2 over the new binary rule in (TR-9). And indeed there does seem to be a bit of evidence in this direction, which is left for the reader to discover in the next exercise.

> **8.5.** Consider the NP *the happy and honest candidate*. Does the existence of this NP provide evidence for the rule in R-2 over the solution in 8.4.1? You should just concentrate here on the *syntax* of this expression. Since we have not yet given a fully general definition for *and*, the tools are not yet available to investigate how the semantics would work in each case, but this will be revisited in Exercise 12.2. Note: The full set of relevant facts is actually a bit complex (and the relevant judgments not entirely clear), so this question is somewhat open-ended, but there is a clear difference in the predictions made by each solution.

There are, moreover, other analogous cases in which there is evidence for the two-step unary rule solution (see, e.g., Jacobson 1999). Hence we will generally prefer this strategy in this book over adding new binary rules. But one should keep in mind that in any given case there is often no strong evidence one way or another, and in some cases the choice might truly might boil down to a matter of taste.

8.4.4. Are all noun modifier adjectives intersective?

Whether one ultimately adopts the binary or the unary rule solution, the claim is that the semantics for something like *red ball* involves intersecting the set of red things with the set of balls. But are all adjectives intersective in this way? After all, *big* seems to have a very different value in a phrase like *big flea* than in a phrase like *big elephant*. It is easy to conclude from this that [[big]] does not pick out any kind of set but rather that [[big]] combines with a noun to give the set of things that are big in comparison to other things in the noun set. If this is correct, the semantics is not intersection; prenominal [[big]] would be a function that maps a set to the subset of things that are big for that set.

The reasoning above turns out to be partly right and partly wrong. It is true that [[big]] by itself does not pick out a set: it needs to be given a comparison class in order to return the appropriate set. However, one can show that the existence of the comparison class argument is independent of the question of how [[big]] combines with the head noun. For the comparison class is needed for "gradable" adjectives in any position (see Kennedy 2007 for much discussion). Thus even in predicative position a comparison class is implicit; recall the discussion in Chapter 2 centering on (4) *Magic Johnson is tall*. Here too one cannot really determine the truth without fixing the comparison class for *tall*. When such an adjective appears prenominally, there is a strong pressure for the comparison class to be the one set by the noun: we tend to understand *a tall basketball player*, for example, to mean someone who is tall for a basketball player. But this is not necessary—it can refer to someone who is quite short for a basketball player but tall compared to the general population. Similarly, let Dumbo be very small compared to other elephants, but still pretty big in comparison to the animals we usually see. We could point to Dumbo and say "Boy, look at that big elephant." In other words, the situation with prenominal adjectives is no different from the situation with predicative adjectives: both need a comparison class. The difference is only that in the prenominal case there is a strong tendency (perhaps due to processing considerations?) to fix the class by the noun.

It is true, then, that the meaning of gradable adjectives is more complex than given here. Such an adjective must always be supplied a comparison class in order to pick out a set. Without giving a full formal account at this point, we adopt a rough-and-ready account by hypothesizing that these all contain a *free variable*. (The semantics for variables is elucidated in Chapters 9 and 15, and an alternative way to model [[big]] without a free variable is discussed in section 15.5.2.) But for now the informal intuition is clear enough: [[big]] means *larger than average for an X*, where X picks up some contextually salient set. This is its lexical meaning; the meaning of the homophonous noun modifier is exactly the elaborated version of this that results from the application of R-2. The intersection semantics embodied in R-2 remains, but the actual meaning of the lexical item *big* has this extra parameter. For expository ease, we continue to ignore the extra parameter for the comparison class until section 15.5.

Incidentally, it is not the case that all things that one might call prenominal adjectives are intersective; things like *former* as in *former senator* crucially combine with the intension of *senator*. It is, therefore, not intersective (there is no set of things that are "former"), and it also (unsurprisingly) has no predicative counterpart. (For that reason *former* is not traditionally called an "adjective," but—like prenominal *tall*—its syntax is indeed $N/_R N$.) *Former* and related words are briefly explored in Chapter 19.

It is also the case that superlative adjectives such as *tallest* are crucially non-intersective (the set of *tallest linguistics majors* is not the intersection of two sets). Nor do superlatives occur predicatively (at least not without a fair amount of contextual support), thus *Nora is tallest* is strange.[9]

> **8.6.** Return to the discussion in section 1.1.1 surrounding the sentences in (1) in that chapter. To simplify the discussion, we took *the tallest* as a single lexical item. You should now be able to go through the compositional semantics of (1a) in somewhat better detail to show how it is put together. Of course, we have given no semantics for superlative adjectives so your analysis will not be complete.

8.5. Relational nouns

This chapter concludes with one more type of category: relational nouns. These are nouns that take PP complements (where the preposition is always *of*) as in:

(12)   the mother of Romeo; the sister of Romeo; the wife of Bert; the author of *Waverley*; the writer of that letter; the builder of the Acropolis; the mayor of Providence; the student of Zellig Harris...)

Notice that expressions like *mother of Romeo* already denote singleton sets, but this is not a necessary fact about relational nouns plus their PP complements (witness *the sister of Romeo*: use of *the* here of course requires a unique contextually salient sister but *sister of Romeo* itself need not be a singleton). And these can of course occur with quantificational determiners (*every student of Zellig Harris, no friend of Sabrina*, etc.). Note also that some of these are kinship terms (*mother, sister*, etc.), but the class is certainly not restricted in this way. It includes many other nouns (*friend, colleague, student*) and includes many forms that are nominalized forms of transitive verbs (*writer, builder*, etc.).

Chapter 6 provided an account of those prepositions that function essentially as case markers; *of* here is one of these. Assume that *of Bert* (in *the wife*

---

[9] We do get sentences like *Nora is the tallest*, where there is an implicit set ("the tallest of some set").

of Bert) is of category **PP[OF]** and *of* of category **PP[OF]/NP**. Assume further that—as with the case of case-marking prepositions in general—[[of]] is just the identity function on individuals. Thus *mother of Romeo, wife of Bert, student of Zellig Harris*, and so forth themselves are complex nouns and have a syntactic distribution which is the same as any simple noun (they occur with determiners like *the* to form an NP), and like other nouns they cannot take subjects:

(13)   *With Krugman writer of today's op ed piece, you'll have to get the *New York Times*.

Syntactically, then, the relational nouns are of category **N/PP[OF]**. Notice that—as discussed in Chapter 6—the traditional morphological category of "noun" is defined in terms of the result: a "noun" is anything whose final result is N. The morphology needs to know about this since even though *wife (of)* and *table* are quite different syntactically (*wife* taking a PP complement and *table* being an intransitive noun) both of them take plural morphology.

Their semantic type must therefore be $\langle e, \langle e, t \rangle \rangle$. This comes as no surprise; the very name "relational noun" suggests that these denote a two-place relation between individuals. As with transitive verbs, English syntax treats this relation as Curry'ed; unlike the case of transitive verbs the $\langle e, t \rangle$ function that results from applying a function like [[daughter]] to its first argument never (directly) gets its second argument.

8.7. Add to our fragment the following lexical items, whose extension at a world w_1 will be shown with the items. We are ignoring the fact that *honest* must be supplied a comparison class, and treat it as a simple function of type $\langle e, t \rangle$. The "universe" will consist of four individuals $\{a, b, c, d\}$.

> <honest, AP, a $\to$ 0, b $\to$ 0, c $\to$ 1, d $\to$ 1.
> <Lear; NP, d>
> <daughter; N/PP[OF]; d $\to$ $\left\{ \begin{array}{l} a \to 1 \\ b \to 1 \\ c \to 1 \\ d \to 0 \end{array} \right\}$

all other individuals (a, b, and c)
are mapped to functions
mapping all individuals to 0.

Give the full syntactic and semantic composition of (i):

(cont.)

> (i) the honest daughter of Lear
>
> In giving the semantics, show the types and also show the extension of each expression at w_1.

Of course many (all?) of these items can also occur without the PP complement as ordinary intransitive nouns. Whether there is a predictable rule mapping items of category N/PP[OF] into N with a regular semantic effect (and with no phonological effect) or whether they are just listed as separate lexical items will be left open here. In at least some cases the corresponding noun has additional aspects of meaning. Thus, Barker (1995) notes that while *child* as an intransitive noun encodes youngness (a child is necessarily young), *child of* does not. At the time of the writing of this book, Chelsea Clinton is approximately 32 years old and hardly a "child," but is still the child of Hillary Clinton.

Finally, note that for many of these it is more natural to use constructions like *Romeo's mother, Sabrina's friend* rather than the form with the of-PP. These look much like constructions with ordinary genitive (or "possessive") NPs with normal intransitive nouns, as in *Dorothy's dog, Sarah's key*, etc. For the latter, though, the semantic relationship between the noun (*dog*) and the genitive NP (*Dorothy's*) is completely free: *Dorothy's dog* really means the dog that stands in some contextually salient relation to Dorothy. (It could, for example, be the dog that Dorothy is in charge of feeding at the local shelter; it could be the dog that was chasing her in a scenario of several individuals each being chased by a different dog, etc.).[10] For the case of relational nouns, however, the genitive can fill the argument slot normally filled semantically by the OF-PP, thus *Romeo's mother* means the same as *the mother of Romeo*.

---

[10] This is similar to the case of noun compounds as in *pumpkin bus*, detailed in Downing (1977), where the relation between the two nouns is completely free and specified by context. A wonderful example illustrating the noun compound case was the term *balloon boy* coined by newscasters in 2009 after a boy named Falcon pretended to be caught in a hot-air balloon that was floating for miles. The entire episode turned out to be a publicity stunt engineered by the parents. *Balloon boy* thus came to refer to a boy who was *not* in a balloon (the contextually salient relation between boy and balloon being, perhaps, "pretending to be in"). With a bit of imagination, one can similarly imagine the phrase *Falcon's balloon* in the same context.

(Since many of these relational nouns can also occur as ordinary intransitive nouns, the genitive can also be similar to cases like *Dorothy's dog*. Take, for example, an NP like *Bill Clinton's child*. This can refer to Chelsea Clinton. However, it of course can also be analyzed as intransitive *child*. Imagine that we are in the context of a daycare center at which Bill Clinton is employed. Each employee is assigned one child who s/he must help with their coloring project. In that scenario, we can talk about *Bill Clinton's child*—note that, predictably, the referent of this NP must be young. (See Partee and Borschev 2003 for much relevant discussion about the two kinds of genitives.)

We will not deal with the cases like *Dorothy's dog* (for interesting discussion see Storto 2000), but it will be useful as we further construct our fragment to have an analysis of the relational noun case (e.g., *Romeo's mother*). Although not the most elegant solution in the world, assume that all relational nouns can shift their syntactic category and semantics by the following unary rule:

R-3. If α is an expression of the form <[α], N/PP[OF], [[α]]> then there is an expression β of the form <[α], NP/$_L$NP[GEN], [[β]] is a function of type <e,e> such that for all x, [[β]](x) is the unique (contextually salient) individual y such that [[α]](x)(y) is true>

(The semantics can be stated much more concisely after the next chapter.)

---

*8.8. As of yet, the system has no way to give an expression like *Lear's honest daughter*. See if you can see why not. You will be able to return to this after section 13.4.

8.6 Summary: The fragment so far

To the fragment in Chapter 6, add the following:

Lexicon:
"open-class" items
S[A]/NP; all of the intransitive adjectives like *honest, red, tall,*...
(S[A]/NP)/PP[OF]; *fond*
N; *table, dog, cat,*...
N/PP[OF]; *mother, child, daughter, employer,*...

"closed-class" items
<[of], PP[OF]/NP, identity function on individuals>

<[the], NP/N, the function mapping a set of individuals to the unique (or most) contextually salient member of that set>

<[is], S[Tense]/(S[A]/NP), identity functions on properties (i.e., on sets of type <e,t>)>
Note: we have given the tensed form here. The more general form of *be* might be S[V]/(S[A]/NP) depending on how exactly the feature system is worked out.

Rules:

R-2.   For any expression α of the form <[α], AP, [[α]]> there is an expression β of the form <[α]; N/N; [[β]] is a function (of type <<e,t>,<e,t>>) which takes a function f and returns the function that characterizes the intersection of f$_S$ with [[α]]$_S$>.
If [α] consists of a single word then the result is N/$_R$N.
(Call this **mod**)

R-3.   If α is an expression of the form <[α], N/PP[OF], [[α]]> then there is an expression β of the form <[α], NP/$_L$NP[GEN], [[β]] is a function of type <e,e> such that for all x, [[β]](x) is the unique (contextually salient) individual y such that [[α]](x)(y) is true>.

9

Interlude: The semantics of variables and the lambda calculus

This chapter detours from the main project of building a semantics (and syntax) for a fragment of English. Instead we pause to build a syntax and semantics for two languages that look very different from English. The first is basically (with modifications) first-order predicate logic which includes a treatment of quantifiers. The second takes the first language and enriches it to what is called the lambda calculus.

Since neither of these looks very much like English, one might wonder why engage in such a project. This might seem especially puzzling because we will see in the next chapter that English quantification is rather different from the treatment of quantifiers in first-order logic, so why bother with the latter? There are two good reasons to digress and build a semantics for these artificial languages. The first, and most immediate, is that the ultimate language developed in this chapter (the lambda calculus with quantifiers) provides a very useful way to name complex model-theoretic objects. The reader has undoubtedly noticed that some of the semantics in the preceding chapters has been stated quite awkwardly. This is fine as long as it is clear:

the language used to name model-theoretic objects is of no consequence for the theory and is only a tool for the linguist (the grammar itself simply pairs expressions with model-theoretic objects). But once the objects get sufficiently complex (e.g., functions with functions as their domains as well as co-domains) it is useful to have a simple way to write out these meanings without excruciating and/or ambiguous prose, and the lambda calculus allows us to do just this. We will, however, take the unusual step of trying wherever possible to also write these out in prose (however excruciating) as a reminder that these name actual model-theoretic objects and that the formulas have no theoretical significance.

The second reason for a detour into the semantics of these artificial languages is that the languages introduced here contain variables, and the semantics for the interpretation of variables translates rather directly into a standard view of the semantics of natural language pronouns. Variables (or their analogue) are also central under one common view of the semantics of relative clauses. But a caveat is in order: Part III develops two competing analyses of pronouns and relative clauses. The view using variables is embedded in an autonomous syntax approach, while the Direct Compositional alternative developed in Part III actually makes no use of variables at all (except as a notational device). And since this book is committed to direct compositionality, one might wonder why spend time discussing variables in terms of the theory of natural language. The reason is that the use of variables in semantics is so widespread that understanding the semantics of variables is a matter of basic semantic literacy. But in any case, it is time to develop more formally a metalanguage that we can use to name model-theoretic objects, since trying to continue with just English as the metalanguage would become more and more difficult.

9.1. First-order predicate logic (modified)

9.1.1. Variables

To depart minimally from what has been done so far, we begin by building a language a bit more English-like than is usual in treatments of first-order logic. We adopt a Categorial Grammar syntax, but with only S and NP as primitives. The correspondence between syntactic category and semantic type remains the same, although intensions play no role here. Hence expressions of category S are of type t, expressions of category NP of type e, expressions of category S/NP of type <e,t>, etc. There is no use of directional features on the slash as the syntax will put all functions before the arguments (making the language verb–object–subject in terms of word order). The noun phrases are all simple with no internal structure. To distinguish the expressions from actual English we notate them as *feed'*, *Fido'*, etc.

Lexicon:
NP: Fido', Porky', Dumbo', . . . (value of each is f, p, d, respectively)
S/NP: walk', chew-gum', squeak', . . . (each of which denotes some function in type <e,t>)
(S/NP)/NP: kiss', kill', feed', . . . (each of which denotes some function in <e,<e,t>>)

Rule (to be revised directly): We number these NER-n ("Not-English Rule") and since this rule is temporary it earns a T.

TNER-1.   Given an expression α of the form <[α], A/B, [[α]]> and an expression β of the form <[β], B, [[α]]>, there is an expression γ of the form <[$\alpha(\beta)$], A, [[α]]([[β]])>.

(Note that we have introduced parentheses into the phonological string in order to make things easier to read. This may seem odd, but since there is no sense in which this language actually has a real phonology, it is harmless.) Thus, TNER-1 combined with the lexicon above gives sentences like *squeak'(Porky')*, *chew-gum'(Dumbo')*, *feed'(Porky')(Dumbo')*, etc. It will also be useful to have rules introducing the logical connectives especially since these will be convenient when this language is used for writing meanings. We give the rules in phrase structure rule:

NER-2: $S_1 \rightarrow S_2 \& S_3$; $[[S_1]] = 1$ iff $[[S_2]] = 1$ and $[[S_3]] = 1$
NER-3: $S_1 \rightarrow S_2 \lor S_3$; $[[S_1]] = 0$ iff $[[S_2]] = 0$ and $[[S_3]] = 0$
NER-4: $S_1 \rightarrow S_2 \rightarrow S_3$; $[[S_1]] = 0$ iff $[[S_2]] = 1$ and $[[S_3]] = 0$
NER-5: $S_1 \rightarrow \sim S_2$; $[[S_1]] = 1$ iff $[[S_2]] = 0$

So far this is little more than a stripped-down version of the English fragment built earlier, with a strange word order. But the first main difference is that we now add in variables. So, in addition to *Fido'*, *Porky'*, *Dumbo'*, etc., the language also contains an infinite number of NPs, each of which is an expression of the form x_i for some positive integer i. In order to give the semantics, we introduce the notion of an *assignment function*— or, for short, an *assignment*. An assignment (function) is a function which takes each variable name and maps it to some object. The set of all assignments will be called G, and g will be used to refer to an arbitrary assignment function. The semantics thus now has an extra dimension from what we have seen so far. A variable name does not have a semantic value in and of itself; it has a value *relative to some way to map it to some object*. In particular, for any g, the value of x_i on g is $g(x_i)$. Another way to say this is that the meaning of x_i is not an individual—it is a function from assignments to individuals (where the assignment itself is a function from variables to individuals). Thus another way to write what was said above is as follows: for any g, $[[x_i]](g) = g(x_i)$. As is the case with world and time parameters, the convention in much semantics literature is to write the g as a superscript, thus $[[x_i]]^g = g(x_i)$ (where there is a hidden "for all g" in front of this formula).[1]

The syntax now gives expressions like *sings' (x₃)*. So far, we have an interpretation for the NP x_3 but not for the whole sentence. Exactly the technique used earlier for world and time arguments will be used here. Thus every expression in the language actually has a value only relative to an assignment. Put differently, the meaning of any expression is a function from the set of assignments to whatever you thought its type of meaning was before reading this chapter. NPs all have as their meanings functions from G to e. Ss denote functions from G to t, and so forth. But the semantics is constructed in such a way that many expressions denote constant functions from the set of assignments. This is true, for example, for all of the lexical items above except the variables. Thus [[Dumbo']] is not d, but is a function

---

[1] This particular definition of an assignment introduces an odd status to a variable: it is both a syntactic expression and a member of a set which forms the domain of an actual function used in the semantics. If we wish the semantics to be concerned with model-theoretic objects only, then we have introduced variable names (a syntactic object) into our toolkit of model-theoretic objects; a rather unnatural situation. This, however, is just an artifact of the particular definition adopted above. One could revise this to take an assignment to be a function from the set of positive integers (clearly unobjectionable model-theoretic objects) to the set of individuals, such that for any g, $[[x_i]](g) = g(i)$. We will not adopt this convention in the remainder of the discussion because section 9.2 introduces variables over other types besides just individuals. We would then have to invoke fancier objects like ordered pairs of integers, ordered triples, etc. in the domain of the assignment functions; this would be needed to distinguish all of these different kinds of variables. All of that can be done but is unpleasant to read. We thus stick to the convention of having an assignment be a function from the variables themselves to other objects.

from G such that for all g in G, [[Dumbo']](g) = d. [[walks']] is similar; it assigns every g in G some function in <e,t>. Hence [[walks']] is a function in <G,<e,t>>. (Of course once we return to English, whose expressions denote functions from world–time pairs to something else, we have one more layer in the functions: [[walks]] is a function from worlds, times, and assignments to a function of type <e,t>. It is constant on the assignment, but not on the world and time arguments. But the language here is purely extensional.)

The semantics of TNER-1 is now to be revised in the obvious way, and we now rename this as NER-1.

NER-1.   Given an expression α of the form <[α], A/B, [[α]]> and an expression β of the form <[β], B, [[β]]>, there is an expression γ of the form <[$\alpha(\beta)$], A, where for all g, [[γ]](g) = [[α]](g)([[β]](g))>. (Again, a more common notation for this last part is: [[γ]]^g = [[α]]^g([[β]]^g).)

Cumbersome though this may seem, it is well worth getting the intuition for what variables are doing here and how this aids in the compositional computation of a formula like *feed's* (x_1) (x_2) which contains two open variables. To illustrate, let us shrink the language to have only two variables x_1 and x_2. Moreover, let us shrink the universe to only two individuals, p and f. Then there are four assignments as follows:

(1) g_1: $x_1 \rightarrow$ p g_2: $x_1 \rightarrow$ p g_3: $x_i \rightarrow$ f g_4: $x_1 \rightarrow$ f
           $x_2 \rightarrow$ p $x_2 \rightarrow$ f $x_2 \rightarrow$ p $x_2 \rightarrow$ f

Let [[*feed'*]] on each g be the function in (2):

(2)   p $\rightarrow \left\{ \begin{array}{l} p \rightarrow 1 \\ f \rightarrow 1 \end{array} \right\}$ f $\rightarrow \left\{ \begin{array}{l} p \rightarrow 0 \\ f \rightarrow 1 \end{array} \right\}$

We—the humans looking at this—can see that [[feed' $(x_1)(x_2)$]] should come out false on g_3 and true on all the others. But that is because we can see the entire formula. We reason that for any g, [[feed']](g)(f)(p) is false while [[feed']](g) applied to any other combination of individuals is true. So we only need to look to see what assignment maps x_1 to f and x_2 to p, and that is g_3. But the grammar is "dumb" and does not get to see the entire formula: it needs a procedure to compute the value in a fully compositional fashion. This is what is accomplished by the method of treating everything as a function from assignments to something else. To illustrate, the computation proceeds as follows:

(3)   [[feed']] = $g_1 \rightarrow$ the above; $g_2 \rightarrow$ the above, etc.
         [[x_1]] = $g_1 \rightarrow$ p, $g_2 \rightarrow$ p, $g_3 \rightarrow$ f, $g_4 \rightarrow$ f

To derive the value of the next larger expression *feed* (x_1) the compositional procedure has access only to the value of *feed'* on each assignment and to value of x_1 on each assignment. By the rule NER-1, it computes the value in (4):

(4) $[[feed'(x_1)]] = g_1 \rightarrow \begin{Bmatrix} p \rightarrow 1 \\ f \rightarrow 1 \end{Bmatrix}$ $g_2 \rightarrow \begin{Bmatrix} p \rightarrow 1 \\ f \rightarrow 1 \end{Bmatrix}$ $g_3 \rightarrow \begin{Bmatrix} p \rightarrow 0 \\ f \rightarrow 1 \end{Bmatrix}$ $g_4 \rightarrow \begin{Bmatrix} p \rightarrow 0 \\ f \rightarrow 1 \end{Bmatrix}$

The interesting point is the next step. To get from here to the value of the full formula, we could perfectly well erase the information in (2) and never look back at it. That information gives the value of *feed'*. But the compositional computation has no access to the meaning of smaller expressions like this, it "sees" only the value of the two expressions that combine to give the full sentence, and these are *feed'* (x_1) and x_2. The value of *feed'* (x_1) is given in (4), and the value of x_2 is (5):

(5) $[[x_2]] = g_1 \rightarrow p,$ $g_2 \rightarrow f,$ $g_3 \rightarrow p,$ $g_4 \rightarrow f$

These two pieces of information are sufficient to compute the right result for the full expression *feed'* $(x_1)(x_2)$ and this is shown in (6):

(6) $[[feed'(x_1)(x_2)]] = g_1 \rightarrow 1,$ $g_2 \rightarrow 1,$ $g_3 \rightarrow 0,$ $g_4 \rightarrow 1$

The moral of this rather plodding exercise is to show that this technique allows the meanings to combine in a fully compositional fashion.

9.1.2. Quantifiers

In addition to their potential use in modeling natural language pronouns, variables are also used in first-order logic as a way to give a semantics for quantifiers like ∀ ("for all") and ∃ ("there exists"). Recall that the goal in this chapter has nothing to do with a direct modeling of the English compositional syntax/semantics. The next additions we make to our Non-English language is very un-English-like; and an account of English quantification that respects the syntax will be the subject of the very next chapter. But working through the semantics for the first-order logic quantifiers again illuminates certain techniques (in particular, the notion of "binding" of the variables) that will be useful later. Moreover, having an explicit semantics for formulas with these quantifiers is useful in naming model-theoretic objects.

Hence we add the following two rules:

NER-6. Given any expression α of the form $<[\alpha], S, [[\alpha]]>$ there is an expression β of the form $<[\exists\ x_i\ [\alpha]], S$, for all g $[[\beta]](g) = 1$ iff there is some assignment g' just like g except possibly for the value assigned to x_i such that $[[\alpha]]^{g'} = 1>$.

NER-7. Given any expression α of the form $<[\alpha], S, [[\alpha]]>$ there is an expression β of the form $<[\forall\ x_i\ [\alpha]], S$, for all g $[[\beta]](g) = 1$ iff for all assignments g' just like g except possibly for the value assigned to x_i $[[\alpha]]^{g'} = 1>$.

Syntactically, these rules prefix a quantifier and a variable to a sentence. (The brackets [...] are used in two senses in the rules above. The outermost brackets in $[\exists\ x_i\ [\alpha]]$ are meant, as usual, to refer to the "phonology" of the expression—rather artificial here since this language is not pronounced—but nonetheless retained from the discussion of English to keep the differences minimal. The inner brackets around α are meant as actual parts of the string, just as parentheses were introduced in NER-1. The addition of these brackets ensures that each string is unambiguous.) NER-6 and NER-7 allow for any indexed variable to be introduced. Notice also that the rules are not formulated to require that there be an instance of x_i within the sentence to which the quantifier and variable are prefixed. There is no particular reason to complicate the rule to require such a variable within the S; if there is none, the effect of these rules on the semantics will just be vacuous—the meaning of β is simply the same as the meaning of α. (This is thus referred to as *vacuous quantification*.)

Let us walk through the semantics. NER-6 ensures that a sentence of the form $\exists\ x_i\ S$ is true on an assignment g if there is some g' which differs only on the value assigned to i such that the lower S is true on g'. What does it take to find such an assignment? Informally it requires there to be some individual a who can be slotted in to the position held by x_i which would make the sentence true. In other words, if the sentence were $\exists x_i\ [walks'(x_i)]$ and we were evaluating this on g, we would look to find some individual a such that $walks'(x_i)$ is true on the g' where x_i is mapped to a. In turn, this means that there has to be some individual who did indeed walk. Note that the phrasing "g' just like g *except possibly* for the value assigned to x_i" means that g' could of course be g itself. For the case of universal quantification, the semantics ensures that $walks'(x_i)$ is true for every assignment which differs from g only in the value that it assigns to x_i. Suppose for example that there are 23 individuals. Then there are 23 assignments that vary only on the value assigned to x_i (for any i). (One of these is guaranteed to be g itself.) Since this must be true on all of these, it is ensured that every individual does indeed walk.

---

*9.1. Show that application of NER-6 and NER-7 in cases where the input sentence does not contain an instance of the variable introduced in these rules has no semantic effect. (In other words, show that vacuous quantification is indeed vacuous.)

There is another way to phrase the semantics which is equivalent. First we introduce a notational convention. For any g and any individual a, let $g^{x\text{-}i \rightarrow a}$ mean the assignment just like g except that x_i is assigned the value a (where of course this again could be g itself). Then the semantic parts of NER-6 and NER-7 could be rewritten as follows:

NER-6′.   …for all g, $[[\beta]](g) = 1$ iff there is some individual a such that $[[\alpha]](g^{x\text{-}i \rightarrow a}) = 1$.
NER-7′.   …for all g, $[[\beta]](g) = 1$ iff for every individual a, $[[\alpha]](g^{x\text{-}i \rightarrow a}) = 1$.

These amount to the same thing as given above. If there are n individuals, then there are n assignments just like g except possibly for the value assigned to x_i. Take the set of all assignments which differ from g only on (possibly) the value assigned to x_i and call that set g/x_i. (A caution on the notation: $g^{x\text{-}i \rightarrow a}$ is a single assignment; g/x_i is a set of assignments.) There is a one-to-one correspondence between the set of individuals and the set g/x_i. NER-6′ ensures that $[[\beta]]$ will be true on an assignment g if we can find an individual a such that $[[\alpha]]$ is true on $g^{x\text{-}i \rightarrow a}$. But if that is the case, then it of course follows that there is a g′ in g/x_i such that $[[\alpha]]$ is true on g′, and this is what NER-6 asks for. Conversely, if there is such a g′, then it follows that there is some individual a such that $[[\alpha]]$ is true on $g^{x\text{-}i \rightarrow a}$. Similar reasoning holds for NER-7 and NER-7′. The key is in noticing that there is a one-to-one correspondence between the set of individuals and the set g/x_i. Some terminology will be useful below. Consider a set A, and imagine "slicing it up" into a set of subsets such that each member of A occurs in one and only one of these subsets. This is called a *partition* of A, and each subset is called a *cell* in the partition (see the Appendix to Chapter 1). We will use the term *cellmates* to refer to members of A which are in the same cell. The relevance of this here is that each variable x_i induces a partition on G (the set of all assignments); each cell in the partition is the set of assignments that differ only on the value assigned to x_i. As noted above by one example, the number of members in each cell will be exactly the number of individuals (and each cell has the same number of assignments in it). Thus g/x_i defined above is a cell in the partition induced by x_i. We will see this played out by example below, but we can note here that the semantics of NER-6 and NER-7 are such that all members of the cell of a partition defined by the variable introduced by the relevant rule will receive the same value.

By way of concrete illustration, consider the composition of the two sentences in (7), given the world set out earlier (two individuals: {p,f} and [[feed']] as shown in (2) and repeated here):

(7)   a. $\exists x_1[\forall x_2 [\text{feed}'(x_1)(x_2)]]$
      b. $\forall x_1[\forall x_2 [\text{feed}'(x_1)(x_2)]]$

(2) $p \rightarrow \begin{Bmatrix} p \rightarrow 1 \\ f \rightarrow 1 \end{Bmatrix}$ $f \rightarrow \begin{Bmatrix} p \rightarrow 0 \\ f \rightarrow 1 \end{Bmatrix}$

We—the all-seeing human beings—know that (7a) should come out true regardless of the assignments (there is indeed someone that everyone fed, namely p) while (7b) should come out false (it is not the case that everyone was fed by everyone; p was fed only by p). But recall again that the compositional computation is not smart and has no access to the meanings of deeply embedded expressions (such as *feed'*). In each step, this computation has access only to the semantics of the input expressions, and—having added in NER-6 and NER-7—it also has access to the structure of the assignments. We will take the assignments as given in (1) (using again only two variables):

(1) g_1: $x_1 \rightarrow p$ g_2: $x_1 \rightarrow p$ g_3: $x_1 \rightarrow f$ g_4: $x_1 \rightarrow f$
              $x_2 \rightarrow p$ $x_2 \rightarrow f$ $x_2 \rightarrow p$ $x_2 \rightarrow f$

We already showed the compositional computation of $feed'(x_1)(x_2)$, the final step in that was (6), repeated here:

(6) $[[\text{feed}'(x_1)(x_2)]] =$ $g_1 \rightarrow 1$, $g_2 \rightarrow 1$, $g_3 \rightarrow 0$, $g_4 \rightarrow 1$

Looking at (7a), the next step is to compute $[[\forall x_2 [\text{feed}'(x_1)(x_2)]]]$ on each g. Here we need access to the structure of the assignments. Computing this for g_1, we look to at its value on all g' just like g_1 except for the value assigned to x_2. In other words, we look to see if it is true for all members of g/x_2. That set is g_1 and g_2. (The partition on G induced by x_2 is { {g_1, g_2}, {g_3, g_4}}.) Looking only at (6), we see that the value of $[[[\text{feed}'(x_1)(x_2)]]]$ is 1 on both g_1

and g_2. Hence, the value of the larger sentence $\forall x_2\ [feed'(x_1)(x_2)]$ maps both g_1 and g_2, to 1. Turning now to the value of the larger sentence on g_3 and g_4, they too form a single cell, and each will receive 1 if and only if the expression in (6) assigns 1 to both assignments. It does not; it assigns 0 to g_3. From this we derive the following:

(8) $[[\ \forall x_2\ [feed'(x_1)(x_2)]\ ]]$ $= g_1 \rightarrow 1,\quad g_2 \rightarrow 1,\quad g_3 \rightarrow 0,\quad g_4 \rightarrow 0$

The next step is to compute $[[\ \exists x_1[\forall x_2\ [feed'(x_1)(x_2)]]\ ]]$ on each g. Consider g_1. Here the relevant set of assignments g/x_1 is the set $\{g_1, g_3\}$ so those two assignments are guaranteed to have the same value. g_1 will of course get the value 1. But so will g_3 even though the line just above assigned 0 to g_3. At this step, however, g_3 no longer cares only about itself—it merely needs to find some cellmate in the partition induced by x_1 that is assigned 1, and g_1 fits the bill. The same will apply to the computation on g_2 and g_4. They are cellmates and hence look to each other; g_2 is assigned 1 by the value of the inner S shown in (8), and so both g_2 and g_4 will be assigned 1. The sentence thus comes out true on all assignments: it is technically a function from assignments to truth values but is a constant function (and so we tend not to detect the assignments, and don't think of it as assignment-dependent).

9.2.   Show the last line of the computation of (7b).

   Notice that at each step shrinks the space of possible ways the assignments can diverge in their value. At the step of interpreting $\forall x_2\ [feed'(x_1)(x_2)]$, we have an equivalence class that partitions the assignments into $\{\{g_1, g_2\}, \{g_3, g_4\}\}$. At the next stage we have the partition $\{\{g_1, g_2\}, \{g_3, g_4\}\}$. By the end we are guaranteed a constant function: g_1 will have to have the same value as g_2 by the first step, but will have to have the same value as g_3 by the second step. And g_3 and g_4 must have the same value by the first step. So at the end, all four have the same value. Incidentally, we can now give a (rough) semantic definition of what it means for a variable to be "bound": x_i is bound within an expression if all members of g/x_i receive the same value. Put differently, it doesn't matter what value one chooses for x_i—the set of assignments in g/x_i in fact differ on just that—but because they are all in the same cell and look to each other, the fact that they disagree on the value of x_i is irrelevant.

Otherwise x_i is free (and so the value of the expression containing it still depends on what value is assigned to x_i). We say "rough" here simply because there are cases that correspond to the intuitive notion of a variable being free but where all assignments are nonetheless assigned the same value (even if we were to fold in worlds) as, for example, the case of a tautology. Thus a statement like *x_3 is x_3* (given a suitable definition for *be* here) is assigned the same value (1) on all assignments and in all worlds, but—should we really care about a precise definition of a "bound variable"—we would probably want to take x_3 to be "free" here. But this is a problem only if we really ever need a precise definition.[2] As we will see later, this is a notion for convenience only. If the grammar never needs to refer to a "bound variable" (or, in the case of English, a "bound pronoun") then our loose definition is perfectly adequate since it is intended just for convenience in discussion. Indeed, the fragment to be developed for the rest of this book has no need for the grammar to refer to a notion of "binding."[3] And this is equally true for the version that makes use of assignment functions to model pronoun meanings as for the variable-free version.

[2] Heim and Kratzer (1998) develop a very interesting system using partial functions. Their system is meant to model English (rather than the artificial toy language here) but the same points would hold. Thus each expression has a value relative to some assignment, but the assignments themselves can be partial functions from the set of variable names to individuals. Moreover, the value of some sentence S is defined only for a subset of assignments (only for those whose domain is the set of variables which occur in what we intuitively think of as "unbound" within S). Space precludes discussion of this here, but it does allow for a definition of "bound" vs "free" variables (or pronouns) that avoids the problem noted above. However, as mentioned above, there will turn out to be no need for a formal semantic definition of "bound" vs "unbound" pronouns (or variables).

[3] There is much work within the linguistics literature that uses the term "binding" to state various constraints relevant to the distribution and readings of pronouns and reflexives. The goal here under Direct Compositionality is to have the empirical generalizations that are packed into constraints on "binding" follow from the way the system is set up without the grammar needing any such definition. This book will not have space to discuss so-called binding constraints, but see Chapter 15 for a discussion of what is known as Weak Crossover effects.

9.3. Take a universe with three individuals {p,f,k}. Take the language given above but with just the two variables x_1 and x_2. We are concerned here with just one world, which is such that on any assignment g, [[kiss]] (g) is:

$$p \to \begin{Bmatrix} p \to 1 \\ f \to 0 \\ k \to 1 \end{Bmatrix} \qquad f \to \begin{Bmatrix} p \to 1 \\ f \to 1 \\ k \to 0 \end{Bmatrix} \qquad k \to \begin{Bmatrix} p \to 0 \\ f \to 1 \\ k \to 0 \end{Bmatrix}$$

(a) First, show the nine assignments.
(b) Then show the compositional computation for each of the following, showing each step as a function from the domain of assignments to some other value:
   (i) $\forall x_1[\exists x_2[\ kiss'(x_2)(x_1)]]$
   (ii) $\exists x_2[\forall x_1[\ kiss'(x_2)(x_1)]]$
   (iii) $\forall x_2[kiss'(x_2)(x_2)]]$

Note that once you have shown the computation of *kiss'(x_2)(x_1)* for (i) there is no reason to repeat this for (ii); just recycle what you have done.

(c) Consider (iv):
   (iv) $\forall x_1[kiss'(x_1)(x_1)]$

The part within the brackets will not be the same as the corresponding part for (iii). But (iv) (regardless of the structure of the world in question) is guaranteed to have the same value as (iii). State why this is so.

9.2. The lambda calculus

9.2.1. Lambda abstraction

Continuing with the digression into languages which are not English, we now take the language above as the point of departure and enrich it, developing what is known as the lambda calculus. As noted earlier, this gives us a precise way to name complex model-theoretic objects. Note, though that developing this language has no theoretical status in that regard—one could continue to use prose to name the object. However, our prose has been getting rather clumsy—and would get even more so more complex objects are developed.

   The first addition to the language is an infinite set of variables over any kind of object (and with every syntactic category). There are variables whose category is S/NP and semantic type <e,t>; we will name these P_1, P_2, etc. There are variables over propositions (category S) which we will label p_1, p_2, etc., and variables of type $<e,<e,t>>$ (category (S/NP)/NP) which we will label R_1, R_2, etc. Recall that, for convenience, we took the domain of the assignments to be the variable names themselves, giving variable names a kind of double status (syntactic objects, and objects in the domain of assignments) and we continue with this convention here. We add the rule in NER-8; X and Y are variables over any category, and y semantic type of expressions of category Y (for any g and any expression β of category Y, $[[\beta]](g)$ is a member of y).

NER-8.   If α is an expression of the form $<[\alpha]$, X, $[[\alpha]]>$ and v is a variable of the form $<[v]$, Y, $[[v]]>$ then there is an expression β of the form $<[\lambda v\,[\alpha]\,]$, X/Y, for any g, $[[\beta]](g)$ is a function from the set of objects of type y, such that for each a in y, $[[\beta]](g)(a) = [[\alpha]](g^{v \to a})>$.

As was the case with NER-6 and NER-7, we are using square brackets in two ways in the "phonology" part of NER-8. The outer brackets indicate "the phonology of" the new expression; the inner brackets around α are actually introduced by the rule (to keep the strings from being ambiguous).

Let us walk through the semantics part in prose. First, let x be the semantic type of expressions of category X and y the type of expressions of category Y. Then our new expression has some meaning which is a function from assignments to something in $<y,x>$. On any assignment g, this new expression takes every member a of the y set, and assigns to it the value that the inner formula (α) assigned to the assignment just like g except where a is the value of the variable v. Prefixing a λ and a variable v to some formula is called *lambda-abstracting* over that variable, but the important point is to see its semantic effects. One effect is it takes a formula which is non-constant on g/v and turns it to a formula whose value is the same for all members of g/v. The other effect is that it takes an expression which, on any assignment, has as its value something in set a, and returns an expression which (on any assignment) is a function from some set b to a. Hence the expression α to which is being prefixed λv has as its value a function in $<G,a>$. Let the variable v be of type b, then the full expression $\lambda v\,[\alpha]$ has as its value a function in $<G,<b,a>>$.

By way of example, take a universe with two individuals {p,f} and put just two individual variables x_1 and x_2 in our language. The four assignments are as given earlier in (1):

(1) g_1: $x_1 \to p$ g_2: $x_1 \to p$ g_3: $x_1 \to f$ g_4: $x_1 \to f$
           $x_2 \to p$ $x_2 \to f$ $x_2 \to p$ $x_2 \to f$

Suppose that we are considering a world in which [[squeaks']] for all assignments is p → 1 and f → 0. Let us compute the value of $\lambda x_1[squeaks'(x_1)]$. First, we compute $[[squeaks'(x_1)]]$ on each g and this gives:

(9) $g_1 \rightarrow 1$, $g_2 \rightarrow 1$, $g_3 \rightarrow 0$, $g_4 \rightarrow 0$

The next step is to compute the value of the whole formula. Once again, the compositional procedure does not need to consult anything about the inner formula; the computation computes the value of $\lambda x_1[squeaks'(x_1)]$ on each assignment purely by looking at (9) and at the structure of the assignments. In particular, the variable that is "bound" here by the λ is x_1; the relevant partition is thus $\{\{g_1, g_3\}, \{g_2, g_4\}\}$. It is guaranteed that for any given cell, each member in that cell will receive the same value; this is because they "look to each other." For example, consider the computation of the value of $\lambda x_1[squeaks'(x_1)]$ on g_1. First, note that the value of this on g_1 is going to be a function of type <e,t>, assigning 1 or 0 to p and 1 or 0 to f. The determination of what value is assigned to p is made by looking at the value of the inner formula on the assignment just like g_1 except that x_1 is mapped to p. This is g_1, so (8) tells us that p will map to 1. For f, the relevant assignment is g_3 so (9) tells us that f maps to 0. Exactly the same remarks hold when we want to find the value of $\lambda x_1[squeaks'(x_1)]$ for g_3. Since g_1 and g_3 are in the same cell, they are guaranteed to be assigned the same value by the full formula. The same holds for g_2 and g_4. But since there is no x_2 at issue, these will come out the same as g_1 and g_3, and in the end we have the constant function from assignments: on any g the value of $\lambda x_1[squeaks'(x_1)]$ is p → 1 and f → 0.

The reader might have noticed that the value of $\lambda x_1[squeaks'(x_1)]$ is exactly the same as the value of *squeaks'*, and was destined to be so. By rethinking the lambda expressions as ways to name functions (which is ultimately the way we will be using them), this is not surprising: the full formula is (on any assignment) a function which asks for an individual, and gives the value of *squeaks'* applied to that individual. So of course this is just a fancy way to write (semantically) exactly the same object as *squeaks'*. Note that of course $\lambda x_2[squeaks'(x_2)]$ is also the same object. As a second example, consider the formula in (10):

(10) $\lambda x_1[\lambda x_2[feed'(x_1)(x_2)]]$

The semantics of this is exactly the same as the semantics of *feed'*. Again, thinking of these as ways to name functions, one can convince oneself of this by noting that for any assignment g, this is a function that takes one individual and then another and returns the value that *feed'* returns when applied to the first individual and then the second. And that, of course, is exactly the *feed'* function (a function of type <e,<e,t>>).

9.4. Given [[*feed'*]] as shown in (2) (and continuing with a language with only two variables and a universe with only the two individuals {p,f}, demonstrate the truth of the remarks above by showing the full compositional computation of (10). Remember that the end product should be a function from assignments to functions of type <e,<e,t>>.

9.5. Like the quantification rules, NER-8 does not require there to be an instance of the variable introduced by this rule within α. If there is none, the rule is not vacuous as in the case of the quantification rule, as the meaning of β is not even the same type as the meaning of α. State what the meaning of β is in general if there is no occurrence of the relevant variable within α.

In view of these equivalences one might wonder what the point is of this notation. It is because other kinds of values can be written in this notation. Take for example (11):

(11) $\lambda x_1[\lambda x_2[kiss'(x_2)(x_1)]]$

This does not have the same meaning as any other lexical item in the language (keeping our lexicon to be just a subset of English), but corresponds to something that we can roughly paraphrase as *was-kissed-by'*. We return to this below.

9.2.2. Lambda conversion

Since the ultimate interest is in the lambda calculus is as a way to name various functions, it is also useful to understand ways in which one can simplify various formulas in the lambda calculus. By "simplify" we mean naming the same object in a shorter way. We can actually give proofs of the equivalences that we show here, but to save space and possible tedium, we will try only to give the intuition behind why the equivalences hold.

Take any formula of the form $\lambda u[\alpha](c)$. Call $\alpha/u \rightarrow c$ the formula derived from $\lambda u[\alpha](c)$ except where all occurrences of u in α are replaced by c. In general (but not always—the exception to be discussed directly) these two formulas will always have the same value. This is called *lambda conversion*. We have already seen a few instances of this. Thus (12a) and (12b) are guaranteed to have the same value; note that (12b) is the result of applying lambda conversion to (12a):

(12)   a. $\lambda x_1[squeak'(x_1)](Porky')$ =   b. squeak'(Porky')

The sign "=" here means *has the same value* (on, of course, all assignments). Another example is (13):

(13)   a. $\lambda x_1[\lambda x_2[feed'(x_1)(x_2)]](Porky')$ =   b. $\lambda x_2[feed'(Porky')(x_2)]$

We also know from the sort of equivalences discussed in 9.2.1 that (b) is equivalent to feed'(Porky'). Similarly, the pair in (14) are equivalent:

(14)   a. $\lambda x_1[\lambda x_2[feed'(x_2)(x_1)]](Porky')$ =   b. $\lambda x_2[feed'(x_2)(Porky')]$

Informally, both of these (on all assignments) denote the set of individuals fed by Porky. We can show cases of two lambda conversions, as in (15):

(15)   a. $\lambda x_1[\lambda x_2[feed'(x_2)(x_1)]](Porky')(Dumbo') =$
       b. $\lambda x_2[feed'(x_2)(Porky')](Dumbo') =$
       c. feed'(Dumbo')(Porky')

(In doing lambda conversions, one needs to make sure to pay attention to the brackets. In (15a) *Porky'* must convert in for x_1 because it is the argument of the function shown in (11).)

9.6. Simplify the following by lambda conversion:

(i) $\lambda x_1[\lambda x_2[feed'(x_2)(x_1)](Porky')](Dumbo')$

However, it is not always the case that $\lambda u[\alpha](c)$ is equivalent to $\alpha/u \rightarrow c$. Rather than giving a full explanation of when and why the equivalence does not hold, we will simply give a recipe for determining when lambda conversion is not valid (i.e., when it is not guaranteed to result in an equivalent formula) along with an example to help elucidate why. This will be followed by a brute-force recipe for allowing conversion on a slightly different formula.

Hence we first give a purely syntactic definition of the notion of a
"bound" variable. (Recall that earlier we gave a rough semantic definition;
a variable x_i is bound in a formula if the value of that formula is the same on
all g/x_i. But for the purposes of the recipe, it easiest and most practical to see
the point with a syntactic definition of the notion bound. Leaving aside
contradictions and tautologies, the two definitions converge on the same
result.) Hence we will define *bound* as follows:

(16)   Let O (for *operator*) stand for any of λ, $\exists$, and $\forall$.
Given any formula of the form $Ox[\dots]$, anything within the brackets is *within
the scope of* O (for x a variable).
A variable x with the name v_i is *bound* by an operator O iff:
  (i) the variable next to O in the formula is v_i;
  (ii) x is in the scope of O; and
  (iii) there is no other O' whose adjacent variable is v_i such that x is in the
     scope of O' and O' is in the scope of O.

Notice that this definition allows for variables which are free within some
subformula even though they may be bound within the main formula. For
example, x_1 is bound within the formula $\lambda x_1[squeaks'(x_1)]$ but is free
within the subformula $squeaks'(x_1)$. Then whenever there is a formula of
the form $\lambda u[a](c)$ one cannot perform lambda conversion (and be guaranteed to preserve equivalence) just in case c is or contains a variable which has
the same name as one which is bound within a. Intuitively, this is because
the variable c or the variable within c will be accidentally "caught" by the
operator inside a.

As an example, take the pair in (17), where (17b) is the result of the
illegitimate lambda conversion:

(17)   a. $\lambda x_i[\exists x_2[feeds'(x_1)(x_2)]](x_2)$ b. $\exists x_2[feeds'(x_2)(x_2)]$

The truth of (17a) is assignment-dependent—it depends on the value
assigned to x_2. Paraphrasing it in prose, it says that x_2 is such that there is
someone who feeds it. This is because the lambda expression within (17a) is
the (assignment-dependent) function that maps an individual to true just in
case there is someone who feeds it. The whole formula then says that this
function truly applies to x_2, but whether or not that is true depends on the
value we assign to x_2. (17b), on the other hand, is constant on all
assignments—on any g, it simply asserts that there is someone who feeds
themselves. What has gone wrong is that the x_2 bound by the existential
quantifier in (17a) and the x_2 outside the lambda expression are not really

the same. The bound one inside the lambda expression could as well have been x_1, x_3, or anything else: it is bound so its name no longer matters. The one outside the expression is not bound, so its name does matter. Put differently, $\lambda x_i[\exists x_2[feeds'(x_1)(x_2)]]$ has the same value on all g/x_2. But the outermost x_2 does not have the same value on all g/x_2, and so neither does the full formula in (17a).

There is also a simple way to avoid mistaken lambda conversions such as those shown in (17). Simply find some new variable that appears nowhere else, take all of the *bound* occurrences of the colliding variable inside a (including the occurrence that sits next to the operator that binds it), and rename it with the new variable. One should be able to convince oneself that once a variable is bound its name no longer matters, so renaming it in this way will have no effect on the meaning of a. Then the lambda conversion can proceed. Given any expression a with a variable a bound within it, call a' the new expression in which every occurrence of a is replaced by another variable b. a and a' are said to be *alphabetic variants*, which means that they are guaranteed to have the same value on all assignments.

---

*9.7. Show that one cannot instead rename the free variable within the expression (or which is the expression) which is being converted in. You can show this by example and/or discuss more generally why the equivalence is not guaranteed to hold in if one renames the free variable.

9.8. Take each of the following formulas, and simplify them as much as possible (i.e., write them in a shorter form that preserves their meaning). Recall that P_1 is a variable of type <e,t> and R_1 is a variable of type <e,<e,t>>.

(i) $\lambda x_1[kiss'\,(x_1)(x_2)](x_2)$
(ii) $\lambda x_1[kiss'\,(x_1)(x_2)](x_1)$
(iii) $\lambda P_1[\forall x_1[P_1(x_1)]](feeds'(x_1))$
(iv) $\exists x_2[\lambda R_1[R_1(x_2)(x_2)](\lambda x_3[\lambda x_1[grooms'(x_3)(x_1)]])]$
(v) $\lambda P_1[\lambda x_1[P_1(x_1)]](chews\text{-}gum')$

9.3. Naming model-theoretic objects

The advantage of having the explicit notation above—along with the principles for rewriting lambda expressions as simpler (syntactically) but equivalent (semantically) expressions—is that it provides a tool to write out complex functions which are difficult to state in prose. It also allows a much less clumsy semantics for some of the earlier rules. Notice that although the meanings of lambda formulas are stated with reference to assignments and variables, we can remain for the moment noncommittal as to the status of these for natural language semantics and still use the relevant formulas. The reason is simple but quite important: for now, at least, *all of the model-theoretic objects that we will name using the lambda notation contain no unbound variables within the formulas.* Thus if assignments were an actual part of the machinery, all of the objects of concern at this point are *constant* functions from the set of assignments. But if everything is a constant function from the set of assignments, we can just as well do without the assignments. Thus the use of assignments, variables, lambda conversion, and so forth is important to understand to make sure that we do correctly represent the meanings of the natural language expressions. But these tools are (so far) not part of the linguistic semantic system. Whether or not something like variables and lambda abstraction do play a role in the semantic theory is addressed in Part III.

To give a few examples of the usefulness of this notation for writing meanings, we will slightly modify the conventions above. First, let us use *feed'* not just as a word in the non-English language, but let us also use it to represent the meaning of English *feed*. In other words, it is the same as [[feed]]. The reason for having both ways to represent the meaning of *feed* has to do with the fact that each notation has certain advantages in terms of readability, and so we will alternate back and forth between the two notations as convenient. Second, the convention of numbered variables is sometimes difficult to read. We will thus use x, y, z, etc. for variables of type e; P and Q for variables of type $<e,t>$; p and q to be variables of type t, and others as needed. When introducing variables whose type is not clear we will subscript them, as for example in the following:

(18) $\lambda R_{<e,<e,t>>}[R(Fido')(Dumbo')]$

This expression names a function in $<<e,<e,t>>,t>$: it characterizes a set of two-place relations. In particular, it maps a relation R to true just in case

R(Fido')(Dumbo') is true or, informally, just in case "Dumbo Rs Fido." Or, take the following (here we omit the subscript, keeping R to be of the same type as in (19)):

(19) $\lambda R[R(Porky')]$

This is a function of type $<<e,<e,t>>,<e,t>>$: it maps any two-place relation R to a function that characterizes the set of individuals who "R Porky." If this function were applied feed' (or, [[feed]]) it would yield the set of Porky-feeders.

We can write out the meanings that we gave above for *to* and for *be*. The former, being the identity function on individuals, is (20a) and the latter is (20b):

(20) a. $\lambda x[x]$ b. $\lambda P[P]$

Or, consider the account of passive in English according to which (21) is not derived by any kind of movement rule, but where there is a productive (morphological) rule mapping an active verb into a passive verb, changing its syntax (and phonology) and its meaning:

(21) The squirrel was chased by Mitka.

We will not formalize the rule here (the reader can easily do so), but we can note that its output would be the verb *killed* with a category roughly (S[Part]/NP)/PP[BY] (we leave it open as to the best feature specification here on the result) and with the meaning shown in (22a) or—just using a slightly different notation—(22b) (whose visual awkwardness reveals the rationale for the prime notation):

(22) a. $\lambda x[\lambda y[$ chase' $(y)(x)]]$ b. $\lambda x[\lambda y[$ [[chase]] $(y)(x)]]$

Note that the rules for λ-conversion are now quite useful as we build up the compositional computation for (21).

> **9.9.** To show the full computation of (21) requires a treatment of the auxiliary. Pretend, then, that the passive verb is actually the single verb *was-chased* with category (S/NP)/PP[BY] and meaning as given above. With that, show the full syntactic and semantic computation of (21), doing λ-conversions wherever (and as soon as) you can to simplify the way in which the semantics is stated. (Note: It is always helpful in terms of the exposition to do the λ-conversions as soon as possible.)
>
> ***9.10.** Assume the Wrap analysis of three-place verbs discussed in Chapter 5 and explicitly folded into the fragment in Chapter 6. That is, assume that all verbs of the form ((S/NP)/NP)/X (for X any category) are

marked as $((S/NP)/_wNP)/X$. (This is actually not crucial for the main point of this question, but since the implementation of the question requires some decision about the structure of three-place verbs, we will make that assumption.)

Since earliest Transformational Grammar, it has been noted that there are a large number of verbs that occur both in the V-NP-PP[TO] configuration and in the V-NP-NP configuration, and where sentences of the form in (ia) have the same truth conditions as those of the form (ib):

(i)   a. NP_1 V NP_2 to NP_3 b. NP_1 V NP_3 NP_2

Examples of this are shown in (ii)–(iii) and this is generally referred to as the *dative alternation*:

(ii)   a. Sabrina gave the toy to Fido.
       b. Sabrina gave Fido the toy.

(iii) a. George told the Cinderella story to the children.
       b. George told the children the Cinderella story.

Many studies of this (beginning with Oehrle 1976) treat these alternations as a unary rule mapping words to others. Take the verbs in the (a) form to be basic. Formulate the rule in question, showing how the output expression differs from the input in syntactic category and in meaning. (The point, of course, is that the use of λs makes it easier to state the meaning of the output verb in terms of the meaning of the input verb. You do not need to use any λs to state the meaning of the input verb; the meaning of the lexical item *give* in (iia), for example, is simply [[give]].)

An interesting sidelight: It is often claimed that the rule is not really productive and regular, for there are many verbs that do occur in the (a) configuration but not in the (b) configuration; examples include *contribute*, *recount*, *donate*, etc. These contrast with *hand*, *toss*, *tell*, *give*, and many others which do occur in both configurations. Leaving aside the verb *promise*, state the generalization of the verbs that do undergo the rule in phonological terms, and think about how one can state the rule so that it is indeed a productive unary rule.

One final example is the Curry'ed meaning for *and* (when it combines two expressions whose meanings characterize sets), which was given earlier in terms of set intersection. We can equivalently give its meaning as follows, where a is meant to be any type:

(23) $\lambda A_{<a,t>}[\lambda B_{<a,g>}[\lambda z_a[A(z) \, \& \, B(z)]]]$

Finally, this notation also allows us to state the semantics of many of the earlier rules in a much more elegant fashion. R-3 (from Chapter 8) serves to illustrate this, but first one more piece of notation. Given an individual x and a function P of type <e,t>, we will use the notation $\iota x[P(x)]$ to mean the unique (or most) contextually salient individual such that P(x) is true. (Often the iota operator shown here is used to mean the unique such individual; here we use it in the same way that English *the* is used.) Note then that any expression of the form $\iota x[\alpha]$ denotes an individual. With this notation, we restate R-3:

R-3.   If α is an expression of the form <[α], N/PP[OF], [[α]]> then there is an expression β of the form <[β], NP/$_L$NP[GEN], $\lambda x \iota y[\, [[\alpha]](x)(y)]]$>.

9.11. Use the λ-notation to restate R-2 from Chapter 8.
9.12. Give the meaning of *didn't* in λ-notation.

PART II

Enriching the Domain

10

Returning to English: Generalized quantifiers

10.1. "NPs" with quantificational determiners

The fragment so far contains no NPs with quantificational determiners, such as the subjects in (1)–(4):

(1) Every husky howled.

(2) Some pig ate Old MacDonald's hay.

(3) No student passed the phonology exam.

(4) Few donkeys appreciate their owners.

Recall that ordinary NPs like *the disobedient husky*, *the ornery pig*, and *Porky* all have the same syntactic distribution and denote individuals. The types of expressions shown in (1)–(4) also all have the same distribution as ordinary NPs (they occur in subject position, they occur as objects of transitive verbs, etc.). But what about their meaning?

10.1.1. First pass: Individuals?

Since other expressions with this distribution denote individuals, the correspondence between syntactic categories and semantic types laid out in
Chapter 6 would lead to the conclusion that these do too. But this seems
to defy common sense: they surely are not individuals on any ordinary
understanding of that term. Of course, we have taken a fairly broad-minded
view of what it means to be an "individual," allowing for abstract individuals such as *modesty*, individuals that name kinds such as *donkeys*, and mass
individuals such as *water*. So perhaps these are just even fancier kinds of
individuals. In this case, though, common sense happens to be correct;
calling these "individuals" will wreak havoc with the semantics. Consider
the intersection semantics for VP conjunction in light of (5):

(5) No student passed the phonology exam and got an A on the semantics final.

If [[no student]] is a fancy individual and that individual is in the intersection
of [[pass the phonology exam]]$_S$ and [[got an A on the semantics final]], then
[[no student]] is in each of these sets. But then that predicts that (5) is
synonymous with (6):

(6) No student passed the phonology exam and no student got an A on the
     semantics final.

Clearly the (at least primary) meaning of (5) is not the reading in (6); it
merely says that there is no student who did both. Note that if we were to
replace *no student* in (5) and in (6) with an ordinary individual-denoting
subject NP such as *Sarah*, then synonymy between the case of VP conjunction and S conjunction does hold. This was discussed earlier, and is
the straightforward result of the fact that if x is in A ∩ B then x is in
A and x is in B.

10.1.   a. Construct an argument to show that [[every student]] also cannot be an
            individual.
         b. Do the same for [[some student]].

In both cases your arguments can be similar to the one above, but you
will need to do more than mechanically switch *no student* in the above
sentences to *every student* or *some student*.

Hence, our semantics for conjunction would be doomed if one tried to force these expressions to be individuals. We will thus for the moment leave aside the ultimate goal of giving these a type of meaning which they share with ordinary NPs like *Babar*, and will concentrate in this chapter on finding some meaning for these expressions which captures the appropriate truth conditions. Chapter 11 returns to the task of unifying these and ordinary NPs. In fact, for now we give quantified expressions a different syntactic category from ordinary NPs—call their category GQ (this stands for *generalized quantifier*, which concept is explained in 10.2).

10.1.2. Second pass: Sets of individuals?

Could the relevant expressions denote sets of individuals (or, equivalently, functions of type <e,t>)? This is tempting at first glance. Let [[every husky]] be the characteristic function of the set of all huskies. An immediate drawback with this hypothesis is that it necessitates a new semantic combinatory rule. Consider (1). Since [[howled]] is a function of type <e,t> a new rule would be needed to combine the two functions to give a result of type t. For the particular case at hand, the semantics here could be as given in (5) (we use the phrase structure rule/semantic rule format for this, and it will go in the category of a fictional rule):

FR-4.   S → GQ   VP $[[S]] = 1$ iff $[[GQ]]_S \subseteq [[VP]]_S$

This gives the right truth conditions when the GQ has *every* as its determiner. But the attempt to treat GQs as denoting sets of individuals along with a rule like FR-4 breaks down in other cases. Take [[no husky]]. What sort of set could this possibly be? The first temptation that springs to mind is that [[no husky]] is the empty set. But then what is the meaning of *no Siamese cat?* It too must be the empty set. Yet this makes the disastrous prediction that the two sentences in (7) are synonymous:

(7)   a. No husky used the litter box.
       b. No Siamese cat used the litter box.

Alternatively, one might try allowing [[no husky]] to be the set of all non-huskies. But then FR-4 gives the wrong meaning: *no husky is howling* would be true if all the non-huskies are howling—obviously an incorrect result. Of course, one could posit a different rule for this case (here, let the VP set be a subset of the GQ set). But now there is no uniform treatment for how VPs combine with GQs, and the rules would need to refer to the internal structure of the GQ (as each determiner would have a separate rule). This is surely not a desirable state of affairs. Moreover, it is not clear at all how to extend the set idea to GQs like *few huskies* (what set of individuals would that be?), *most huskies*, etc.

10.1.3. Third pass: English as first-order logic? Straw Man makes a cameo reappearance

At this point, Straw Man reappears. Straight from his logic class where he has learned all about quantifiers, variables, and assignment functions, he is eager to apply his new-found knowledge to the semantics of English. Why not, he says, assume that the grammar maps the sentences in (1) to representations like the language developed in section 9.1? *Every husky is howling* is mapped to (8a), *Some husky is howling* is mapped to (8b), and *No husky is howling* to either (8c) or (8c') (these are equivalent):

(8)   a. $\forall x_1[\text{husky'}(x_1) \rightarrow \text{howl'}(x_1)]$
       b. $\exists x_1[\text{husky'}(x_1)\ \&\ \text{howl'}(x_1)]$
       c. $\sim\exists x_1[\text{husky'}(x_1)\ \&\ \text{howl'}(x_1)]$ c'. $\forall x_1[\text{husky'}(x_1) \rightarrow\ \sim \text{howl'}(x_1)]$

The idea, then, is that the grammar assigns meanings by the two-step process of mapping English sentences into LFs like those in (8), and these in turn are compositionally interpreted by the procedure given in Chapter 9.

What is the price? First of course, by abandoning Direct Compositionality, Straw Man is advocating a more complex model of grammar. The syntax computes representations and there is an additional series of rules mapping those into representations of the sort in (8). Moreover, the consequence is that although *every husky*, *some husky*, etc. behave syntactically like constituents, they have no meaning. Notice that in (8a), for example, there is no subformula which corresponds to *every husky*. The "meaning" of *every husky* is simply the contribution that it makes in terms of a direction for how to build the relevant LF.

Of course, Straw Man is not committed to Direct Compositionality, and so is not particularly moved by these arguments. But there are other reasons to question this solution. First the rules *are* complex: the rules mapping the English sentences to the requisite LFs need to be formulated, and this is not that simple (we leave it to the reader to see how to state these). Note too that the relevant rule cannot be stated completely generally; the rule mapping (2) its LF (8b) introduces "&," whereas the rule mapping 1 to (8a) introduces "→." So there is no single rule mapping sentences with expressions of the form [Quantifier N] into the relevant LF.

And it gets worse. Consider (9):

(9)   Most Siamese cats have lovely voices.

Can we map this to some formula of first-order logic to give the right truth conditions? First, we note a tangential problem: *most* is arguably vague— one might be unsure as to whether (9) requires 51% of the Siamese cats to have lovely voices, or perhaps more (and if so, how much more). Fortunately, this question is not central to the point below, so simply assume that a sentence like (9) is true provided that more than 50% of the Siamese cats have lovely tails. We will introduce a new quantifier M that we can read informally as *for most*. Following the strategy for *all* and *some*, we might try to assign to (9) either the representation in (10a) or in (10b). The semantics of these will be analogous to the semantics for quantifiers given in Chapter 9, except that the full formula is true on an assignment g just in case the inner formula is true for more than 50% of the assignments in g/x:

(10)   a. Mx[Siamese-cat'(x) & have-lovely-voices(x)]
       b. Mx[Siamese-cat'(x) → have-lovely-voices(x)]

It is immediately obvious that (10a) is incorrect; this is true if more than 50% of the individuals are Siamese cats and have lovely voices. The problem with (10b) is more subtle, but it too is incorrect. (9) is true if it's the case that for most things, if they are Siamese cats then they have lovely voices. But for (10b) the inner formula is true on any assignment g for which g(x) is not a Siamese cat. Thus consider a universe with 100 individuals, 90 of which are not Siamese cats, and where only three of the actual Siamese cats have lovely voices. Then (9) is false, but our semantics assigns true to (10b). Of course we have only tried formulas with the two connectives "&" and "→"—perhaps we just need to be clever and try a different one. It need not even correspond to any of the standard ones for which we have names (i.e., &, v, and →) as long as it can be defined. But it is quite easy to show that no possible connective will do. There are only sixteen logically possible ones and none gives the right result.

10.2. Show the sixteen logically possible connectives (remember, these all take as input two values in {1,0} and return one value in {1,0}, and show that none of them gives the right truth conditions.

*10.3. Although somewhat off the main topic, once you have constructed the logically possible connectives asked for in Exercise 10.2, it becomes obvious that many of these are "stupid"—i.e., it is not surprising that only a few of these remotely correspond to any actual natural language words. Discuss which ones would be rather "stupid" for a natural language to encode as a lexical item.

Finally, once again facts centering on conjunction challenge this solution. For quantified expressions happily conjoin with each other (the facts are similar for *or*):

(11)　a. Every coyote and most wolves howl at the moon.
　　　　b. No pig and no turkey remained on the farm when the gates were left open.

One would hope to subsume these under the cross-categorial definition (syntactically and semantically) for *and* (and *or*). But under Straw Man's view, *every coyote* is not a meaningful expression and so there is no way to directly give a semantics for expressions like *every coyote and most wolves*. Once again, then, he would be reduced to positing the hidden S conjunction analysis (see Chapter 5). Unlike the case of VP conjunction, the 2-S analysis here is not disastrous for the semantics: (11a) for example does happen to have the same meaning as (12):

(12)　Every coyote howls at the moon and most wolves howl at the moon.

Still, this requires the adoption of additional rules, and it obviously would be desirable to account for (11) with the more general treatment of conjunction. We thus part ways with Straw Man.

10.2. Generalized quantifiers

10.2.1. The semantics

The remarks much earlier in Chapter 5 concerning the Curry'ing of transitive verbs showed that it is not necessarily difficult to have the semantics truly respect the syntax. Sometimes the first way that springs to mind concerning the meaning of an expression won't work, but this might only mean that the semantics has actually packaged the meaning in slightly more sophisticated ways. Unless these ways turn out to be torturously complex, a reasonable hypothesis is that this is indeed how the semantics works. Hence, let us return to taking seriously the notion that *every husky*, *most Siamese cats*, *no wolf*, etc. all have meanings. Consider where the discussion left off before Straw Man reappeared. We eliminated the possibility that these expressions denote individuals, and the possibility that they denote sets of individuals. What if we try just one level of complexity beyond sets of individuals, i.e., sets of sets of individuals? Happily, this turns out to be exactly what is needed and accounts for all of the facts considered so far. (Initially we will show the point in set terms; it will be easy enough to then convert this into function terms.) Indeed, this solution, proposed for English in Montague (1973), was highly influential, and has been accepted in most work in formal semantics ever since. Any set of sets of individuals (or, equivalently, a function of type $<<e,t>,t>$) is called a *generalized quantifier*.

Take *every pig*. In pure set terms, let the every-pig set (given a world and time) be the set of sets that have the [[pig]] set as a subset. Thus [[every pig]]$_S$ = $\{S| \,[[pig]]_S \subseteq S\}_F$. Returning to function terms, [[every-pig]] is of type $<<e,t>,t>$; here the domain of [[every pig]] is the set of functions of type $<e,t>$, the co-domain is just t. Thus it maps a function P (of type $<e,t>$) to true iff for all individuals x such that [[pig]](x) is true, P(x) is true. (Assume that it is false otherwise.) Using the notation developed in Chapter 9, we can write the meaning (extensionally) in any of the ways shown in (13)—they all say the same thing (we use the prime-notation rather than double brackets for readability):

(13)   a. [[every pig]] = $\lambda P_{<e,t>}[\text{ pig's} \subseteq P_S\,]$
       b. [[every pig]] = $\lambda P[\forall x\ [x \in \text{pig's} \rightarrow x \in P_S]]$
       c. [[every pig]] = $\lambda P[\forall x\ [\text{pig'}(x) \rightarrow P(x)]]$

Incidentally, (13c) contains within a first-order formula which might seem odd since the first-order rendering of the meaning is exactly what was argued against above. But in fact nothing here contradicts that discussion. (13c) is used only as a way to write the model-theoretic object. Any of the other notations shown above (or the prose description) will do just as well. And a sentence containing *every pig* is not mapped into an LF using this first-order quantifier; it is just part of the notational system for writing the meaning.

In order for this meaning to do any work, this needs to fold into the rest of the compositional semantics. Consider (14):

(14)   Every pig grunted.

Since *every pig* does not denote an individual, (14) cannot be put together in the way already seen for a sentence like *Porky grunted*. In fact, recall that we are temporarily ignoring the commonality of ordinary NPs and expressions like *every pig* (this is the subject of Chapter 11) and we are calling the category of *every pig* a GQ. We get exactly the right truth conditions if we reverse the function argument structure from what happens in the case of a VP combining with an ordinary NP. That is, since the subject in (14) is a function of type $<<e,t>,t>$ and the VP of type $<e,t>$, one would expect that [[every pig]] applies to [[grunted]]. Indeed, this gives exactly the right result.

It is easiest to see this at first in set terms. The sentence is true if the [[grunt]] set is a member of the set of sets denoted by *every pig*. What does it take to make that true? [[every pig]] is the set of all sets with [[pig]] set as subset; and so if the [[grunt]] set is in the [[every pig]] set, then the [[pig]] set is a subset of the [[grunt]] set. And indeed this is what it takes to make (14) true. (Of course the sentence need not be about every pig in the universe but only every pig within some contextually salient domain. But this is a separate issue, postponed until section 10.6.) One other issue that we will not deal with is whether or not (14) presupposes that there are pigs (this is reminiscent of the situation with *the*). The meaning written out above in (13) predicts not: if there are no pigs then [[every pig]] maps every VP meaning to true. Whether or not this is a good prediction is an open question. It might be that (14) should be undefined in a pigless world (or context), or it might be that conditions of language *use* (i.e., the pragmatics) make (14) deviant in such a world/context (and hence the existence requirement here is not a semantic matter). Nothing in the subsequent discussion crucially hinges on the outcome of this question (for the meaning above could easily be modified if pig existence were a presupposition), and so we leave the semantics as stated.

10.2.2. The syntax

What about the syntactic category of *every pig*? For convenience we have called this GQ. But given the Categorial Grammar syntax, one would hope that the fact that it can combine with a VP is subsumed under the general rule schemata given earlier rather than introduce a new rule combining GQ with S/NP. This is easily done: assume that the category of *every pig* is S/(S/NP) (the directional slashes will be discussed directly). This preserves the correspondence set up earlier between syntactic categories and semantic types, and with suitable directional slashes allows the combination of a VP with a subject like *every pig* to be subsumed under R-1.[1]

The astute reader might notice two obvious problems with this solution. Both of these problems will disappear in Chapter 11, but at least the first one needs to be given a temporary fix before proceeding. And this concerns the directional features on the slashes. Notice that the general word order rules spelled out in (3) in Chapter 6 predict that the more fine-grained category here should be $S/_L(S/_LNP)$. Obviously this gives the wrong word order (allowing for, e.g., *grunted every pig*). The desired category for *every pig* is $S/_R(S/_LN)$. So the word order rules must be overridden. For now we will help ourselves to the notion that the lexical specification overrides the default rules and just build the exceptionality into a lexical entry. Of course *every pig* is not listed in the lexicon, so the exceptional part comes from the lexical entry for *every* which we (temporarily) take to be $(S/_R(S/NP))/N$. (Although this works it is somewhat embarrassing: for this lexically specified R-slash just happens to give the same word order one would get if *every pig* were an ordinary NP. Again this embarrassment disappears later.) The rest of the slash-directional features will be correctly specified by the rules, ultimately giving *every* the ultimate category $(S/_R(S/_LNP))/_RN$, which means that *every pig* is $S/_R(S/_LNP)$. Second, we surely don't want to have *every pig* (or *every*) defined as a "verb." But if the result category is S, it is. A suitable use of features could circumvent this, but actually the discussion in Chapter 11 eliminates this worry as well. We will, incidentally, often continue to use the term GQ as a shorthand for $S/_R(S/_LNP)$.

---

[1] A different solution is taken in Partee and Rooth (1983) where they treat these as NPs, and allow a single syntactic category (here, NP) to correspond to more than one semantic type. However, their solution is not rooted within a Categorial Grammar.

10.4. Consider a universe with six individuals {a,b,c,d,e,f} and a world w_1 in which [[pig]]$_S$ = {a,b}, [[elephant]]$_S$ = {c,d,e}, and [[wolf]]$_S$ = {f}. Moreover, [grunt]]$_S$ = {a,b,e}. Take the following sentence:

(i) Every pig grunted.

First, show the extension of [[every pig]]$_S$ in w_1 in set terms. (That is, show the set of sets in [[every pig]]$_S$, keeping in mind that this is not just sets that we have names for (such as *grunt*) but all of the relevant sets. Show the syntactic computation of (i), and how the extensions are put together, although you need not show the extension of [[every]]; just begin with [[every pig]]

10.2.3. Extending to the other quantified cases

The beauty of this solution is that all of the GQs can be given meanings of the same type. Take *some pig*. The set version of this is the set of sets which have a non-empty intersection with the [[pig]] set. The function version can be notated in—among others—any of the following ways:

(15)   a. {S| pig's ∩ S ≠ ø }$_F$
       b. λP[pig's ∩ P$_S$ ≠ ø]
       c. λP[∃x[pig'(x) & P(x)]]

Take a sentence such as *Some pig ate.* In set terms, this is true if the [[eat]] set is in the above set of sets, and for that to be the case there must be some individual which is in both the [[pig]] set and the [[eat]] set. And that of course gives exactly the right truth conditions. [[no pig]] is similar; it is (in set terms) the set of sets with an empty intersection with the [[pig]] set. [[three pigs]] is the set of sets whose intersection with the [[pig]] set has a cardinality of at least 3; we will write this as shown in (16):

(16) λP[| pig's ∩ P$_S$ | ≥ 3]

(Note that we have used at least 3 rather than exactly 3; we return to this in 10.4. But nothing here hinges on that decision; should *Three pigs stayed home* mean that exactly three pigs stayed home, one can trivially revise (16).) Expressions with complex quantificational determiners like *at most three pigs* are also amenable to this treatment; [[at most three pigs]] is shown in (17):

(17) $\lambda P[\,|\,\text{pig's} \cap P_S\,| \leq 3\,]$

Expressions like *many pigs* and *few pigs* are also generalized quantifiers, but the details are postponed until section 16.3.2.

Recall that giving a semantics for sentences such as (9) *Most pigs have lovely voices* (we let the Siamese cats mutate into pigs here) was one of the problems for Straw Man. It is no problem here. The meaning for *most pigs* is shown in (18) (this of course is also the meaning for *at least half of the pigs*):

(18) $\lambda P \left[\, |\text{pig's} \cap P_s| > \dfrac{|\text{pig}|}{2} \,\right]$

Notice incidentally that all of the above generalized quantifiers have been defined in terms of intersection with the exception *every*. But this too could be defined this way, since for any two sets A and B, A is a subset of B if and only if the intersection of A and B is A.

10.5. Take the universe as given in Exercise 10.4, and w_1 as laid out there. Show the extension of [[no elephant]], [[most elephants]], and [[two pigs]] at w_1.

10.3. The determiners

So far the discussion has centered on the meanings of the full expressions *every pig, no pig*, etc. But of course these ultimately need to be compositionally computed from the meanings of the lexical items, and so we now pull this apart. The quantificational determiners themselves combine with nouns to give generalized quantifiers, so their syntactic category is $(S/_R(S/NP))/N$ and their meaning is of type $<<et,>,<<e,t>,t>>$. This type looks complex but it really is not: put in set terms, these determiners take a set and map it into a set of sets. This means that each determiner is simply a Curry'ed relation between sets of individuals (more technically, they are Curry'ed relations between functions which characterize sets of individuals). Take for example [[every]]. In set terms, this is nothing more than the Curry'ed version of the subset relation. [[some]] (in set terms) is the Curry'ed relation between two sets A and B which can be paraphrases as the "has a non-empty intersection" relation. Put slightly more formally, it takes a set A and then a set B and returns true iff the intersection of A and B is not empty.[2] Using the lambda notation, one can write [[every]] and [[some]] as in (19):

(19) $[[\text{every}]] = \lambda P_{<e,t>} [\lambda Q_{<e,t>} [P_S \subseteq Q_S]]$
       $[[\text{some}]] = \lambda P_{<e,t>} [\lambda Q_{<e,t>} [P_S \cap Q_S \neq \emptyset]]$

10.4. Interlude: Scalar implicature

The above discussion concerning *some* used singular forms such as *some student*. The points to be made below are more naturally exposited using plurals like *some students*. Hence, while there may well be differences between *some student* and *some students*, we will overlook these here and switch to the plural form. Thus consider the meaning given above for *some* and consequently for sentences like (20):

(20)   Some students (absolutely) love formal semantics.

Given our semantics, this is true as long as the intersection of the student set and the set of lovers of formal semantics is not empty. This includes the situation in which all of the students love formal semantics. Yet at first glance that often strikes speakers as incorrect; on hearing (20) in an actual conversational context most listeners would conclude that there are also students who don't love formal semantics. This, incidentally, is true even if we are given a restricted domain. If I am talking about the students I have taught over the years (and hence the domain is restricted) and I utter (20), the listener will conclude that there are some students within the relevant domain (i.e., those who have taken formal semantics from me) who do not love formal semantics.

It might therefore seem that [[some]] should be revised as follows:

(21) $[[\text{some}]] = \lambda P_{<e,t>} [\lambda Q_{<e,t>} [P_S \cap Q_S \neq \emptyset \ \& \ P_S \nsubseteq Q_S]]$

[2] There is an extremely rich literature exploring possible constraints on determiner meanings cross-linguistically: while there are many relations between sets that one could write out, there are hypotheses that only some of these can actually be realized as single lexical items. See, e.g., Keenan and Stavi (1986).

But there turns out to be good reasons to reject this revision. (The discussion below is just a small sample of the vast amount of work under the rubric of Gricean pragmatics, scalar implicature, etc.). First, if this truly were the meaning of *some*, then (22a) would be a contradiction; note that the meaning given above is the meaning for the complex determiner *some but not all*, and indeed (22b) is a contradiction:

(22)   a. Some students love formal semantics, in fact they all might!
       b. Some but not all students love formal semantics, in fact they all might!

In addition, ordinary sentences like (23) would be odd. Why add *but not all* if *some* had the same meaning as *some but not all*?

(23)   Some but not all students love formal semantics.

A temptation might be to claim that *some* is ambiguous. Suppose there are two homophonous lexical items *some₁* and *some₂*, where *some₁* has the (weaker) meaning shown in (19) and *some₂* has the stronger meaning shown in (21).

Before addressing this possibility, note that the discussion here is parallel to the discussion of the meaning of *or* in Chapter 3. Recall that at first glance, a sentence of the form S_1 *or* S_2 seems to require at least one but not both sentences to be true; informally *or* seems to have "not and" as a part of its meaning. But we showed that this was not part of the truth conditions. (24a) is not a contradiction while (24b) is:

(24)   a. Sabrina will go skydiving on her vacation or she will go bungee jumping on her vacation and (in fact) she might do both.
       b. Sabrina will go skydiving on her vacation or she will go bungee jumping on her vacation but she won't do both; and (in fact) she might do both.

Nor is *or* ambiguous; this was demonstrated in Chapter 3 with respect to course prerequisite scenario where the student who had taken both Phonetics I and Phonology I could not be banned from registering in Phon/Phon II. (See the discussion surrounding (3) in section 3.2.)

The same point can be repeated with *some*. Suppose that—instead of (3) in Chapter 3—the linguistics department in question had the following description of the prerequisites:

(25)   Prerequisites are strictly enforced. Everyone who has taken some Phonetics course is allowed to enroll in Phonology I, and no one else is.

Once again the instructor in charge can hardly ban a student who had taken *all* of the Phonetics courses from enrolling in Phonology I. And this is not just a matter of saying that the context biases in favor of the *some₁* meaning (the weaker meaning), because we can add background assumptions that should bring out the *some₂* (stronger) meaning if it were available. Suppose the linguistics department in question is such that every Phonetics course covers a certain amount of phonology, that having taken all of the Phonetics courses one might well have covered just about everything that is covered in Phonology I, and that the department does not like students to get credit for courses whose material they already know. The instructor of Phonology I might well frown upon the enrollment of the student who has taken all of the Phonetics courses, but she simply cannot use the language of (25) as a reason to ban the student from the course. Yet if *some* were ambiguous, she would be within her rights to do so.

Thus the situation with *or* and the situation with *some* are quite parallel: *or* does not have the exclusive *or* meaning and *some* does not have the "some and not all" meaning. Just as *or* often—but not always—suggests "not and," *some* often—but not always—suggests "not all." As shown in the course catalogue scenario, the suggestions at issue disappear in the same sorts of environments (we have seen only one such place here, but others will be discussed in Chapter 17). Incidentally, most speakers are quite convinced that even if *or* really has only the inclusive reading, *either . . . or* surely is exclusive, as in (26):

(26) Either Mitka or Kolya has been digging in the yard.

There is a very strong suggestion here that both have not been digging. But even with *either . . . or* the exclusive reading goes away in the kinds of contexts we have been considering, as evidenced by the following:

(27) Everyone who has taken either Phonetics I or Phonology I is allowed to enroll in Phon/Phon II (and no one else is).

Once again this has no exclusive *or* reading; our instructor cannot ban the student who has taken both courses.

The fact that the situation with *or* and the situation with *some* are similar is not entirely surprising; there are parallels between *or* and *some* just as there are between *and* and *all*, as can be discovered in the exercise below.

10.6. Show that *or* is to *and* and *some* is to *all*. One way to think about this is to imagine a finite domain, and think of possible paraphrases of *Every student left* and *Some student left*.

In fact these similarities give another reason to doubt the hypothesis that these words are actually ambiguous: it would be a strange accident if *or* and *some* were both ambiguous, and in just the same ways. And so we turn now to a pragmatic explanation for why *or* often suggests "not and" while *some* often suggests "not all"—an explanation rooted in how language is used rather than in the literal meanings of the words. And ultimately the kind of pragmatic explanation to be developed immediately below combined with a closer look at the semantics will provide an explanation for just where the stronger understandings do emerge and where they don't, as will be shown in section 16.6.

The explanation here is quite standard, and is rooted in what is known as Gricean pragmatics. This is based on the observation from Grice (1975) that there is a distinction between the literal *meanings* of linguistics expressions and their *use*. Humans are rational beings engaged for the most part in cooperative conversation, and hence able to draw certain inferences in various conversational contexts that go beyond literal entailments. Some of these inferences can be drawn in virtue of what is *not* said, as well as what is. One of the relevant principles of cooperative conversation is that speakers in general will be as informative as possible (without being overinformative); Grice dubbed this the *Maxim of Quantity*. Given two sentences S_1 and S_2 where the first entails the second, the first is stronger; i.e., it gives more information about the world. Suppose then a speaker uttered S_2 when it would have been just as easy to utter S_1 (by this we mean that, for example, S_1 is not significantly longer, more awkward, etc.). A listener will reason that the speaker is communicating in a rational and cooperative way, and so given that the speaker did not utter the stronger sentence S_1 it must be because s/he is not in a position to truthfully utter S_1. Perhaps S_1 is false, or perhaps it is simply the case that the speaker does not have enough information to be sure that S_1 is true. These inferences are known as *scalar implicatures*, a term first introduced in Horn (1972) and studied in detail in many subsequent works (see Horn 2004 for a survey).

Applying this to the case at hand, consider the relationship between (28a) and (28b):

(28) a. Some students (absolutely) love formal semantics.
  b. Every student (absolutely) loves formal semantics.

Given the semantics in section 10.2.1, (28b) does not—strictly speaking—entail (28a). For the (b) sentence can be true in a world (or context) with no students, while the (a) sentence cannot. But assuming that we are looking at these in a context where speaker and hearer agree that there are students, then (28b) combined with background assumptions about the context does entail (28a). From now on we will speak a bit sloppily and say that *every* entails *some*, keeping in mind that this is a shorthand for: a sentence with *every* combined with the background assumption that the domain is not empty entails the corresponding sentence with *some*. Hence on hearing (28a) (in the nondefective context where there are students), a hearer will conclude that a rational and cooperative speaker would have uttered (28b) if they were in a position to. If we add to this an assumption on the part of the hearer that the speaker is in a position to know whether (28b) is true or false, the conclusion follows that it must be false. Hence the illusion that *some* means "some but not all." The same logic holds for the case of *and* and *or*; hearing (29a), a hearer can conclude that the speaker was not in a position to say (29b). Add to that the assumption that the speaker is in a position to know whether (29b) is true or false, one can conclude that it must be false:

(29) a. Kolya was playing or fighting.
  b. Kolya was playing and fighting.

Finally, we have also been assuming that the meaning of *three pigs* is as given in (16), which means that *Three pigs stayed home* is true even if four did. The reason that this suggests that exactly three pigs stayed home is the same.[3]

Two points about scalar implicatures are worth stressing as they are often oversimplified. First it is technically incorrect to speak of sentences having implicatures; implicatures are drawn only in the context of actual utterances. (Sentences have truth conditions, but not implicatures.) The remainder of this book will at times also be guilty of using the terminology of a

---

[3] Recently, however, the issue of whether ordinary numbers like *three* really mean *at least three* or *exactly three* has been revisited; the facts regarding numerals are much less clear than the facts discussed above with respect to *some* and *or*.

sentence implicating something, but keep in mind that this is just shorthand. When claiming that a particular *sentence* has an implicature, what one really is saying is that the implicature arises in the plausible contexts that one supplies when no overt context is given. Second, the direct implicature from, for example, (29a) (given a suitable context) is only that the speaker does not know (29b) to be true. The stronger implicature that (29b) is false comes from the additional step of assuming speaker knowledgeability (and therefore is not present in contexts where one can reasonably assume that the speaker is not in a position to know whether (29b) is true). Finally, there are many open questions about scalar implicatures. For example, one must be careful about just how the competing utterances are computed. Consider (30):

(30)   a. Chris used to have a dog.
      b. Chris used to have a pug.

(30b) is stronger than (30a), but surely on hearing (30a) a listener will (generally) not conclude that (31b) is false (or that the speaker does not know that (30b) is true). This inference would arise only in contexts where the dog breed is relevant, as for example, if I asked you whether Chris used to have a pug and you answered with (30a). (In that case, I would conclude that either you don't know if the dog was a pug or else that it wasn't.)[4]

10.5. Generalized quantifiers and conjunction

10.5.1. VP Conjunction

We now return to the two conjunction problems facing Straw Man. First, recall from Chapter 5 that Curry'ing the meanings of transitive verbs allows

---

[4] The pragmatic picture developed above has been challenged in recent work such as Chierchia (2004), Fox (2007), and Chierchia, Fox, and Spector (2012). These authors take the view that the computation of implicature is not just a matter of human reasoning, as is taken in the Gricean program. Rather they posit that the compositional computation in the grammar itself computes not just the literal meanings but also a strengthened meaning; i.e., the "implicatures" are part of the system of grammar. A similar although not identical position is put forward in Levinson (2000). We will not address this here. The interested can consult the above works, and see also Russell (2006) and Geurts (2009), among others, for critiques of the grammatical computation of implicature view.

for a very simple semantics for (31); the conjunction of the two VPs in (31a) is just set intersection, and in (31b) is set union:

(31) a. Sam fed the pig and meditated.
      b. Sam fed the pig or meditated.

Recall further that the only option available to Straw Man was to conclude that these actually involve hidden S conjunction. But, as discussed earlier, this (without invoking yet additional apparatus) makes the wrong predictions about the meanings of (32a) and (33a), which have meanings different from the meanings of the two-sentence conjunctions in the (b)-sentences:

(32) a. Some pig squealed and grunted.
      b. Some pig squealed and some pig grunted.

(33) a. Every pig squealed or grunted.
      b. Every pig squealed or every pig grunted.

The earlier discussion in Chapter 5 left it open as to how to account for the meanings of the (a) sentences as we had no semantics at that point for subjects with quantificational determiners.

But we can now show that the semantics here succeeds in giving the right meanings to these sentences. Take (33a). [[squealed or grunted]] is the union of the squealers and the grunters. The full sentence says that this set is in the set of sets denoted by [[every pig]]. In order for that to be true, the [[pig]] set must be a subset of the [[squeal or grunt]] set. But notice that all that requires is that each pig is a squealer or a grunter—it is not necessary for all the pigs to have the same property. Consider the pigs Strawbuilder, Stickbuilder, and Brickbuilder. If Strawbuilder squeals and Stickbuilder and Brickbuilder both grunt, the sentence is true, which is exactly as our semantics predicts. (The secondary reading, which is brought out with the continuation of *but I don't remember which*, is accounted for in Chapter 11.) (32a) comes out exactly right as well: a single pig must do both. The semantics here requires the intersection of the squeal set and the grunt set to have a non-empty intersection with the pig set. Thus there must be at least one pig in that VP intersection set; but that itself contains only those individuals that do both.

10.7. Take the universe and w_1 as shown in Exercise 10.4. Add to that the following: $[[howl]]_S = \{c,e\}$. Show the syntactic and semantic computation (showing the extensional value of each expression at w_1) for both (i) and (ii) (as usual, simply ignore *is* and the progressive morphology). Do *not* show the actual extension of $[[no]]$, $[[and]]$, and $[[is]]$; this would be unbelievably laborious. You can write these out using the λ-calculus. These remarks hold for subsequent exercises as well.

(i) No pig grunted and howled.
(ii) No pig grunted and no pig howled.

10.5.2. Generalized quantifier conjunction

In addition to VP conjunction, we have seen that generalized quantifiers can also conjoin with each other, a fact which should be subsumed under the generalized lexical entries for *and* and *or* given in the fragment summary in Chapter 6. Recall that we have not yet finalized the meanings of these items, but have concluded that whenever they conjoin two set denoting expressions, the result is intersection and union. The semantics of sentences like (34) thus works out exactly as expected:

(34) a. Every student and some professor meditated.
      b. Every cat and no wolf stayed behind.
      c. Three phonology students or every syntax student will come to the colloquium.

Take (34a). $[[every\ student]]_S$ is the set of sets with $[[student]]_S$ as subset, and $[[some\ professor]]_S$ is the set of sets with a non-empty intersection with $[[professor]]_S$. Since these are conjoined by *and*, the full GQ will denote the set of sets that occur in each of these. Thus in order for (34a) to be true, $[[meditated]]_S$ must be both in $[[every\ student]]_S$ and in $[[some\ professor]]_S$. This in turn means that $[[student]]_S$ is a subset of $[[meditated]]_S$ (and hence indeed every student did meditate) and that $[[mediated]]_S$ also has as member at least one professor. These are the right truth conditions. For (34b), we will display the full syntactic and semantic composition, keeping in mind that *and* has the Curry'ed meaning written out in λ-notation in (23) in Chapter 9. We begin with lexical items already fully specified for directional slashes, and until the last step we will use GQ as an abbreviation for $S/_r(S/_LNP)$. It will also be clearest to recast the semantics for *and* into the function version (given in (23) in Chapter 9). In reading this, one should make sure to understand each line, and how the lambda conversions shown here help to simplify the formula.

(35) no, GQ, $\lambda P_{<e,t>} [\lambda Q_{<e,t>} [P_S \cap Q_S = \varnothing]]$
   wolf, N, wolf
   no wolf, GQ, $\lambda P_{<e,t>} [\lambda Q_{<e,t>} [P_S \cap Q_S = \varnothing]](wolf') =$
                              (by the λ-conversion equivalence)
        $\lambda Q_{<e,t>} [wolf'_S \cap Q_S = \varnothing]$
   and, $(X/_LX)/_RX$, $\lambda A [\lambda B[\lambda z[A(z) \& B(z)]]]$
       X is instantiated by GQ, so the next step is:
   and no wolf, $GQ/_LGQ$,
       $\lambda \mathcal{P}_{<<e,t>,t>} [\lambda \mathcal{Q}_{<<e,t>,t>} [\lambda P_{<e,t>}[\mathcal{P}(P) \& \mathcal{Q}(P)]] (\lambda Q_{<e,t>} [wolf'_S \cap Q_S = \varnothing]) =$
       $\lambda \mathcal{Q}_{<<e,t>,t>} [\lambda P_{<e,t>}[\lambda Q_{<e,t>} [wolf'_S \cap Q_S = \varnothing] (P) \& \mathcal{Q}(P)]] =$
       $\lambda \mathcal{Q}_{<<e,t>,t>} [\lambda P_{<e,t>}[wolf'_S \cap P_S = \varnothing \& \mathcal{Q}(P)]]$
   every, $GQ/_RN$, $\lambda V_{<e,t>} [\lambda T_{<e,t>} [V_S \subseteq T_S]]$
   cat, N, cat'
   every cat, GQ, $\lambda V_{<e,t>} [\lambda T_{<e,t>} [V_S \subseteq T_S]](cat') = \lambda T_{<e,t>}[cat'_S \subseteq TS]$
   every cat and no wolf, GQ, i.e., S/R(S/LNP)
       $\lambda \mathcal{Q}_{<<e,t>,t>} [\lambda P_{<e,t>}[wolf'_S \cap PS = \varnothing \& \mathcal{Q}(P)]](\lambda T_{<e,t>}[cat'_S \subseteq TS]) =$
       $\lambda P_{<e,t>}[wolf'_S \cap P_S = \varnothing \& \lambda T_{<e,t>}[cat'_S \subseteq T_S] (P)] =$
       $\lambda P_{<e,t>}[wolf'_S \cap P_S = \varnothing \& cat'_S \subseteq P_S]$
   stayed behind, $S/_LNP$, stayed-behind'
   every cat and no wolf stayed behind, S,
       $\lambda P_{<e,t>}[wolf'_S \cap P_S = \varnothing \& cat'_S \subseteq P_S](stayed-behind') =$
       $wolf'_S \cap$ stayed-behind'$_S = \varnothing \& cat'_S \subseteq$ stayed-behind'$_S$

10.8. Take (34b) again. As best you can, describe *in prose* how the semantic computation proceeds. This is similar to what is done in the text for (34a) except that in the informal prose description there we made our lives simpler by de-Currying *and*. Your task then is to try to state in prose the meanings of each of the complex expressions (*no wolf, and no wolf, every cat, every cat and no wolf,* and finally the whole sentence).

10.9. Using the model in (35), take the sentence below in (i) and show its syntactic and semantic composition (take *attended the rally* as a single unanalyzed VP to avoid busywork irrelevant to the point here):

(i) Three students and no professors attended the rally.

Show that this turns out to be synonymous with (ii):

(ii) Three students attended the rally and no professor attended the rally.

*10.10. The sentence in (i) below involves both GQ and VP conjunction:

(i) No cat and no wolf howled and screeched.

Work through the full syntactic and semantic computation along the lines shown in (35), doing lambda conversions wherever possible (and as soon as possible). Note that this is synonymous with (ii) and not with either (iii) or (iv).

(ii) No cat howled and screeched and no wolf howled and screeched.
(iii) No cat and no wolf howled and no cat and no wolf screeched.
(iv) No cat howled and no cat screeched and no wolf howled and no wolf screeched.

Try to get the intuition for why this is so. One might mechanically work through the derivations of all four sentences to see that our semantics does indeed give the right results, but the best thing to do would be to try to get an intuition of how the patterns are working here, and why.

A fork in the road

At this point in the text there is a choice. Readers now have enough background to proceed directly to Chapter 16 which takes up the distribution of so-called Negative Polarity Items (as well as additional material on scalar implicatures). This might be especially rewarding for readers who are anxious to see the formal tools developed so far pressed into service for making order out of what at first glance appears to be a rather chaotic domain. However, one can also just move on to Chapter 11 and postpone the material in Chapter 16. (Another reasonable path is to insert Chapter 16 after Part II.) In any case, the next section in this chapter—on domain restriction—should be read before Chapter 16 and also Chapter 17; it is also useful for section 13.2.2 which itself is a starred section). It merits an asterisk before it at this point because readers who are not planning to look at Chapter 16 at this point can skip it for now. But unlike the other starred sections (which can be skipped altogether with little or no loss for later material), this one will be crucial later. Thus it is included now both for readers planning to move directly on to Chapter 16, and also of course for readers interested in the topic.

*10.6. Domain restriction

It has been noted from time to time in this text the interpretation of expressions with quantificational determiners is limited to some domain. If we are farmers and I turn to you mid-morning and say *Every pig was fed*, you would certainly not interpret this to mean every pig in the world, or even every pig in the region, but every pig on our farm. Similarly if I say *No pig ate this morning* we again understand this as no pig from the relevant set—in this case once again the pigs on our farm.

The particular way in which the domain is restricted of course depends entirely on context. But an interesting question arises. Is the fact a GQ is interpreted relative to some (contextually set) domain built into its meaning itself? Or is this simply a consequence of the fact that sentences are always interpreted not with respect to full worlds but rather smaller situations? The first point of view (that the semantics of a GQ has a slot for a domain restriction as part of its meaning) has been taken by von Fintel (1994), Stanley and Szabo (2000) and others; the second has been argued for by Kratzer (2004). Here we consider the first view, in fact one argument for this (put forth originally in von Fintel 1994) will be explored in section 16.4; another potential advantage emerges in Chapter 17.

Saying that the domain restriction is part of the semantics means that a QP like *every pig* does not actually have quite the meaning given earlier, since it has an extra piece in its meaning which is for the domain restriction. Of course the particular domain cannot be part of the meaning since that varies wildly from context to context, but the expectation that there will be a contextually set domain can be part of the meaning. At this point, we will informally use the notion of a *free variable* in order to flesh out the domain restriction proposal, even though we have yet to really give a full semantics for variables in natural language. (In fact, Chapter 17 recasts this without use of a variable.) In other words, suppose that [[every pig]] is not as shown in (36a) but rather (36b):

(36)   a. $\lambda P[\text{pig's} \subseteq P_S]$
      b. $\lambda P[\text{pig's} \cap D \subseteq P_S]$

Although a discussion of variables is postponed, it is fairly easy to get an intuitive understanding of (36b). D is a free variable over sets of individuals, and its value is ultimately set by the context (note that this is reminiscent of the understanding of the free variable over comparison classes in the meaning of adjectives as was discussed in section 8.4.4).

Assuming that (36b) is the meaning for *every pig*, the next question is how to arrive at this from the compositional semantics. We will follow von Fintel (1994) in treating the domain restriction variable as part of the meaning of the determiner. Thus [[every]] is actually:

(37) $\lambda Q[\lambda P[Q_S \cap D \subseteq P_S]$

Suppose further that all determiners come with a domain restriction as part of their meaning. We have already seen that domain restriction is at play in the interpretation of sentences with *no* and with *every*, and it is easy to see that it will also be in play for sentences like *At most three pigs ate this morning*. Moreover, a sentence like *Some student passed the exam* is not understood as saying some student anywhere, but rather this asserts that some student out of some relevant set passed. So [[some]] is:

(38) $[[\text{some}]] = \lambda Q[\lambda P[Q_S \cap D \cap P_S \neq \emptyset]]$

(We have not put brackets around the three sets above because intersection is associative and so the bracketing would make no difference.) Note that it is also reasonable to think that there is a domain restriction as part of the meaning of *the*. Thus, as noted already in Chapter 1, a sentence like (39) might be taken to be about the tallest linguistics major at Brown University:

(39)   We didn't order a gown long enough for the tallest linguistics major.

In view of this, the meaning of *the* might be revised as (40):

(40) $[[\text{the}]] = \lambda P[\iota x[x \in P_S \cap D]]$

For the moment, little in the discussion in this text hinges on whether or not the lexical entries here for *some*, *every*, etc. do contain the domain restriction piece. It is easier to work with these meanings if we ignore this part, and so we will generally do just that. The official fragment includes both versions of the lexical entries for *the* and for quantificational determiners (with and without the domain restriction).

11

Ordinary NPs and type lifting

Chapter 10 began with the observation that expressions like *every pig, some pig*, etc. have the same distribution as ordinary NPs like *Porky* and *the mayor of Providence*. We then proceeded to give them meanings quite different from those of ordinary NPs, and also renamed their syntactic category. The fact that GQs—like ordinary NPs—occur in subject position has been taken care of in virtue of their full category $S/_R(S/_LNP)$, and their ability to occur in object position is a complex topic that forms the subject of Chapter 14. But there is another way in which ordinary NPs and GQs behave alike: they can conjoin with each other (hereafter we use the term *conjunction* to mean combining with either *and* or *or*):

(1) a. Dumbo and every seal escaped from the circus.
     b. Obama and some Republican senator will appear at the fundraiser.
     c. Obama or some Republican senator will appear at the fundraiser.

Our syntax does not yet admit of these: *and* and *or* are of category (X/X)/X but GQ and NP are different categories. And even if conjunction of unlike categories were allowed, there remains the more pressing question: how to assign a meaning to these conjoined expressions?[1] We saw that the

---

[1] Indeed there are cases of apparent coordination of different categories; see Chapter 6, n. 9. As noted there, Bayer (1996) shows that these can be reduced to coordination of like categories in a Categorial Grammar.

conjunction of two GQs can be handled as instances of set intersection or union, but ordinary NPs do not denote sets.

In fact, the problem is somewhat independent of the cases in (1). For ordinary NPs themselves can conjoin:

(2)   Bachmann and Perry spoke at the Tea Party rally.

While our syntax predicts these to be well-formed, the semantics has nothing to say about them: it makes no sense to talk about the intersection of individuals! Now in the case of (2), one might suspect that *and* in (2) is a different lexical item from the *and* that intersects sets. Perhaps it takes two atomic individuals and returns a plural individual (such that *Bachmann and Perry* is quite similar to *the candidates*). In fact, there may well be a second *and* that does just this. But ordinary NPs also conjoin with *or* and no similar story could be told for that case. Again *or* has been taken to involve set union, but the NPs in question do not (as we have set things up so far) denote sets:

(3)   Bachmann or Perry spoke at the rally.

So the tasks are as follows: (a) to provide a complete account of the identical distribution of NPs and GQs; (b) to have the syntax be such that GQs can conjoin with ordinary NPs, and (c) to provide a semantics for (1)–(3). As mentioned above, (a) will be postponed until Chapter 14; the other tasks will be addressed here.

11.1. Montague's solution

Montague's analysis (Montague 1973) provides an ingenious solution. Once again it relies on the idea that perhaps the meanings are not always what they appear: perhaps the semantics has packaged things in clever ways. Thus, while one can retain individuals as basic building blocks in the semantic ontology, Montague's hypothesis is that ordinary definite NPs (including proper names) don't actually denote (world/time-dependent) individuals, but rather they have a fancier meaning. The solution rests on the observation that every individual can be repackaged as a set of sets that contain that individual; the individual r whom we are used to thinking of as the individual denoted by *Romeo* can be repackaged as the set of sets containing r. In function terms, this is the function of type $<<e,t>,t>$ that maps any function P of type $<e,t>$ to true if P(r) is true. This is shown in (4) in both set and function notation:

(4)   [[Romeo]]$_S$ = {S| r ∈ S}
     [[Romeo]] = λP[P(r)]

One might worry that potentially allows two NPs to "collide"—are we guaranteed that there could not be two individuals with all the same properties? The answer is yes, we are: the property of being identical to r is true only for r. In set terms, the singleton set {r} is the Romeo set of sets and not in the set of sets corresponding to any other individual. Thus any individual is mapped to a unique generalized quantifier, and that generalized quantifier corresponds to no other individual. The function that maps any individual to the corresponding generalized quantifier is called the *lift* function (and notate this as *l*). For any generalized quantifier generated by an individual there is a function *lower* that takes the set of sets and recovers the individual (it is the only individual in every set in the GQ). Of course, lower is not defined for every GQ; if it were we would have had no need for GQs in the first place. (Recall that there was no sensible way to take *no husky* to be an individual.) Thus *l* is a total function from individuals to generalized quantifiers, and lower is a partial function from generalized quantifiers to individuals; it maps any GQ which is *l*(x) to x. Note incidentally that now the extension of an NP like *Romeo* differs from world to world (as it should since the property of being in love with Juliet might hold for r in one world but not another), but the idea that proper names are rigid designators has not gone away. For at the center of the whole thing remains the individual r who is constant across worlds; and [[Romeo]] in any world w is the set of properties that that individual r has at w.

  The above deals just with proper names, but of course definite NPs like *the disobedient husky* will also have lifted meanings. Let m be the individual who is indeed the (most or only) contextually salient disobedient husky, then the [[the disobedient husky]] will be λP[P(m)]. Under this hypothesis, *the*—like the other determiners—would be listed in the lexicon with category (S/$_R$(S/NP)/N and with meaning of type <<e,t>,<<e,t>,t>>.

11.1. Give the meaning for *the* under this account. To write it out, you can use notation that includes the iota-operator in section 9.3 in the discussion surrounding R-3.

This solves the problems elucidated above. Ordinary "NPs" of course have the same distribution as GQs because they are GQs. The two always also have the same semantic type, namely $<<e,t>,t>$. Since "NPs" like *Obama* and *Boehner* both denote sets of sets, it is not surprising that they can conjoin. This is just like any other case of conjunction with *and* and *or* of set-denoting expressions; the semantics is intersection or union. And of course the same holds true for cases of conjunction of these with the kind of GQs discussed in the preceding chapter. We will informally walk through just one example here shown in (5) (this is more natural with *but* than with *and*; we assume that the two have the same semantics for our purposes):

(5)   Mitka and/but no cat escaped.

[[Mitka and no cat]]$_S$ is the set of sets which is the intersection of [[Mitka]]$_S$ and [[no cat]]$_S$. The former is the set of sets with m as member, and the latter is the set of sets that have a non-empty intersection with the [[cat]] set. Thus in order for [[escaped]]$_S$ to be in the set of sets denoted by the subject, it has to be both in [[Mitka]]$_S$ and in [[no-cat]]$_S$ from which it follows that m must be a member of [[escape]]$_S$, and that [[escape]]$_S$ has an empty intersection with [[cat]]$_S$. These are exactly the right truth conditions.

11.2. Consider a universe with four individuals {a,b,c,d} and a world w_1. Let [[Babar]] in w_1 (and of course in all worlds) be $\lambda P[P(b)]$ and [[Dumbo]] be $\lambda P[P(d)]$. Let [[seal]] in w_1 be {a,c}, [[elephant]] be {b,d}, and [[intelligent]] be {a,b,c}.

(a) Show the full compositional computation extensionally for w_1 of *the intelligent elephant*. (Thus show the extension of each expression at w_1.) Remember to fold in the shift of a predicative adjective to the prenominal adjective.

(b) Show the computation of this for any world. In other words, this question asks you to write out [[the intelligent elephant]] using the lambda notation, to show what the value would be regardless of what are the facts of the world in question.

(c) Show the extension of *Dumbo* at w_1 (i.e., show the actual set of sets, rather than naming the object as a formula).

11.3. Add the following to the facts above: $[[\text{Silkie}]] = \lambda P[P(c)]$ (at w_1 and, of course, for all worlds), and $[[\text{escaped}]]$ in $w_1 = \{b,c\}$. Show the compositional computation for the following sentences. In each case, first show the value of each expression extensionally for w_1, and then also show in general how the semantics is put together using λ-notation.

  (i) Silkie and the intelligent elephant escaped.
 (ii) Dumbo and every seal are intelligent.
(iii) Dumbo or Silkie
(iv) Dumbo and no seal

11.2. Partee and Rooth's solution: Lift as a unary rule

But Montague's solution does have drawbacks. First, individuals are part of the ontology and part of the basic building blocks for meanings, yet there are no linguistic expressions whose extensions are just individuals. The least complex type of meaning would be the meaning of a VP (which is a function of type $<e,t>$).[2] (Under CG, the syntax has a similar peculiarity: NP is a basic category and yet there are no linguistic expressions of category NP.) Moreover, following some observations in Keenan and Faltz (1985), note that there are proper names for individuals, but no proper names for other types of GQs. For example there is no name *Droloryman* picking out the set of sets which is the union of $\{S|\ d\ \epsilon\ S\}$ and $\{S|\ m\ \epsilon\ S\}$. Were proper names listed in the lexicon as having type $<<e,t>,t>$, the fact that they always correspond only to individuals does not follow.

    Partee and Rooth (1983) thus proposed an interesting modification of Montague's analysis. They suggested that ordinary definite (both proper names and those with *the* as determiner) do indeed denote individuals in their basic meaning. In other words, a proper name like *Barack Obama* is listed as picking out (in all worlds), some individual—call it o. And *the* has the meaning given in Chapter 8: it is of type $<<e,t>,e>$ and maps a set to the unique (or most) contextually salient member of the set. Thus $[[\text{the disobedient husky}]]$ is, as discussed earlier, an individual. (And, in the CG syntax, its

---

[2] A different solution to this anomaly was proposed in Bennett (1974) where he indeed takes VP-meanings as the lowest type in the ontology.

category would be just $NP/_R N$.) However, they also proposed a unary rule (which they dubbed a type shift rule) which allows these to map with no phonological effect into the generalized quantifiers of Montague. Hence an expression like *the disobedient husky* has two meanings; it can denote an individual, or it can denote the generalized quantifier built from that individual.

Partee and Rooth were not assuming a Categorial Grammar syntax, but adapting their proposal into the framework here, we posit the following unary rule (to be generalized below):

TR-10.   Let a be an expression of the form $<[a], NP, [[a]]>$. Then there is an expression β of the form $<[a], S/_R(S/NP); \lambda P_{<e,t>}[P([[a]])]>$.

11.4. Return to the world and lexicon as laid out in Exercises 11.2 and 11.3. Given the Partee and Rooth proposal, we of course must modify the meanings for the lexical items given there; now [[Babar]] (in all worlds) = b, [[Dumbo]] = d, and [[Silkie]] = c. Redo your answers to (11.3i) and (11.3iii) using the Partee and Rooth proposal.

11.3. Generalizing the rule

It turns out that generalizing TR-10 will have nice consequences as we built the system further. First, we generalize the definition of l (lift). For any member x of a set X and any set of functions F from X to Y, there is a function $l(x)$ from F to Y, such that for all f in F, $l(x)(f) = f(x)$. Put informally, $l(x)$ is something which takes any function g as argument (provided that x is in the domain of g), and gives back that which one would have gotten had g applied to x. A somewhat subtle point is that as defined here, the domain of $l(x)$ is every single function which has x in its domain—not just those functions whose domain is some particular set of interest. Similar remarks apply to the co-domain. Since it is often convenient to consider just those functions in $l(x)$ which are functions from some specific set X to some specific set Y, we will use the notation $l_{<X,Y>}(x)$ when needed (but subscript on the l operation will be omitted when not necessary). Thus $l_{<X,Y>}(x)$ is a function of type $<<X,Y>,Y>$. The original lift of individuals to functions of type $<<e,t>,t>$ is just one instance of the general *l* operation. Given an individual a, $l_{<e,t>}$, (a) is the function that takes any <e,t> function P and returns the value of P(a); it is $\lambda P[P(a)]$. We can now generalize TR-10 as follows (the syntax will be further generalized in 11.5):

TR-11. Let *α* be an expression of the form <[*a*], A, [[*a*]]>. Then there is an expression *β* of the form <[*a*], B/R(B/LA) or B/L(B/RA), $\lambda f_{<a,b>}[f([[a]])]$ (i.e., $l_{<a,b>}([[a]])$)>, where a is the type for expressions of category A and b for expressions of category B.

Of course the syntax here looks a bit dismal. In the first place there are two possible categories for the output expression (depending on the slash directions). And we surely should be embarrassed about what looks to be an accidental fact that the directionality on the slashes just happens to give the new expression a category that preserves word order. In other words, it just happens to ensure that the new lifted expression combines with an expression of category B/A to give just what would have resulted in the syntax from using the unlifted version. Temporarily, we will live with this embarrassment.

Consider a simple example like *Mitka howls*. Notice that we now have an infinite number of derivations for this sentence. The first is the obvious one; the lexical meaning of *Mitka* is the simple individual m is the argument of [[howls]] (of type <e,t>). The second involves lifting *Mitka* to the GQ with meaning $\lambda P[P(m)]$ and that takes ordinary [[howls]] (still of type <e,t>) as argument. But now we have introduced a third derivation, in which [[howls]] is lifted to be of type <<<e,t>,t>,t>; that is, it takes a generalized quantifier as argument.

> **11.5.** Show this derivation (showing both the syntactic and semantic composition). Do as many *λ*-conversions as you can to show that the meaning is the same as the meaning that results from the two it is equivalent to the two derivations given above.

But there is no harm in allowing in these extra derivations: they all converge on the same meaning. Indeed this is guaranteed by the very definition of *l*; for any function f *l*(a)(f) is destined to give the same result as f(a), for that is exactly how lift is defined.

What, then, could possibly be the advantage of incorporating the generalized rule in TR-11 which allows for all of these extra derivations? The
advantages come from cases where the output of the lift operation itself
"does something" other than immediately taking the would-be function as
its argument—as, for example, when it conjoins with another expression of
the same category. As one such case, recall the extra reading of a sentence
like (6) discussed in Chapter 5 (the material in parentheses is there to bring
out the relevant reading):

(6)   Every wolf howled or sang (but I can't remember which).

This reading is now predicted; it is the reading that results if *howl* and *sing* are
both lifted over GQ meanings. That is, each of these denote sets of GQs; they
combine with *or* (to give the union of the relevant sets), and then they take
the subject GQ as argument. The derivation is spelled out in (7), using
function rather than set notation throughout. We leave off those slash
directions which are predictable from the word order rules given in
section 6.3, and put in only those which are stipulated either as part of the
lexical category (in this case, of *every*) or are given by TR-11 (those stipula-
tions themselves will be removed in section 11.5). The derivation in (7) also
simplifies the full analysis of *or*; since *or* in actuality is Curry'ed, the expression *howl or sing* involves two steps, but we collapse these here into one:

(7)   howl, S/NP, howl' (of type <e,t>) → by TR-11
      howl, (S/$_L$(S/$_R$(S/NP)), $\lambda P_{<<e,t>,t>}[\,P\,(\text{howl'})]$
      sing, S/NP, sing' (of type <e,t>) → by TR-11
      sing, (S/$_L$(S/$_R$(S/NP)), $\lambda Q_{<<e,t>,t>}[\,Q\,(\text{sing'})]$
      howl or sing, (S/$_L$(S/$_R$(S/NP)), $\lambda R_{<<e,t>,t>}[\lambda Q\,[Q(\text{sing'})](R)] \vee \lambda P[P\,(\text{howl'})](R)]$
      $= \lambda R\,[R\,(\text{sing'}) \vee R\,(\text{howl'})]$
      every wolf, S/$_R$(S/NP), $\lambda P[\forall x[\text{wolf'}(x) \rightarrow P(x)]]$
      every wolf howl or sing, S, $\lambda R\,[R\,(\text{sing'}) \vee R\,(\text{howl'})](\text{every-wolf'}) =$
      every-wolf'(sing') $\vee$ every-wolf'(howl') =
      $\lambda P[\forall x[\text{wolf'}(x) \rightarrow P(x)]](\text{sing'}) \vee \lambda P[\forall x[\text{wolf'}(x) \rightarrow P(x)]](\text{howl'}) =$
      $\forall x[\text{wolf'}(x) \rightarrow \text{sing'}(x)] \vee \forall x[\text{wolf'}(x) \rightarrow \text{howl'}(x)]$

11.6. The derivation shown in (7) derives the relevant reading by lifting
each of the VPs separately and then combining them with *or*. What
would be the reading for the derivation in which they are first conjoined
with *or* (that is the unshifted lexical items conjoin), and then the resulting
VP *howled or sang* lifts by TR-11?

11.4. The lowest types hypothesis

11.4.1. Some additional predictions

Partee and Rooth made the interesting speculation that in processing a sentence, a listener will first interpret expressions in their lowest types (that is, the types given by the lexicon without additional rules), and will posit the higher type meanings only if there is evidence for this. (Notice that this is phrased as a principle *of the processor* and not of the *grammar*. Some modern work recasts this as a *grammatical* principle, we return to this in 11.4.2.) The idea is that the processor will recompute and use higher types if there are either grammatical or pragmatic reasons for this. For example, in the sentence in (6) the continuation *but I don't remember which* forces the more complex reading. Or, there could be other pragmatic or contextual cues leading a listener to the more complex reading. This also means that in processing an ordinary sentence like *Porky grunted* a listener computes the meaning using the individual-denoting meaning of *Porky*. However, in hearing a sentence like *Porky or Strawbuilder grunted* or *Porky or every wild boar grunted* the existence of the conjunction causes a reanalysis whereby the lifted meaning of *Porky* is accessed. A nice consequence of this proposal is that it succeeds in predicting that the extra reading for *every wolf howled or sang* is less available and is a secondary reading, which accords with most people's (admittedly unsystematically collected) intuitions.[3]

A second example of the advantage of both generalizing the lift rule and adopting the lowest types hypothesis concerns the ambiguity of sentences like (8):

(8)   Every student didn't pass the exam.

---

[3] This hypothesis is reminiscent of some other proposals in the syntactic processing literature according to which listeners compute the "minimal" derivation available such as the "Minimal Attachment" hypothesis of Frazier (1978). In some of these other cases, however, it is unclear how this actually could take place for no algorithm is provided (nor is any algorithm obvious) that would guide the processor to the minimal derivation. The lowest types hypothesis, however, is quite clear and avoids this problem: the processor initially accesses the lexical meaning and then recomputes only when needed.

On one reading (arguably the most accessible one), the sentence claims that all the students failed. But it has an additional reading: one which is often referred to under the rubric of *not* scoping over *every*; in this reading (8) says only that at least one student failed. This is not as immediately accessible but can certainly be brought out with the right context (and/or intonational contour). To show this with a slightly different example, it used to be standard protocol on Amtrak trains running between Boston and Washington that—as the train approached smaller stations such as New London, New Haven, etc.—the conductor would announce (for example):

(9)   Next station stop, New Haven. All doors will not be open.

Surely the passenger scheduled to disembark in New Haven would not say "But conductor, my ticket is to New Haven—how can I possibly get off this train?" (Fortunately, should there have been a pragmatically challenged passenger the conductor did generally follow this announcement with something like "Please exit at the rear of the train.")

One kind of account for the "wide-scope negation" reading is the one embedded in a theory that maintains that a sentence is mapped into an LF which inputs to the model-theoretic interpretation. Under this view, *not* can raise and take scope over the full sentence giving the secondary reading. (Such accounts generally treat the primary reading in a somewhat different way than has been done here, but we will develop that here.) But notice that the relevant reading can also be accounted for under the Direct Compositional model without invoking a level of LF.

First is a small housekeeping detail. In the fragment in Chapter 6, *didn't* has as its category (S/NP)/(S/NP). It was not given a cross-categorial definition (the way *and* and *or* were) and so can combine with VPs but not necessarily with members of other categories. Indeed, it should not have a completely general category since it does not combine with NPs, APs, and so forth. However, to account for the secondary reading we do need to assume that it can combine both with ordinary VPs and with lifted VPs (and hence it also has the category (S/(S/(S/NP)))/(S/(S/(S/NP)))). Although the existence of this extra category does not follow from anything, recall that we are oversimplifying in any case: *didn't* is not really a single lexical item and the actual negation is either *not* or *n't* which follows (and in the case of *n't* is cliticized to) the first in a string of auxiliaries. We have avoided a full treatment of negation in English because a treatment of the syntax of auxiliaries is far beyond the current scope. Thus simply assume that the lexical entry for *didn't* from Chapter 6 is revised as follows: <[didn't], X/X, $\lambda F_{<a,t>}[\lambda A_a[\sim F(A)]]$, where X is restricted to S/NP or S/(S/(S/NP))>. With this, the secondary reading is accounted for; showing this is the task of the next exercise.

11.7. Show the simplest (lowest types) derivation (both the syntax and the semantics) for (8) and then show the derivation which yields the weaker meaning to the effect that at least one student failed the exam (but not necessarily all). You can treat *pass the exam* as a single lexical VP (with meaning of type <e,t>) for simplicity.

11.8. Show a third derivation in which *didn't* first combines with the <e,t> meaning of *pass the exam* and then that VP lifts over generalized quantifier meanings. What are the truth conditions that result from this derivation?

There remain some unsolved problems with the adoption of the fully generalized lift rule in TR-11, for indeed there are many cases in which the additional readings do not exist. For example, the relevant reading is impossible in (10):

(10)   Some student(s) failed syntax and forgot to come to the phonology exam.

The extra reading—analogous to the secondary reading for (6)—would be one in which some students failed syntax and some forgot to come to the phonology exam, but they need not be the same students. (This, of course, is the reading one would expect also under the Conjunction Reduction analysis discussed and rejected in Chapter 5.) Notice that even when the context is loaded so as to give this reading every chance to emerge, it is absent. Suppose for example we are discussing where students go on their spring vacations, and I report:

(11)   Some students go skiing for the week and stay home and study.

The only reading this sentence has is the contradictory one in which the same students did both; there is no way to force this into the pragmatically sensible reading. Similarly, there does not seem to be a second ("wide-scope negation") reading for (12):

(12)   No student didn't go skiing.

The only available reading is that every student skied; there is no weaker reading which simply asserts that at least one student skied. Incidentally the problem here is not a problem just for the type-lifting account; any other account of the ambiguity of (6) and (8) will need to ensure that the mechanisms for that do not generalize to give additional readings for (11) and (12).

*11.4.2. The lowest types hypothesis: Processing vs grammar

The lowest types hypothesis (or variants thereof) is sometimes phrased in terms of a constraint in the grammar within theories that do not maintain a Direct Compositional architecture. In particular, suppose that the input to the semantics is a syntactic representation (whether it be the surface or an LF representation). Consider a compositional interpretation of an expression of category A containing two daughter expressions of category B and C. (We are not using a Categorial syntax here.) Suppose that [[B]] is a function of type <c,a> and [[C]] is of type c. The idea is that the only possible semantic derivation is the one in which [[B]] applies to [[C]]. Thus C cannot map to the lifted meaning which is the output of (the semantic part of) TR-11. This means that, for example, the meaning of *Mitka howls* can be put together in only one way. There is, however, a type-lifting rule along the lines of Partee and Rooth, which can apply "as a last resort." That is, if the semantics encounters an expression like *[Mitka and every wolf]* the only way to combine these meanings is for the expression *Mitka* to lift, and in that case this is allowed. Thus here the claim that the meaning of *Mitka howls* is put together using the lowest types is not a claim about processing, but indeed the grammar does not allow the derivation where *Mitka* lifts to take *howls* as argument (nor any of the higher derivations). In fact, more generally a number of researchers have posited that any type shift rule (a unary rule shifting the meaning of an expression into a new meaning with a different type) applies only "when needed" or "to repair type mismatch."

   The "type lift (or, more generally, type shift) as a last resort" view as a principle of *grammar* (rather than processing) makes no sense under Direct Compositionality. Nor does the idea that such rules exist in order to "repair" type mismatches (another slogan that one sometimes sees). This rubric presupposes a view where there is an already computed object which the semantics is "trying" to interpret. Note of course that this view means that the additional readings discussed above for (6), (8), and (9) cannot be accounted for in the way suggested here (using type lifting). This is because the grammar has a perfectly good way to put together the meanings without this, and if type lifting is allowed in the grammar only when there is no other way to compose the meanings, it will not be allowed here. This illustrates a key difference between the last-resort strategy as a principle of *processing* vs a principle of *grammar*. A human being processor (such as our poor Amtrak traveler wishing to de-train in New Haven) can (hopefully!) reason that the lowest types meaning is pragmatically inappropriate, and recompute. The grammar, however, is not "smart" in this way; it is a purely algorithmic device with no ability to reason about trains and stations and conductors. Thus a theory that maintains "type lifting as a last resort in the grammar" would need a different account of, for example, the Amtrak reading.

The Direct Compositional view of grammar taken in this book has no notion of unary rules (such as type lifting) existing "in order to repair mismatches" and no notion that these rules can apply only when needed. For there can be nothing to repair; the syntax and semantics work together to prove expressions well-formed and assign them a meaning. There can be no notion of a rule *needing* to apply, for the grammar itself has no needs or goals. Only the human processor does: the goal of the processor is to interpret the sentence, but the grammar is a purely static system predicting the well-formedness of expressions and pairing them with meanings. Thus, with Partee and Rooth, we will assume that the lowest types hypothesis is a hypothesis processing, not grammar.[4]

---

[4] Sometimes one sees claims that the existence of unary (or, type shift rules) is explained by the slogan that they "exist to repair type mismatches" (this goes along with the notion that they apply only as a "last resort"—i.e., when need to repair type mismatches). But it is unclear what—if anything—this is supposed to explain. First, why would one want an explanation for the existence of these rules as opposed to any of the other sorts of rules in the grammar? Perhaps the driving intuition is that because these rules do not affect the phonology of an item, their existence is peculiar and needs "explanation" in a way that other rules don't. But even if we grant this, there are problems with the claim that the last-resort principle explains the existence of these rules. For one thing, there are many unary rules (especially ones mapping single words into others) that do not clearly have this function. Consider for example the verb *give* which can appear with both two NP complements and an NP and

11.5. Resolving some syntactic loose ends

We can now clean up some of the aspects of the syntax which seemed problematic. First, recall that the generalized lift rule given in TR-11 had the embarrassing property that the syntactic category of the derived expression was such that it happened to preserve word order. That is, when the lifted version of *Porky* (which is $S/_R(S/_LNP)$) combines with a VP like *grunted* (of category $S/_LNP$) the lift rule ensures that it takes its VP argument to its right. In the first place this was just stipulated as part of the rule. We might have expected the lift rule itself to give an underspecified category. But then the general word order directional slash rules (given in (3) in Chapter 6) would make the category $S/_L(S/_LNP)$. So we need an extra stipulation here to override the general case: this is reminiscent of the discussion earlier about the lexical entry for *every* (see section 10.2.2). Worse, this stipulation makes it a complete accident that the lifted material takes the function as its argument to give exactly what we would have gotten had the function expression taken the original expression as its argument. And of course we also have the possibility of output expressions of the general form $A/_L(A/_RB)$. This is the general form of the category of lifted VPs (thus these are $S/_L(S/_R(S/NP))$ and here we need to ensure that they take the generalized quantifier to their left (just as the generalized quantifier would have taken the unlifted version to its right), again making it looks like an odd coincidence that the lifted VP combines with a GQ to give exactly what we would have gotten had the GQ combined with the unlifted VP.

But it actually is no accident that it works this way if lift is an operation on syntactic categories as well as on the meanings. Recall that section 6.5 posited that any category of the form $A/_DB$ (for D some directional feature) corresponds to a (Curry'ed) function taking two strings as argument and returning a third. Given that, there is a natural connection between the semantic operation *l* and the syntactic operation performed by the lift rule. Speaking informally, what it means to be a *lift* of a category A means to

PP[TO], where one can derive one meaning from the other (see Exercise 9.10). But since both meanings are of type $<e,<e,<e,t>>>$, a type mismatch hardly "explains" the difference in meaning. Second, one must still predict which shifts exist and which don't. And third, under this sort of teleological view of the grammar, there is no explanation as to which mismatches are allowed by the syntax in the first place (nor, of course, any explanation as to why the syntax would allow these mismatches).

return a category B/(B/A) which is such that when an expression in this category combines with an expression of category B/A, the result is the same as when the B/A combines with the homophonous (unlifted) expression in B. To formalize this, we define **L** as an operation on syntactic categories where **L** is defined in terms of the functions that correspond to each category.

(13) *Definition:*
  For any category A, $L_B(A)$ is any category such that for all expressions x of category A and all expressions y and z such that [x] = [z], $F_{L_B(A)}([y])([z]) =$ $F_{CAT(z)}([z])([x])$.

This looks slightly different from ordinary lift for the simple reason that the strings themselves are not functions (unlike the meanings of those strings). Rather, the category of a string corresponds to a function and it takes one argument more than does the corresponding meaning of the string, and this fact is reflected in the above definition. To see the connection between this we can state this in prose: the lift of any category A is a category with the following property: for any x in A, the new category is such that when applied to an expression y and then an expression z (whose phonology is the same as that of x) the result is the phonological string that one gets by taking the function associated with the category of z and applying it to x. Since x is an expression whose category is A, it follows that z must have as its category B/A (for some B), and that x must therefore be of category B/(B/A). Notice also that for any category A, $L_B(A)$ is not unique (hence L_B is not a function). For NP, for example, $L_S(NP)$ is both $S/_R(S/_LNP)$ and $S/_L(S/_RNP)$.

This might seem like quite a bit of trouble to generalize the two outputs of L(A) rather than simply listing them as $B/_R(B/_LA)$ or $B/_L(B/_RA)$, but it has at least three advantages. First, it makes the details of the lifted categories nonaccidental, capturing the idea that the fact that word order is preserved is not stipulated but is part of the definition of the operation. Second, it naturally extends if there are additional operations such as Wrap. (See the extended fragment in Chapter 6.) Thus if there are items of category $A/_WB$ whose corresponding function is as defined in the fragment in Chapter 6 there needs to be one additional slash which is $A/_IB$ (I for infix); the definition of $F_{A/_IB}$ can be supplied by the reader. Thus giving a general definition of L allows an A to lift to $B/_I(B/_WA)$ and so forth. The third advantage concerns the lexical category of quantificational determiners, to which we return directly.

From here on we will use the convention of bold italics to notate semantic operations (operations on model-theoretic objects); bold capital letters for operations on syntactic categories, and bold lower-case non-italics for names for the full rules. Moreover, whenever there is need to specify the ultimate result category of some category $L(A)$, we notate that as $L_B(A)$, as was done above. As usual, subscripts will be omitted when not needed.

Armed with this, we can recast the lift rule so that it does not stipulate the slash directionality on the output—it simply says that the input category A maps to $L(A)$. Hence we revise TR-11 to rule R-4, which will also be referred to as **l**:

R-4.   Let a be an expression of the form $<[a], A, [[a]]>$. Then there is an expression β of the form $<[a], L_B(A); \lambda f_{<a,b>}[f([[a]])]$ (i.e., $l_b([[a]]))>$.

(Since $L_B(A)$ is not unique, R-4 actually allows an expression to map to more than one output expression.)

We now also have a solution to the problem of the lexical category of quantificational determiners. Recall that we have listed these as $(S/_R(S/NP))/N$ where the R feature was stipulated in order to override the default rules. But we can now solve this by saying that the category itself in the lexicon is not spelled out as above, but is simply $L_S(NP)/N$. Note, incidentally, that this means the category can be spelled out in two ways, either as $(S/_R(S/_LNP))/_RN$ or as $(S/_L(S/_RNP))/_RN$, hence expressions like *every dog* are both $S/_R(S/_LNP)$ and $S/_L(S/_RNP)$. Finally, there is no problem with the grammar being "tricked" into thinking that an item like *every* is a verb and undergoing verbal morphology. Although its ultimate result category is S, it is not specified in the lexicon the way verbs are.

11.6. Summary: The fragment so far

The following lexical items and rule are added to the fragment from Chapter 8:

Lexicon: because these are all constant functions from worlds, we leave off the world parameter:

The determiners without domain restriction:

$<[every], L_S(NP)/N, \lambda P[\lambda Q[P_S \cap Q_S = P_S]]>$
$<[some], L_S (NP)/N, \lambda P[\lambda Q[P_S \cap Q_S \neq \emptyset]]>$
$<[no], L_S(NP)/N, \lambda P[\lambda Q[P_S \cap Q_S = \emptyset]]>$
$<[three], L_S(NP)/N, \lambda P[\lambda Q[|P_S \cap Q_S| \geq 3]]>$
$<[most], L_S(NP)/N, \lambda P[\lambda Q[|P_S \cap Q_S| > |P_S|]]>$

The determiners with domain restriction (temporary; to be revised in Chapter 15 without use of a free variable for the domain):

<[every], L_S(NP)/N, $\lambda P[\lambda Q[P_S \cap D \cap Q_S = P_S]]$>

and so forth for all of the others above.

In addition there are complex determiners like *exactly three, at most three, less than half*, but since these ultimately need to be compositionally derived from their parts, we will not include them here:

<[didn't], X/X, $\lambda F_{<a,t>}[\lambda A_a[\sim F(A)]]$, where X is restricted to S/NP or S/(S/(S/NP))>

Definition of l: For any x (of any type) in a set X and any set Y, $l_Y(x)$ is a function in <<X,Y>,Y> such that for all f in <<X,Y>,Y>, = $l_Y(x)$ = f(x).

Definition of L: For any category A, L_B(A) is any category such that for all expressions x of category A and all expressions y and z such that [x] = [z], $F_{L_B(A)}([y])([z]) = F_{CAT(z)}([z])([x])$.

Rule l:

R-4.   Let a be an expression of the form <[a], A, [[a]]>. Then there is an expression β of the form <[a], L_B(A), $\lambda f_{<a,b>}[f([[a]])]$ (i.e., $l_{<a,b>}([[a]])$)>.

12

Generalized conjunction

12.1. Generalizing *and* and *or*

The last several chapters featured instances of *and* and *or* conjoining expressions of a variety of categories, where the semantic contribution of *and* and *or* is often intersection and union respectively (more accurately, as the Curry'ed versions of these two binary operators). But to say that the semantics is always intersection/union is not quite right. In the first place, as was hopefully discovered in Exercise 5.6, one cannot collapse S conjunction and VP conjunction in this way. In the case of S conjunction, intersection is of the set of worlds characterized by each of the daughter Ss, which means that intersection crucially is of *intensions*. The case of VP conjunction involves intersection only once the world argument has been supplied; here it is intersection of the *extensions*. Moreover, there are cases of more complex expressions which can conjoin. Take for example the case of transitive verbs:

(1) a. Br'er Fox chased and caught Br'er Rabbit.
    b. Tim watched and hated the movie.

Transitive verbs have meanings of type $<s,<e,<e,t>>>$. Even considering just their extensions, they are of type $<e,<e,t>>$—they do not characterize a set, and so they do not denote the kind of object that can be intersected. Still, one might have the intuition that these all involve intersection "at the end of the day." In other words, [[watched and hated]] (ignoring the world argument) is λx[watched'(x)$_S$ ∩ hated'(x)$_S$]. For that matter, one can see everything as ultimately tied in to ordinary first-order propositional &, for to be in the intersection of two sets A and B is to be in A *and* to be in B. All of the remarks above hold for the parallel case of union with respect to *or*.

This is exactly the idea that Partee and Rooth (1983) pursue in giving a single cross-categorial definition and meaning for *and* and *or*. They first recursively define a binary operator *meet*, notated Π. Π is defined for any two members of the set of truth values, and for any two functions f and g, f Π g is defined if for all x, f(x) Π g(x) is defined. Moreover, for the base case—where Π takes two truth values and returns a third—its semantics is just &. This is given in (2i). The recursive definition allows it to take two complex functions (of the same type), each of whose ultimate result is a truth value and return a function of the same type as the inputs, and the definition is given in (2ii) (here we use the notation (a,b) for ordered pairs):

(2)   i. Given two truth values a and b (i.e., members of {1,0})
        a Π b = a & b (i.e., Π = (1,1) → 1, (1,0) → 0, (0,1) → 0, and (0,0) → 0)
   ii. Given two functions f and g such that f Π g is defined, f Π g =
        λx[f(x) Π g(x)].

Then *and* can be listed in the lexicon as being of category (X/X)/X, with meaning λA[λB[A Π B]]. This meaning is just Curry'ed Π.

A similar treatment is available for *or*. First we recursively define *join*, notated ΙΙ. As above, it is defined for any two members of the set of truth values, and for any two functions f and g, f ΙΙ g is defined if for all x, f(x) ΙΙ g(x) is defined. The base step again is the same as first-order v, and the recursive step is parallel to the definition of Π:

(3)   i. Given two truth values a and b (i.e., members of {1,0})
        a ΙΙ b = a v b (i.e., ΙΙ = (1,1) → 1, (1,0) → 1, (0,1) → 1, and (0,0) → 0)
   ii. Given two functions f and g such that f ΙΙ g is defined, f ΙΙ g =
        λx[f(x) ΙΙ g(x)].

The full lexical entry for *or*, then, is <[or], (X/X)/X, λA[λB[A ΙΙ B]]>. Both of these, then, are given a generalized meaning that applies to a variety of semantic types, and are given a cross-categorial syntax.

Notice that, since English contains no expressions that are of type t (the lowest type are expressions of type <s,t>) the lowest meaning of *and* is λp$_{<s,t>}$[λq$_{<s,t>}$[p Π q]] which is the same as λp$_{<s,t>}$[λq$_{<s,t>}$[λs$_s$[p(s) & q(s)]]], and this is found in ordinary S conjunction cases such as *Porky grunted and*

Trickster howled. However since we are systematically ignoring intensions, we can for practical purposes in this text take the lowest type meaning of *and* to be just $\lambda p[\lambda q[p \ \& \ q]]$ and this is what is used in conjoining S. For the case of VP conjunction (keeping everything extensional again, as always), the recursive definition gives *and* the meaning $\lambda P_{<e,t>}[\lambda Q_{<e,t>}[\lambda x_e[P(x) \ \& \ Q(x)]]]$ which is the meaning we've been using all along. Thus the intersection of two sets is everything that is in both sets, which is equivalent to $\lambda P_{<e,t>}[\lambda Q_{<e,t>}[P_S \cap Q_S]]$.

Now consider a more complex case, such as the case of transitive verbs as in (1a). We show this using the full syntactic and semantic composition in (4). We add the directional slashes throughout, but of course in all cases these are not part of the lexical entries but are supplied by the word order rules given earlier in (3) in Chapter 6.

(4) caught, $(S/_LNP)/_RNP$, caught'
    and, $(X/_LX)/_RX$, $\lambda A[\lambda B[A \ \Pi \ B]]$
    and caught, $((S/_LNP)/_RNP)/_L(S/_LNP)/_RNP))$, $\lambda R_{<e,<e,t>>}[\text{caught'} \ \Pi \ R]$
    chased and caught, $(S/_LNP)/_RNP$, caught' Π chased' $=$
       $\lambda x[\text{caught'}(x) \ \Pi \ \text{chased'}(x)] =$
       $\lambda x[\lambda y[\text{caught'}(x)(y) \ \Pi \ \text{chased'}(x)(y)]] =$
       (since we are ignoring the world argument)
          $\lambda x[\lambda y[\text{caught'}(x)(y) \ \& \ \text{chased'}(x)(y)]]$
    Br'er Rabbit, NP, r
    chased and caught Br'er Rabbit, S/LNP, $\lambda x[\lambda y[\text{caught'}(x)(y) \ \& \ \text{chased'}(x)(y)]](r) =$
      $\lambda y[\text{caught'}(r)(y) \ \& \ \text{chased'}(x)(y)]$
    Br'er Fox, NP, f
    Br'er Fox chased and caught Br'er Rabbit, S, $\lambda y[\text{caught'}(r)(y) \ \& \ \text{chased'}(x)(y)](f) =$
      caught'(r)(f) & chased'(r)(f)

In prose, what *and* does when it conjoins two transitive verbs such as *chased and caught* is create a new complex transitive verb which is the relation that holds between two individuals a and b just in case a chased b and a caught b. Notice that in showing the composition of (4), we rewrote *caught' Π chased'* by two steps to the equivalent $\lambda x[\lambda y[caught'(x)(y) \ \& \ chased'(x)(y)]]$. This has the opposite effect, as does λ-conversion; here a formula is being rewritten as a longer one. But it is useful as it is more readable. Once again one should bear in mind that converting one formula to another is just a way to write meanings in a way which might be easier to read, but it is not necessary (except, of course, when asked for in an exercise).

> **12.1.** Show the full syntactic and semantic computation for (i) (treat *briar patch*) as a single unanalyzed noun. Use the model in (4).
>
> (i) Every rabbit or some fox entered the briar patch.
>
> **12.2.** a. Show the full syntactic and semantic computation for (i):
>   (i) The rabbit is happy and healthy.
> b. Now do the same for (ii). Caution: Keep in mind the word order rules for adjectives that modify nouns.
>   (ii) the happy and healthy rabbit

12.2. Remarks on noun conjunction

Noun conjunction presents an interesting problem. Consider (5):

(5)   Every man and woman voted in the election.

There are two points to notice here. The most striking is the fact that the lowest type meaning is absent: this does not have a "hermaphrodite" meaning, where it claims that everything which is both in the [[man]] set and in the [[woman]] set voted. On the other hand, (5) is quite easily understood as synonymous with *every man and every woman voted in the election*.

> **12.3.** Show how the grammar developed so far predicts the existence of the reading in which (5) means the same as *every man and every woman voted in the election.* You will need to think about how to type-lift *man* and *woman* to get the appropriate meanings.

As shown by Exercise 12.3, it is not surprising that *every man and woman* can have a meaning which is the same as *every man and every woman*. But what is surprising, perhaps, is the lack of the hermaphroditic meaning. Now in this particular case it is tempting to place the entire burden on the pragmatics. Such a reading is obviously absent (or at best difficult to access) because our world does not contain hermaphrodites. One might push this reasoning further. Recall the remarks in Chapter 8 that many of the concepts that get lexicalized as nouns (at least as those which are often referred to as *basic-level* nouns) tend to be sets that are mutually exclusive—a tiger is not also a lion and a table is not also a chair. Thus in many cases the pragmatics will rule out the intersection of the lowest types reading (that is, the intersection of the sets which correspond to the basic lexical meaning of the two nouns will necessarily be empty, and hence a listener assuming a cooperative speaker will recompute to the higher types). Unfortunately, this cannot be the whole story. For even when we choose nouns whose sets are very easy to intersect, and even when we stack the context to bring out this reading, the relevant reading still seems to be absent or, at least, extremely difficult.[1] For example, take the context of a club for both students and faculty who enjoy any kind of outdoor activity, including skiing, hiking, and bungee jumping. If we saw a notice that the club would be hosting a meeting that was open only to *every bungee jumper and professor,* we would be unlikely to conclude that the invitees to the meeting are just those who are both professors and bungee jumpers. A student bungee jumper and a professor hiker would seem to be invited as well.[2] (The judgments are, however, delicate, and the interested reader is invited to construct other examples and perhaps do some systematic informant work in order to elucidate the full pattern.)

Similar facts hold with relational nouns. Thus expressions of the form *RN₁ and RN₂* generally lack the reading: $\lambda x[RN_1{}'(x)_S \cap RN_2{}'(x)_S]$ (for RN an abbreviation for N/PP[OF]). This is again true even when the pragmatics makes such a reading quite available, as in (6).

(6)   a.   Every cousin and fellow student of John is coming to his party.
     b.   Every professor and employer of Maria will write her a very good recommendation.

---

[1] There are cases where this reading does emerge, as in (i) (discussed in Partee and Rooth 1983 and attributed to unpublished work by R. Cooper):

(i)   Every wife and mother is underpaid.

[2] Further complexities arise when the determiner is *a*; here it often becomes much easier to get the "missing" reading, as in:

(ii)   A student and bungee jumper is running for election.

(ii) is most naturally understood with the lowest type meaning where a single person who is in the intersection of students and bungee jumpers is running.

We thus leave this as an interesting and unsolved problem. (See also n. 2.)
Interestingly, *or* is quite well behaved in this regard. Note the following:

(7) a. Every professor or bungee jumper is invited to the meeting.
    b. Every man or woman will be allowed to vote in the special election.
    c. No student or bungee jumper came to the demonstration.

Certainly the primary reading of, for example, (7b) is the reading obtained
by having [[every]] take as argument the union of the men and the
women sets.

12.4. i. Show the full derivation for this reading (showing only the
derivation of the GQ *every man or woman*) and show that this
GQ is equivalent to the GQ *every man and every woman*.
ii. Show the full derivation using the simplest types for *no student
or bungee jumper*.

Not surprisingly, (7b) also has a secondary reading which can be brought
out with the continuation "but I can't remember which" (see Exercise 12.3
for the derivation of this reading), but in this case this is definitely the less
accessible reading, as the lowest types hypothesis predicts.

Looking ahead, section 13.4.4.2 will entertain the possibility of adopting
a slight variant of the Partee and Rooth proposal, in which *and* and *or* are
both listed in the lexicon with their simplest meanings and categories (where
they conjoin only sentences) and where the extra meanings and categories
are derived by a unary rule.

12.3. Summary: The fragment so far

To the fragment in Chapter 11, add the following lexical items:

<[and], (X/X)/X, $\lambda A_x[\lambda B_x[A \sqcap B]]$> (for x the semantic type of expressions of
category X)
<[or], (X/X)/X, $\lambda A_x[\lambda B_x[A \sqcup B]]$>

PART III

Relative Clauses, Scopes, and Binding: Some Theoretical Controversies

13

Relative clauses: Sketching two accounts

13.1. Preliminaries

This chapter and the following two approach three phenomena (relative clauses, GQs in object position, and pronominal binding) from two different points of view. For each case we present a relatively standard non-Direct Compositional account of the domain, followed by a Direct Compositional account. There are several reasons for developing two different accounts of each phenomenon—not the least of which is to introduce some of the theoretical controversies in the literature. Beyond that, seeing what the different points of view have in common gives a deeper understanding of the domains and of the generalizations that hold across theories. And of course an understanding of more than one account enables one to read literature written from a variety of theoretical perspectives. That said, a reader approaching all of this material for the first time might worry about a possibly confusing overload. Such a reader might want to initially work through the technical details of just one of the approaches across the three chapters while skimming the other, and return to the details of the other account only on a second pass.

The concern in this chapter is the syntactic and semantic composition of NPs and GQs which contain relative clauses, such as those in (1):

(1) a. the house which Jack built
     b. the house that Jack built
     c. the house Jack built
     d. every rat which the cat chased
     e. no mouse who chased Calico

Some initial caveats are in order. Both theories developed here are intended as sketches, for we ignore a number of interesting issues and details have been amply documented in the syntactic literature. For example, no account will be given of cases involving the phenomenon known as *pied-piping*. This term refers to examples in which the front of the relative clause contains not just a single relative marker, such as *that* or *which*, but a more complex phrase containing a relative pronoun (*which*, *who*, etc.) within it (in all the examples below, the pied-piped phrase is italicized); the last example is (slightly modified) from Ross (1967) and shows that the pied-piped material can be quite complex:[1]

(2) a. the house *into which* Jack ran
     b. the rat *whose mother* Calico chased
     c. the king *the cousin of whom* the Duchess was engaged to
     d. the reports *the height of the lettering on the covers of which* the government proscribes

Moreover, for both theories developed below, the treatments of the actual relative pronoun (*which*, *who*, *whose*, etc.) are almost certainly incorrect. In both cases, the treatments are designed purely for expository convenience. In fact there is little point in worrying too much about how to fold in the contribution of the relative pronoun without also giving an analysis of the cases in (2) since an adequate treatment must generalize to the pied-

---

[1] The colorful terminology comes from Ross (1967). His observations were framed in a theory in which the *wh*-word and the material surrounding it "moves" to the front, and the metaphor involves the *wh*-word as the Pied Piper and the rest of the material that tags along with it as either the rats or the unfortunate children of Hamlin.

piping cases.[2] Relatedly, we will say little about relative clauses with *that* (as in (1b)) and with no relativizer (as in (1c)). Finally, we ignore many of the syntactic complexities that are well known in the literature under the rubric of *island constraints*. The goal is only to develop two different approaches to the basic semantic composition coupled with (in each case) a general sketch of how the syntax works. Interestingly, the two approaches do converge on the meaning of the relative clause itself, even though they get there by very different methods. And those different methods themselves will figure in quite prominently in the discussion in the next two chapters.

13.2. What do relative clauses modify?

13.2.1. The noun modification argument

But before considering the internal composition of relative clauses, we turn to a question hinted at briefly in section 1.1: does a relative clause combine the noun or with the entire NP or GQ? (This question is independent of the theoretical debate elucidated later in this chapter.) In other words, is a phrase such as *every table which Martha refinished* put together as illustrated in (3a) or as illustrated in (3b)?

(3)   a. every [table which Martha refinished]
       b. [every table][which Martha refinished]

> **13.1.** As shown above in (1), relative clauses occur both within expressions where *every* is the determiner and within those where *the* is the determiner. Thinking only about the syntax, does this fact bear on the choice of the two possibilities illustrated in (3)? Can both theories handle this fact with no additional complexities in terms of the syntactic combinatory rules (or, in CG terms, the category of a relative clause)?

[2] Accounts of this phenomenon compatible with the general framework assumed here can be found in Sharvit (1998) and Jacobson (1998), both of which should be accessible after Chapter 15. A somewhat different type of account goes under the rubric of "reconstruction" (see Chomsky 1977) and a more recent version of this known as the "copy theory of movement" (see Fox 2002, 2003).

The question was discussed in syntactic terms at least as early as Stockwell, Schachter, and Partee (1972) (much earlier work simply assumed the structure in (2b); see, e.g., Ross 1967).[3] But in a seminal paper, Partee (1975a) pointed out that the semantics can be used to help answer this question; the semantic composition is much more straightforward under (3a) than under (3b).[4]

To show this, we make the assumption that the relative clause *which Martha refinished* denotes (relative, of course, to a world and a time) the characteristic function of the set of things that Martha refinished. (Or perhaps it is a fancier packaging of this, as in the treatment of prenominal adjectives in section 8.4.3. But since that will not affect the discussion, we use the simpler type for exposition.) The semantic composition of (3a) is thus straightforward: the relative-clause meaning—a set of individuals—intersects with the noun meaning (another set of individuals). The determiner then combines with a complex noun (which denotes a set of individuals) in the perfectly routine fashion. So, whether the noun happens to be complex (e.g., *table which Martha refinished*) or simple (e.g., *table*), it denotes a set. Obviously fancier cases like *every table which Martha refinished which Jack sold* are equally straightforward—the complex noun *table which Martha refinished* combines with another relative clause to give another complex noun and the semantics is again intersection.

Now consider how the semantic composition would have to work under (3b). For the sake of discussion, we quite crucially ignore the possibility that [[every table]] has a domain restriction slot (see section 10.6), and take [[every table]] to be the set of sets of individuals that have the table set as a subset.[5]

---

[3] Prosodic evidence would also seem to favor the account in (3b) since there is generally a prosodic break after *table*. However, as pointed out at least as early as Chomsky (1965) the prosodic evidence can be quite misleading.

[4] These remarks assume a Direct Compositional approach to at least this construction. That is, the semantics gives evidence only under the assumption that (at least in this case) the syntactic composition and the semantic composition are the same. In a theory in which they are divorced and where a syntactic representation is mapped into a different LF, one could break these apart, and one could assume that the syntax is as in (3b) and mapped into an LF more like (3a). As far as this author is aware, this has not been explored in the literature.

[5] This is not a trivial simplification. As will be noted in 13.2.2, the argument elucidated in 13.2.1 actually needs to be rethought if the domain restriction "slot" (which we have represented so far as a free variable) is part of the meaning of the GQ.

If the material is put together as in (3b), we need to define an operation that maps the set of sets having [[table]] as subset to the set of sets having as a subset the set of things that are both tables and are things that Martha refinished. In other words, the model-theoretic object shown in (4a) (given here in function terms) needs to be mapped to the object in (4b):

(4)   a. $\lambda P[\forall x[\text{table'}(x) \rightarrow P(x)]]$
       b. $\lambda P[\forall x[[\text{table'}(x) \ \& \ \text{refinished'}(x)(\text{martha})] \rightarrow P(x)]]$

The term model-theoretic object is stressed here to ward off the temptation to think that the solution lies in mapping the *formula* in (4a) into the more complex one in (4b). Obviously this can be done: simply define an operation that takes any string "S_1" on the left of the arrow and within the narrowest bracket / and converts that into the string "$S_1 \ \& \ S_2$" where "S_2" is the representation of the relative clause in some symbolic representation such as the non-English language defined in section 9.1. But this is not an operation on meanings but rather on syntactic formulas, and thus not a possible way for the semantics to work. Since (4a) and (4b) both name functions of type <<e,t>,t>, the task is to formulate the operation that maps the (4a) function to the (4b) function. Or, returning to set terms, the operation will—for any set A (the denotation of the relative clause)—map (5a) to (5b):

(5)   a. $\{B| \text{ table's} \subseteq B\}$
       b. $\{C| \text{ table's} \cap A \subseteq C\}$

There is such an operation but it is complex, and so is left as an advanced exercise for the ambitious.

---

*13.2. Be ambitious. In other words, show the operation that will derive the set of sets [[every table that Martha refinished]] from [[every table]] and more generally will derive for any set S [[every-N S]] from [[every-N]]. A hint to get started: think first about how—given the set of sets—one can recover the set of tables from [[every table]], i.e., how one can map [[every table]] into [[table]].

Regardless of the complexity of the operation, the implausibility of this solution becomes evident upon noticing that different quantificational determiners require different operations. Thus things would have to either be very non-compositional or the grammar would need to assign a different category to, e.g., *some* as it assigns to *every* (and yet other categories to other determiners). To show this, notice first that the operation for *every* (i.e., the operation that maps (5a) to (5b)) involves mapping some set P (a set of properties) into some superset of P. To convince oneself of this, note that any property P in the set [[every-table]] (i.e., every property P that holds for every table) certainly holds for every table that Martha refinished (since, after all, each such table is a table). But the reverse does not hold. If every table that Martha refinished is made of wicker then [[is made of wicker]] is in (5b) but not necessarily in (5a). Thus there are properties in the (5b) set that are not in the (5a) set. (Readers who have already read Chapter 16 can note that this is the same as the observation that [[every table that Martha refinished]] is weaker than [[every table]].)

It is now easy to see that the operation that derives the meaning in (5b) from (5a) cannot possibly be the same operation that derives [[some table that Martha refinished]] from [[some table]]. For clearly [[some table]] has more sets in it; there might be a crooked table (hence [[is crooked]] is in [[some table]] but it is not necessarily in the set [[some table that Martha refinished]] (she could be quite careful to only refinish uncrooked tables). So here the operation that combines the relative clause meaning with the GQ meaning would have to map a set into a subset. (Again, for readers familiar with the notion of strength in Chapter 16, one can note that here [[some table which Martha refinished]] is stronger than [[some table]], reversing the pattern for *every*.)

Thus (given the assumptions made here about the meanings of the GQs and the relative clauses), the only way to have two different operations at work without abandoning compositionality would be to say that *some table* and *every table* are actually of different syntactic categories. This would allow the grammar to use a different operation when each of these combined with the relative clause. And yet other operations would be needed for the case of other GQs like *no table*. At this point it is quite clear that the compositional semantics is much simpler under the analysis in (3a); the set denoted by the relative clause simply intersects with the noun set, as in other cases of noun modification.

> ***13.3.** State what the operation would need to be for combining [[some N]] with a relative clause meaning and do the same for [[no N]]. Once again begin by considering how one could map [[some N]] (for any N) into [[N]], and similarly for the case with *no* as determiner.

*13.2.2. But—not quite so fast...

Like so many other things in semantics, the story does not end here. (Since the further twist has no effect on the subsequent discussion in this book, this section can safely be skipped.) Bach and Cooper (1978), drawing on evidence from Hittite, argued that the grammar must be able to put things together in the way shown in (3b) and that, moreover, there are ways that this can be done without positing different categories for each GQ.[6] We will neither give their Hittite evidence here nor spell out their proposal in detail, as it requires some complex use of variables, but we will sketch the idea. Recall that the discussion directly above crucially ignores the possibility that GQs such as *every table* come with a domain restriction slot or "variable" as part of its meaning; see the discussion in section 10.6. Bach and Cooper's proposal makes use of the existence of this piece of meaning: it combines the semantics of the relative clause with the semantics of the GQ in such a way as to have the relative clause satisfy the domain restriction. This is not enough, for there must be a new slot or variable for a domain restriction even after the relative clause combines with the GQ. There are two reasons for this. First, additional relative clauses are possible (so-called *stacked relatives*) as in:

(6) a. every table which Martha refinished which was brought to the Antiques Road Show

b. every table which Martha refinished which was brought to the Antiques Road Show which was appraised for more than a thousand dollars etc.

---

[6] But we really don't need to consider only Hittite to suspect that language does allow the semantics to put things together in the way shown in (3b). And this is because English contains lexical GQs (*everybody, nobody, someone*, etc.) and these of course can combine with relative clauses, as in *nobody who voted for the proposal* or *everybody who loves the snow*, etc.

Each subsequent relative clause presumably would be filling the domain restriction in the GQ with which it combines, and therefore a new domain restriction piece must be added with each subsequent relative clause. Secondly, even when a GQ contains a relative clause, it is still understood relative to some contextually set domain. Thus if I tell you that *every student who took formal semantics got an A* you once again will not interpret this as meaning every student in the world who took formal semantics but more likely would restrict this to the students in my formal semantics class this year (or some other contextually relevant domain). Thus an analysis in which the relative clause fills the domain restriction piece must be supplemented with something that introduces a new slot or variable each time. See Bach and Cooper (1978) for one proposal and Jacobson (1983) for an alternative cast without use of variables.

For the remainder of this chapter, however, we will adopt the analysis in (3a), since supplying the details of an alternative analysis is beyond our scope. As noted above, nothing in the subsequent discussion hinges on this, for the concern for the rest of the chapter is with the internal semantic (and syntactic) composition of the relative clause. And either way, the relative clause itself denotes a set of individuals (or perhaps a fancier packaging of a set).

13.3. An account with movement and traces: Assignment functions in grammar

We now return to the question of how the meaning of the relative clause is put together. The first account to be considered here is relatively standard, and is generally phrased in terms of a theory with a non-Direct Compositional architecture where the syntax computes representations which are interpreted by the semantics. For the case at hand, it suffices to view "surface structure" as what is interpreted (but see section 14.2), and where that structure itself is derived by a series of rules mapping one syntactic representation into another. In particular, this theory assumes movement rules in the syntax. For a relative clause as in (7), the relative pronoun *which* moves from its original position as object of *built* to the front of the relative clause (as indicated by the lines). Thus the syntax computes these representations in a series of steps and the representations serve as the input to the semantics. This account is also usually coupled with the (logically independent) assumption that each NP comes with an index (a positive integer), and that when it moves it leaves a phonologically empty "trace" in the original position, where that trace bears the index of the original item. We have arbitrarily picked the index 8 here:

(7)   every house [which$_8$ [Jack built t$_8$]]

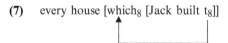

The semantics thus interprets a structure roughly like (7). Since the goal in this text is not to develop an explicit fragment within this framework, we will not actually formulate the movement rule in any generality; a variety of versions can be found in almost any introductory syntax text within the group of theories that go under the rubric of Government and Binding, Principles and Parameters, or Minimalism (as well as many other earlier theories maintaining transformations).

We will, however, elaborate the internal structure a bit for the purposes of developing the semantic composition. Thus assume that the structure after movement (and which inputs the semantics) is actually the more elaborated version in (8). (Part of the motivation here for some of the particular details is to be able to generalize this to another case discussed in Chapter 14.) Note that this assumes that when *which* moves, its index is copied onto the node labeled Λ here, (8) also assumes that the index on *which* remains after movement, but since it plays no role in the semantic computation it actually makes no difference whether it remains or not. Very often we will omit the index on the moved *wh*-item. We use label RC for the relative clause; the name is inconsequential:

(8)

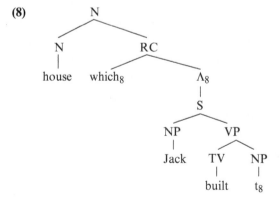

There are, incidentally, a variety of slightly different notations that could have been adopted. Following, for example, the treatment of a related case in Heim and Kratzer (1998) one could treat "8" as a phonologically null element which is a sister to S rather than recording it as a feature on the node labeled Λ. The choice is purely a matter of notation.

Since we are not using the Categorial Grammar fragment here, we need to say something about how structures of this sort in general are interpreted. Leaving aside for the moment the contribution of the trace, and leaving aside the interpretation of the node labeled Λ, we can essentially take the fragment up through Chapter 5 and recast the semantics as rules that work compositionally (hence, bottom-up) to interpret local trees (as was done in Exercise 5.1). In other words assume that there is a rule to the effect that an S with two daughters NP and VP will have as its value (extensionalizing) [[VP]]([[NP]]). All of this can be cast more naturally in a type-driven framework (see section 6.5): for any node A with two daughters B and C, if [[B]] is a function in <c,a> and [[C]] is a member of c, then the denotation of the mother (A) will be [[B]]([[C]]). Following Heim and Kratzer (1998) assume that another type-driven principle is that for any two sisters B and C which are such that they both have meanings of type <a,t> (for any type a), the meaning of the mother is the characteristic function of the intersection of the sets that each daughter characterizes. (See the relevant discussion surrounding APs in section 8.4.1.)

But the full interpretation of (8) involves one major new piece of apparatus that our treatment of English has so far not required: the use of assignment functions. To add this to the semantic toolbox involves essentially the moves that were introduced earlier in Chapter 9 for the two non-English languages. Thus assume that in addition to worlds, times, individuals, and truth values we have a set of *assignment functions* (or simply *assignments*) G. For now, take each assignment g to have as its domain the set of positive integers, and as its co-domain the set of individuals. Assume further that the interpretation of any actual linguistic expression is relative to assignments. Put differently (and somewhat non-standardly) the meaning of any expression is a function from the set of assignments to something else. (For example, a sentence denotes a function from G to functions of type <s,t>; a VP is a function of type <G,<s,<e,t>>> and so forth.) As seen earlier in the artificial languages with variables, any expression that contains nothing "unbound" within it is a constant function from G. Thus [[every dog]] is a function G to a function of type $<<e,t>,t>$ but it is a constant function from G, and each g in G receives the by now familiar value.[7]

As is undoubtedly obvious, the role of the assignments is of course to give an interpretation to the trace (and later to pronouns). Thus while "normal" expressions like *Jack, build, house, the,* and so forth have the same value on all assignments, traces do not. They function just like the variables introduced in Chapter 9; their value varies with assignments, and depends on just what the assignment assigns to their index. (Since all NPs come with an index, the reader might wonder whether the same is true of ordinary NPs such as *the house* or, for that matter, even *Jack.* For these too will have an index: and so one might wonder whether [[the house]]$_8$ is different from [[the house]]$_9$? We will assume not and will assume that the indices play a role only in the interpretation of traces and pronouns. The function of the indices on the full NPs is relevant only when that NP moves and leaves a trace.) Thus for any index n and any assignment g, [[t_n]](g) is g(n). We will use the more normal convention of putting the assignment as a superscript: thus, for any g, [[t_n]]^g = g(n). This changes all the semantic rules, but in a perfectly straightforward way. For example, the rule interpreting a local tree whose mother is S and whose daughters are NP and VP now says that for all g, [[S]]^g = [[VP]]^g([[NP]]^g). The assignments are thus folded into the combinatorics just like the world and time arguments are once the rules are fully intensionalized.[8] If everything is bound in some expression, its value is a constant function on the set of assignments.

Consider, then, the tree in (8). The interpretation of the VP-node is a function from assignments to $<e,t>$ functions (as usual ignoring the worlds and time) such that for all g, [[VP]]^g = [[built]]^g(g(8)). Note [[built]] is constant on all g, and that g(8) is some individual; hence the VP is a function that maps any g to the set of individuals who built whatever it is that g assigns to 8. Moving up the tree, for any assignment g, the value of

---

[7] Heim and Kratzer (1998) develop an interesting alternative where the assignments are partial functions, and assign values only to those integers which correspond to indices on "unbound" material within the relevant expression. This does have some advantages; see Chapter 9, n. 2.

[8] Hence the value of an expression is a function from worlds, times, and assignments to something else. Incidentally, the order in which these different arguments are taken makes no difference: just as the worlds and times are independent of each other so too are the assignments independent of worlds and times.

S is the proposition that Jack built whatever it is that g assigns to 8. This is a non-constant function from assignments to propositions. The actual proposition that it denotes depends on what assignment one uses.

The interesting action comes in the next step: the interpretation of the node labeled Λ_8. This is similar to the non-English rule NER-8 of Chapter 9, and is given here in (9). Because this is not going to be a part of the ultimate Direct Compositional fragment developed in the book, no rule number will be assigned to it. Moreover, since this is embedded in a framework in which the input to the semantics are trees, we will formulate the rule that way:

(9) $\left\| \begin{array}{c} \Lambda_n \\ | \\ S \end{array} \right\|^g = \lambda a_e [[[S]]^{g: n \rightarrow a}]$

In prose, this says that for any assignment g and any local tree labeled Λ_n whose daughter is the single node S, the value of Λ_n on g is the function from individuals to propositions which maps any individual a to the value of the daughter S on the assignment function just like g except that (if it differs at all) the integer n is mapped to a.

To illustrate, suppose that Jack built the Vanderbilt mansion and the White House, but did not build the Breakers. Suppose that g_1 assigns 8 to the Vanderbilt mansion; g_2 is exactly like g_i except that it assigns 8 to the Breakers, and g_3 is exactly like the others except that here 8 is assigned to the White House. Then the value of the S-node in 8 is 1 on g_1, 0 on g_2, and 1 on g_3. Now we compute the value of Λ_8 in (8) on each assignment, beginning with g_1. This value is the function that takes each of Vanderbilt, Breakers, and White House and assigns either 1 or 0. First we see that Vanderbilt is mapped to 1 because [[S]] on g_1 is 1. The reason that the value of S on g_1 is the crucial one to consider is that g_1 is the assignment just like g_1 in all respects except (if there is any difference) 8 is mapped to Vanderbilt. In this case, it happens that that there is no difference; here the assignment that g_1 "looks to" is itself. The Breakers is mapped to 0 on g_1, because here g_1 "looks to" g_2 (which is the assignment just like g_1 except that in this case 8 is mapped to Breakers). The value of the S on g_2 is 0; for [[S]] on g_2 is the proposition that Jack built $g_2(8)$, which is the proposition that Jack built the Breakers (which is false). Similarly, White House will be assigned 1. It is easy to see that g_1, g_2, and g_3 are all assigned the same value (a function of type <e,t>) at the level of the node labeled Λ_8 since they all "look to" each other. In this way, just like NER-6 in Chapter 9, what happens here is that the value of the S-node is a (generally) non-constant function from assignments to propositions, while the value of the Λ-node is now a function from assignments to <e,t> functions, and for all assignments that differ only on the value assigned to the relevant integer, it is a constant function.

Moving up the tree, the next question concerns the contribution of *which*. We have set things up here in such a way that *which* actually makes no contribution: its ultimate contribution was just to mark where it had moved from in such a way that that position (the object of *built*) is a trace. To use a technique which has already been introduced, we will take the tack of having [[which$_8$]] (on any g) be the identity function on functions of type <e,t>.[9] (Note that there are actually an infinite number of lexical items *which* since it has an index: even if the index is removed after movement it has to be there before movement and so there must be these different items. But they all have the same meaning as things are being set up here.) Thus [[which$_8$ Jack built t$_8$]] is (on any g) the characteristic function of the set of things that Jack built. Note too that so will be [[which$_7$ Jack built t$_7$]]; once the trace is "bound" at the Λ step its index does not matter.

Finally, the meaning of the expression *house which Jack built t$_8$* is put together by the intersection of [[house]]$_S$ and [[which$_8$ Jack built t$_8$]]$_S$. Of course, this is oversimplified in that neither of these two expressions denote just sets of individuals, but rather have as their value functions from assignments to sets. In both cases they have the same value on all assignments, so one can assume that the semantics will specify that the value of the mother node N on an assignment g is the value of [[house]]$_S{}^g$ intersected with [[which Jack built t$_8$]]$_S{}^g$. And of course this need not be specified for this particular construction, but would follow from a type-driven principle as discussed above.

---

[9] An alternative is to simply have *which* have no meaning, and have a convention that for any local tree with two sisters A and B where one is meaningless, the meaning of the mother is the meaning of the meaningful daughter.

Many of the details here could have been worked out slightly differently. But the key point of this analysis is that it makes use of (a) movement of the relative pronoun to leave an indexed trace; (b) the use of assignments in order to interpret the indexed trace; (c) the rule that "binds" the trace—i.e., the rule which is the interpretation of the node labeled Λ, and (d) a view of grammar in which the input to the semantics is representations (and in this case representations that are derived in the syntax not just by something like phrase structure rules but also by movement rules).

13.4. Consider a case of so-called *stacked relatives*, as in (i):

(i) the house which Jack built which Sarah sold

The two occurrences of *which* could happen to have the same index, but nothing would ensure that. Take, then, the following structure (for the complex N portion only) which is one structure the grammar would assign to the N:

(ii)

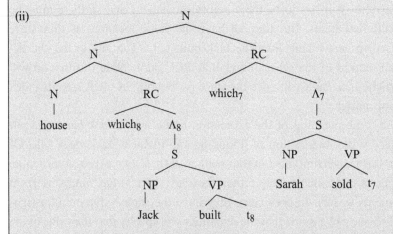

Show, for any assignment g, the value of each node in this tree. (The simplest way to write this out is to first number every node in the tree so that you can refer to each distinct node.) Suppose that the second occurrence of *which* (the one that moves from object position of *sold*) had had the index 8 instead of the index 7. Would this have made any difference in terms of the meaning of the entire expression shown in (ii)? Why or why not? Would this have given some of the subparts different meanings?

13.4. A Direct Compositional (and variable-free) analysis

We now consider this domain in a Direct Compositional setting (and also a setting without movement or indices). The basic idea for an account of constructions like relative clauses that makes no use of movement goes back to at least Gazdar (1982) and later work within Generalized Phrase Structure Grammar (see Gazdar, Klein, Pullum, and Sag 1985). Several similar proposals were subsequently put forth within the Categorial Grammar literature. Here we initially adopt one CG version which is roughly that in Steedman (1987), although it will contain various modifications.

13.4.1. Preliminaries: Function composition

First we introduce the operation known as function composition. Take a function f from A to B and a function g from B to C (any two of those sets could happen to be the same). Then the two functions can be composed into a new function notated as gof which is a function from A to C, where for any x in a, gof(x) = g(f(x)). (Thus gof = $\lambda x[g(f(x))]$.) The basic intuition becomes clear with a single example. Let f and g both be functions illustrated in (10), where the members of set A are in the left-hand column, the members of B in the middle column, and the members of C in the right column.

(10)   f   g

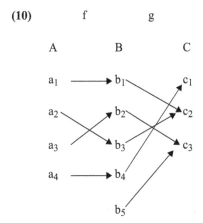

Then g of maps a_1 to c_2, a_2 to c_1, a_3 to c_3, and a_4 to c_1. Since f and g are functions (i.e., each member of A is assigned a unique value in B by f, and each member of B is assigned a unique value in C by g), it is easy to see that the gof is also destined to be a function.

We now (temporarily) add two rule schemata to the fragment. In section 13.4.4 it will be shown that each of these can be unpacked into a different rule followed by the ordinary application schemas (R-1a and R-1b). But even after making this move, the rules here are convenient to refer to as a shorthand for two rules, and so we will call them CR-5a and CR-5b (Collapsed Rule) and will refer to them as the function composition schemata (we give these just extensionally):

CR-5a.   Let a be an expression of the form $<[a], A/_RB, [[a]]>$ and β is an expression of the form $<[\beta], B/_RC, [[\beta]]>$ then there is an expression γ of the form $<[a\text{-}\beta], A/_RC, [[a]]\circ[[\beta]]>$.

CR-5b.   Let a be an expression of the form $<[a], A/_LB, [[a]]>$ and β is an expression of the form $<[\beta], B/_LC, [[\beta]]>$ then there is an expression γ of the form $<[\beta\text{-}a], A/_LC, [[a]]\circ[[\beta]]>$.

Suppose there are three expressions: a of category $A/_RB$, b of category $B/_RC$, and c of category C. Notice that the grammar now allows two different ways to compose the string [a-b-c] and prove this a well-formed expression of category A. One is the normal "application-only" derivation shown in (11a) and the second is a derivation involving function composition followed by application as shown in (11b) (we will represent these with trees, showing the rule used for the composition of each of the larger expressions):

(11)   a.

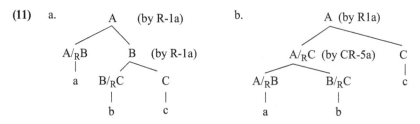

Both modes of combining these expressions give rise to the same ultimate string [a-b-c]. They also give the same meaning. Thus note that the first application-only derivation puts the meanings together so that the ultimate string has the meaning a'(b'(c')). (The prime notation is used here rather than brackets for readability; recall that these are interchangeable.) The derivation represented in (b) puts the meanings together as follows: a'ob'(c'). But by definition of function composition, for all x a'ob' is the same as a'(b'(x)), and so the meaning of the final result in (11b) is a'(b'(c')). Thus the two different ways to put the string together converge on the same word order and the same meaning.

One might notice that so far, it is just a stipulation that CR-5a and CR-5b happen to preserve word order. That is, CR-5a for example stipulates that the expression of category $B/_RC$ will go to the *right* of the expression of category $A/_RB$, but as written here this is an accident. It would have been just as easy to write a rule which put the $B/_RC$ expression to the left of the other. Similarly, it appears to be an accident of the way we have written the rules that the output is $A/_RC$ and not, say, $A/_LC$. Either possibility would have wreaked havoc with the fragment, and gives all sorts of strange word orders that do not exist. But in fact, we need not think of this word-order-preserving property of the function composition schemas as an embarrassing accident. (This is reminiscent of the remarks made earlier with respect to type lifting.) Recall that for any expression x of category X, there is an associated function F_X such that $F_X([x])$ is a function from strings to strings. Hence the actual syntactic categories in CR-5a and CR-5b can and ultimately should be restated in terms of actual function composition. After all, the very definition of function composition ensures that the string put together by the combinatorics aob(c) has the same word order as the "application-only" derivation a(b(c)). More specifically, for any string x of category $A/_RB$, y of category $B/_RC$, and z of category C, $F_{A/_RB}([x]) \circ F_{B/_RC}([y])([z]) = F_{A/_RB}([x])(F_{B/_RC}([y])([z]))$ so it follows that the composite of the two relevant functions is the function corresponding to the category $A/_RC$ (similar remarks, of course, hold for the left-slash cases). For this reason, this view also ultimately allows CR-5a and CR-5b to be collapsed as one function composition rule (just as R-1a and R-1b can be collapsed). However, for present purposes we simply continue to list the two composition schemata separately (and stipulatively), but number them in such a way as to indicate that they can be collapsed.

Consider now some actual English examples such as those in (12):

(12)   a. Every fox chased Br'er Rabbit.
　　　b. Calista loves model-theoretic semantics.

Every fox in (12a) is a GQ; its full category is $S/_R(S/_LNP)$ (recall that we arrive at this category by listing *every* in the lexicon as being of category $L_S(NP)/N$; see the discussion in section 11.5.) Thus (12a) can be derived not only in the usual application-only way but also as shown in (13) (for simplicity, no domain restriction piece is included as part of the meaning of the GQ):

(13)   every fox; $S/_R(S/_LNP)$; $\lambda P[fox's \subseteq P_S]$
chased' $(S/_LNP)/_RNP$; chased'
every foxed chased; $S/_RNP$; $\lambda P[fox's \subseteq P_S]$ o chased' (by CR-5a) =
$\lambda x[\lambda P[fox's \subseteq P_S](chased'(x))]$ =
$\lambda x[fox's \subseteq chased'(x)_S]$
in prose: this is the set of individuals x such that the fox set
is a subset of the chasers of x
(hence: the set of individuals that every fox chased)
Br'er Rabbit; NP; b
every fox chased Br'er Rabbit; S, $\lambda x[fox's \subseteq chased'(x)_S](b)$ =
$fox's \subseteq chase'(b)_S$

Should the last line appear confusing, one can convert that into the follow-ing equivalent but perhaps less confusing way to write it: $\forall x[fox'(x) \rightarrow chase'(b)(x)]$. Since an ordinary "NP" like *Calista* can lift to be a GQ, a parallel derivation exists for (12b). We leave this as Exercise 13.5; note that [[Calista loves]] is the set of individuals that Calista loves.

> **13.5.** Show the full syntactic and semantic composition for (12b) under the derivation where *Calista* first combines with *loves*. Treat *model-theoretic semantics* as an unanalyzed NP as if it were listed in the lexicon (i.e., you need not give its internal composition).

13.4.2. Interlude: Coordination

Enter a thoroughly appalled syntactician: "But wait! How can one possibly be as naive as to propose that sentences like (12a) or (12b) have a structure in which the subject and the transitive verb form a constituent rather than the transitive verb and object forming a VP constituent? Don't we learn from our most elementary syntax books that there is a VP constituent and that therefore the transitive verb must always combine first with its object?" Actually, we (presumably) do know that the verb *chased* **can** combine with its object first to form a VP, but it does not follow from this that this is the only possible derivation (i.e., "structure") for these sentences.

Recall the discussion in section 5.1. What is the evidence for a VP constituent? The most robust piece of evidence concerns coordination; we find conjoined cases like (14):

(14)   Calista loves model-theoretic semantics and hates syntax.

But this shows only that there is one derivation in which *loves* combines first with *model-theoretic semantics* (to conjoin with *hates syntax*); it does not show that there can't also be a second derivation of (12b). (Readers familiar with other standard arguments for constituent structure might also be worried about those; we address some in the Appendix to this chapter.)

Conjunction cases like (14) show that the derivation for (12b) that fits the compositional picture illustrated in (11a) does in fact exist, and this of course is the evidence that there is a "VP" constituent in English. But is there any evidence that the derivation illustrated in the abstract in (11b) also might exist? That is, is there any evidence that *Calista loves* can also be a constituent in (12b)? Quite strikingly, the answer is yes: we need only turn the conjunction argument around. For there are also sentences like (15), which have traditionally gone under the rubric of *Right-Node Raising*:

(15)   Calista loves and Gollum hates model-theoretic semantics.

It is well worth pausing for a moment to consider the common wisdom on sentences like (15). Many textbooks argue that only constituents may conjoin—as has been assumed throughout this book—and that conjunction is therefore a test of constituency. But under "standard" accounts there is no way for *Calista loves* and *Gollum hates* to be treated as constituents. Faced with such apparent counterexamples to the generalization that "only con-stituents conjoin," various additional mechanisms are proposed for cases like (15). For example, one common view is that (15) underlyingly consists of two sentences (*Calista loves model-theoretic semantics and Gollum hates model-theoretic semantics*), and the two instances of the object NP *model-theoretic semantics* move to the right and merge into a single NP. And there are other proposals as well (see, e.g., Williams 1978; McCawley 1987), but all involve additional complexities in the grammar. In fact, it is somewhat ironic that many introductory textbooks contain the adage (accepted here) that conjunction is a test for constituency, and then go on to call cases like (15) and other related cases instances of "non-constituent conjunction." Assuming that conjunction is indeed a test for constituency, we must conclude that *Calista loves* and *Gollum hates* are both well-formed constituents (i.e., well-formed expressions). This is part of the beauty of the CG account of these: the addition of the function composition schema CR-5a is sufficient to predict that *Calista loves* is an expression of category $S/_R NP$ as is *Gollum hates*. That the two can conjoin is completely expected by the cross-categorial treatment of *and*. The semantics works out exactly as it should; this is left for the reader to verify in the next exercise.

> **13.6.** Give the syntactic and semantic composition of (15), adding nothing to the fragment except for the function composition schemata in CR-5a and CR-5b.

Before returning to relative clauses, it is worth noting that there are many other cases of so-called "non-constituent coordination" that are accounted for by the addition of FC. Consider for example each of the cases in (16):

(16)　a. Calista loves and believes that Gollum hates model-theoretic semantics.
　　　b. Mitka dashed into and destroyed the chicken coop.

We have not yet folded prepositions like *dash* into our fragment, nor have we yet incorporated embedded sentences (as in simple cases like *Barbara believes that Paul hates model-theoretic semantics*). But an interested reader can easily figure out the syntactic categories involved for all of the items above within a CG syntax, and can show just how it is that the syntax will allow these. The semantics will also be straightforward once we have the semantics for basic items like *believe* (which involves incorporating intensionality into the fragment and hence is postponed) or *into* (which involves a more thorough treatment of prepositions), but again an interested reader can see how the semantics would work for these additional cases of "non-constituent" coordination. In each case, the term "non-constituent coordination" is incorrect; these simply involve the coordination of constituents.

> ***13.7.** An especially interesting case of "non-constituent coordination" which falls out under the analysis here is (i), which is discussed in Dowty (1988):

i. Captain Jack served lobster yesterday and bananafish today.

Assume first that *yesterday* and *today* are VP modifiers (in CG terms, they are of category $VP/_LVP$, where the L feature is given by the word order rules in (3) in Chapter 6. To give their meanings clearly requires an intensional semantics since they each take time-dependent sets as their input and crucially return new time-dependent sets. For the purposes of this question, then, we need to oversimplify (having not yet fully folded in intensionality); simply assume (counterfactually) that [[yesterday]] and [[today]] are each of type $<<e,t>,<e,t>>$ and don't worry about the details of their meaning.

   With that oversimplification, show that (i) can be derived from the fragment developed here (with the addition of the function composition schemata), and show that its meaning will be the same as the meaning of (ii):

ii. Captain Jack served lobster yesterday and Captain Jack served bananafish today.

Hint: Feel free to help yourself to the use of the fully generalized type-lifting rule R-4 in Chapter 11, especially as concerns the object NP.

13.4.3. Returning to relative clauses

13.4.3.1. The basic account
Other than the coordination facts, is there any other evidence that expressions like *Barbara loves* are well-formed expressions in the language? Do they exist in any other environments? The answer again is yes: these are exactly the sort of expressions that combine with relative pronouns in relative clauses, and with questions words in *wh*-questions (as in, for example, embedded questions like *I wonder what Barbara likes*). In short, these occur in traditional *extraction* or *wh-movement* constructions. We can thus speculate that relative pronouns and question words themselves are listed with some category like $X/(S/_RNP)$, where X here is a placeholder (it will have one value in the case of questions and another in the case of relative clauses).

Before fleshing out the full details of the syntactic and semantic composition for the relative-clause case, we should note that expressions of category $S/_R NP$ (such as *Calista loves*) do of course have a far more limited distribution than ordinary "VPs"—i.e., expressions of category $S/_L NP$ (as in *loves model-theoretic semantics*). The latter (with varying morphologies) occur as complements of auxiliary verbs like *will*, *have*, *be*; and as complements of verbs like *like*, etc.

(17)   a. Calista will [love model-theoretic semantics]
    b. Calista has [loved model-theoretic semantics] (for at least 30 years)
    c. Calista is [loving model-theoretic semantics]
    d. Calista likes [teaching semantics]

Auxiliaries thus presumably are of category $(S/_L NP)/_R(S/_L NP)$ (in each case the complement is specified for a certain morphological feature, and the reason that auxiliaries and verbs like *want* are not treated by the grammar as modifiers is that the fine-grained category for which they select is not identical to the result category). There are, however, no auxiliary-like items which ask for an $S/_R NP$ complement; we do not find hypothetical auxiliaries like *fung* that occur as follows:

(18)   *Sally fung [Calista love]

But this is not surprising. After all, note that the auxiliaries in the lexicon merely say that they take complements of the form S/NP. The fact that these complements are $S/_L NP$ and not $S/_R NP$ is a fact about the general word order rules spelled out in (3) in Chapter 6. If the auxiliary *has*, for example, is listed simply $(S/NP)/(S[PERF]/NP)$ then the general word order rules will spell this out more fully as $(S/_L NP)/_R(S/_L NP)$. Thus it is predicted that expressions like *Calista love(s)* occur only with items that specifically override the default rules or in conjunction which is entirely cross-categorial.

Presumably, then, relative pronouns and *wh*-question words have the special status that they are listed in the lexicon as combining with $S/_R NP$. (They also combine with expressions of category $S/_L NP$ as in *every mouse who/which chased Calico*. A more sophisticated treatment of these words would remedy this; here we just list two separate syntactic categories for these in the fragment.) We can now turn to the full composition of *every table which Martha refinished*. Recall that the movement account developed in 13.3 posits the structure in (8), where the trace has an index and where the S *Martha refinished* t_8 has as its interpretation a proposition relative to assignments. But it shifts its meaning (by the rule in (9)) to denote on each assignment the set of things that Martha refinished. This is constant on all assignments and so, for all intents and purposes, the expression *Martha refinished t_8* (as a constituent of category Λ_8) denotes a set. We formulated things in such a way that [[which Martha refinished t_8]] also is (on all assignments) a set.

The Direct Compositional version sketched here—which makes no use of traces and no use of indices or assignments—ends up with the same result but gets there in a different way. Notice that function composing the lifted (GQ) [[Martha]] with [[refinish]] directly results in an expression *Martha refinished* which denotes the set of things that Martha refinished. The derivation of this is exactly analogous to the derivation of *Calista loves* which was worked out in Exercise 13.6. There is no need to assume that *refinish* combines in the syntax with an actual NP (such as a trace) and no reason to assume that [[refinish]]—of type $<e,<e,t>>$—needs to actually find an argument of type e to combine with. Indeed it does not find such an argument, but is composed with the GQ subject.

As in the view sketched in 13.3, we need to say something about the syntactic and semantic contribution of *which*. Keeping in mind that we are simplifying for the sake of exposition, assume a new primitive syntactic category, which we will label RC whose semantic type is $<e,t>$.[10] The syntactic function of the relative word *who* or *which* is to map an $S/_R NP$ into an RC, so we give this the category in the lexicon $RC/(S/_R NP)$. (The fact that *which* takes the $S/_R NP$ to its right follows from the general slash-directional rules in (3) in Chapter 6.) As done in 13.3,

---

[10] In standard movement views this is not the usual category label for relative clauses—they are usually considered to be some kind of "CP," where CP is the label for embedded clauses in general. But they do not have the same distribution as ordinary CPs such as the complement of *think* in *Chris thinks that the world is flat.* Nor do they have the same internal structure, and—as will be shown below—they do not have the same kind of meaning either. There are various ways in the standard view to account for those differences; one is to have a feature on the CP node which distinguishes relative clauses from ordinary CPs. In the end, then, some difference must be found and there seems to be no real reason to think of these as CPs. But the label is arbitrary, and should one wish, one could take "RC" to be really something like CP[REL]. This is merely a matter of nomenclature.

we take its meaning by the identity function over functions of type $<e,t>$. Thus [[which]] is $\lambda P[P]$.

The remaining step is to allow an expression of category RC to combine with the noun to give a noun. As was the case with noun-modifying adjectives discussed in Chapter 8, there are two possibilities. One is to simply add a new rule schema to the effect that an RC can occur to the right of a noun, and the meanings of the two combine by set intersection. This, incidentally, is essentially parallel to the tack taken in "standard" approaches.[11] The other is to posit a unary rule shifting an RC to an N/N with the semantics exactly like that of the shift from AP to N/N. We will choose the latter here for this can be achieved with very little that is new. Since the output category is the same as that in R-2 and the semantics is also the same, we need merely slightly amend R-2 (**mod**) as follows:

(R-2)   Let a be an expression as follows: $<[a],$ AP or RC, $[[a]]>$. Then there is an expression β: $<[a], N/N, \lambda P_{<e<e,t>>}[\lambda x[P(x) \& [[a]](x)]>$.

13.8. Show the full syntactic and semantic computation of (i) and (ii) under the Direct Compositional approach:

(i) every table which Martha refinished
(ii) the woman who Calista saw the cousin of
(iii) every course which Calista loves and Gollum hates

---

[11] Thus some rule or principle is needed to ensure that expressions of the form *which Mabel refinished* etc. combine with nouns. It is often suggested in elementary discussions of X-bar theory that the fact that certain kinds of "adjuncts" (or modifiers) occur with certain items need not be stated on a case-by-case basis, but follows from a general X-bar theory rule of the form X-Bar → X-Bar YP, where the relative-clause category simply instantiates YP here. But of course this is not enough; the theory needs to be supplemented with rules/principles specifying *what* instances of YP go with what categories instantiating X. In other words, let CP [REL] be the category for relative clauses; it can instantiate YP when X is instantiated by N but not if X is instantiated by, e.g., V. In the end, the X-bar rule schemata are not schemata in the sense here; they do not fully specify exactly what particular rules do and do not exist.

Finally, it is well known that relative clauses can be indefinitely complex in terms of embedded sentences; we find, for instance, examples like (19):

(19) the planet which Chris believes that Sarah said that Calista saw

Consider first a simple case like (20):

(20) Chris believes that Calista saw Jupiter.

We have actually not introduced embedded sentences yet because (as already noted) a full semantic treatment requires the full intensional apparatus, for the semantic object which combines with [[believe]] is not a truth value but a proposition. Hence [[believe]] is of type $<<s,t>,<e,t>>$. But we can simplify at this point and take [[believe]] and [[say]] to be of type $<t,<e,t>>$. We also introduce a new primitive syntactic category CP which is the category for *that Calista saw Jupiter* and we take expressions of this category to have meanings of type t (ultimately, of course, of type $<e,t>$). Let *that* be listed in the lexicon as $<[that]; CP/S; \lambda p_t[p]>$ and let *believe* be listed $<[believe]/; (S/NP)/CP; [[believe]]>$. (The listing for *say* is analogous.) With this apparatus, (19) can be derived.

13.9. Show the syntactic and semantic computation of (19).

13.4.3.2. Syntactic loose ends

There are some awkward details in the account here. In particular, the category RC is (borrowing terminology from Gazdar and Sag 1981) a *phantom category*. It is the category for *which Mabel refinished*, but there is no item (at least not in the fragment developed here) that asks for such a category as argument. In fact it shifts to N/N and only then combines with the noun, and so it seems a bit silly to posit this intermediate category. Why not simply have *which* and *who* take the $S/_R NP$ and directly give the noun modifier? In other words, why not list *which* as in (21) (and similarly for *who*):

(21) $<[which], (N/N)/(S/NP), \lambda P_{<e,t>}[\lambda Q[\lambda x[P(x) \& Q(x)]]]>$

In fact, this is the solution in Steedman (1996). We have resisted the temptation to do this (at the expense of needing the strange category RC) for several reasons. First, it does not capture the commonality between the semantics of modification by APs and by RCs (here R-2 takes both AP and RC as input to yield N/N). Second, in the long run, the category RC can be revised to be simply the label for S with a certain feature on it, a feature that indicates that it has a pronoun within it, making it a less odd category. In the variable-free treatment of pronouns that will be discussed in Chapter 15 this is quite natural and the fact that the type of this expression is of category <e,t> is also automatic. And third, under the variable-free view the semantics of the relative word can be subsumed under the semantics of pronouns in general, which ultimately allows a treatment of the pied-piping cases (see Jacobson 1998). The category and meaning for *which* in (21) extends in no obvious way to cover the pied-piping cases. This book, however, will not have space to discuss pied-piping (nor the semantics of relative pronouns) any further, and so here we will just live with the awkwardness of the category RC and the (perhaps somewhat unintuitive) idea that the relative word has as its meaning $\lambda P_{<e,t>}[P]$.

There are other loose ends. We have provided no account of relative clauses where the "gap" is internal, such as those in (22) (where ___ indicates the gap site):

(22)   a. the book which Bill believes [__ pleased George]
       b. the story which George read __ to the children

Indeed the function composition schemata put things together in such a way that the "missing argument" can only be on the right edge of an expression or on its left edge. There are many actual and potential variants of the proposal discussed here designed to remedy this. One would be to extend the whole system to incorporate Wrap slashes. Another is to allow some additional schemata (see, for example, Steedman 1996). Still another strategy is proposed in Oehrle (1990) which combines some of the insights of the Steedman (1987) proposal discussed here with ideas that are much more similar to the (related) proposal in Gazdar, Klein, Pullum, and Sag (1985). We leave it to the interested reader to pursue some of this literature, which should be accessible at this point. Finally we have said nothing about various ill-formed cases—in particular the cases known in the literature as island constraint violations (Ross 1967). The above literature contains some discussion of relevance, and there is a vast literature questioning whether such violations really should be accounted for in the grammar or are instead derivable from facts about information structure (see, e.g., Kuno 1975) or other processing considerations (see, e.g., Kluender 1998).

---

*13.10. One of the constraints discussed in Ross (1967) is the Coordinate Structure Constraint; in movement terms this was phrased as "no movement out of a coordinate structure." This was designed to predict the ill-formedness of expressions like:

(i) *the table which Sally built chairs and Mabel refinished __

There has, however, been considerable discussion in the literature as to whether this is really a syntactic problem or simply violates various constraints on information structure. Advocates of the non-syntactic explanation point to perfectly well-formed cases like those in (ii):

(ii)   a. the beer which Sam went to the store and bought __
       b. the piece of property which either Sally is going to win the lottery or she
           will have to sell __

Does the account of coordination here predict the ill-formedness of (i) or not? Are there assumptions about *and* that one could make that would change the answer? *Note:* Your answer will depend on exactly what it means to say that *and* is cross-categorial and is listed as (X/X)/X. For the purposes of this question, take that statement to mean that X is an underspecified category in the lexicon which is more fully specified before *and* combines with anything. Thus, for example, *and* can receive the full specification (S/S)/S or (VP/VP)/VP and these items then combine by the normal rules. You might want to revisit this question after reading 13.4.4.2.

13.4.4. A refinement: The Geach rule

13.4.4.1. The rule and its application to relative clauses (and coordination)

The function composition analysis presented above can be modified slightly to recast function composition as a unary rule; this has some advantages which will be shown below. The revision involves what is known in the CG literature as the *Geach rule* (see Geach 1970) or alternatively *Division*, and is a very simple mapping from functions to functions. In particular take any function f of type <a,b> and any set c. Then f can be mapped to a function which we will call $g(f)$ of type $<<c,a>,<c,b>>$, where $g(f) = \lambda C_{<c,a>}[\lambda x_c[f(C(x))]]$. In prose: the new function $g(f)$ takes as argument any function C from c to a, and then any member x in c, and returns the value that f assigns to C(x). Of course, as with other operations that we have discussed, g is really a family of operations, because for any function f of type $<a,b>$, g is not uniquely defined; it can yield a function of type $<<c,a>,<c,b>>$ or $<<d,a>,<d,b>>$, etc. We can use g just to mean the set of all of these functions, and when we need to distinguish one from the other we can use the notation, for example, $g_c(f)$. The interesting thing to notice is that this is nothing more than a unary version of the function composition operator. (Recall that any binary operator such as function composition which simultaneously takes two arguments—in this case two functions— to return some value can be Curry'ed to take its argument one at a time. Thus g is the Curry'ed version of the binary function composition operation.)

One can easily get the intuition of g combined with an appreciation of its value for the Direct Compositional program by an example. Ignoring worlds and times, consider the relationship between the first-order proposisitional negation $\sim$ and the meaning of English *didn't* which is VP negation. The latter can be defined in terms of the former as follows:

(23) $[[didn't]] = \lambda P_{<e,t>}[\lambda x[\sim P(x)]]$

Notice that $[[didn't]]$ is $g(\sim)$ (more technically, it is $g_e(\sim)$); in this case g maps a function of type $<t,t>$ into one of type $<<e,t>,<e,t>>$. We are not suggesting that *didn't* is derived from $\sim$ by a productive rule in the grammar here; rather, its lexical meaning boils down to $g(\sim)$. This example also illustrates the usefulness of this notion for the Direct Compositional program. At first glance, the contribution of the negation in *Porky didn't grunt* would seem to correspond to ordinary first-order logic $\sim$ which is a proposisitional operator. In the syntax, on the other hand, *didn't* combines with a VP to give a VP. (Of course, as pointed out earlier, even this is an oversimplification, since the real negation is *n't*; we return to this point directly.) One temptation, then, for reconciling this apparent mismatch between the syntax and the semantics is to posit that the negation raises at LF so that the relevant representation for this which inputs the semantics is [not [Porky grunted]]. But the Direct Compositional strategy is simply to posit that the obvious meaning is just packaged in a slightly fancier way, and in this case taking [[didn't]] to be $g(\sim)$ does the job. The moral can be applied to many other cases as well: whenever there is something that at first glance seems to scope over sentences in the semantics but takes smaller scope in the syntax, one can posit that it is actually the Geach'ed version of the obvious meaning.

In fact, as noted repeatedly, positing a primitive lexical item *didn't* is still not quite true to English grammar; negation is expressed by the word *not* or the clitic *n't* which actually combines with auxiliaries. But one can simply apply another round of the *g* operation to give the actual meaning for *n't*. (For simplicity, we will leave our fragment as is with *didn't* as the negation, but the revision would be simple and an interested reader can work this through; part of this is suggested in the next exercise.)

13.11. Ignoring the fact that each auxiliary selects for a VP with a certain kind of morphology, auxiliaries are of the category VP/VP (i.e., (S/NP)/(S/NP)) with meaning of type $<<e,t>,<e,t>>$). The syntax of English must also be set up in such a way that only the first auxiliary in a chain of these combines with *n't* (an interested reader might try to find ways to ensure this via a judicious use of features and giving auxiliaries more fine-grained categories in terms of the featural composition of the VPs that they select).

The task here, though, is not to give a full account of the syntax, but to show that the meaning of *n't* can be given in terms of the meaning of ~ using two applications of *g*. Show how this can be done. (Keep in mind that—ignoring intensions—auxiliaries are of type $<<e,t>,<e,t>>$.) Note too that the syntactic category of *n't* is such that it takes an auxiliary to its left to produce an auxiliary. Of course, more needs to be said to account for the fact that *n't* is not an independent word. Finally, the English auxiliaries crucially refer to the world and time parameters of the VPs with which they combine; *will* for example obviously really combines with expressions of type $<i,<e,t>>$ since it says something about times, and *can*, *may*, etc. crucially combine with expressions of type $<w,<e,t>>$ as statements containing these are statements about possible worlds. Hence the semantics you give above will be just a sketch without folding

(cont.)

in intensions, but the basic sketch should be clear using the simplified extensional types. Simply take as your task to have the sentence in (ia), for example, have the same truth conditions as the paraphrase in (ib), and similarly for other auxiliaries:[12]

(i) a. The crocuses won't bloom in February this year.
     b. It is not the case that the crocuses will bloom in February this year.

Similar remarks hold for other items that seem to have semantic scope over sentences but in the syntax have a much smaller scope such as past-tense morphology.

Returning to the analysis of relative clauses, notice that since g is nothing more than the unary (Curry'ed) version of the function composition operator, the two rules in CR-5a and CR-5b can be recast instead as unary rules; we do so in R-5:

R-5a. Let a be an expression of the form $<[a], A/_RB, [[a]]>$. Then there is an expression β of the form $<[a], (A/_RC)/_R(B/_RC), g_c([[a]])>$ (for c the semantic type of expressions of category C).

R-5b. Let a be an expression of the form $<[a], A/_LB, [[a]]>$. Then there is an expression β of the form $<[a], (A/_LC)/_L(B/_LC), g_c([[a]])>$ (for c the semantic type of expressions of category C).

---

[12] There is actually an interesting complication that we ignore here. In general, an auxiliary with *n't* attached at the end gives rise to a meaning where the negation scopes over the auxiliary, as is shown in the paraphrases in (i) and (ii). Hence *can't*, for example, means (roughly) "not can"; *You can't go home that way* can be paraphrased as *It is not the case that you can go home that way*. But *must* has the opposite behavior: *You mustn't drive without a license* doesn't mean "It is not the case that you must drive without a license" but rather "You are obligated to not drive without a license." This has the odd result that *can't* and *mustn't* mean more or less the same thing. To make matters even stranger, this fact is not general: the auxiliary-like item *need*—which on the face of it has a meaning similar to *must*—is well behaved. This can be observed by thinking about the meaning of "You needn't drive without a license." The observation about *must* and *can* is due to Horn (1972).

We will refer to these rules as the **g-sl** schemata ("sl" here is for "slash" and
the reason for this name will be clarified in Chapter 15 when a second **g** rule
is introduced). As with the case of CR-5a and CR-5b and the earlier case of
type lifting, the actual directional features on the slashes in the syntax need
not be stipulated under the view that the syntactic category of a string x
corresponds to a function F, such that F([x]) is a function from strings to
strings. We will not work through the details here, but see the discussion
above with respect to CR-5. Since the *g* operation is just a Curry'ed version
of the function composition operator, those remarks extend straightforwardly to this case. Should there be slash features using wrap, this too can
be incorporated. Moreover, these two rules will ultimately be collapsed into
one under that view; again we list them separately here for expository
convenience.

> **13.12.** Redo the derivations for (15) in the text and for (ii) from Exercise
> 13.8 using R-5a instead of CR-5a. If ambitious, do the same for (i) in
> Exercise 13.7.

Is there any particular reason to prefer the two-step version (**g-sl** plus **app**)
over direct function composition? Indeed there is, and this is reminiscent of
other cases where it turns out that a unary rule rather than a new binary
combinatory rule was useful. That is, the two-step solution gives the intermediate step (i.e., a step in which the relevant expression has just undergone
g-sl), which might be the input to other rules. And one of those rules that
could apply to the intermediate step is **g-sl** itself; in other words with the
intermediate step the rule can apply recursively. The advantage of this is the
subject of Exercise 13.13. It is also interesting to note that the revised
solution here is actually somewhat closer to the spirit of the similar analyses
in the Generalized Phrase Structure Grammar literature and the Head-
Driven Phrase Structure Grammar literature (see the slash-passing conventions in these theories).

> **13.13.** Show that recursive application of this rule predicts the possibility
> of coordination in cases like (i) (you can give just the syntax; you need not
> give the semantics, and refer to the category CP and the category of

(cont.)

believe given above in the discussion surrounding (20). (Notice that this sentence is more natural with *but* instead of *and*, but for simplicity we give the version with *and*.) You don't need to worry about the internal structure of *was corrupt*.

(i) Raymond admitted that some and denied that every candidate was corrupt.

*13.4.4.2. Generalized *and* as generalized g-sl?

There is an obvious way to generalize the **g** operation such that it applies to n-place functions, and "opens up" each of the argument slots to themselves be functions. Without giving this in fullest generality, we illustrate with the case of the generalization to a function f of type $<a,<b,c>>$. This can be mapped to something that we will call **gen-g$_d$**(f) which is a function of type $<<d,a>,<<d,b>,<d,c>>>$ such that:

(24) $gen\text{-}g_d(f) = \lambda X_{<d,a>}[\lambda Y_{<d,b>}[\lambda D_d[f(X(D))(Y(D))]]]$

It should be obvious that this can be generalized for functions of any number of places.

What is especially interesting here is that the recursive definition of Π and ΙΙ given in (2) and (3) in Chapter 12 involves precisely successive applications of **gen-g** to the Curry'ed first-order & and v (i.e., the operators of type $<t,<t,t>>$. To show this, we begin with the base step of Curry'ed & which we will call AND, which is $\lambda p[\lambda q[q \& p]]$. Then the case of conjoining two expressions of type $<e,t>$ to give a new one of type $<e,t>$ involves the generalized operator shown in (25a), which is exactly (25b):

(25) a. $\lambda P_{<e,t>}[\lambda Q_{<e,t>}[\lambda x[AND(Q(x))(P(x))]]]$
      b. $gen\text{-}g_e(AND)$

The meaning of *and* used to conjoin two generalized quantifiers is $gen\text{-}g_{<<e,t>,t>}(AND)$. This item takes AND of type $<t,<t,t>>$ and maps it to a new meaning of type $<<GQ,t>,<<GQ,t>,<GQ,t>>>$ (where GQ is shorthand here for $<<e,t>,t>$). Since conjunction always works on expressions whose final result is a truth value (notice that the generalized definition of Π ensures this), every instance of [[and]] can be derived from AND by a succession of application of **gen-g**.

Does this have any interest beyond the sheer fun of noticing the relationship between the various tools discussed so far? Actually, it might (the remarks here are speculation and are designed to invite the reader to think more about these issues). Thus, one might entertain the possibility that *and* and *or* are not listed cross-categorically in the lexicon. Rather, suppose there is a single lexical item *and* as follows: <[and], (S/S)/S, AND>. (This of course cannot be exactly right since the lowest type for *and* is actually of type <<s,t>,<<s,t>,<s,t>>> while AND is of type <<t,t>,t>, but—as usual—the appropriate refinement is straightforward.) Similar remarks hold for *or*. Then we can derive other versions of *and* and *or* by application of **gen-g** to these items. Notice that we have left off the slash directionality in the above; if this is the right way to think about the cross-categorial status of *and* and *or* the rules need to be stated more fully to give the appropriate directional features on the slashes. We leave further discussion of this for the intentionally quite open-ended exercises below.

*13.14. Assume that the above suggestion is correct as an account of the polymorphicity of *and* and *or* (i.e., there is actually just one lexical entry and all other uses are derived by a generalization of the **g-sl** rule). Then first, state the appropriate rule or rules, and state what needs to be assumed about the slash-directional features. Second, notice that it was pointed out that the simple **g-sl** rule (like function composition) need not stipulate the slash-directional features under a view of grammar where the syntactic categories themselves are functions. The definition of **g-sl** to such a function will predict the output. The generalized **g-sl** rule, however, does not have quite the same property and this might well militate against thinking of this as a real generalization of **g-sl**. Discuss why this is so. (Note: this is truly an advanced exercise.)

*13.15. One potential problem with the suggestion above concerns cases involving noun conjunction. In other words, in addition to *and* and *or* of category (S/S)/S we might need additional basic lexical items of category

(cont.)

(N/N)/N. Are these additional items necessary? Make sure to revisit the discussion of noun conjunction and the answers to Exercises 12.3 and 12.4. The answer here is actually rather complex, so don't expect a simple "yes" or "no" answer.

13.5. Appendix: Reassuring the Appalled Syntactician

Many people familiar with the standard arguments in syntax regarding constituent structure are initially shocked that anyone would suggest that *Calista loves* can be a constituent in *Calista loves model-theoretic semantics*. In fact, the addition of **g-sl** (or the function composition schemata) allow for all sorts of substrings of sentences to be analyzed as constituents (i.e., as well-formed expressions with a category and a meaning) which are quite standardly thought to resist all the standard tests for constituency. We have already addressed some of the objections that one might raise against this non-standard notion of constituents, but since elementary linguistics and syntax textbooks contain a battery of other arguments about constituent structure, it is worth a brief discussion of this here.

Obviously, space precludes going through each of the textbook arguments against the sort of odd constituents allowed here, but we briefly comment on the logic of these arguments to reassure the appalled syntactician that the fragment developed here is not insane. Consider one classic argument concerning "movement" (parallel arguments concerning "deletion" and "substitution by anaphoric elements" can be answered in similar ways). Here, then, is an argument found in literally almost any introductory linguistics or syntax textbook.

The textbook: Certain expressions may move to the front of a sentence, as shown in (27), where (27a) is the version of the sentence with no movement. (The construction here is known as the Topicalization construction and needs special discourse conditions and/or special prosody to make it natural sounding; we surround the relevant sentences with extra material to make them more natural). The moved material is put in italics and the sentences that we are primarily interested in are underlined:

(26)   a. Kelly predicted that Chris would adopt the Siberian husky puppy.
  b. *The Siberian husky,* Kelly predicted that Chris would adopt;
     the malamute, she predicted that he would leave.
  c. Kelly thought that Chris would adopt the Siberian husky, and indeed,
     adopt the Siberian husky he will.

In (26b) an NP is found at the front of the clause rather than in normal object position; in (26c) an entire VP (which occurs with an auxiliary verb) is found at the front. The logic then goes on to assume that the (b) and (c) sentences are derived by a transformation moving material to the front of a sentence, and that only constituents can move in this way. Thus the ungrammaticality of things like (27b) is used to argue that the material at the front cannot ever be analyzed as a constituent. We will not go to the trouble to try to improve this sentence by embedding it in relevant discourse contexts, since it is fairly clear from the outset that it is hopeless:

(27)   a. Kelly believed that every dog howled.
  b. **Dog howled,* Kelly believed that every.

Of course the argument itself is phrased in terms of a theory with movement rules, which are not being adopted here. But that fact does not undermine the potential force of the argument since any theory does need to account for the existence of cases like (26b) and (26c) while ruling out (27b). The cases in (26) are not difficult to accommodate in the framework here: simply assume (for example), that there is a unary rule which takes any expression of category $S/_R X$ and shifts it to one of category $S/_L X$ (for X a variable here over categories). Then even though the textbook argument for the non-constituency of *dog howled* would need to be rephrased, the argument would still seem to survive. One might assume that there must be no category X such that *dog howled* is of that category, and/or no way to analyze *Kelly believed that every* to be an expression of category $S/_R X$ (for some X).

So the very generous notion of constituent structure assumed here appears to be in trouble: for it predicts that *dog howled* can indeed be analyzed as a single constituent, as can *Kelly believed that every*. The (ambitious) reader should be able to show that *dog howled* can be analyzed as an expression of category $S/_L Det$, where Det is an abbreviation for the category of quantifiers, which is $(S/_R VP)/_R N$. (To show this, you will need to lift *howl* to take GQs as argument.) Moreover, *Kelly believes that every* can be analyzed as a well-formed expression of category $S/_R(S/_L Det)$ (with the help of some fancy footwork involving **g-sl** and **l**). So why can't the category

$S/_L$Det instantiate X in our Topicalization schema? Or, to use the more traditional movement terms, why can't this category "move"?

The answer is quite simple. The way the textbook argument is phrased assumes that constituency is both a necessary *and sufficient* criterion for "movement" (or for an ability to appear in this fronted position). But the latter assumption is incorrect: under no theory is it the case that constituents of any category can occur at the front of the Topicalized construction. In movement terms, this means that constituenthood is a necessary condition for movement; it is not a sufficient one. In the terms of the non-movement Direct Compositional theory developed here, the Topicalization unary rule that shifts $S/_R$X to $S/_L$X is stated too generally: there have to be restrictions on what can instantiate X. After all, there are many cases of perfectly "standard" constituents which cannot occur at the front in a topicalization construction, as in:

(28)   a. *Man who built The Breakers, Mary hired the.
       b. *Who built the Breakers, Mary hired the man.
       c. *Is flat, Mary thought that Chris believed that the world.

Tensed VPs, complex nouns (*man who built the Breakers*), relative clauses, and many other expressions are disallowed in Topicalized position. To be sure, a fully adequate theory would have something more to say about just what categories can and can't "Topicalize" (in the terms here, what categories can and can't instantiate X in the topicalization unary rule), but since it can be shown independently that there are many such restrictions, there is no real reason to conclude that the fact that many of these "odd constituents" do not occur in this construction threatens the conclusion that they are indeed constituents. Similar logic holds for the traditional arguments which are usually framed in terms of "substitution by an anaphoric item" and "deletion."

13.6. Summary: The fragment so far

To the fragment in Chapter 12 add the following:

Lexicon:
<[which], RC/$(S/_R$NP) and RC/$(S/_L$NP), $\lambda P[P]$>
<[who], RC/$(S/_R$NP) and RC/$(S/_L$NP), $\lambda P[P]$>

Rules:

R-2   **(mod)** (revised). Let a be an expression as follows: $<[a], RC, [[a]]>$. Then there is an expression β: $<[a], N/N, \lambda P_{<e,t>}[\lambda x_e[P(x) \,\&\, [[a]](x)]>$;
if $[a]$ consists of a single word, the result is $N/_R N$.

R-5a. Let a be an expression of the form $<[a], A/_R B, [[a]]>$. Then there is an expression β of the form $<[a], (A/_R C)/_R (B/_R C)>, g_c([[a]])$ (for c the semantic type of expressions of category C).

R-5b. Let a be an expression of the form $<[a], A/_L B, [[a]]>$. Then there is an expression β of the form $<[a], (A/_L C)/_L (B/_L C)>, g_c([[a]])$ (for c the semantic type of expressions of category C).

Comments:

• R-5a and R-5b should ultimately be collapsed into one, and the directional features on the slashes would not be stipulated. That rule might ultimately be generalized further to Generalized **g**.

• The treatment of *which* and *who* should ultimately be revised, and revised in such a way as to account for the pied-piping cases. See Jacobson (1998) for some discussion.

14

Generalized quantifiers in object position: Two approaches

Chapter 10 focused on the syntax and semantics of GQs like *every wolf, no goose*, and *some professor*. In particular, the hypothesis that these have meanings of type $<<e,t>,t>$ and are of syntactic category S/(S/NP) (or simply $\mathbf{L_S}$(NP)) provides an elegant account of how these combine in the syntax and semantics with VPs. Moreover, it was noted that GQs have the same distribution as ordinary NPs (such as *the big bad wolf* and *Porky*). This is partially accounted for by the assumption that ordinary NPs can input the lift rule R-4, which means that, for example, an expression with the phonology [porky] can also be a GQ. And so, it follows that wherever a GQ is allowed, so is an ordinary NP. But this gives only half the story: nothing so far precludes the possibility of an environment which allows ordinary NPs but not GQs. Yet no such environment exists.

    In more concrete terms, the fragment so far has no account of GQs in, for example, object position, as in (1):

(1) a. Romulus loves every wolf.
b. Carolyn saw no stars.
c. Wolfie chased every pig.

Assuming that [[love]], [[saw]], [[chase]] etc. are of type $<e,<e,t>>$, some extra device is needed to allow for these GQs in object position. To this end, this chapter will explore two different types of solutions which have been proposed. The first (in section 14.2) is not Direct Compositional and makes use of a level of Logical Form as the input to the semantic interpretation, and where LF is distinct from the pronounced sentence. Hence, this approach posits a rule which moves the object GQ to a different position at LF. In other words, as far as the semantics is concerned, GQs do *not* in fact occur in object position. The second solution (in section 14.3) is Direct Compositional and requires no revisions to the architecture assumed here. Rather than adding a rule mapping one representation into another, it adds instead a unary rule, mapping a function that has an e-type argument position to one asking for an $<<e,t>,t>$ argument. After developing the two views, section 14.4 provides some comparison.

14.1. A tempting but inadequate solution

But first we should dispense with a simple hypothesis which—while elegant in that it requires adding nothing more to the fragment developed so far— does not give the full range of facts. This rests on the observation that one possible derivation for (1a), for example, involves combining (lifted) *Romulus* with *loves* in the way discussed in Chapter 13, to give the expression *Romulus loves* of type $<e,t>$ and of category $S/_RNP$. Moreover, recall the speculation that *every* is listed in the lexicon as having category $L_S(NP)/N$. This means that this category can be more fully fleshed out as either $(S/_R(S/_LNP))/_RN$ or $(S/_L(S/_RNP))/_RN$. And that in turn means that *every wolf*—in addition to the category $S/_R(S/_LNP)$ that it has when it occurs in subject position—also has the category $S/_L(S/_RNP)$ and can take the $S/_RNP$ *Romulus loves* to its left. The reader can verify that the derivation sketched here not only gives the result that (1a) is well-formed, but also gives (1a) the right meaning as well. Indeed, this derivation does exist according to the fragment here.

14.1. Show the full syntactic and semantic details of the derivation sketched above.

But this cannot be the whole story about quantified NPs in object position, First, the grammar still needs something more to account for cases of coordinated VPs with GQs in object position (in one of the conjuncts or in both) as in (2):

(2)   a. Carolyn extinguished every lamp and (still) saw no stars.
          b. MacDonald milked every cow and fed every pig.
          c. MacDonald milked Bessie and fed every pig.

A derivation analogous to the one noted above allows *Carolyn extinguished* to be an expression that can combine with a GQ to its right, but that provides no way to coordinate *extinguish every lamp* and *saw no stars*, which is needed for (2).

Second, consider the following sentences:

(3)   a. A doctor has examined every patient.
          b. Some wolf chased every pig.

These exhibit what is known as a scope ambiguity. Take (3a). On one reading, *a doctor* has wide scope over *every patient*; in this reading there is a single doctor who did all of the examining. The second reading is weaker; it requires only that every patient has been examined by some doctor, but not necessarily the same doctor for each one. Thus here *every patient* has wide scope over *a doctor*.[1] The second reading is definitely harder to get but is brought out with the proper context. Imagine a medical clinic wishing to

---

[1] In the case of a sentence containing two GQs one of whose determiner is *some* and the other *every*, it is difficult to definitively show that there is a genuine ambiguity rather than a vagueness. This is because one of the possible readings happens to entail the other. Thus in (3b), if the wide-scope subject reading is true, it is also the case that every wolf is chased by some pig—it just happens to be the same pig. However, any solution based on giving a semantics for this in which the sentence has only one reading (the weaker one, in which every wolf was chased by some pig) will then give the wrong semantics for the corresponding sentence in which the quantifiers are reversed, as in:

(i)   Every pig chased some wolf.

shut down for the night, but whose rules do not permit closing until every single patient has been seen by at least one doctor. The receptionist announces that at last we can close, for indeed "A doctor has (by now) examined every patient." (We are using *a doctor* here interchangeably with *some doctor*.) (3b) is similar; some find it difficult to get the wide-scope reading on *every pig*, but it emerges with appropriate context (and with the help of the right prosody). But consider what happens according to the account under consideration here. While (3a) can be derived, it has only one meaning: the meaning in which *a doctor* has narrow scope.

14.2. Show the full syntactic and semantic details of the derivation of (3a) in which *a doctor* combines first with *examine* (ignore the auxiliary here) by function composition (or, by **g-sl** plus application). Show that it results in the meaning where *every patient* has wide scope.

14.3. Construct a context to bring out the wide-scope reading of *every pig* in (3b).

Thus not only does this solution give only one reading for these scopally ambiguous sentences, but it also gives the least preferred reading, not a happy consequence. So something more is needed.[2] Thus we now turn to

---

In other words if one were to set up the semantics for (3b) such that the only reading is wide scope on the object, then (i) should also have only the wide-scope object reading. But that makes the incorrect prediction that (i) is false in a world in which each pig did some wolf-chasing though the pigs did not chase the same wolf.

[2] It is also not clear that the above type of solution can fully generalize to GQs in all positions, although this depends in part on the status of Wrap operations. The data at issue concerns the fact that GQs combine with three-place verbs as in (i) (and we get both scope possibilities):

(i)   George read every child a story about goats.

This type of observation was made originally in Hendriks (1993) with respect to Dutch and German where, in embedded sentences, both the subject and the object precede the verb (and where either can be GQs, with the same scope ambiguities as we find in English). But it should be noted that cases like (i) (and the Dutch/German cases involving subjects and objects) are not necessarily fatal for the type of solution under consideration here. The ability of that solution to extend to these cases depends on exactly how and if Wrap operations are folded into an expanded

two different solutions. Like the two accounts of relative clauses in Chapter 13, one (in section 14.2) does not maintain Direct Compositionality; the second (in 14.3) does.

14.2. Quantifier (Lowering)/Raising

The first solution considered here is embedded in a theory with a level of representation (LF) which is input to the compositional semantics, and at which only a trace or pronoun (of type e) is actually in object position at that level. This view also crucially makes use of variables and assignments as part of the semantic machinery for natural language; traces (and pronouns) have indices in the syntax, and thus they are analogous to the variables in the artificial languages developed in Chapter 9.[3] (In fact, this view, as usually implemented, claims that all NPs have indices in the syntax; as will be shown below, the index on full NPs plays no role in their interpretation.) Thus to say that the trace/pronoun "is of type e" is to say that its semantic value is an assignment-dependent individual. Crucially, then, as far as the semantics is concerned, GQs actually do *not* exist in direct-object position—all direct objects at the level of semantic interpretation are expressions with meanings of type e.

One of the earliest versions of this view was put forward (without full semantic detail) within the framework of Generative Semantics (Bach 1968; McCawley 1971). The fundamental premise of Generative Semantics was that the phrase structure rules define a level of LF which is the level relevant for semantic interpretation, and subsequent transformations map that into a different, surface level. Thus all quantified NPs (i.e., all GQs) were actually generated by the phrase structure rules not in subject, object, etc. position, but rather were higher in the tree. The normal NP positions at LF are filled with silent "variables" (or, if you will, silent pronouns, or what is now known as a

---

fragment. But in any case, we have seen other reasons that additional apparatus is needed to fully account for the existence of GQs in object position.

[3] Keep in mind that the Direct Compositional fragment developed so far uses variables and assignments merely for the metalanguage being used as a convenient way to name model-theoretic objects (as discussed in Chapter 9). It does not use them as an actual part of the semantic machinery for natural language, and they could be dispensed with entirely with any other system for naming these objects (such as the use of prose descriptions, done here whenever possible).

trace), and the full material such as *every pig, no wolf*, etc. is lowered into those positions by a transformation known as Quantifier Lowering.

A variant of this was subsequently taken up in Chomsky (1976) and May (1977). Because this variant is much more common in recent literature it is the one to be considered here, and—at the risk of overlooking various revisions which have been explored since these original proposals—will be referred to as the *modern LF view*.[4] This variant shares with Generative Semantics the assumption that the level relevant for interpretation is LF, that quantified NPs are not in object position at that level, and that the surface position and the LF position of GQs are related by a movement rule. The difference lies in the general architecture of the grammar. In the modern LF view, the syntax proves well-formed surface representations by a series of rules (including perhaps movement rules of the sort moving relative pronouns that were discussed in Chapter 13). But in addition to the movement rules that happen "in the overt syntax," there are movement rules that map a surface representation to an LF, and this (as in Generative Semantics) is the input to the semantics. (By a rule applying "in the overt syntax" we mean one that applies in such a way as to have an effect on the actual surface, pronounced sentence.) In other words, the main difference between this view and the Generative Semantics view of relevance to GQs is in the direction of the rules. In Generative Semantics there is a rule of *Quantifier Lowering* (since the rules map LFs to surface representations); in the modern view the rule is known as *Quantifier Raising* (since surface representations are mapped to LFs).[5]

---

[4] Revisions of the general picture of the organization of the grammar have been explored in a number of works that have gone under the rubric of "Minimalism" (see, e.g., Fox and Nissenbaum 1999). But the differences primarily concern the question of just how to state the rules that give LFs as output; the LFs in the end and the interpretation of these are generally assumed to be something like the view that will be exposited here. And different researchers also advocate slight differences in the actual form of the LFs from that are looked at here, but these differences have no consequence for the discussion in this chapter.

[5] There is actually an earlier Direct Compositional variant of the Quantifier Lowering/Quantifier Raising account due to Montague (1973) and known as the *Quantifying-In* solution. Montague's particular proposal contained additional assumptions to be discussed below. But leaving those aside, a version of his proposal would be much like the Generative Semantics view except it makes no use of an actual *level* of Logical Form. The syntax and semantics work in tandem; surface strings are directly built, and each expression is interpreted as it is "built" in the

Incidentally, the LF view is perfectly compatible with the movement theory of relative-clause interpretation developed in section 13.3 although at first glance it might appear that it is not. For in section 13.3 it was assumed the input to the compositional semantics was the *surface* representation, derived through a series of rules applying in the syntax (including one which moved the relative pronoun to the front and left an index trace). In reality, though, the full model in which that view is embedded takes LF (not the surface representation) to be the input to the compositional semantics. But there is no need to revise the presentation in Chapter 13: simply assume that in the cases discussed there nothing of interest happens to map the surface representation to the LF. Thus, what was taken there to be the surface representations are identical to the LFs and so again it is an LF which is interpreted.

Returning to the case at hand, the idea is to posit a rule (most easily seen as an optional rule) which allows both quantified and simple NPs to move from their surface positions to higher positions. This is much like the rule moving a relative pronoun in the "overt" syntax. (Since this theory is generally not coupled with a Categorial Grammar syntax, it posits a single category both for ordinary NPs like *Porky* and for generalized quantifiers like *every pig*. We will continue to call this *NP*, although in much literature it is called *DP*.) The rule in question is known as *Quantifier Raising* (QR for short). The difference between QR and the rule which moves relative pronouns is that QR applies in the component of the grammar that maps surface representations to LFs. Put differently, it has no phonological consequences, and so is often called *covert* rather than *overt* movement. Incidentally, while the rule is known as *Quantifier* Raising, it is formulated here to allow any NP to raise, including ordinary definite NPs like *the book*. The rationale for this generalization will be pointed out in 14.4.2.1. Assume

syntax. Where the Quantifying-In solution differs from the Direct Compositional approach to be discussed in 14.3 is in using a more complex set of syntactic operations than are being used here. In particular, this approach builds up an expression like *Romulus loves he$_5$* (or one can use *Romulus loves t$_5$*) whose meaning is the same as the meaning of the node labeled S in (4) below. This then is converted to the sentence *Romulus loves every wolf* by a rule substituting the GQ onto *he$_5$*; the semantics performs the two operations that correspond to the interpretation of the higher portions of the tree in (4). The point, then, is that there is no actual level of representation in which the GQ is higher in the tree (as in Generative Semantics and in the "modern" LF view) and thus it is Direct Compositional, but it does require a more complex view of the syntax.

further that each NP comes with an index and that QR leaves an indexed trace in the position from which the NP raised. While we adopt a convention according to which the index remains on the raised NP, it should be noted that the index on that NP plays no role in the interpretation. We will not formalize the rule here because its precise formulation depends on a variety of theoretical assumptions. It suffices to assume that (1) can have an LF as in (4) (other LFs are also possible if, for example, the subject NP also raises):

(4)

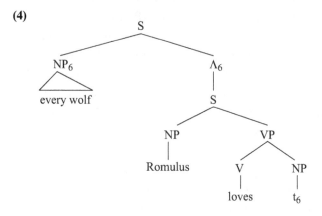

To take stock: this solution requires the addition of QR and, of course, does not maintain Direct Compositionality. The grammar keeps track of representations which are interpreted, there are various levels of representation, and there is movement without phonological consequence as well as movement with phonological consequences. That said, the apparatus set up in section 13.3 (see in particular the rule in (9) in Chapter 13) is now sufficient to interpret this LF and nothing more needs to be said. The step-wise semantic interpretation of the expression labeled Λ_6 is akin to the interpretation of Λ_8 shown in (8) in Chapter 13, and so we leave the details to be spelled out in the exercise directly below. Notice that this, of course, also requires the use of variables and assignments, but the (informal) non-Direct Compositional fragment in section 13.3 already added that, so nothing new is needed here if this is embedded in the same general theory as that explored in section 13.3. Note that $[[\Lambda_6]]$ will have a constant value on all assignment functions (as it contains no other unbound traces or pronouns within it), and on all assignments it is the characteristic function of the set of things that Romulus loves. This then is taken to be the argument (on any assignment g) of $[[every\ wolf]]^g$.

> **14.4.** Work through the full semantic details for the interpretation of (4) showing the value for each node in the tree.

The fact that (3b) is ambiguous between both scope possibilities also follows. For the wide-scope object reading, the most straightforward way to derive this is via an LF where only the object has raised. That LF is exactly like the one in (4) except that there is an NP of type <<e,t>,t> in subject position; it is shown in (5a). It is also possible to raise both the subject and the object but have the object have wider scope than the subject; this results in exactly the same reading as if only the object raised. (See Exercise 14.6.) However, another possibility is for both the subject and the object to raise, but the subject to have wider scope than the object; that LF is shown in (5b). Below these two LFs we work through the semantics for (5b). We have numbered all of the nodes in (5b) purely for convenience to refer to them; the numbering is not part of the system itself. Moreover, here we use *chase'* to mean not just the semantic value of the word *chase* (since that is a function from assignments to functions of type <e,<e,t>> but rather to refer to the value that this receives on all assignments (since it is a constant function). (Similarly for *pig'* and *wolf'*.)

(5)

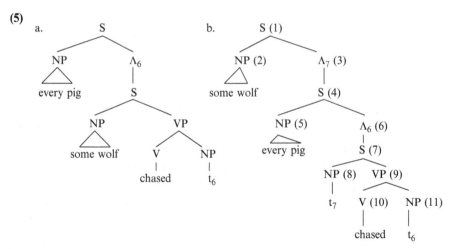

for any g:

$[[11]]^g = g(6)$
$[[10]]^g = chase'$
$[[9]]^g = chase'(g(6))$

$[[8]]^g = g(7)$

$[[7]]^g = \text{chase'}(g(6))(g(7))$

$[[6]]^g = \lambda x_e[\text{chase'}(x)(g(7))]$ (this is by Rule 9 given in Chapter 13)

$[[5]]^g = \lambda P_{<e,t>}[\forall y[\text{pig'}(y) \rightarrow P(y)]]$

$[[4]]^g = \lambda P_{<e,t>}[\forall y[\text{pig'}(y) \rightarrow P(y)]](\lambda x_e[\text{chase'}(x)(g(7))]) =$

$\quad \forall y[\text{pig'}(y) \rightarrow \lambda x_e[\text{chase'}(x)(g(7))]\ (y)] = \forall y[\text{pig'}(y) \rightarrow \text{chase'}(y)(g(7))]$

$[[3]]^g = \lambda x_e[\forall y[\text{pig'}(y) \rightarrow \text{chase'}(y)(x)]]$

$[[2]]^g = \lambda P_{<e,t>}[\exists z[\text{wolf'}(z)\ \&\ P(z)]]$

$[[1]]^g = \lambda P_{<e,t>}[\exists z[\text{wolf'}(z)\ \&\ P(z)]](\lambda x_e[\forall y[\text{pig'}(y) \rightarrow \text{chase'}(y)(x)]])=$

$\quad \exists z[\text{wolf'}(z)\ \&\ \lambda x_e[\forall y[\text{pig'}(y) \rightarrow \text{chase'}(y)(x)]](z)]] =$

$\quad \exists z[\text{wolf'}(z)\ \& \forall y[\text{pig'}(y) \rightarrow \text{chase'}(y)(z)]]$

14.5. Using the above as the model, show the computation for the meaning associated with the LF in (5a).

14.6. Construct a second LF for the wide-scope object reading in which both subject and object are raised, but the object is above the subject and show the computation of its meaning.

14.7. To the extent possible, take each of the lines shown in the semantic computation of (5b) above, and state the model-theoretic objects in prose. For example, [[6]] is, on any g, that function that characterizes the set of objects that g(7) chased.

14.8. It was assumed above that ordinary NPs like *Romulus* can also undergo QR. We leave it open in this exercise as to whether in the theory under consideration in this section such an NP can only have a meaning of type e (its lexical meaning) or whether it can also type-lift to have a meaning of type $<<e,t>,t>$. The conclusion to be drawn from this exercise will turn out to be the same either way.

Note that—unlike the sentence in (3b)—the corresponding sentence with an ordinary NP such as *Romulus* in (surface) subject position is not ambiguous:

(i) Romulus chased every pig.

Since QR is the mechanism used to account for scope ambiguities, a (naive) conclusion that someone might be tempted to draw form the lack of ambiguity in (i) is that QR should not indeed be able to raise the NP *Romulus* out of the sentence at LF.

(cont.)

Show why this conclusion is incorrect and that there is no harm in allowing it to raise. One can show this using either the e-type meaning for *Romulus* or the <<e,t>,t> meaning, so show it both ways. (If it has the e-type meaning, general type-driven principles will presumably work so that the meaning of its sister node labeled Λ is the function which takes the individual r as argument.)

One might have observed that—as presented here—the minimal derivation (i.e., the one involving the least steps in the computation of the LF) is the derivation resulting in (5a) which gives the wide-scope object reading. Since this reading is greatly dispreferred to the narrow-scope object reading, one might take this as a criticism of this approach. This, however, would be hasty, for two reasons. First, there might be an independent explanation (perhaps having to do with processing) for the strong preference for subject wide scope. Second, the QR view is often embedded in a theory or theories with additional assumptions that we are ignoring here but which make the situation more complex. Suffice it to say here that readers familiar with the *VP-internal subject hypothesis* can explore how this would interact with more fully fleshed out LFs and how this would interact with the scope predictions. There also remains the question of how (or whether) this basic approach accounts for the coordination cases in (2) (without positing that VP coordination always involves hidden coordination of two Ss). This is left for the reader to explore in the following exercise. (Further interactions between scope and coordination are discussed in section 14.3, and Exercises 14.16 and 14.18 will return to how to think about those in the QR approach.)

*14.9. As noted in Exercise 13.10, it is often assumed (since Ross 1967) that there is a constraint according to which material may not move (in the syntax) out of a coordinate structure (this is known as the *Coordinate Structure Constraint*). It is further often assumed in the general framework under discussion here that QR is subject to the same constraints on movement as are the other movement rules (such as the rule fronting *which*) that are posited within that framework. However, the assumption that QR should also be subject to the Coordinate Structure Constraint is independent of the basic approach towards GQs in object position being exposited here. For the purposes of this exercise, then, ignore this assumption.

Given this, show how the QR approach can give a *representation* for the sentence in (2) (there are in fact two possible representations) without having to posit that the two conjoined VPs are really "hiddenly" Ss.[6] (That is, use the VP conjunction analysis that has been assumed throughout this book.) Then, carefully work through the truth conditions of your representation(s) and see if they are correct. *Note*: This is subtle and challenging, so work through it carefully. The best method is to work through all the semantics making all possible λ-conversions until you arrive at a first-order logic formula for each representation, and then compute the truth conditions for that formula.

14.3. A Direct Compositional solution

The fact that generalized quantifiers occur in object position (usually thought of as an e-type argument position) combined with the existence of the scope ambiguities is often used as the poster child evidence for the claim that the semantics does not work in tandem with the syntax, but is instead read off a level of LF at which items are rearranged. But such a conclusion is premature: we have seen over and over that fancier ways to package meanings allow a theory in which the semantic composition

---

[6] Readers familiar with the VP Internal Subject Hypothesis (VPISH) might be tempted to solve this problem using that hypothesis. Note, though, that this still requires something extra, and actually is very similar to simply saying that the conjoined VPs are actually two "sentences." That is, under VPISH there are two subject positions (even though they are called "VP subjects" rather than "S subjects") and the two moved or raised subjects merge into one. This is thus not substantially different, for the present purposes, from some version of a Conjunction Reduction analysis.

respects the syntax and works in tandem with it. Actually, there are quite a number of available ways to accommodate the distribution (and readings) of GQs in a Direct Compositional fashion; just one such strategy will be explored here. This involves a unary rule operating on the verbs (and on other items that combine with NPs).[7]

By way of background, we turn first to an account of GQs in object position proposed in Montague (1973). The general strategy throughout much of Montague's work is to "fancy up" the types of the basic meanings of lexical items (i.e., the meanings that they are listed as having in the lexicon). What would this strategy lead to? It would lead to the assumption that we have been wrong all along about the meaning of ordinary transitive verbs. They are not of type <e,<e,t>> but rather of type <<<e,t>,t>,<e,t>>—they expect generalized quantifier meanings in object position. This hypothesis is, of course, in no way incompatible with the fact that ordinary NPs like *Mitka* and *the big bad wolf* can appear in object position, since these too can have the lifted meanings of type <<e,t>,t>. (And recall that—under Montague's strategy of packing all of the complexity into the lexical meanings—definite NPs have only meanings of this type. The fragment here revises this so that the lexical meanings of definite NPs are of type e, but they can lift to GQ meanings by the rule l.) The corresponding syntactic category—under the Montague treatment—would of course be parallel; the lexical category of *chase* would not be (S/NP)/NP but rather (S/NP)/(S/(S/NP)).

Just what is the meaning of *chase* in this view? To exposit, let *chase*'* be the ordinary Curry'ed two-place relation "chase" between individuals—that is, the meaning that we have assumed for *chase* until this point. Then let actual [[chase]] be the following, which we from now on call *chase'*$_{MONT}$:

(6) $\lambda P_{<<e,t>,t>}[\lambda x[P (\lambda y[chase_*'(y)(x)])]]$

To get the intuition of the relation between the ordinary (Curry'ed) two-place relation *chase*'* of type <e,<e,t>> and *chase'*$_{MONT}$ (of type <<<e,t>,t>,<e,t>>) it is helpful to say the above in prose. (6) is a function that first takes a GQ-type meaning and then some individual x as argument,

---

Some other Direct Compositional accounts can be found in Montague (1973) (see n. 5), Moortgat (1997), and Barker (2001) which uses quite a different set of techniques.

and returns true if the property of being ordinary-chased by x is in the set of sets mapped to true by the GQ. For example, if $chase'_{MONT}$ combined with [[every pig]] it would return the function that maps an individual to true just in case the property of being chased by that individual is in the [[every pig]] set. Put differently, it returns the function that maps an individual x to true just in case the set chased by x has the [[pig]] set as a subset. And this of course gives the right meaning for the expression *chased every pig*. The syntax is straightforward; given the revised category for *chase*, it can of course combine with any GQ in object position.

But this revision of the lexical meaning of *chase* is still not enough. For this gives only the wide-scope subject meaning for (3b), as shown in (7):

(7) [[chased every pig]] = $\lambda x[every\text{-}pig'\ (\lambda y[chase_*'(y)(x)])]$ =

$\lambda x[\lambda P_{<e,t>}[\forall z[pig'(z) \to P(z)]](\ \lambda y[chase_*'(y)(x)])]$ =

$\lambda x[\forall z[pig'(z) \to \lambda y[chase_*'(y)(x)](z)]]$ =

$\lambda x[\forall z[pig'(z) \to chase_*'(z)(x)]]$

[[some wolf chased every pig]] = $some\text{-}wolf'(\lambda x[\forall z[pig'(z) \to chase_*'(z)(x)]])$ =

$\lambda P[\exists y[P(y)\ \&\ wolf'(y)]](\lambda x[\forall z[pig'(z) \to chase_*'(z)(x)]])$ =

$\exists y[\lambda x[\forall z[pig'(z) \to chase_*'(z)(x)]]\ (y)\ \&\ wolf'(y)]$ =

$\exists y[\forall z[pig'(z) \to chase_*'(z)(y)]\ \&\ wolf'(y)]$

We have laboriously worked through all the steps here, but it may be easier to get the intuition using prose. [[chase every pig]] characterizes the set of individuals x which are such that the set x chases has all the pigs in it. Combining this with the subject says that this set has a non-empty intersection with the wolf set. And hence there must be at least one wolf who chased all the pigs. This solution, then, takes us only halfway there. It does not give the wide-scope object meaning (which in this case is the weaker meaning) whereby each pig is chased by some wolf but not necessarily the same wolf. Incidentally, it will not help to invoke the derivation in which *some wolf* combines first with *chased* (by **g-sl** on *some wolf* plus application) and then combines with *every pig*. Recall that **g-sl** + application is equivalent to function composition. But notice now that by the very definition of function composition, [some-wolf' o chase$_{MONT}$'](every-pig') is equivalent to some-wolf(chase$_{MONT}$'(every-pig')). So this too results in the narrow-scope reading for the object.

But there is an easy fix. The next step is to take the strategy proposed by Partee and Rooth (which is consistent with their general strategy discussed in Chapter 11). Assume that ordinary transitive verbs like *chase* are indeed

listed in the lexicon with the ordinary meaning of type <e,<e,t>> but map
by a unary rule to a homophonous item that allows instead for a generalized
quantifier in object position. In other words, assume that our original
understanding of [[chase]] is correct: it is simply *chase*$_*$' (we henceforth
omit the subscript asterisk since we are using *chase'* and [[chase]] interchangeably to be the meaning of *chase*). But, according to the Partee
and Rooth proposal, it maps to *chase'*$_{MONT}$ by a unary rule given below
in TR-12. In the Categorial syntax assumed here this would be accompanied
by a syntactic part as well; for the moment we state just the semantic part as
the rule will be generalized below):

TR-12.   Let a be an expression whose meaning is of type <e,<e,t>>. Then there is a
homophonous expression β whose meaning is of type <<<e,t>,t>.<e,t>>
where $[[\beta]] = \lambda P_{<<e,t>,t>}[\lambda x[P(\lambda y[a'(y)(x)])]]$

For the data considered so far we could stop here. The reading of (3b)
where the object has wide scope is accounted for in the way discussed in
section 14.1, and the reading where it has narrow scope is accounted for in
the way shown above. But Hendriks (1993) noted that the Partee and Rooth
rule can easily be generalized to allow any e-type argument slot to "lift" to
allow for a GQ instead, and this also allows for both scope possibilities.
(Hendriks argued for this solution on the grounds that the function composition approach will not help in the case of a language like German where
the two NPs are on the same side of the verb; but as noted in n. 2, this
depends on whether and how a Wrap operation is folded into the system.
Still we pursue the Hendriks' generalization here as it is quite interesting and
has advantages with respect to coordination.) Although the formalism for
stating the generalized rule is a bit clumsy (merely because we need to
introduce some new notation), the rule itself is just a fairly natural generalization of the Partee and Rooth rule. Modifying Hendriks' terminology
slightly, we will refer to the generalization as Argument Slot Lift (**argslot-l**).

It is initially easiest to state the rule in prose. Let f be any function that
takes n arguments (including 0) of any type, then an e-type argument, and
then m other arguments (including 0) of any type to return 1 or 0. Then
argslot-l(f) is a function which also takes the same n arguments, then a
generalized quantifier argument $\mathcal{P}$, and then the same m arguments. It
returns 1 just in case $\mathcal{P}$ maps to 1 the set of individuals x which are such
that had f applied to the same n arguments and then to x and then to the

same m arguments, f would have returned 1. To put this in notation we need to introduce a few notational conventions. Let $K^{\rightarrow}$ be any sequence of semantic types (of any number, including none), similarly for $L^{\rightarrow}$. Let $X_K^{\rightarrow}$ be any sequence of variables each of the same type as the sequence notated by $K^{\rightarrow}$ (again of any number, including none), and similarly for $X_L^{\rightarrow}$. Finally let $\lambda X_K^{\rightarrow}$ be a sequence (of any length, including 0) of λs and variables of the relevant type (similarly for $\lambda X_L^{\rightarrow}$). Then we define **argslot-l** as follows:

(8) *Definition of Argument Slot Lift (**argslot-l**):*

Let f be any function of type $<K^{\rightarrow},<e,<L^{\rightarrow},t>>>$. Then **argslot-l**(f) is a function of type $<K^{\rightarrow},<<<e,t>,t>,<L^{\rightarrow},t>>>$, where **argslot-l**(f) = $\lambda X_K^{\rightarrow} [\lambda P[\lambda X_L^{\rightarrow} [P(\lambda x_e[f(X_K^{\rightarrow})(x)(X_L^{\rightarrow})])]]]$.

As formulated here, **argslot-l** is not uniquely defined; if there is a function with more than one e-type argument it can apply to either one. When needed, we will use the notation **argslot$_i$-l** to refer to the operation that lifts the ith argument slot (where the object slot of a transitive verb, for example, is the first slot; lifting the subject position would be **argslot$_2$-l**). Thus note that the Partee and Rooth rule is simply **argslot$_1$-l** applied to a function of type $<e,<e,t>>$. Armed with **argslot-l**, we can add to the fragment the full unary rule in R-6; $A^{\rightarrow}$ here means any sequence of syntactic categories as does $B^{\rightarrow}$; once again in both cases the sequence can be empty.

R-6.   Let a be an expression of the form $<[a], ((S/A^{\rightarrow})/NP)/B^{\rightarrow}, [[a]]>$ where A is of length n. Then there is an expression β of the form $<[a], ((s/A^{\rightarrow})/GQ)/B^{\rightarrow}$, **argslot$_{n+1}$-l**([[a]])>.

Because the notation is indeed clumsy it might be obscuring the more important model-theoretic intuition of what **argslot-l** does; the reader is thus encouraged to revisit the prose description given above to internalize the operation.

Now consider the case of a transitive verb like *chase*. As has already been shown, when this inputs **argslot$_1$-l**, this gives *chase'*$_{MONT}$. This allows a GQ in object position, and if this verb is taken as argument of the subject GQ, the result is the narrow-scope reading on the object for a case like (3b).

*14.10. Another way to derive (3b) is by application of *argslot₁-l* followed by *argslot₂-l*. That is, the object argument slot is lifted first to a GQ slot, and then the subject slot is lifted. This gives exactly the same reading as one would get by lifting the object slot and then applying the result to the *every pig* to give the VP *chase every pig* and then having that be the argument of the subject. In other words, this gives the same reading as the derivation shown above in (7) and results in a narrow-scope object. Work through the full syntactic and semantic details to show this.

*14.11. Related to the discovery above, consider a function of type <e,t>. *argslot₁-l* maps this to a function of type <<<e,t>,t>,t>. Work through the semantics of *argslot₁-l*(f). What other operation gives exactly the same result?

But there is an additional derivation: one in which both argument slots lift but where the subject slot lifts first and then the object slot does. And this gives wide scope to the object:

(9)   chase, (S/NP)/NP, chase' → (via *argslot₂-l*)
    chase, (S/GQ)/NP, $\lambda y_e[\lambda P[P(\lambda x_e[\text{chase'}(y)(x)])]]$
        call this expression chase₂
            → via *argslot₁-l* applied to chase₂:
    chase, (S/GQ)/GQ, $\lambda Q[\lambda R[Q(\lambda z_e[\text{chase}_2\text{'}(z)(R)])]]$
    chase every pig, S/GQ, $\lambda Q[\lambda R[Q(\lambda z_e[\text{chase}_2\text{'}(z)(R)])]](\text{every-pig'}) =$
        $\lambda R[\text{every-pig'}(\lambda z_e[\text{chase}_2\text{'}(z)(R)])] = $ (by unpacking chase₂')
        $\lambda R[\text{every-pig'}(\lambda z_e[\lambda y_e[\lambda P[P(\lambda x_e[\text{chase'}(y)(x)])]](z)(R)])] =$
        $\lambda R[\text{every-pig'}(\lambda z_e[\lambda P[P(\lambda x_e[\text{chase'}(z)(x)])](R)])] =$
        $\lambda R[\text{every-pig'}(\lambda z_e[R(\lambda x_e[\text{chase'}(z)(x)])])]$
    some wolf chased every pig, S,
        $\lambda R[\text{every-pig'}(\lambda z_e[R(\lambda x_e[\text{chase'}(z)(x)])])](\text{some-wolf'}) =$
        $\text{every-pig'}(\lambda z_e[\text{some-wolf'}(\lambda x_e[\text{chase'}(z)(x)])])$

In prose, this says that the pig set is a subset of the set of individuals z who are such that the set chasing z has a non-empty intersection with the wolf set. Or, put more simply: the pig set is a subset of the set of individuals each of whose chasers include a wolf. And this is the reading we are after here.

14.12. (This exercise is parallel to the one in 14-8 framed within the LF theory.) The Direct Compositional fragment here allows the NP *Romulus* to lift to a GQ with a meaning of type <<e,t>,t>, and thus allows one derivation of (i) exactly analogous to the derivation shown in (9):

(i) Romulus chased every pig.

Yet (i) is not ambiguous in the way that (3b) is. Does this pose any problem for the assumption that *Romulus* can type-lift? Show why or why not.

We will not give further examples, but it is clear that this strategy will generalize to cases of three-place verbs such as those in (4), and indeed will allow any scope possibilities between different NP positions of the same verb. But we should note that generalizing this strategy to account for the existence (and readings) of GQs in *all* NP positions is not automatic; a bit more needs to be said. First, and most important, notice that AS-L is defined in the semantics only for those functions whose final result is a truth value (see Exercise 14.13 to discover why this is so). But prepositions (at least some of them) have been taken to be the identity function on individuals and so would need to also be given a meaning in which they are the identity function on GQs, since we of course get expressions like *read the book to every child*. Perhaps they should be listed as the identity function on NP and lift(NP), where those two categories can be collapsed in some way. Moreover, how exactly should we generalize the syntax in R-6 so that PP as well as NP argument positions can lift? A plausible answer is that the category PP is really simply the same as the category NP but with the addition of a special feature (in other words, this is just like a case-marked NP). We will leave the full details open, acknowledging that some (hopefully minor) modification is needed to account for the full range of GQs under this solution while the LF solution covers all of the cases straightforwardly. (Of course, this is true only given some actual formulation of QR, but assume it can be formulated to raise any NP from any position whatsoever.) Finally, the rule R-6 applies only to expressions whose syntactic category has S as the final result. The syntax can (and probably should) be generalized to include any category whose final result category is of semantic type t (as, for example, the category N).

---

*14.13. The syntactic categories in R-6 can be generalized in various ways, as suggested in the discussion above. However, the semantic definition of *argslot-l* cannot be generalized to apply to functions whose final result is e rather than t. The basic idea crucially requires the input function to be one whose final result is t. Think through why this is so. (Hint: it has to do with the type of GQs themselves.)

There are some interesting predictions of this general approach with respect to coordination. Consider a sentence like (10):

(10)   A/Some doctor examined every inpatient and released every outpatient.

The salient reading for this is one in which the subject has wide scope. There is no problem getting this sentence with this reading. Here both *examine* and *release* simply undergo AS$_1$-L to give what we have been calling *examine*$_{MONT}$ and *release*$_{MONT}$; each take the relevant GQs as argument and the two VPs are conjoined in the normal way.

14.14. Show the details of this derivation. To save steps, feel free to de-Curry *and* and combine the two VPs in a single step.

But it is predicted that there should also be a reading in which *every inpatient* and *every outpatient* both scope over the subject. This would involve applying *argslot$_1$-l* to both verbs. The two are of the same type (and category); both VPs are of type S/GQ and should conjoin. It is simply not clear (to this author at any rate) whether this is a good or bad prediction; informants seem to vary on whether they accept this reading. To help bring out this reading (if it exists), we can set up the following context. The chief resident at the local hospital is allowed to go home for the night only after every outpatient has been released by some doctor and every inpatient has been checked over by a doctor. The resident announces that she is now able to go home, for, after all, *Some doctor (or other) has examined every (single) inpatient and (has) released every last outpatient.* Again we leave it open as to whether this reading does emerge. Of course that reading is expected in any case to be quite difficult to access. First, it is generally the

case that wide-scope objects are dispreferred. Combining this with coordination might just push things too far to make the reading accessible. The
reader is invited to try to construct other such cases and also to explore the
parallel facts with *or* (in which the wide-scope reading in some cases actually
seems easier to get).[8]

14.15. Show the details of the derivation of (10) under the reading in
question. Again, feel free to de-Curry *and* to save steps.

*14.16. Assuming that there is no constraint precluding QR from out of
a coordinated VP, show that the LF account also allows both readings
discussed here (using only VP conjunction).

14.4. Some comparisons

14.4.1. The generality of the solutions

The two different approaches considered here make quite different commit-
ments to the organization and architecture of the grammar. Under the first
approach, representations (i.e., trees) are referred to in the grammar, and
there are rules mapping one representation to another. The input to the
semantics is a representation computed by a series of steps "in the overt
syntax" followed by a series of steps (including so-called covert movement)

---

[8] Notice that it is predicted that this should also have a "mixed" reading, one
which can be paraphrased as "For every patient, there is some doctor who examined
him/her, and there is some particular doctor who released every patient." This is
because there are two forms of *examine* and of *release*. In one, **argslot$_1$-l** is followed
by **arglost$_2$-l** and the other reverses these. But the two end up being of the same
syntactic category (S/GQ)/GQ and the same semantic type and so should be able to
conjoin. It is quite clear, however, that this reading is completely hopeless and will
not emerge no matter how much one tries.

Hopefully this can be explained by some sort of processing principle. Note that a
version of this problem potentially arises in the LF view as well. There too there will
be a mixed reading if the quantifiers can raise out of conjoined VPs (as is necessary if
there is no additional hidden subject for each VP). The actual mixed reading there is
slightly different, but it is equally impossible.

yielding an LF representation. We did not explicitly formulate the rule of QR since some of the details depend on other theoretical assumptions, but some formulation is needed. The resulting LF is compositionally interpreted. The second approach adds a rather symbol-heavy type shift rule, but maintains a Direct Compositional architecture and adds no new devices. One can hope that the symbol-heaviness of the rule is in part an artifact of the notation; the model-theoretic basis of the rule, while not trivial, is not that difficult to see.

There are, however, arguments that are rather traditionally taken to support the QR (or Q Lowering) view which should be addressed here. The first is that the device needed to allow quantifiers in object position in the first place generalizes to give both scopes. But this true on the second approach as well: Hendriks' generalized version of the Partee and Rooth rule which allows GQs in object position allows both scope possibilities. A second argument sometimes given for the QR approach is that the apparatus developed for the quantifier scopes automatically generalizes to account for pronominal binding in general. We return to this in the next chapter. To anticipate: it is indeed the case that given the apparatus of the QR approach, pronominal "binding" can also be accounted for quite easily with suitable lexical entries for pronouns. But this ends up being a mixed blessing. For it will be shown in section 15.2.2 that using the QR approach for pronominal binding overgenerates, and needs to be reined in by an additional constraint.[9] One area where the LF approach arguably does

---

[9] Another quite standard argument for the QR approach, dating back to Generative Semantics (see, e.g., Lakoff 1971; Postal 1974), is that rules which presumably move things like relative pronouns to the front are subject to a set of constraints, and the rules moving GQs into (in Generative Semantics) or out of (in the QR view) a sentence are subject to the same constraints. Of course, this is phrased in theory-internal terms: the view of relative clauses developed in section 13.3 does not assume a movement rule. But it could be rephrased more theory-neutrally. The claim is that the gap (or "missing argument") in a relative clause cannot be in certain syntactic environments (known as *islands*; see Ross 1967) and that the same is true of the position from which a GQ "raises." In reality, however, the generalizations are quite murky and there is actually only partial overlap between the environments disallowing wide-scope quantification and those allowing "extraction." (The former is much more limited than the latter.) Moreover, our understanding of the principles that give rise to island effects is quite hazy, and there is a good deal of controversy as to whether these have any syntactic basis at all.

have a small advantage is that it is easy to generalize it to account for both the syntax and the semantics of GQs in all positions that can be occupied by an ordinary NP. (Of course the rule remains to be formulated, but it is easy enough to formulate it to raise any NP leaving an e-type trace in that position.) As noted above, the particular Direct Compositional solution explored here does need some refinements to extend to the case of PPs; how serious a problem this is remains open.

On the other hand, the LF approach faces some difficulties concerning the existence of GQs in object position in coordinated VPs (see Exercise 14.9; readers who did not do that exercise can guess that incorrect truth conditions result from the most straightforward solution). And along the same lines, the LF account needs something additional (beyond the treatment of *didn't* developed here) in order to account for scope interactions with GQs and negation, as can be discovered in the exercises below. Nothing extra is needed for these scope interactions under the Direct Compositional fragment developed here. Again, this is left for the reader in the subsequent exercise.

14.17. Notice that (i) is ambiguous between a reading in which the negation has scope over the GQ and one where the scopes are reversed (the reading where *every pig* has wider scope than the negation is more difficult to get, but one can construct a context to bring it out):

(i) MacDonald did not feed every pig.

How are the two readings accounted for in the Direct Compositional fragment developed so far?

*14.18. What will the LF account need to say in order to account for the two readings?

14.4.2. Antecedent-Contained Ellipsis

14.4.2.1. The "textbook" argument
There is another very interesting argument for the QR approach worth considering—not only to answer it, but also because it provides an illuminating illustration of the interconnectedness of various theoretical assumptions.

It also allows a brief introduction to another rich empirical domain (ellipsis). The argument was originally put forth in Sag (1976) albeit in slightly different terms (based on observations from Bouton 1970), and has become (literally) a textbook argument for QR; see, e.g., Heim and Kratzer (1998). By way of background, consider first the phenomenon known as *VP Ellipsis* or *VP Anaphora*. This involves sentences in which an auxiliary occurs without its complement but where the "missing" complement is (usually) understood as the meaning of some other overt VP in the discourse context:

(11)   a. Bode will ski the course in four minutes. Lindsay will too.
       b. Sally said she would complete the marathon, and indeed she did.

The second sentence in (11a), for example, is most naturally understood as conveying the proposition that Lindsay will also ski the course in four minutes. We henceforth use the term VP Ellipsis (VPE) in an analysis-neutral way to refer to the phenomenon in question.

Whether the missing meaning needs to be supplied in virtue of being the meaning of some other VP which is overt in the discourse context or can instead be supplied by some sort of inference in a given context is the subject of a long-standing debate. For the present purposes, it is sufficient to observe that at least generally the missing meaning is the meaning of some other overt VP in the discourse context; call that the *antecedent VP*.[10] Given that, the phenomena of VPE can be used as a tool for determining the exact meaning of the antecedent VP.

Before proceeding further, more needs to be said about how the grammar accounts for these cases where an auxiliary is missing its complement and the missing meaning is supplied via some antecedent VP. Does the sentence *Lindsay will too* in (11a) actually have as its representation at some level *Lindsay will ski the course in 4 minutes too* where the VP *ski the course in 4 minutes* is silent or deleted? If so, is this material present and deleted "in

---

[10] This term is a bit misleading in that the VP which supplies the meaning can actually follow the ellipsis site, as in the following discourse (a full discourse is given here to highlight the point that the missing meaning does not come from any other sentence):

(i)   Speaker A. Did Sarah finally decide which candidate to endorse?
       Speaker B. Yes. Once Todd did, she finally endorsed Newt.
              (the first sentence can be understood as "Once Todd endorsed Newt")

the overt syntax" or is it copied in during the computation of LF? Or might we instead think of these as containing no VP like this at any level, but where instead the function [[ski the course in 4 minutes]] is somehow supplied as part of the understanding of the sentence? For example, one might think of the semantics of (11a) as containing a "free variable" of type $\langle e,t \rangle$, whose value is supplied by the discourse context.

Unfortunately, space precludes doing justice to these questions here. And so we will just pick one way to think about this construction where the choice is motivated by two considerations. First, the view chosen here is compatible with the general assumptions made throughout this book. And second—although this view is not shared by most researchers who do advocate LF—it does not in any way impact on the argument to be developed below and is therefore a safe and theory-neutral way to exposit the textbook argument for QR. Assume, then, that there is no linguistic VP (at any level); for now we can think of the semantics as containing a "free variable" of type $\langle e,t \rangle$ as argument of the auxiliary, where the value of this variable is ultimately supplied by context. More concretely, assume that an auxiliary such as *will* is listed in the lexicon as having the category (S/NP)/(S/NP) and has a meaning of type $\langle\langle e,t \rangle,\langle e,t \rangle\rangle$.[11] Call this *will₁*. Assume further that there is a unary rule mapping all auxiliaries to homophonous forms that occur with no VP complement; for the case of *will* call this second item *will₂*. There are, incidentally, a number of ways in which those items traditionally called "auxiliary verbs" share syntactic properties, so it is reasonable to posit a feature [AUX]; items with this feature input the rule in question. (Lest it appear to the reader that we are adding unary rules willy-nilly it should be noted that any theory needs some device to predict that auxiliaries can occur without an explicit (or overt, or pronounced) complement. The devices vary, but some such device is needed no matter what.[12]) Thus *will₂* has as its category just S/NP, and its meaning is

---

[11] Here is a case where times are actually crucial: obviously *will'* maps a time-dependent set into another time-dependent set and so its meaning is really of type $\langle\langle e,\langle i,t \rangle\rangle,\langle e,\langle i,t \rangle\rangle\rangle$. Its full meaning is not difficult to spell out: it takes a function P of type $\langle e,\langle i,t \rangle\rangle$ (a time-dependent set), then an individual x and then a time i and returns true if there is a time i' later than i such that P holds of x at i'. Since adding in the extra time layer makes the exposition more cumbersome and is irrelevant to the basic point, we will ignore it here.

[12] For example, under some accounts an auxiliary may select for an "empty operator" E which occurs as sister to the VP and suppresses its phonological content;

[[will$_1$]](P), where P is a free variable over functions of type <e,t> whose value is ultimately fixed by picking up some salient <e,t> function in the discourse context. (Chapter 15 will give a more explicit account of "free variables" in general, including ultimately eliminating them in a variable-free context.) In (11a), then, the relevant function that fixes the value of P is [[ski the course in four minutes]]. Recall that (for reasons left open here) in general the function that sets the value for P is made salient by being the meaning of an actual VP which is uttered in the discourse context.

With this background, consider the phenomenon known as *Antecedent-Contained Ellipsis* first noted in Bouton (1970) and exemplified in (12):

(12)   Sarah will read every newspaper which Katie will.

It is quite reasonable to suspect that the mechanisms for VPE in general extend to this case. And so, at first glance, this leads to the conclusion that *will* in the second clause is *will$_2$* and is of category (S/NP) but with meaning [[will$_1$]](P). In more theory-neutral terms: whatever allows for a silent or missing VP meaning in (11a), those same mechanisms should allow for the missing VP meaning within the relative clause in (12). Hence under the set of assumptions made so far, the value for P is the meaning of some other overt VP in the discourse context. Since (12) is fine without elaborating the discourse context any further, this must be the meaning of the matrix VP. Notice that a key premise in the development of the argument is that the missing or silent meaning in (12) *must be a VP type meaning*. This follows (in the textbook view) not only because this is crucially seen as *VP Ellipsis*, but also because the textbook argument is always embedded in a theory maintaining the view of relative clauses developed in section 13.3 (the movement/trace account). Crucially, under that view, *which* combines with some expression whose meaning is of type <e,t>.

In other words, take the non-elliptical version in (13):

(13)   Sarah will read every newspaper which Katie will read.

Recall that *which Katie will read* is (under the movement/trace account) analyzed syntactically as *which [$_{A-8}$ Katie will read t$_8$]*, where [[Katie will read t$_8$]] is—on any assignment g—the proposition that Katie will read g(8). The meaning of [$_{A-8}$ Katie will read t$_8$] is—on any g—the set of things that

see Merchant (2001) for this type of account. And so something is needed to predict what can and can't select for E.

Katie will read. Moving up the tree, the meaning of *which Katie will read t_8*
is the same, and this set (on any g) intersects with [[newspaper]]$_S$ (on any g).
Thus, in order to provide a semantic composition for (12) in such a way that
all the types can mesh, the ultimate understanding of the free variable
P (which stands in for the "missing meaning" that combines with the
auxiliary) must be [[read t_8]]. That is, it has to be a *full VP meaning* which
contains in object position an "open individual" (i.e., a non-constant function from assignments to individuals). If this meaning is supplied, then the
meaning of the relative clause in (12) can be put together exactly like the
meaning of the relative clause in (13) is.

But what VP can supply the missing meaning? As noted above, without
any further context this is perfectly interpretable (where (12) is understood
as the same as (13)). And so, the antecedent VP can only be the matrix
VP. But as it stands, it can't be the matrix VP! After all, the matrix VP itself
is *read every book which Katie will*, whose meaning is [[read every book
which Katie will P]]. But if the <e,t> function to be assigned as value of
P itself contains P, there is an infinite regress. Or, as it is sometimes phrased,
we arrive at the antecedent containment paradox.

How can this paradox be resolved? Enter QR to the rescue. There is no
problem if the object NP *every book which Katie will* has undergone QR
leaving an indexed trace in the object position of the matrix. Under this
view, the matrix VP can have as its LF representation *read t_8* which is
(relative to an assignment) a completely sensible function of type <e,t>.
This function thus supplies the value for P, and the antecedent containment
paradox disappears. The full details are left for the subsequent exercise.

14.19. Show the LF after raising. For the purposes of how this has been
exposited here, assume that both *which* and *every book which Katie will*
are indexed 8, so both leave t_8 in the relevant position. Then show how
the matrix VP is interpreted to have a meaning of the right sort to fix the
value of the free variable P.

Incidentally, we can now return to why QR was formulated to allow any
NP to raise (including definite NPs). This is because we also find Antecedent
Contained Ellipsis when definite NPs occur in object position as in (14), and

the paradox would arise here too unless *the candidate that Todd will* is raised at LF so that the matrix VP is [endorse t_i] (for some i).

(14)   Sarah will not endorse the candidate that Todd will.

14.4.2.2. Antecedent-Contained Ellipsis as Transitive Verb Phrase Ellipsis

We have dwelt on this case in some detail not only because it is relevant to the QR debate, but also because it dramatically illustrates the interconnectedness of various assumptions, and shows how changing some fundamental assumptions can significantly alter the conclusions. The astute reader will already have noticed that the argument is framed within the trace/movement account of relative clauses and relies on assumptions that are not shared by, for example, the Direct Compositional account in section 13.4. In particular, the argument rests on the assumption that *will* in the relative clause in (12) needs to find an <e,t> type meaning—i.e., the meaning of some VP.[13] But consider again the non-elliptical version (13) under the Direct Compositional account in section 13.4. The compositional semantics puts this together by combining *will* only with an expression of category (S/NP)/NP (which we will refer to henceforth as a Transitive Verb Phrase or TVP), and combining its meaning with a two-place relation of type <e,<e,t>>. In particular, ordinary *will* undergoes the **g-sl** rule so that it maps to something looking for an <e,<e,t>> expression to give back a meaning of that same type. If (12) can be put together in a fashion analogous to (13) there is no need to assume that some actual full VP is required in the discourse context to supply the missing meaning; all that is needed is TVP to supply the meaning. And of course the lexical meaning of *read* is available. And so, the argument that the object must have moved out by covert QR leaving a trace vanishes. This point was first noticed in Cormack (1984) and developed further in Evans (1988) (see also Jacobson (1992, 2003, and 2008 for elaboration and extension to a wide range of cases). In a nutshell is that all that is missing here (and picked up by

---

[13] The remarks here are oversimplified in that in many LF accounts it is assumed that *will* raises to take a full sentence as its scope; its meaning is thus actually of type <t,t> (or, more accurately, <<i,t>,<i,t>>). But the same point will go through: it ultimately needs to find an expression of type t with which to combine, which will still lead to the conclusion that there has to be a trace in object position.

context) is *read'*—this is exactly as expected under the account of relative clauses developed in section 13.4.

It is worthy pursuing this in a bit more detail. Listed in the lexicon is *will$_1$* whose category is (S/NP)/(S/NP) and whose meaning is of type $<<e,t>,<e,t>>$. In the derivation of (13) (the non-elliptical version), it maps by **g-sl** to what we can call *will$_3$* of category ((S/NP)/NP)/((S/NP)/NP) or, for short, of category TVP/TVP. In (13), it finds its complement *read* of category TVP (and with meaning $<e<e,t>>$); the result is a TVP. The rest of the composition is left to the reader to work out; it is exactly analogous to cases already discussed. What about (12)? The only additional assumption that needs to be made is that the unary rule shifting auxiliaries in such a way that they occur without their complements can easily be stated to allow **g-sl** (*will*) (i.e., *will$_3$*) to do the same. Thus corresponding to *will$_2$* (which is a VP with meaning [[will]](P)) the generalization of the rule allowing an auxiliary to occur without its complement will allow *will$_4$* of category TVP and with meaning [[will$_3$]](R). (That meaning can be further unpacked as λx_e[will$_1$'(R (x))]. To be sure the actual rule allowing for "missing complements" has not been formulated here; one set of explicit details is worked out in Jacobson (2003) (in a variable-free framework), but the reader can on their own formulate a rule in such a way as to accomplish the necessary generalization.)

The rest is straightforward. R must have its value supplied by being the meaning of some overt expression in the discourse context, but in the case that expression is just a TVP rather than a VP. There is one point worth noting. In the matrix sentence, *read* must undergo **argslot$_1$-l** in order to occur with the quantified NP in object position, and so this item does not have a meaning of type $<e,<e,t>>$ (rather, it is of type $<<<e,t>,t>,<e,t>>$. But there is no problem with the analysis; this item is listed in the lexicon as *read* of category (S/NP)/NP with meaning of type $<e,<e,t>>$ and so presumably the ordinary two-place relation *read* (or what we called earlier *read$_*$*) is indeed the meaning of this item (it just has the second meaning as well).

An ambitious reader is invited to sketch out the full derivation of (11a) in both theories. One will see that the QR/movement/trace account involves a series of representations and thus rules mapping representations to representations. The Direct Compositional account, on the other hand, involves application of a series of unary rules mapping local expressions to others but makes no crucial use of representations. (Note too that it is misleading to think of the unary rules as changing the meaning of expressions; these rules are simply proofs that the relevant output expressions are well-formed on the basis of the well-formedness of input expressions.)

14.5. Generalized quantifiers in embedded sentences

We have sketched two accounts of generalized quantifiers in object position and their scopal interaction with GQs in subject position, but have not looked at all at the distribution of GQs (and their scope possibilities) in embedded sentences. Consider for example a sentence like (15):

(15)   Some candidate thinks that every proposal will be rejected.

The **argslot-l** solution to scope ambiguities developed in section 14.3 does not readily allow for a reading where *every proposal* scopes over *some candidate* here. This is because it involves the manipulation of argument *slots* and so predicts (without additional machinery) that the sort of scopal interactions shown in (3b) are restricted to what we might call co-arguments of the same verb.

Arguably, this is a good prediction. Although the facts are a bit murky, the general wisdom is that (15) does indeed lack a reading in which *every proposal* has wide scope over *some candidate* (see, e.g., May 1985).[14] Indeed much of the literature within the QR tradition formulates QR to be "clause-bounded," meaning that an NP within an embedded sentence can raise only to have scope over that sentence and not higher. However, in the Direct Compositional fragment developed here there is an interesting additional prediction: the reading with wide scope on *every gun control bill* should emerge in cases like (16):

(16)   Some senator plans to vote against every gun control bill.

Notice that we have switched here to a case where the embedded material is a subjectless infinitive VP. This is because, for reasons which remain unclear, it is extremely difficult to get the relevant reading with a full embedded tensed S. But the existence of a wide-scope reading for *every gun control bill* in (16) is sufficient to make the point. This reading should

---

[14] Hendriks' actual proposal did allow an embedded GQ to scope over a GQ in the matrix for he posited an additional rule (called Value Lift) which accomplished this. We will not explore this here.

(and presumably does) emerge because—however one analyzes embedded infinitive VPs like the one in (16)—the use of **g-sl** predicts that *plans to vote against* can combine to give a complex transitive verb. That, then, can undergo the two **argslot-l** steps exactly as sketched in (9).

14.6. Summary: The fragment so far

Add to the fragment in Chapter 13 the following:

Definition:

Let f be any function of type $<K^{\rightarrow},<e,<L^{\rightarrow},t>>>$. Then ***argslot$_{n+1}$-l***(f) is a function of type $<K^{\rightarrow},<<e,t>,t>,<L^{\rightarrow},t>>>$ (where n = the number of slots in K) where $AS_{n+1}\text{-}L(f) = \lambda X_K^{\rightarrow} [\lambda P[\lambda X_L^{\rightarrow} [P(\lambda x_e[f(X_K^{\rightarrow})(x)(X_L^{\rightarrow})])]]]$.

Additional rule: **argslot-l** (argument slot lift):

R-6. Let a be an expression of the form $<[a], ((S/A^{\rightarrow})/NP)/B^{\rightarrow}, [[a]]>$ where A is of length n. Then there is an expression β of the form $<[a], ((S/A^{\rightarrow})/GQ)/B^{\rightarrow},$ ***argslot*** $_{n+1}$***-l***$([[a]])>$.

15

The interpretation of pronouns: Two accounts

15.1. Introductory remarks

15.1.1. Variables or not?

The previous two chapters considered relative clauses and GQs in object position from two points of view. The most striking difference between the two views is the one that has been stressed all along in this book. One uses a Direct Compositional architecture in which there is no notion of a level of representation that inputs the semantics; indeed the grammar does not actually refer to representations (in the sense of, e.g., trees). The other view—the LF view—makes crucial use of representations, and the representation inputting the semantics is not the one representing the pronounced sentence, but is an abstract LF in which a constituent can move to a position other than where it is pronounced.

There is a second major difference between the two approaches sketched in Chapters 13 and 14. The LF theory crucially uses assignment functions as part of the semantic apparatus (and indices in the syntax). Thus, like the artificial language developed for convenience in Chapter 9, expressions have as their semantic value a function from the set of assignments (G) to something else. The Direct Compositional fragment makes no use of variables, indices, and assignments. The semantic composition of a relative clause does not use an indexed trace whose index is lambda-abstracted over. Rather, the grammar puts relative clauses together using the **g-sl** rule (or function composition). What is seen as movement in the standard theory—which is what leaves the indexed trace—is instead a case of a function that happens not to combine with its expected argument. Rather, the function in question itself is the argument of another function. So, for example, in *which Martha refinished*, [[refinish]] does not combine with a variable of type e nor with any object at all. Rather, (lifted) *Martha* undergoes **g-sl** and in turn takes *refinish* as argument. The LF view and the Direct Compositional view also part ways on the interpretation of GQs in object position. Under the LF view, such a GQ raises and again leaves an indexed trace, allowing a transitive verb not only to find as its object an expression of type e. Crucially, the value of that e-type expression is dependent on assignments (as it is an indexed trace). And this trace corresponds to a variable which is lambda-abstracted over in order to create an expression of type <e,t> to serve as argument of the raised GQ. The Direct Compositional alternative developed in Chapter 14 just maps the transitive verb to one expecting an <<e,t>,t> argument in object position.

Thus (in addition to an arguably simpler architecture), the Direct Compositional theory developed so far has the advantage of avoiding assignments as part of semantic apparatus for the interpretation of natural language. It might be worth stressing again that although we are using the λ-language and variables as a way to write out complex functions, this is just for notation. One can—as we have often done—restate these model-theoretic objects in prose, and there are other logical systems which could have been used to write these meanings which do not use variables.[1] But in the fragment so far, no expression of English has as its semantic value an assignment-dependent object, and so assignments play no role.

As in the previous two chapters, this chapter also considers a phenomenon— pronominal binding—from two points of view. The first makes use of both LF

---

[1] One such system is the Combinatory Logic developed in Curry and Feys (1958) in which all of the meanings that can be written using the lambda calculus can be written without variables.

and variables; the second is a variable-free and Direct Compositional approach. But it is important to point out that the issue of Direct Compositionality is not crucially tied in with the question of whether or not the grammar makes use of assignment functions and variables (although the two positions do go rather nicely together). There are Direct Compositional accounts which do use variables. But space—and potential overload for the reader—preclude developing such an account here. For interested readers, a fully Direct Compositional account using variables is available on the textbook website at <http://sites.clps.brown.edu/compositionalsem>. After developing the two different accounts (in sections 15.2 and 15.3) the rest of this chapter returns to some observations of relevance to both theories (sections 15.4 and 15.5).

Before proceeding, one further remark is in order about the overall simplicity of the two views developed here. Readers might be struck by the fact that the LF view with variables (section 15.2) takes far fewer pages to exposit than does the variable-free view in 15.3. This might well give the impression that the former is considerably simpler. But this is only because this incorporates quite a bit of machinery developed in earlier chapters which has no analogue in the Direct Compositional view, including the use of LF, movement (QR) to get that LF (which rule was never explicitly formulated), assignment functions as developed in Chapter 9, the use of an interpretive rule akin to lambda abstraction in order to interpret the relevant LFs, and so forth. Also, no explicit syntax was given in conjunction with the LF view; rather a kind of informal syntax was just assumed. Hence an overall comparison of the two theories requires full and explicit fragments for both theories—starting from scratch and including both a syntax and a semantics. That cannot be accomplished in this book; here we develop only the Direct Compositional fragment (and even then some details are left out or are just hinted at). And of course the tools here are used only in the service of an account of English, so an ultimate reckoning of the types of tools needed in language in general is quite far off from what is done here. Hopefully, though, the Direct Compositional fragment developed here can serve as a starting point for theory comparison.

15.1.2. Pronominal binding: The empirical phenomenon

The empirical domain of immediate interest is the interpretation of pronouns. Imagine asking someone who knows nothing about semantics: what is the meaning of a pronoun such as *he, she, they*, etc.? The answer that a semantically naive person usually gives is that a pronoun picks out some contextually salient individual in a given context. A scenario like that in (1) makes this a perfectly plausible conjecture; here *he* picks up the contextually salient individual Elmo:

(1)   We are at a party and our friend Elmo makes his goodbyes and walks out the door, forgetting to put on his hat. I turn to you and say "uh oh, he forgot his hat."

But it is easy to show that pronouns don't simply pick out individuals. Sentences like those in (2)—whose intended reading is quite clear— immediately defeat the naive hypothesis.

(2)   a. Every woman$_i$ invited the man who she$_i$ had met at the rally.
      b. No fourth grade boy$_i$ called his$_i$ mother (on Mother's Day).

What is the individual referred to by *she* in (1a)? Even more strikingly, what could possibly be the individual *his* in (1b)? In the face of (1), the immediate temptation is to think of pronouns as having as their meanings variables, and this is the line pursued in the next section. Of course, this alone would accomplish nothing unless coupled with some notion of a semantics for variables. Otherwise, to say that a pronoun like *he* corresponds to a variable merely restates the question (what does a variable mean?). Indeed, though, we already have a semantics for variables—both for the artificial languages in Chapter 9 and in the account of traces in Chapters 13 and 14—so we can take that as the point of departure in section 15.2.

A notational point: recall from the very first chapter of this book that indices are being used to indicate the intended reading. Whether or not indices are part of the actual grammatical apparatus is of course part of what is at issue. To keep the different uses of indices straight, when a pronoun or GQ is indexed with a subscript such as i and j, this is intended *only* as a way to indicate a particular reading. When indices are being used as part of the grammatical apparatus (in the theory that maintains this), we continue to pick arbitrary integers for the indices. Also, a terminological point: we continue to use the terminology of a "bound pronoun" and the "binder of a pronoun" in a purely informal but hopefully clear way. Take for example (2b). As will be discussed below, neither theory actually posits any direct relationship between *no fourth grade boy* and *his*. We will none-theless continue to refer to the former as the "binder" of the pronoun for expository purposes. Moreover, the variable-free view contains no real notion of "binding" in any sense, and as has been seen at various earlier points in the text, a definition of "binding" of a pronoun in a theory with assignments is actually a bit complex (and is not really necessary). Again, then, the term *bound pronoun* is just an expository convenience.

15.2. The LF (variable-ful) view

15.2.1. The basic account

Given the apparatus for the interpretation of traces in Chapter 13 and the mechanisms for binding traces left by QR, the machinery needed to provide a meaning for sentences like (1) is largely already in place. All that is needed is lexical entries for pronouns. Thus assume that a pronoun has an index as part of its lexical entry which plays a key role in its interpretation, and the bound reading of a pronoun is a consequence of the fact that the NP which binds it can undergo QR. This means that there are an infinite number of pronouns in the lexicon: he_1, he_2, etc., and there must be some kind of schema over lexical meanings to the effect that for any lexical item he_n, and for any g, $[[he_n]]^g = g(n)$. Incidentally, the fact that a pronoun has an index is not just an automatic consequence of the more general fact discussed earlier that (in the LF account) all NPs have an index. For the index on an NP like *every third grade boy* is on the entire NP node, not on a single lexical item. Moreover, as shown in Chapter 14, that index plays no role in the interpretation of the expression *every third grade boy* (to highlight this fact, QR was formulated so as to actually remove the index from that expression). Its sole purpose is to leave that index on the trace, where it is interpreted. For a pronoun, the index is a key part of its semantics.

Consider (2b). Here *his* is a genitive pronoun which combines with a relational noun; one can use R-3 introduced in section 8.5. (R-3 was formulated within a theory using a Categorial Grammar syntax, which is not usually assumed under the LF view, but this is orthogonal to the points here.) Thus, *his* has some index—say, 5. Then the value of his_5 is an assignment-dependent individual; on any g it is g(5). Similarly, the value of his_5 *mother* is also assignment-dependent; for each g, it is the unique individual who is the mother of g(5). Now consider the subject NP *no fourth grade boy*. It can also be indexed 5 (if it has a different index, then *his$_5$* remains free; we return to free pronouns in 15.2.3). Since *no fourth grade boy* can undergo QR, one LF for the sentence *no fourth grade boy called his mother* is the following:

(3)

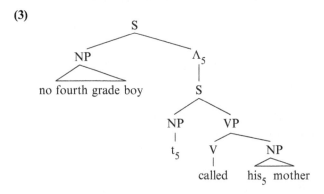

This gives the bound reading on the pronoun, and the compositional details are straightforward. As discussed above, the NP *his$_5$ mother* on any g denotes the mother of g(5). The value of *called his$_5$ mother* on any g is the characteristic function of the set of individuals who called the mother of g(5). The value of the S [*t$_5$ called his$_5$ mother*] on any g is the proposition that g(5) called the mother of g(5). The next node up—Λ_5—has a value which is constant on all assignments. It is (on all assignments) the characteristic function of the set of individuals who call their own mother (see the rule in (9) in Chapter 13). And that function is taken as argument (on any g) of [[no fourth grade boy]]; the latter (on any g) is the set of individuals with an empty intersection with the fourth grade boy set, and we arrive at the correct truth conditions.

Thus given the apparatus of QR, the notion of indexed traces, and the use of assignments for the material already covered, pronominal binding becomes automatic, provided that pronouns come with indices in the lexicon and have the same semantics as traces. Another consequence of this system is that it extends immediately to the case of multiple pronouns and multiple binders, as will be brought out through the next exercise.

15.1. In order to show the point above, we need to deal with an embedded sentence. As has been noted multiple times, the full semantics of sentences embedded under verbs like *think* requires giving an intensional semantics (the object of someone's thoughts is not a truth value but

(*cont.*)

280   15. PRONOUNS: TWO ACCOUNTS

something about the way the world might be; technically then it is a set of worlds). But for simplicity, simply extensionalize here, and take *think* and *hope* to both have meanings of type <t,<e,t>>. Then show the LF and the semantic computation for each of the following sentences:

(i) Every fourth grade girl$_i$ hopes that no third grade boy$_j$ thinks that her$_i$ dog chased his$_j$ cat.

(ii) Every fourth grade girl$_i$ hopes that the boy$_j$ who she$_i$ invited will bring his$_i$ dog (to the party).

In (ii), omit *will* and *to the party* from the computation; these are put in to make the sentence more natural but need not be dealt with here. Further, treat *third grade boy* and *fourth grade girl* as single unanalyzed nouns. Finally, for *her dog* and *his cat* we have no account of these in the fragment (recall that R-3 in Chapter 8 dealt with genitives for relational nouns, but not for this kind of genitive). So simply take something like *Dorothy's dog* to be an individual which we will just write out as [[the-dog-of(d)]], keeping in mind that this is a shorthand, and take it as being of type e. Using this as the model for writing out *her dog* etc. should be straightforward.

15.2. Now consider a sentence like (i), again on the reading indicated by the indexing:

(i) Every third grade boy$_i$ said that he$_i$ (already) fed his$_i$ dog.

Assume that both pronouns here (and *every third grade boy*) are indexed 5 in the syntax. Then show that there are two different LFs which give the meaning above; keep in mind that all NPs—including pronouns—can optionally undergo QR. There are additional LFs where *his dog* raises, but this is not at issue here; neither of the LFs of relevance for this exercise involves QR on *his dog*.

As noted in section 15.1, one will often hear it said of an example like (2b) that *no fourth grade boy* binds *his*. And here too that terminology will be used where convenient *as a way to indicate a certain reading*. But this terminology is potentially misleading, for under the account above (as well as in the variable-free account in 15.3) there is no direct semantic relationship between the pronoun and the subject GQ. Rather, the two are coindexed in the syntax and it is this fact which allows the trace left by QR to be coindexed with the pronoun. This is the only sense in which there is a relationship between *no fourth grade boy* and *his*. In fact, it was pointed out in Chapter 9 that the notion of the *binding* of a pronoun or a trace with index n is most naturally defined as the point in the computation where an expression shifts from one whose value varies on the assignments g in G/n to one whose value is constant on all g in G/n. Hence here the binding of a pronoun he_n happens at the stage where the node labeled Λ_n is interpreted. Again, then, binding has nothing to do with the GQ itself. Of course none of this really makes any difference as it is mere terminology. The way the grammar has been set up here—even in the view above making use of LF and indices—the grammar itself never refers to a notion of binding.[2]

---

[2] A common slogan in much of the literature that endorses something like the account of pronouns developed just above is that "binding requires c-command." (For a definition of c-command, see n. 4, this chapter.) This is used in two different ways, depending on whether one is talking about c-command at LF or c-command at some syntactic level (such as the surface representation). The most common use of this slogan refers to LF, and in this case it is really nothing more than an observation rather than any kind of principle that must be stated in the grammar. That is, it means that the relevant reading in sentences like those in (1) emerges as a result of QR, and consequently the "binder" (the NP which undergoes QR) c-commands the pronoun at LF. But this is just a fact about the way the semantics has been set up and not an additional principle in the grammar. The second use of this slogan refers to a version of the Weak Crossover Constraint which is discussed directly below in section 15.2.2. Here the idea is that there is an actual constraint within the grammar. Again, though, it need not refer to any notion of "binding"; a version of this constraint is given in (8) which does refer to c-command but not to a binder, and is a constraint on the relationship between the trace left by QR and the pronoun.

Note also that the syntactic literature—especially that beginning with Chomsky (1981)—is full of discussion of constraints on "binding" under the rubric of so-called "Binding Theory." Under this view, one might think that the grammar does access such a notion. But the notion of "binding" at issue in these discussions has little to do with the use of that term here. Rather the so-called "Binding Theory" refers to constraints on the interpretation and distribution of reflexive and reciprocal pronouns ("Principle A"), and on some principles constraining the interpretation of ordinary pronouns including principles that would need to block certain understandings of free pronouns ("Principle B" and "Principle C"). This book has not and will not deal with these phenomena, save to say that there are Direct Compositional and variable-free accounts of the relevant phenomena. See, e.g., Szabolcsi (1987) and

15.2.2. A wrinkle: Weak Crossover effects

Thus the QR approach generalizes quite readily to handle the semantics of bound pronouns. But the ease with which it generalizes is a mixed blessing. For the ability of a GQ to take scope over other material does not in fact correlate completely with the distribution of binding. The consequence of this fact is that the approach sketched so far needs to be supplemented with an additional principle relevant to pronouns so as to rein it in. Otherwise, it is predicted that certain sentences have meanings that they do not in fact have.

The phenomenon in question centers on the fact that although a GQ in object position can generally scope over a subject, it cannot bind a pronoun in subject position. Consider the following contrasts:

(4)   a. No fourth grade boy$_i$ called his$_i$ mother (on Mother's Day).
      b. *His$_i$ mother called no fourth grade boy$_i$ (on the first day of school).

(5)   a. Every patient$_i$ was discharged by some doctor who had seen him$_i$.
      b. *Some doctor who had seen him$_i$ has discharged every patient$_i$.

Notice that in (5b), for example, the problem is not one of scopes. We have already seen that in a corresponding sentence like (6) it is possible to get a wide-scope object reading as, for example, in the scenario where a clinic may close for the night only after every patient has been discharged (and no single doctor needs to sign off on all the discharges):

(6)   We can finally close, since some doctor has discharged every patient.

The same scenario does not help for (5), verifying that the problem is located in the binding of the pronoun. Nor is there anything odd about the intended readings in (4b) and (5b); we can bring out the intended reading for (4b) by using a passive:

(7)   No fourth grade boy$_i$ was called by his$_i$ mother (on the first day of school).

This lack of the bound readings here is generally known as the *Weak Crossover* effect (henceforth WCO). The term *Crossover* was coined originally

Steedman (1996) for two different accounts of reflexives both compatible with the general architecture here, and see Jacobson (2007) for an account of so-called Principle B effects within the framework here. None of these accounts require the grammar to make use of a notion of "binding" (nor of indices).

by Postal (1971) who discovered a similar asymmetry with respect to relative clauses (and questions). Thus Postal noted the following contrasts (again we use indices on the relative pronoun *who*, just to indicate the intended reading):

(8)   a.   No woman who$_i$ had invited her$_i$ father (to her graduation) received an extra ticket.

   b.   *No woman who$_i$ her$_i$ father had invited (to his retirement party) received a ticket.

(The use of *no* in the determiner here is not really central to the point, but is helpful since substituting in *the* improves these, for reasons that will not be pursued here.) Postal assumed a rule fronting the relative pronoun (as in the view in section 13.3); he adopted the term *Crossover* to refer to a constraint to the effect that a *wh*-word could not cross over a coindexed pronoun in its movement path. Since his original work, it is generally agreed that whatever is responsible for the effect in (8) is also responsible for the effect in (4) and (5).[3] The primary focus here will be on the case with GQs in object position, but we will show that the two accounts of WCO effects discussed in this book do generalize to the relative clause case.

There are literally dozens of accounts of the WCO effect on the market, and obviously space precludes comparing and contrasting them. The important point is that something extra is needed to block the intended readings in (4) and (5); the simple account using QR predicts that these readings should exist. One fairly standard solution assumes that in addition to the apparatus developed so far in the non-Direct Compositional theory (indices, traces, movement in the syntax, and covert movement mapping surface representations into LFs) there are also constraints on well-formed LFs. In other words, the rules that apply to yield LFs (such as QR) can

---

[3] The addition of the term "Weak" here is from Wasow (1972). The rationale for this is that the effect is not entirely robust and can be ameliorated in a variety of ways. There is a special case of the phenomenon known as "Strong Crossover" which is much more robust and cannot be ameliorated, as in (ia) (the quantificational case) and (ib) (the relative-clause case), where here the pronoun is not embedded in other material:

(i)   a.   *He$_i$ praised no man$_i$. (cannot mean: No man praised himself)

   b.   *No man$_i$ who$_i$ he praised will win the modesty prize. (cannot mean: No man who praised himself will win the modesty prize)

apply freely but there is an additional set of rules specifying that certain LFs are ill-formed; call these *LF filters*. WCO effects can thus be accounted for if the grammar contains the following LF filter:

(9)   An LF which contains a trace which is coindexed with a pronoun is ill-formed unless the trace c-commands the pronoun.[4]

Incidentally, for the cases at hand it would have worked just as well to require that the trace precede the pronoun (rather than c-command it).[5] We use the c-command version both because it is more common, and because it also lends itself more easily to comparison with the account to be developed in section 15.3. As the reader can easily verify, the LF needed to give the relevant (non-existent) reading for (4b) and (5b) violates (9) since the GQ raises from object position and hence its trace does not c-command the pronoun embedded in the subject. The LFs for (5a) and (5b), on the other hand, are admissible. Notice that this generalizes immediately to the relative-clause contrasts in (8); this is the subject of Exercise 15.3.

15.3. Show the LFs for (4a) and (4b) to demonstrate that the remarks above are correct.

15.4. Show the LFs for just the relative-clause portions of (8a) and (8b) to demonstrate that the remarks above are correct. You can ignore the material in parentheses and the auxiliary *had*.

---

[4] C-command is a notion defined in terms of trees. A node A c-commands a node B if the first node above A (the "mother" of A) dominates B. Intuitively, then, if A c-commands B this means that A is at least as high in the tree as B. Put in terms of things combining to give well-formed expressions, the c-commanding material is introduced later (or at the same time as) the c-commandee.

[5] Most early accounts of this were actually based on linear order (see, e.g., Postal 1971; Jacobson 1977) while many later accounts were based on c-command (see especially Reinhart 1983). But there continue to be accounts based on linear order. See Barss and Lasnik (1986), and an especially interesting account is found in Shan and Barker (2006).

15.2.3. Free pronouns

Recall the discourse in (1) above, repeated here:

(1) We are at a party and our friend Elmo makes his goodbyes and walks out the door, forgetting to put on his hat. I turn to you and say "uh oh, he forgot his hat."

Here the pronoun *he* (and also *his*) has nothing binding it, nor need it even have any mention in the linguistic context of the name of the referent (here, *Elmo*). This point can be made even more dramatically with the following kind of contexts (based on observations of Lasnik 1976).

(10) We are at a party and a particularly obnoxious man who no one likes walks in the door. Because everyone so dislikes this person, no one speaks to him all evening, nor even utters his name. Eventually he takes the hint and leaves, and after he finally walks out the door I turn to you and say "Thank goodness he left."

(11) Exactly the same context as above, but when I turn to you I say "Boy, everyone (sure) dislikes his style."

How are we to understand the semantics of *he/his* in these cases? Clearly they are not instances of bound pronouns. In early work in transformational grammar (Postal 1966; Ross 1969; Langacker 1969) it was assumed that all pronouns are represented as fuller NPs at the level that inputs the semantics and are reduced to pronouns under linguistic identity with something else in the discourse context[6] (compare this to the remarks about VP Ellipsis in section 14.4.2). But since the above contexts were deliberately constructed to ensure that there could be no identical linguistic material in the discourse context, that cannot be the way to think about the semantics of these pronouns either.

Notice, though, that under the theory developed in this section, nothing forces the binding of a pronoun. Take (10). Suppose this is just he_5. Under the LF view, there is no QR here, nothing happens, and the LF for this is just essentially [he_5 left]. Similarly for (11). In this case the subject *everyone* can indeed undergo QR, but in the reading of interest it is not coindexed

---

[6] Variants of this view have been resurrected in modern work as well; see especially Elbourne (2005) who argues that all pronouns do contain hidden fuller linguistic material.

with *his* and so *his* remains free. Thus the final sentence has as its value an *assignment-dependent* proposition rather than an ordinary proposition. But presumably in ordinary discourse contexts listeners are looking for propositional information. It is propositions that are used to convey facts about this world (they denote sets of worlds, and in main clauses are taken to assert that this world is in the relevant set). It is also propositional information that is used for inferences, and so forth. Ultimately, then, the interpretation of a sentence with an unbound pronoun is such that the listener applies the assignment-dependent proposition to some actual assignment in order to extract propositional information. So in the case of (10) (where the pronoun is indexed as he_5), the context makes salient or available an assignment in which 5 is assigned to Elmo. We will not pursue here just how that happens. We will, moreover, often continue to speak informally of the "pronoun picking up a contextually salient individual" even though technically speaking what is picked up is an assignment. Notice, by the way, that *all* sentences have as their values functions from G to propositions. However, in the case of a sentence with an unbound pronoun there is no mystery as to how the listener arrives at propositional information: the value of a sentence is a constant function from assignments, so it does not matter which assignment is chosen. Technically, though, an assignment must be supplied. We will have more to say about so-called "free variables" in section 15.5.

15.3. A Direct Compositional and variable-free approach

As noted in the introductory remarks to this chapter, both quantification in object position (and scope ambiguities) and relative clauses can be handled smoothly under Direct Compositionality, and can be handled without use of indices, assignments, and/or variables as part of the syntactic or semantic machinery. We thus turn our attention now to an approach to the semantics of pronouns which similarly requires no LF (and hence of course no QR) and also makes no use of indices, assignments, or variables.

This approach has generally gone under the rubric of *variable-free semantics*, and it has its roots in the variable-free logic of Curry and Feys (1958) (known as Combinatory Logic), although that was not intended as a theory of natural language semantics. The idea that natural language makes no use of variables was perhaps first put forth (albeit in programmatic form) in

Quine (1960). It has subsequently been explored by a number of researchers particularly in Categorial Grammar and related traditions (Szabolcsi 1987, 1992, Hepple 1990, Dowty 1992, Jäger 1996, Shan and Barker 2006, and a number of papers of the present author, including Jacobson 1991, 1999, 2000). The discussion here will focus on the particular implementation in especially Jacobson (1999) (with some modifications). The proposals by the other authors cited above include interesting alternative ways to implement the basic idea, but obviously a comparison is beyond the present scope.

15.3.1. Pronouns and "binding"

Consider the underlined portions of the sentences in (12) under the reading indicated by the indices there:

(12)   a. Every third grade boy loves <u>Jim's mother</u>.
      b. Every third grade boy$_i$ loves <u>his$_i$ mother</u>.

(13)   a. Every male candidate thinks (that) <u>Rick lost</u>.
      b. Every male candidate$_i$ thinks (that) <u>he$_i$ lost</u>.

In the LF view exposited above, the object NPs in both (12a) and (12b) are of the same type: both have as values functions from the set of assignments (G) to individuals. The object NP in (12a) is a constant function while the object in (12b) is not. Moreover, in (12a) *his* has an actual index in the grammar. (13) is parallel; in both cases the underlined portion is a function from G to propositions. By contrast, the variable-free view takes *Jim's mother* to denote an individual but *his mother* does not—its value is a function from individuals to individuals. In general, an expression with an unbound pronoun within it is a function from individuals to whatever is the type of a parallel expression with no unbound pronoun within it. Once again the term *unbound* (or *free*) is being used here in an informal way for exposition, but its use is hopefully clear. If there are two unbound pronouns within an expression then it is a function of type <e,<e,X>> (for some X).

   To work out the details, three questions need answering. First, what is the meaning (and syntactic category) of a pronoun itself? Second, consider a sentence like (14):

(14)   Every man$_i$ thinks that his$_i$ mother lost.

The lexical meaning of *lost* is of type <e,e>. Since it was said above that *his mother* denotes a function of type <e,e>, how can the two combine? (For that matter, how it is that *his mother* has the meaning that it does?) And third, how do we ultimately get the effect of what is informally being called binding? That is, how do we get the intended reading in, e.g., (12b)?

To begin with the pronoun itself, it was hypothesized that any expression containing a pronoun unbound within has as its value a function from individuals to something else. Extending that to pronouns themselves, let a pronoun such as *he* also have as value a function from individuals to individuals—hence of type <e,e>. Since there are no indices, there is a single pronoun *he* in the lexicon, and we assume that it denotes the identity function on individuals. (We ignore the contribution of gender, and treat *she* and *he* alike, although eventually gender information can be folded in. Moreover, strictly speaking, *he* stands here for a lexeme without case marking; case-marking rules will more fully specify the syntactic category and map the abstract lexeme into the various case-marked versions.)

This also needs to be married to a syntax. Given the tight correspondence in Categorial Grammar between the syntactic category and semantic type, *he* cannot be an NP since NPs are of type e. Assume, then, that pronouns are NP-like, but have a special feature (which will be notated as a superscript). Hence we give a second recursive definition of categories as follows: If A is a category and B is a category, then A^B is a category. The semantic type of A^B is a function from B-type meanings to A-type meanings. Semantically, then, A/B and A^B are of the same type, but the latter does not actively want to combine in the syntax with a B. Rather the superscript feature (in general) records that there is an unbound pronoun within it, and records its semantic type. Hence a pronoun is listed in the lexicon with category NP^{NP} with meaning $\lambda x_e[x]$. And, more generally, any expression that has an unbound pronoun within it has a superscript in its category.[7] The category of *his mother* is also NP^{NP} while the category of the underlined material in (13b) is S^{NP}.

---

[7] However the reverse does not hold: not everything with a superscript has an actual unbound pronoun within it. See 15.5 for additional uses of the superscript feature, and see also Chapter 17. The analogue to this in variable-ful theories is that some expressions contain unbound variables within them as part of their meaning even though there is no overt pro-form within these expressions. See, e.g., Mitchell (1986), von Fintel (1994), Stanley and Szabo (2000), and others.

Now consider the semantic composition of the underlined expression in (13b), where *he* combines with *lost*. Since *lost* is S/NP and [[lost]] is of type $<e,t>$, it cannot directly combine with *he* which is of category NP^{NP} and of type $<e,e>$. But a simple unary rule—already familiar from R-5 (**g-sl**) in Chapter 13—will accomplish the task. We need only a slightly different version of R-5; one whose semantics is the same, but whose syntax has the effect of passing the superscript feature from an argument to the result category. The fragment in the Appendix actually suggests collapsing the two **g** rules, but for now we keep them distinct. The new one is formulated in R-7 and will be referred to as **g-sup**:

R-7.   (**g-sup**): Let α be an expression of the form $<[a]; A/B; [[a]]>$. Then there is an expression β of the form $<[a]; A^C/B^C; g_c[[a]]>$ (for c the type of expressions of category C).

With this, *he lost* is put together as follows:

(15)   lost, S/NP, lost' $\rightarrow_{\text{g-sup}}$
lost, S^{NP}/NP^{NP}, $\lambda f_{<e,e>}[\lambda x[\text{lost'}(f(x))]]$
he, NP^{NP}, $\lambda y[y]$
he lost, S^{NP}, $\lambda f_{<e,e>}[\lambda x[\text{lost'}(f(x))]](\lambda y[y]) = [\lambda x[\text{lost'}(\lambda y[y](x))]] = \lambda x[\text{lost'}(x)] = \text{lost'}$

Note then that *he lost* means the same as *lost* (modulo the contribution of gender), but has a different category. As expected, its category is S^{NP}.

It is worth pausing to observe an interesting similarity between the LF account with variables developed in section 15.2 and the account here, which is that both posit a commonality between "gaps" in constructions like relative clauses and pronouns. The LF account treats one as a trace while the other is of course a lexical item, but both have indices and the two have the same semantics. The account here has nothing analogous to a trace, but treats the semantics of an expression containing a gap and an expression containing an unbound pronoun within it as a function of type $<e,X>$ for some X. The argument slot is passed up in both cases by a **g** rule which has two different versions in terms of the syntax—one passing up a slash and one a superscript—but both have the same semantics.

15.5. Take *his* as listed in the lexicon as $NP[GEN]^{NP[GEN]}$ with meaning $\lambda x_e[x]$. Show the syntactic and semantic composition of *his mother lost*.

The next step is to introduce machinery to get the effect of what we have informally been calling binding. In other words, how is it that (12b) and (13b) have the readings indicated by the indices there? This is accomplished by an additional unary rule. Before giving its formulation, a comment is in order lest it appear that unary rules are being added willy-nilly. For recall that the LF account also has a unary rule (or something analogous) to effect binding: this is the interpretation rule (9) in Chapter 13. This rule maps an *open proposition* (one which has different values on G/i for some i) to one which is the same proposition on all members of G/i. Its semantics is analogous to the semantics in Chapter 9 of lambda abstraction. The rule to be introduced in the variable-free framework is different in that it does not, of course, use assignments and variables. Another interesting difference is that it is more local—a fact which will be quite advantageous in some of the material to be considered later. But both accounts make use of a unary rule (or something analogous) for binding.

Hence we first define an operation on functions which called z as follows (to be generalized later):

(16)   Let f be a function of type $<b,<e,a>>$. Then $z(f)$ is of type $<<e,b>,$ $<e,a>>$, and is $\lambda Y_{<e,a>}[\lambda x_e[f(Y(x))(x)]]$.

The informal intuition is that z maps f to a new function whose first argument will not be something in set a but rather will be a function from individuals to members of a. Its next argument will be an individual, and it "merges together" the two individual slots. Incidentally, there is no real reason to restrict z to functions of type $<a,<e,b>>$ rather than functions of type $<a,<c,b>>$ (for any c); this is done here for expository ease. We can then define the full unary rule at work as follows; we refer to this rule as **z**:

R-8.   Let a be an expression of the form $<[a], (A/NP)/B, [[a]]>$. Then there is an expression β of the form $<[a], (A/NP)/B^{NP}, z([[a\square]])>$.

By way of illustration, consider (12b). As already noted, [[his mother]] is the function mapping each individual to his mother; call this the-mother-of function. Now take *love*. Its lexical type is $<e,<e,t>>$, and so cannot combine directly with *his mother* which is of type $<e,e>$. But one of two things can happen. One is that *love* maps to **g**(*love*), whose meaning is of type $<<e,e>,<e,<e,t>>>$; we return to that derivation below. Here we are interested in the bound reading; this results from the mapping to **z**(*love*), whose meaning is of type $<<e,e>,<e,t>>$. It is easiest to get the intuition of the semantics of z informally. To z-love some function f (of type $<e,e>$) is to be an x who ordinary-loves the value that f assigns to x. So in this case, *z-love* combines with the-mother-of function, and to be an x who z-loves the-mother-of function is to be an x who loves the-mother-of x. In function terms, the meaning of the VP is $\lambda x[\text{love'(the-mother-of'(x))(x)}]$; in set terms it is the set of self's mother-lovers. And the full meaning for (11b) is derived by taking this as argument of the GQ subject. The whole S, then, is true just in case the set of self's mother callers has the third grade boy set as a subset.

It is again worth comparing this to the LF theory with variables. In that theory *every third grade boy* undergoes QR, so that the LF is (17):

(17)   every third grade boy $[_{\Lambda_8}$ [s t8 loves his8 mother]]

The value of the embedded S is—on any g—the proposition that g(8) loves the mother of g(8). By the rule in (9), the value of the node labeled Λ_8 is, on any g, the set of self's mother lovers—exactly the same (modulo the use of the assignments) as the meaning of the VP *loves his mother* in the variable-free account. Thus the step that accomplishes binding happens at the S-level, where there is a trace in subject position coindexed with the pronoun. In the variable-free theory it happens through the mapping of *love'* to *z-love'*. But the rest of the composition is essentially the same. In the LF theory, $[[\Lambda_8]]^g$ is taken as argument of $[[\text{every third grade boy}]]^g$ to give the final meaning. In the variable-free account, $[[\text{z-loves his mother}]]$ is taken as argument of $[[\text{every third grade boy}]]$.

This discussion centered on the semantics only, but z has a syntactic side too. Since *his mother* is not an ordinary NP but is of category NP^{NP} it would also be syntactically of the wrong category to be argument of ordinary *loves* whose category is $(S/_L NP)/_R NP$. But z maps this to an expression whose category is $(S/_L NP)/_R NP^{NP}$—i.e., to something wanting to combine with a pronoun-containing expression.

We further illustrate the z rule with (13b). Recall from (15) that *he lost* is of category S^{NP} with meaning $[[\text{lost}]]$ (of type $<e,t>$). Now consider *thinks*. As usual, we ignore the fact that *thinks'* takes an intensional argument (i.e., it is of type $<<s,t>,<e,t>>$) and simplify its lexical type as $<t<e,t>>$.

Then z-*think* is of type $<<e,t>,<e,t>>$, and to z-think some P of type $<e,t>$ is to be an x who thinks that P holds of x. So (13b) is put together as follows:

(18)   thinks, $(S/_LNP)/_RS$, thinks' $\rightarrow_z$
thinks, $(S/_LNP)/_RS^{NP}$, $\lambda P_{<e,t>}[\lambda x[thinks'(P(x))(x)]]$
he lost, S^{NP}, lost' (from (3) above)
thinks he lost, $S/_LNP$, $\lambda P_{<e,t>}[\lambda x[thinks'(P(x))(x)]](lost') =$
  $\lambda x[thinks'(lost'(x))(x)]$
this VP is then taken as argument of the subject GQ *every male candidate*

15.6. Show the full syntactic and semantic composition of (14). The first part is already done in your answer to (15.5).

*15.7. By way of comparison, work through the derivation of (14) using the LF account, seeing step by step where this differs from the variable-free account. Try to see just where this is similar to the variable-free account and where it is different.

Now consider a sentence like (19):

(19)   Every first grade boy$_i$ thinks that Santa loves his$_i$ mother.

Here the pronoun is not bound within the lower clause but only within the *thinks* clause. But recall that the lexical verb *loves* can also map to **g**-*loves* (rather than **z**-*loves*). Informally, this keeps the pronoun "free" and available for binding from higher up. In this case, the lower VP is put together as follows:

(20)   loves, $(S/_LNP)/_RNP$, loves' $\rightarrow_g$
loves, $(S/_LNP)^{NP}/_RNP^{NP}$, $\lambda f_{<e,e>}[\lambda x[loves'(f(x))]]$
his mother, NP^{NP}, the-mother-of
loves his mother, $(S/_LNP)^{NP}$, $\lambda f_{<e,e>}[\lambda x[loves'(f(x))]](the\text{-}mother\text{-}of) =$
$\lambda x[loves'(the\text{-}mother\text{-}of'(x))]$

The meaning of g-*loves his mother*, then, is of type $<e<e,t>>$.

A worry might arise: when this combines with the subject *Santa* (which denotes the individual s), why is that not taken as argument of this function? If it were, the sentence would be saying something about someone loving the mother of Santa, obviously an unfortunate result. But in fact a derivation in which the above function applies to the individual denoted by the subject is not countenanced by the syntax. The lexical entry for *Santa* is an NP, and nothing allows this to directly combine with an $(S/_LNP)^{NP}$. The derivation of (19) involves **g** on the GQ (type-lifted) version of *Santa*, as shown below; the remainder of the derivation of (19) is left for the reader in Exercise 15.8.

(21)   Santa, NP, s →₁

Santa, l(NP) (hence, $S/_R(S/_L NP)$), $\lambda P_{<e,t>}[P(s)]$ →$_{\text{g-sup}}$

Santa, $S^{NP}/_R(S/_L NP)^{NP}$, $\lambda R_{<e,<e,t>>} [\lambda y[\lambda P_{<e,t>}[P(s)](R(y))]]$ =
$\lambda R_{<e,<e,t>>} [\lambda y[R(y)(s)]]$

Incidentally, Exercise 15.12 will suggest a way to generalize the **app** rule (R-1) so that the ordinary NP *Santa* can directly combine with *loves his mother* in (19) (without use of l or **g-sup**). This gives s a much shorter derivation resulting in the same string and meaning. Should there be some advantage to adopting a theory allowing for shorter derivations, this option is quite possible, and an interested reader is invited to explore this further on their own.

> **15.8.** Show the rest of the syntactic and semantic computation for (19). (For the treatment of *that* see the fragment at the end of Chapter 6.)

15.3.2. Free pronouns

Nothing in the system forces the application of **z** at some point in the derivation of a sentence with a pronoun: there could be just applications of **g** "all the way up." Suppose, for example, a sentence like *Santa loves his mother* were derived using the steps shown above (thus *loves* undergoes **g** rather than **z**), and where this is not embedded further and is just a main clause. For that matter, a sentence like *Every boy thinks that Santa loves his mother* also has a reading in which *his* is not bound by either *every boy* or by *Santa* and is just a free pronoun. In that case, then, we end up with the final "sentence" being of category S^{NP} and with meaning of type <e,t>.

> **15.9.** Show the derivation of *every boy thinks (that) Santa loves his mother* where *his* remains free.

Recall that a similar situation holds in the LF theory; there nothing forces binding either. In the LF theory, a sentence like *Santa loves his mother* where *his* is not bound denotes an assignment-dependent proposition, and its ultimate propositional value is supplied not in the semantics proper. Rather, the listener presumably applies this to some contextually salient assignment. The situation here is a bit different, but analogous. In the variable-free account, the "sentence" is ultimately of category S^{NP} and not S. Its value is not a proposition but a function from individuals to propositions. Here, then, the propositional information is supplied by the listener applying this to some contextually salient *individual* (rather than a salient assignment). Lest it seem odd to conclude that *Santa loves his mother* (on the free reading) or a simple sentence like *He left* do not denote propositions but rather functions into propositions, we need merely note that the full value of such expressions is not a proposition in the variable-ful view either. These are assignment-dependent propositions, which is equivalent to saying that they are functions from assignments to propositions. Thus there is no proposition unless some contextually salient assignment is picked. (In fact, arguably the notion of an individual being contextually salient is somewhat less mysterious than the notion of an assignment being salient.)

One might also wonder in the variable-free view why ordinary VPs like **Left* are not well-formed sentences in their own right in English. After all, this has the same meaning (modulo the gender contribution of the pronoun) as *He left*. The reason is purely one of syntax: S/NP and S^{NP} are not the same syntactic category. The latter but not the former can stand alone (and any theory needs some account of what can and cannot be free-standing expressions). An obvious speculation is that this might be the right analysis for so-called pro-drop languages; there perhaps tensed VPs are allowed to stand alone, and have <e,t> meanings as their value, just as *he left* does in English.[8]

*15.3.3. Generalizing the rules

This section generalizes some of the rules in the fragment. One reason for these generalizations centers on cases with multiple pronouns to be discussed below. Another is that in general the combinatorics need to be able to ignore superscripts. The generalizations required are straightforward, and are easily accomplished by defining (at least some of) the rules recursively, a move which may well have other benefits throughout the system.

---

[8] Note that wondering why it is that some languages allow tensed VPs as stand-alone expressions and some do not is no different than wondering why some languages are pro-drop and some are not.

Consider (22):

(22)   Every third grade boy$_i$ saw the man who his$_i$ mother kissed (under the mistletoe).

The initial focus is on how it is that the relative clause *who his mother kissed* can occur as a postnominal modifier. Recall that the fragment as developed so far allows expressions like *who Ms Claus kissed* to occur as nominal modifiers via R-2; this rule maps an RC to an N/N. Although that treatment might ultimately be revised, that rule nonetheless serves well to illustrate the general point. The details of the internal composition of *who his mother kissed* are postponed until Exercise 15.11, but assume that it is (as we would expect) an expression of category RC^{NP}. The point is that R-2 is formulated to take as input RC and not RC^{NP} and so needs to be modified. Moreover, the output should not be N/N but rather (N/N)^{NP}. And, while we have so far dealt with cases containing only one pronoun, any expression can of course contain any number of pronouns, such as the relative clause in (23):

(23)   the table which her mother built for his father

Here *her mother built for her father* is presumably of category (RC^{NP})^{NP} and maps to ((N/N)^{NP})^{NP}.

This presents no serious problem. We simply generalize R-2 by defining the syntactic and semantic mappings recursively. First, we define the base step, which is the operation that shifts a function of type $<x,t>$ to one of type $<<x,t>,<x,t>>$ with the associated semantics of intersection. Call this **int**^{0} and define **int** recursively as follows (note the connection to the recursive definition of [[and]] given earlier):

(24)   a.   Let f be a function of type $<x,t>$. Then **int**^{0}(f) is of type $<<x,t>,<x,t>>$ and is $\lambda g_{<x,t>}[f_s \cap g_s]$.
            b.   Let f be a function of type $<a,b>$ such that **int**^{i} is defined for b (for some i). Then **int**^{n}(f) = $\lambda A_a[\textbf{int}^{n-1}(f(A))]$.

The same can be done with the syntactic side. Recall that some of the syntactic operations on categories (such as **l** and **g-sl**) are related to the corresponding semantic operations; hence the use of the same names. For R-2, however, this is not the case; the syntactic mapping of RC (or AP) to N/N has nothing to do with the intersection of strings, so we adopt a new name for the syntactic mapping—call it **NMOD**. Thus we define this as follows:

(25) a. Let C be the category RC or AP (and perhaps some others). Then
NMOD^0(C) is N/N. If C consists of just one word, then **NMOD^0**(C) is
N/$_R$N.

b. Let C be any category X^Y such that **NMOD^i** (for some i) is defined for
X. Then **NMOD^n**(C) = (**NMOD^{n-1}**(X))^Y.

R-2 can now be generalized as follows:

R-2′:   Let a be an expression of the form <[a], C, [[a]], for C any category for
which **NMOD** is defined>. Then there is an expression β of the form
<[a], **NMOD^n**(C), **int^n**([[a]])>.

Other unary rules can be generalized in exactly this way. (Since **z** will
have a different generalization, and since it is not clear that that there is any
reason to generalize **z** in this way, we will not extend this to **z**, although it
would do no harm to do so.) To save space, the generalizations will not be
given here; the reader can work through some examples via the exercises
below. Incidentally, in the particular case at hand, the numerical superscript is not necessary, but it is included for exposition since the analogue is
needed for some of the other rules. This is because in some cases the
semantics could work in more than one way if the generalized rule did
not keep track of the recursion. Take for example a function f of type
<a,<b,c>> and consider how a generalized **g** rule could apply to this. There
are two ways: it could map f to a function of type <<d,a>,<d,<b,c>> or to
a function of type <a,<<d,b>,<d,c>>>. But (for both the slash version of **g**
and the superscript version), the syntax of the two applications is different,
and the use of the numerical superscript will make sure that the syntax
traces the semantics. Of the two mappings of f noted above, the first is g^o(f)
and the second is g^l(f).

---

*15.10. Generalize **g-sl** (R-5), **g-sup** (R-7), and **l** (R-4) in the way shown
above.

Armed with the answer to Exercise 15.10, the apparatus is in place to give
the full syntactic and semantic composition of *who his mother kissed* in (22).
We leave the demonstration of this for Exercise 15.11, but a few hints are in
order. It is helpful to first work again through the composition of *who Ms
Claus kissed*, and keep in mind that the composition of *who his mother kissed*
should be (more or less) parallel, just using the generalized versions of the

relevant rules. There is, however, one difference to be aware of. Once you have gotten *his mother* to be of the appropriate type, you should note that it cannot immediately take *kissed* as argument, and so a few more steps are needed. Feel free to help yourself to **l** and **g**. But, as will be explored in section 15.12, another possibility (which gives the same result but in a shorter derivation) is simply to generalize R-1 in a way parallel to the generalization of the unary rules. Since the exercises below are somewhat technical, a less ambitious reader can skip them and simply take it on faith that *who his mother kissed* can be composed into an expression of category RC^{NP}.

---

*15.11. Show the syntactic and semantic composition of *who his mother kissed.* Then show the composition of *the man who his mother kissed.* (The details of the composition of *his mother* can be skipped as this was done in Exercise 15.5.)

*15.12. Generalize R-1 in the way suggested above, and show how this simplifies the derivation of *his mother kissed.* More generally, comment on just how it is that superscript features are "passed" (in terms of functions vs arguments) in the two different ways to do this. Go back to the derivation of *Santa loves his mother* (in which *his* is free) shown in (20) and (21) and show a shorter derivation for this with this generalization (making sure that the meaning is the one intended in that discussion).

A slightly different generalization is needed for **z**, for R-8 gives it only for the narrow case of binding a pronoun within some expression C by the argument slot that is the very next one after C is introduced. But in fact, a pronoun can be bound by any later argument slot. This is most obvious in the case of three-place verbs. If the analysis of these in Chapter 6 is correct, the merging of the subject position with the pronoun within the PP skips over the object position:

(26) No fourth grade boy$_i$ sent flowers to his$_i$ mother.

Send is of category ((S/NP)/NP)/PP and it should map by an extended version of **z** to ((S/NP)/NP)/PP^{NP}. (See the discussion in 15.3.4 for one reason for adopting this category.) Similarly, [[send]] is a function of type $<e,<e,<e,t>>>$ and should map to one of type $<<e,e>,<e,<e,t>>>$ with meaning $\lambda f[\lambda y[\lambda x[send'(x)(y)(f(x))]]]$. It is obvious that we need a generalization that allows binding across argument positions. Incidentally, the need for a generalization of **z** which skips over argument positions is independent of this particular analysis of *send*. The other possibility is that it combines first with its adjacent NP and then with the PP and so is of category ((S/NP)/PP)/NP. But then there would still be need for the generalized version of **z** for sentences like *No fourth grade boy$_i$ showed his$_i$ picture to Nora.* Moreover, argument positions given as superscripts also need to be skipped over; examples illustrating this point will be given later.

The rule should thus be generalized to bind across any argument slot. In the syntax, the generalization is that it can skip over both ordinary slashes and superscripts. To notate this, let A|B mean either A/B or A^B. Then, borrowing the notational conventions used in Chapter 14, we state the generalized **z** rule. (In this case it is again not clear that there is any need for the grammar to keep track the various versions of the rule, but to be safe we will distinguish them by using the name of the result category.) Hence, we first generalize the semantics, and then state the generalized rule:

Definition: Let f be a function of type $<b,<c^{\rightarrow n},<e,a>>>$ (where $c^{\rightarrow n}$ means n number of argument positions of any time, for $n \geq 0$). Then $z^a(f) = \lambda Y_{<e,b>}[\lambda Z^{\rightarrow n}[\lambda x_e[f(Y(x))(Z^{\rightarrow n})(x)]]]$.

R-8   Generalized: Let α be an expression of the form $<[\alpha], ((A/NP)|C^{\rightarrow n})/B, [[\alpha]]>$. Then there is an expression β of the form $<[\alpha], ((A/NP)|C^{\rightarrow n})/B^{NP}, z^a([[\alpha]])>$.

We will generally omit the superscript except where needed for clarity. While the notation looks clumsy, this is arguably an artifact of the notational system; conceptually the rule is straightforward. The semantics merely takes a function that wants some argument in b, then any number of other arguments, and then an individual argument, and maps it to one that takes an argument in $<e,b>$, then the same other arguments and then an individual, and "merges" the last individual slot with the individual-argument slot in $<e,b>$ argument. The syntax is similar; it basically can skip over both slash and superscripts.

15.3.4. Weak Crossover

Recall the discussion in section 15.2.2 of Weak Crossover effects as exemplified in (4):

(4)   a. No fourth grade boy$_i$ called his$_i$ mother (on Mother's Day).
       b. *His$_i$ mother called no fourth grade boy$_i$ (on the first day of school).

The LF view there adopted the LF filter (9), which rules out any LF in which a pronoun and trace are coindexed unless the latter c-commands the former. (We should caution, though, that while this is a common strategy for accounting for these effects, there are also many other accounts. Still the use of some sort of filter is quite common.)

In the variable-free view developed here, the asymmetry between (4a) and (4b) is built directly into the formulation of z: it maps a function of type $<b<e,a>>$ to one of type $<<e,b>,<e,a>>$ (or—for the generalized version given in 15.4.3—it maps a function of type $<b,<c^{\to n},<e,a>>>$ to one of type $<<e,b>,<c^{\to n},<e,a>>>$) and it merges the "later in" e-argument slot with the slot occupied by the pronoun. In other words, in (4a) it maps *call*—which expects an ordinary e-type object—to something wanting an $<e,e>$ object, and it binds the newly introduced e-position to its subject slot. It is automatic, then, that the effect of binding works in the direction that it does. And so one nice consequence of the variable-free approach is that nothing extra is needed to give Weak Crossover effects. The rules do not in any sense require an additional filter to rule out certain representations or derivations; the effect follows directly from the way the binding rule (z) works.

Of course the system developed here also allows subjects to first combine with transitive verbs (see, for example, the discussion in section 13.4.1). Does this interfere with the generalization above about the binding pattern? The answer is no: the asymmetry is unaffected by the fact that the combinatory order is flexible, because the binding step (the rule z) effects the argument structure of a very local expression. To demonstrate, note first that indeed *his mother* can combine with *called* to give *his mother called* of category $(S/_R NP)^{NP}$. This was demonstrated in Exercises 15.10 and 15.11, but readers who skipped that section can simply take this on faith. But the fact that *his mother called* can combine to be a single expression does not disturb anything; the effect of binding does not take as input a full expression of this sort. Rather the binding effect happens more locally—in this case on *call*—and that gives only an output in which the subject slot binds a pronoun in the object. In fact, *call* can first undergo z (before combining with the subject), but combining this with *his mother* results in something of category $(S/_R NP^{NP})^{NP}$ and with meaning $\lambda x_e[\lambda f_{<e,e>}[z\text{-call}'(f)(x)]]$. Recasting that meaning in slightly more readable form, this is $\lambda x[\lambda f_{<e,e>}[\text{call}'(f(x))(x)]]$. Thus it takes an individual x and a function f of type $<e,e>$ and returns true if x called the value of f applied to self. (And it is waiting for an NP^{NP} in object position, but will "hold off" on the superscript introduced by the pronoun in subject position.) But this does not change the binding pattern. For example, this could combine with *her dog* in such a way that *his mother* binds *her dog*, but this does not lead to the WCO-violating reading. The details of these derivations are space-consuming and hence left as an exercise for the ambitious reader; the important point here is that recasting the effect of binding in this very local way means that the existence of expressions like *his mother loves* (which are waiting for NPs in object position) cause no problem for the account of WCO.[9]

---

*15.13. Show the details of the syntactic and semantic composition of (i):

(i) His mother$_i$ called her$_k$ dog.

Note that *his* is a free pronoun; once its value is set then *his mother* picks up some individual. Therefore, the reading notated above is accessible via a derivation in which *her* happens to pick up the same individual. We are interested here, however, in showing how we get (i) on the bound reading.

15.14. Taking as point of departure the fact that *his mother called* has the meaning and category shown above, show the composition of a relative-clause case like:

(i) the woman who his mother loves

Convince yourself that this does not have the WCO-violating reading, but only has a reading in which *his* is free (and could be bound from higher up).

It should, however, be noted that although the WCO effect requires no extra constraint or stipulation, it does not follow from any deep principle of the general theory here. For there could have happened to be the reverse binding rule **s**,[10] formulated below (using the FR designation, for fictional rule):

---

[9] This is not to say that **z** always applies only to a single lexical item. Take, for example, *Every man$_i$ thinks that Mary loves his$_i$ dog.* One possible way to get the relevant reading is for **z** to apply to *thinks*. But another possibility is that *thinks that Mary loves* combines (by various applications of **g-sl** and **r-app**), and that then undergoes **z**. The result is the same either way.

[10] This is essentially the operation that Curry and Feys (1958) dubbed **S**. Hence the reason for naming the binding rule **z**; it is a "backwards" version of **S**.

Definition of s:

Given a function f of type <e,<x,y>>, s(f) is a function of type <e,<<e,x>,y>> such that $s(f) = \lambda x[\lambda Z_{<e,x>}[f(x)(Z(x))]]$.

FR-5. Let α be an expression of the form <[α], (X/Y)/NP, [[α]]>. Then there is an expression β of the form <[α], (X/Y^{NP})NP, s([[α]])>.

This does just the reverse of **z**: it maps an expression that expects both an NP and a later argument of category Y into one which now expects the NP and a later pronoun-containing Y, and semantically it merges the earlier slot with the pronoun in the later argument. This is exactly what would give WCO violations.

15.15. Show how one can get the WCO-violating reading of (i) with FR-5:

(i) *no girl who$_i$ her$_i$ father invited

15.16. Show how adoption of FR-5 also allows for a derivation of the WCO-violating (ii):

(ii) *His$_i$ mother called no fourth grade boy$_i$.

It might even be that **s** is available in a limited range of cases, for there are well-known exceptions to WCO which are poorly understood (such cases would also require exceptions to the LF filter in (9) under the variable-ful theory). Here we continue to assume that only **z** exists and not **s**, leaving open the question of whether there might be limited cases of **s**. It is, however, worth stressing again that no extra piece of machinery such as a filter is needed.

15.3.5. What happens when there is more than one pronoun?

15.3.5.1. Multiple pronouns which are "the same"

One of the nice properties of the system with variables and assignments is that cases with more than one pronoun—including cases where these are bound by different things—present no difficulty. It is built into the system that these follow just the way cases with just one pronoun do; Exercises 15.1 and 15.2 were designed to elucidate that point. Hence, no competitor to a theory with variables could possibly be taken seriously if it could not handle such cases equally well. Having generalized the rules in the way done in section 15.4.3, it turns out that such cases are also unproblematic in the variable-free view. The derivations themselves can be space-consuming when written in the λ-notation (as opposed to being written using just the operations **g** and **z**), but no new apparatus is needed. We will keep the discussion here somewhat informal, and let the interested reader work through the details on their own. (Details can also be found in Jacobson 1999, although the generalizations of the rules proposed in this chapter differ slightly from the ones given there.) Moreover, although this section does not quite merit an asterisk, the more casual reader wanting just the basic outline of how the variable-free system works can safely skip this section. Little else—including most of the further applications in Chapter 17—depends on a full understanding of this material.

First, consider sentences with two pronouns where the two pronouns are—speaking informally—"the same," as for example (27) on the reading indicated by the indices:

(27)   Every third grade boy$_i$ thinks that he$_i$ should call his$_i$ mother.

There are actually at least two different derivations that result in this reading. On one, *call* undergoes **z** so its subject position binds *his*, while *thinks* also undergoes **z** so that its subject position binds *he*. The LF variable-ful view also has a possible analysis of this which is analogous; this is explored in Exercise 15.18.

15.17. Give the full details of the above derivation for (27). You can write this out using just the **z** operator rather than in the λ-notation if it makes it easier to see what is going on. Also ignore *should*, and ignore internal details not relevant (such as the full syntactic and semantic composition of *every third grade boy*).

15.18. If you did Exercise 15.2, discuss which of the derivations shown there is analogous to the derivation in Exercise 15.17. Of course the theories are different, but it is hoped that the notion of one being analogous to the other will be clear.

But there is another way to get the appropriate meaning, which is best illustrated by noting that there are cases where the position occupied by one pronoun cannot bind the other; often these are referred to as cases where the two pronouns are *co-bound*:

(28)   Every third grade boy$_i$ thinks that the man who his$_i$ mother loves (should) feed his$_i$ dog.

This does not lend itself to the strategy above; neither pronoun is in a position whereby **z** allows its slot to bind the other pronoun. As it turns out, (28) is unproblematic. One meaning of the embedded S is such that the two pronouns do not "know" they are the same; its meaning is (using an informal representation) $\lambda x[\lambda y[$the man y's mother loves (should) feed x's dog]], and the category of the embedded clause is $(S^{NP})^{NP}$. But two applications of **z** on *thinks* will result in the appropriate meaning. Readers working through the next two exercises can see this in more detail. Notice that (27)—on the reading represented there—can also be derived in a fashion exactly analogous to the derivation here of (28).

---

*15.19. Show the syntactic and semantic composition of *the man who his mother loves (should) feed his dog*. Ignore *should*, and you can begin with *the man who his mother loves* as already composed. Its meaning is $\lambda y[$the man who y's mother loves], of category NP^{NP}. Similarly begin with *his dog* as meaning $\lambda x[$the-dog-of'(x)] of category NP^{NP}.

*15.20. Show that two applications of **z** on *think* give the desired reading for (28).

---

*15.3.5.2. And yet another possibility

Interestingly, there is another way to arrive at the reading in (28), which is to generalize **g-sub** yet further in a way already explored for **g-sl** in section 13.4.4.2. This is to allow **g** on an expression of category (A/B)/C to map to one of category $(A^D/B^D)/C^D$. The semantic operation is just as one would expect. Let f be a function of type $<c<b,a>>$. Then this generalization maps f to a function of type $<<d,c>,<<d,b>,<d,a>>>$ with meaning $\lambda X_{<d,c>}[\lambda Y_{<d,b>}[\lambda D_d[f(X(D))(Y(D))]]]$. (And of course presumably this should be generalized to apply to any number of argument slots.) Were this to apply to *feed*, the lower clause would have as its meaning $\lambda x[$the man who x's mother loves should feed x's dog] and be of category S^{NP} and a single application of **z** on *thinks* will give the reading in (28). (Note that the other derivation is available too; that there can be two applications of **z** is an automatic consequence of the system.) The difference between the derivation here and the one sketched in the above exercises is that here the meaning of the embedded S is such that the two pronouns are already "merged," and the embedded S is thus of type <e,t> rather than being of type <e,<e,t>>. As noted directly above, both derivations are automatic in the system here. Notice that this derivation is analogous to one in which the two embedded pronouns have the same index (if you did Exercise 15.2, this is analogous to one of the derivations there).

---

*15.21. Beginning with the meanings of the subject NP and the object NP as shown in 15.19, show the syntactic and semantic composition of (28) using the generalization of **g** above.

*15.22. If you did Exercise 15.2, show which of the derivations is analogous to the derivation in 15.21. The remarks in 15.18 about the notion of the finding analogies between the two different theories hold here as well.

15.3.5.3. More than one pronoun—different binders

One can also construct cases of multiple pronouns which in the end are bound by different positions. This presents no problem: these different readings arise simply through combinations of **z** and **g** applied in different orders. We sketch just one example to illustrate the point. Consider (29a) and (29b) (*no man* in (29a) is recast as *every man* in (29b) to help make sure that the relevant binding pattern is pragmatically salient in each case):

(29)   a. Every boy$_i$ hopes that no man$_j$ will realize that his$_i$ dog chased his$_j$ cat.
    b. Every boy$_i$ hopes that every man$_j$ will realize that his$_j$ dog chased his$_i$ cat.

As the interested reader can verify, *his dog chased his cat* has the meaning $\lambda x[\lambda y[y$'s dog chased x's cat]]. The key to the two different binding patterns lies in what happens to *realize* (as usual, we ignore *will* here). Both involve an application of **z** and of **g** to *realize*, but in different orders. The application of **z** binds a pronoun to the subject position of *realize* while application of **g** "passes this up" for higher binding. Therefore, if **z** applies first to *realize* followed by **g**, the subject position of *realize* binds the instance of *his* corresponding to the dog-owner; the cat-owner *his* is passed up as an open slot and is bound by **z** on *hope*. If **g** applies first then the dog-owner *his* is passed up. Binding the other *his* (the cat-owner) by the subject position of *realize* involves the application of **z** that skips over the super-script that was introduced by **g**; this is thus $\mathbf{z}^S$. The derivations are sketched more fully in (30) which schematize both the syntax and semantics:

(30) a. every-boy(**z**(hopes)(**g-sup**(no-man)(**g-sup**(**z**(realize))(his-dog-chased-his-cat)))) (= 29b)

  b. every-boy(**z**(hopes)(**g-sup**(every-man)($\mathbf{z}^S$(**g-sup**(realize))(his-dog-chased-his-cat)))) (= 29a)

---

*15.23. Take the derivations shown above and recast them showing the details both of the syntactic computation and also show the semantics using the λ-notation.

15.4. More on Weak Crossover

15.4.1. Definite NPs and WCO

15.4.1.1. An apparent problem (for both theories)

The contrasts shown earlier in (4) and (5) illustrate the WCO effect: a GQ in object position cannot bind a pronoun within the subject. Under the QR/LF view, the LF filter in (9) was posited to account for this; under the variable-free view this followed from the formulation of **z**. While there are many other formulations of Weak Crossover, the remarks below are of relevance to just about all of them. Note too that the discussion in this section is relevant to both the LF variable-ful and the Direct Compositional variable-free theory, and the discussion below should therefore be of interest regardless of one's theoretical persuasion.

The point of departure is that the empirical generalization regarding the WCO effect would seem to be threatened by perfectly good sentences in which quantified NPs are replaced by definite NPs or proper names. Thus, although some speakers find sentences like the following slightly awkward, most agree that these are clearly better than those in (4) and (5):

(31) a. The woman who had endorsed him$_i$ introduced McCain$_i$ (at the convention).

  b. The woman who had endorsed him$_i$ introduced the winner of the Iowa caucus$_i$ (at the convention).

And, while speakers vary in whether they accept cases like (32) where the pronoun is in genitive position (and not within a relative clause as in the above cases), here too it is generally agreed that these are far better than the corresponding case in (4).

(32)   a. His$_i$ mother called Jack Sprat$_i$ (the minute he got to school).
  b. His$_i$ mother called the winner of the spelling bee$_i$ (almost immediately after he won).

Since these have the readings indicated by the indices above, one might wonder whether they pose a threat to the twin claims that proper names and definite NPs can be GQs but that this kind of binding is blocked. If the reading here is a result of binding—whatever mechanism one uses for that— why should these be good?

15.4.1.2. Not a problem after all

As it turns out, these are entirely unproblematic. Indeed, just about any theory automatically predicts that the sentences in (31) and (32) can be understood in the way indicated by the indices used there. Recall that— regardless of which theory one chooses—there are pronouns which are free. This was shown by the Elmo discourse in (1) at the outset of this chapter. With that in mind, then, consider (33) under the understanding indicated by the indexing there:

(33)   Jack Sprat$_i$ called his$_i$ mother.

There are two ways that (33) could have this understanding. The first is that *his* is a bound pronoun, exactly as in the case of *Every fourth grade boy$_i$ called his$_i$ mother*. The details of course vary by theory, but both allow for a bound reading. In the LF variable-ful theory, the subject NP can be coin-dexed with *his* and can undergo QR. (Section 14.4.2.1 contained discussion of why the QR approach is formulated in such a way as to allow ordinary definite NPs to undergo QR as well allowing GQs to undergo QR.) In the variable-free approach, *call* undergoes **z**, and the meaning of the VP is the function characterizing the set of self's mother callers. Whether *Jack Sprat* in (33) is a GQ or an ordinary NP actually makes no difference; the binding is a consequence of **z** on *call*.

But *his* in (33) can also be free. Under a theory with variables it has some index, let us say 5. Assume that it happens not to be coindexed with *Jack Sprat*. Then the value of the sentence is a non-constant function from assignments to propositions. And presumably then there is an available g such that g(5) is Jack Sprat. (This is just like the case of the context making available an assignment where the relevant variable is assigned to Elmo in the obnoxious guest scenario.) This is often referred to in the literature as a case of *accidental coreference* between [[Jack Sprat]] and the value assigned to free *his*. (It is also sometimes called *covaluation*.) Analogous remarks hold in the variable-free version. Here *call* undergoes **g** and the subject lifts and also undergoes **g** (although once again see Exercise 15.12 for a way to get this via a shorter derivation). The result is a sentence of category S^{NP} with meaning of type <e,t>, and the function is applied by the listener to the contextually salient individual Jack Sprat.

   With this in mind, consider again (32a): *His$_i$ mother called Jack Sprat$_i$.* It is not at all surprising that this is good. The binding derivation is blocked, just as there can be no binding in something like **His$_i$ mother called every third grade boy$_i$.* But the free reading is not blocked: here *his* remains free and can pick up the contextually salient individual Jack Sprat. More technically: on the view with variables it has an index (say, 5) and the sentence is understood on the assignment g such that g(5) = Jack Sprat. On the variable-free view the sentences denotes a function from individuals to propositions, and is applied to the contextually salient individual Jack Sprat.

15.4.1.3. Independent evidence: Ellipsis and the notion "sloppy identity"

Striking confirmation for the remarks above comes from ellipsis phenomena. This will be exposited primarily using the variable-free approach, but similar remarks hold under the variable-ful LF approach and some of the exercises are designed to bring this out. Thus note that two key points emerged from the above discussion. *Point 1*: In a sentence like (33), the understanding that Jack Sprat called Jack Sprat's mother comes about in two different ways (the pronoun can be free or bound). In variable-free terms, *call* can undergo **z** (giving the bound reading) or it can undergo **g**, where the entire sentence is then a function of type <e,t> applied to a contextually salient individual, who can certainly be Jack Sprat. *Point 2*: Whatever accounts for WCO effects in the case of quantified NPs predicts that for a sentence like (32), the only way that the relevant understanding can emerge is via a free pronoun. Ellipsis provides a nice probe to verify both of these.

Now consider (34) on the understanding of the first sentence where what is at issue is Jack calling Jack's mother. Even keeping that constant, there is a well-known ambiguity in the second sentence:

(34)   Jack$_i$ won't call his$_i$ mother. But Bill will.

On one reading, it is understood as asserting that Bill—unlike Jack—will be a dutiful son and will call Bill's mother. This is especially easy to bring out in a context where Jack and Bill are two boys at a boarding school, and it is Mother's Day. (Call that the Mother's Day scenario.) The other way to understand the second sentence is that once again Jack is not a dutiful son, but Bill will call Jack's mother. This easily emerges in the following scenario: Jack's mother is in the hospital, Jack and his mother have always been estranged, but Bill also knows Jack's mother and is quite fond of her. (Call that the Hospitalized Mother scenario.) The first of these readings was dubbed the *sloppy identity* reading in Ross (1967) and this terminology has been used ever since. The second reading is what Ross dubbed the *strict identity* reading.

That the "missing" VP in (34) can be understood either way is exactly what one would expect. Once again, concrete discussion of this point requires choosing some theory of ellipsis (and of binding), and so we use the account developed in section 13.4.2, though similar remarks hold under other accounts as well. There it was hypothesized that what is generally known as VP ellipsis involves the mapping of the lexical item *will* (of category VP/VP) to a second word that does not actually expect to get a complement in the syntax. Continuing to use the notion of a "free variable" as an expository device, the meaning of this second item is *will'(P)*. Thus P here is a free variable over <e,t> type meanings, and its value is fixed by the context. Obviously in the full variable-free setting we need to modify this since there could not, of course, be free variables; see section 15.6. But using the notion of a free variable for exposition is convenient, so we continue with that informal notion for now. Then a sentence like *Bill will* is ultimately [[will'(P)(b)]] and something in the context supplies the value for P. In (34) it is obviously the meaning of the VP in the *Jack* sentence.

Since the VP in the *Jack* sentence contains a pronoun, one possible meaning for it is $\lambda x[x$ *called x's mother*$]$. That is, it denotes the set of self's mother-callers. And if this is picked up as the value of P, the result is the so-called sloppy reading. The *Bill* sentence ends up saying that Bill has the same property, from which it follows that Bill calls Bill's mother. Notice, incidentally, that the term "sloppy identity" is a misnomer: the *meaning* supplied in the second sentence is exactly the same as the meaning of the first VP. And so the existence of this reading is completely unsurprising.[11] The parallel story under the LF approach is not exactly the same, for here the VP itself in the first clause does not have as its value $\lambda x [x\ call\ x's\ mother]$ but is, rather, just the assignment-dependent set such that for any g its value is the set of individuals who called the mother of g(5). Nonetheless, a similar point holds in the LF approach as well, and we leave the detailed exposition of this to the reader in the exercise below.

15.24. Proponents of the LF theory usually make somewhat different assumptions regarding VP Ellipsis, according to which there is some actual level of linguistic representation of the second sentence containing material which is identical to material in the first sentence. But because it is unduly cumbersome to compare this to the view taken here, use the view of VP Ellipsis discussed above (and in section 14.4.2) when doing this exercise. Thus, show how the LF theory also accounts for the sloppy reading under the assumption that the missing VP is understood as a free variable P, whose value is set by being the meaning of some other expression in the discourse context. Comment on the crucial role that LF is playing in supplying the "missing" meaning.

The strict reading—brought out in the Hospitalized Mother scenario—is simply the reading that results when *his* in the first sentence is free and picks up contextually salient *John*. And so the understood value for P for the second sentence is the set of individuals who call John's mother. Incidentally, *his* can also refer to any other salient person in the discourse context. Take, for example, the following which we will call the Sam's Mother scenario. Sam, Jack, and Bill are all good friends, have been since childhood, and so they all know Sam's mother. Sam's mother has been in an accident and is in hospital. We are discussing the fact that Sam is out of the country (with no access to Skype) and wonder if anyone will be able to call Sam's mother. Here the natural understanding of the first sentence is that

---

[11] That the so-called sloppy identity reading can be analyzed this way was proposed at least as early as Keenan (1971).

Jack will not call Sam's mother. In that case (and without any further context to set the value for P) the second sentence is understood as claiming that Bill will call Sam's mother. Notice that this reading—where *his* is Sam—and the strict reading discussed above are basically the same. Whoever *his* happens to pick up in the first sentence results in an <e,t> function which is picked up as the value of P. The strict reading, then, is just a special case of the more general case where *his* picks up someone in the discourse context. (This point is worth stressing, as it is sometimes lost in discussions about these.)

The existence of the strict/sloppy ambiguity thus confirms Point 1 above: the prediction that there are two ways to get the understanding of *his* in (33) shown by the indexing there. Point 2—that in cases like (32a) there can be no binding—cannot be shown by using VP Ellipsis for obvious reasons. But we can show this by broadening the landscape of ellipsis phenomena. Before giving the relevant sentences, consider the following scenario. Jack, Bill, and Sam are all childhood friends and go off to boarding school on the same day. Their three mothers are all worried that the boys will be lonely, and so they designate Jack's mother to call each boy some time during the first week. A and B are discussing whether or not Jack's mother has fulfilled her obligations yet, and they have the following dialogue:

(35)   A. Well, his mother did call Jack today.
       B. Yes, but not Bill.

It should again be noted that some speakers find A's sentence itself (on the intended reading) to be somewhat marginal; it is most natural with stress on *Jack*.[12] (It also requires stress on *did* in this context.) But for most speakers it is at least tolerable. The point to notice is that the B sentence is completely natural in this scenario. Assume—as in the case of VP ellipsis—that a sentence fragment as in B is understood by some process according to which the meaning of [[his mother (did) call]] is supplied here. (Notice that in the CG fragment it makes perfect sense to say that this has a meaning since this material can be composed up to be a well-formed expression with a meaning. The LF view one would need to say something a bit different about the understanding of the B-sentence, but that debate would take us

---

[12] This is known as focal stress or contrastive stress; a discussion of focus is contained in Chapter 18. Many of the remarks in this section on ellipsis can be made also with respect to focus and there is a well-known connection between ellipsis and focus (see, e.g., Rooth 1992).

too far afield. The ultimate point about the pronoun will go through regardless of the exact theory of ellipsis.) So the B-sentence is fine, but it can only be understood on the strict reading. This follows if *his* in the A-sentence can be understood as a free pronoun.

Strikingly, no sloppy reading is available. This can be confirmed by a simple variant of the above scenario which is designed to bring out a sloppy reading. The same boys go off to boarding school, the same mothers worry about their loneliness. But instead of one mother being the designated caller, each mother decides that at some point during the week she will call her own child. Once again A and B are discussing whether or not all of the boys have yet gotten their phone calls. (35B) cannot (at least not without great difficulty) be understood as conveying that Bill's mother did not call Bill, even though this scenario was loaded in such a way as to try to bring out the sloppy reading.

This follows given the claim that *his* cannot be bound by the object position. Putting this more technically in variable-free terms, *his mother called* can be assembled into an expression with a meaning, but the way the binding rule **z** works, this cannot have the meaning $\lambda x[x$'s mother call $x]$. That can only be assembled if there were a backwards version of **z** that applied to *call*. The LF theory—supplemented by the WCO filter in (9) in Chapter 13—also has no way to compose up an LF for (35A) such that there is a part of that LF with that meaning. In (35A) *Jack* can undergo QR, but if it was coindexed with the pronoun then its trace would not c-command the pronoun, and the WCO filter would be violated. Notice too that the attempted meaning of the dialogue in (35) in the relevant scenario is possible if we simply change the structure of the sentences a bit, and so (36) easily allows for the sloppy reading:

(36)   A. $Jack_i$ was called by his_i mother today.
        B. Yes, but Bill wasn't.

This of course is not surprising, since *his* in A can be a bound pronoun.

Thus, summarizing the situation in theory-neutral terms, the fact that definite NPs in object position can "co-refer" to a pronoun within a subject does not threaten the WCO generalization, since this pronoun can be free. And the pattern of strict and sloppy identity with ellipsis confirms the suspicion that such cases only involve free and not bound pronouns.

15.25. Consider the following:

(i) Every third grade boy$_i$ thinks that he$_i$ should call his$_i$ mother and that every fourth grade boy should too.

This has a sloppy reading, where the third grade boys think that the fourth grade boys should call their own (fourth grade boys') mothers. Show how this is predicted to be a possible reading using the variable-free approach and discuss this (at least informally) with respect to the LF approach. Consult Exercises 15.17 and 15.18.

It is worth noting that this also has a strict reading even where the pronoun is bound—i.e., a reading in which the second clause is understood in such a way that each third grade boy thinks that each fourth grade boy should call the mother of that third grade boy. We will not explore here how this is accounted for in either theory. It is actually fairly easy to see what would be going on in the LF theory, and the interested reader is invited to work that out. For the variable-free theory, a more detailed account of ellipsis is needed; the account spelled out in Jacobson (2003) allows for this.

*15.4.1.4. A more formal account of the strict reading

There is more to say about the strict reading, as an interesting issue arises (under either theory). The key generalization is that however *his* is understood in the *Jack* sentence, it has the same understanding in the *Bill* sentence. Under what we've been calling the strict reading (as in the Hospitalized Mother scenario) *his* is understood as *Jack* in both cases. In the Sam's Mother scenario, *his* is understood as *Sam* in both cases. As noted above, the strict reading is just a special case of the more general free reading. But what is interesting is that there is no way for the first *his* to be understood one way and the second a different way. (Of course that is exactly what happens in the sloppy reading, so in order to show the point we need to construct a case where we rule out the possibility of *his* being bound by the subject. Once that is controlled for, we can show that there is no way to understand the two occurrences of *his* differently.) To convincingly show the point it is necessary to construct a scenario in which the non-existent reading is pragmatically quite felicitous, but is nonetheless unavailable. Here, then, is an appropriate scenario. Sam, Jack, Bill, and Tony have all been good friends since childhood. Sam's mother is Thelma, Bill's mother is Louise, and

Thelma and Louise are also good friends. Thelma and Louise are in a car which plunges off a cliff; both are injured and rushed to the hospital. Now imagine two people—A and B—who are talking about this. There is a third person—C—who knows all of the above facts. Moreover, C misses the first part of the conversation, but does overhear the interchange in (37):

(37) A. Well, Jack won't call his mother.
     B. True. But Tony will.

It is perfectly reasonable for C to conclude that A meant that Jack won't call Sam's mother (Thelma) or to conclude that A meant that Jack won't call Bill's mom (Louise). But whichever proposition speaker A's utterance is meant to convey, C assumes that B's utterance is about the same mother. C cannot come away from this conversation thinking that (on the basis of what he has heard) Jack won't call Thelma but Tony will call Louise.

Consider, now, the value of [[call his mother]] where *his* is free under either of the theories discussed here. In the variable-ful theory, it is not strictly speaking a function of type <e,t>, but an assignment-dependent function of this type: i.e., a function of type <G,<e,t>>. In the variable-free theory, it is a function of type <e,<e,t>>. Now consider what that entails in terms of the fact that some kind of missing meaning is supplied in the B sentence. We have not spelled out in full the details of just how it is that a missing VP-type meaning is supplied, and will continue to be informal on that score. But regardless of the details, the following question arises: is what is supplied as understanding in the second sentence a function *into* <e,t> meanings (in variable-ful terms, the domain of that function is G; in variable-free terms the domain of that function is e)? Or is it instead the case that what is supplied is not literally the value of the first VP, but an <e,t> meaning arrived at by applying the value of the first VP to some assignment (in the variable-ful theory) or some individual (in the variable-free) theory?

The simplest way to ensure that Thelma and Louise do not get mixed up in (37) is to assume the latter. That is, what is supplied as the "missing" meaning in the B sentence is not a function from some domain into a function of type <e,t>, but rather a full-blown <e,t> meaning itself. Interestingly, there is independent evidence for the hypothesis that in this type of construction what is picked up is a full-blown <e,t> rather than a function into such functions. This evidence comes from the domain of indexical pronouns such as *I, you*, etc. Obviously their value depends on the speech context: assume that an indexical pronoun denotes a function from speech contexts to individuals.[13] One way to work this into the full theory of the compositional semantics is to take every expression as having a value which is a function from contexts to something else. The value of a sentence, for example, is a function from speech contexts to propositions—i.e., from contexts to functions of type $<s,t>$. Hence, for example, the proposition expressed by a sentence such as *I believe in variables* depends on the context of utterance. Obviously folding this into the full compositional apparatus is beyond the present scope and so we will continue to ignore this context parameter for the rest of this book, save to note its relevance to the analysis of VP Ellipsis.

So take a VP like *call my mother tonight*. Leaving aside the worlds and times, its value is not a function of type $<e,t>$ but rather a function from speech contexts to such a function. Now consider the dialogue in (38), the implications of which are discussed in Hankamer and Sag (1984):

(38)   A: Jack is going to call my mother tonight.
         B: Really? I'll bet Bill won't.

Here the understanding of the "missing" material is not the set of individuals who call B's mother, but rather those who call A's mother. Yet since the value of *call my mother* in A's utterance is actually a function from speech contexts to sets, it denotes the set of callers of A's mother *only* once the speech context parameter is supplied. If B's sentence picked up the speech-context-dependent set, then the understanding would be that Jack would not call B's mother. Hence indexical pronouns provide evidence that in cases of ellipsis, what is supplied as the missing meaning is not a function into $<e,t>$ meanings, but an $<e,t>$ meaning itself. The case with free pronouns is analogous: what is picked up is the meaning of the antecedent VP after it is applied to some assignment (in the variable-ful view) or some individual (in

---

[13] This is oversimplified; beginning with Partee (1989b) it has been noticed that indexical pronouns like *I* also function like "variables," since "sloppy" readings are available in cases like (i) (where the relevant reading is such that no one else called their own mother):

(1)   Only I called my mother.

For relevant discussion of how to account for this in the variable-free view, see Jacobson (2012); an account using variables is spelled out in, among others, Kratzer (1998).

the variable-free view). Thus Thelma and Louise are not mixed up in (37) any more than A's mother and B's mother are mixed up in (38).

*15.4.2. A note on three-place verbs and WCO interactions

The discussion throughout this book has for the most part been restricted to sentences with intransitive or transitive verbs, ignoring cases of three-place verbs, as in *give the milkbone to the puppy, read the story to the children,* etc. However—using only the CG terminology for the moment—it was noted in Chapter 5 and 6 that there is some evidence that in cases like the above *give* first combines with *to the puppy* and then the direct object NP (*the milkbone*) combines with that string by Wrap. It was also pointed out in section 5.5 that a similar strategy has been adopted in non-CG frameworks with movement (see, e.g., Larson 1988). Under that view there is a level of representation at which *give to the puppy* is a single constituent with *the milkbone* as its sister, and a movement rule applies to give the final surface order. (See the discussion in section 5.5 about various implementations of this.) But in the earlier discussions, no actual evidence was given for these conclusions. We are now in a position to give one piece of evidence for this: it has to do with WCO interactions. Since we are focusing here on VPs of the form V-NP-PP, it will simplify the discussion (under either theory) to think of PPs as just fancy NPs. That PPs with case-marking prepositions like *to* have the same semantics as NPs has already been established. Assume that their syntax is more or less the same too (with the addition of the case-marker). In particular, in the Direct Compositional view, assume that they can lift to generalized quantifiers (see the discussion in section 14.3), and assume that in the LF view they can undergo QR.

With this in mind, note that while (39) is good, (40) is degraded (the judgments do not seem to be as sharp here as in the cases in (4) and (5); we leave it open as to why not):

(39)   a. Gail sent every package$_i$ to its$_i$ intended recipient.
       b. Gordon gave every painting$_i$ (in his collection) to someone who could really appreciate it$_i$.

(40)   a. ?*Gail sent a package that contained his$_i$ favorite cookie to every soldier$_i$ (in that battalion).
       b. ?*Gordon gave a portrait of her$_i$ grandfather to every girl$_i$ (in the class).

In order to conclude that this is an instance of a WCO violation, one needs to ensure that when no binding is involved, the second NP can scope over the first. Indeed the wide-scope reading for *every* emerges with no difficulty at all in (41):

(41)   a. Gail sent a package to every soldier (in that battalion).
       b. Gordon gave one of his paintings to every girl (in the class).

Let us first consider what this shows under the variable-free view, making use of **z**. Under the formulation of **z** in R-8, the object slot (the slot occupied by *every package*) can be merged with the pronoun slot only if the category of *send* is $((S/_LNP)/_WNP)/_RPP$. The **z** rule allows this to map to $((S/_LNP)/_WNP)/_RPP^{NP}$ with meaning $\lambda f_{<e,e>}[\lambda x[send'(f(x))(x)]]$ (which can be equivalently written as $\lambda f_{<e,e>}[\lambda x[\lambda y[send'(f(x))(x)(y)]]]$. The reverse binding pattern is not possible as shown in (40). In other words, this is parallel to the subject–object asymmetry with respect to binding. Under an account of WCO effects that builds it in to **z** via the order of the arguments, the conclusion follows that verbs like *send* and *give* have the Wrap category.

Similar remarks hold under the LF view. Given the WCO filter in (9) it must be that—at LF—the trace of *every package* in (39) c-commands the pronoun within the PP. On the other hand, should the PP raise in (40a) it must be that its trace does not c-command the coindexed pronoun within the *package*-NP. The details of just what the LFs look like depend on the precise analysis of the movement rules at work in these cases, but the main conclusion is analogous to the conclusion in the variable-free view.

Incidentally, one might take the binding patterns in (39) and (40) to show that we have been wrong all along in our discussion of WCO effects—that the effect is one based on linear order and not the order of argument introduction (or, c-command). In that case, no wrap or movement would be necessary for the three-place verbs. That WCO is about linear order was actually assumed in early accounts of this construction, and has been revived from time to time (see, e.g., Shan and Barker 2006). If this turns out to be the case, the LF filter in (9) can easily be modified to refer to precedence rather than c-command. In the variable-free view, the requisite modification would involve a more general binding rule (where any argument position could be "merged" with a pronoun within any other) and where the rule was sensitive to the slash directions. We will, however, not pursue this here, because WCO effects are not the only reason to adopt a

Wrap analysis (or its analogue in theories with movement). The distribution of reflexives and reciprocals has also been used in support of this.

15.5. More on free "variables"

The preceding sections made precise the notion of free pronouns under both views. In the variable-ful view, a sentence such as *He₅ left* has as its value an assignment-dependent proposition; for each g, it is the proposition that g(5) left. Some principle predicts that this is applied (by the listener in a discourse context) to some assignment g. In the variable-free view, the value of *He left* is a function of type <e,t>, which the listener applies to a contextually salient individual. But recall that throughout this book we have made use of other kinds of "free variables" in addition to those that pick up individuals. For example, an adjective such as *big* was hypothesized to contain as part of its meaning a "variable" of type <e,t> which supplies the comparison class. In section 10.6 it was hypothesized that quantificational determiners have as part of their meaning a "variable" that restricts the domain. And in section 14.4.2 it was hypothesized that VP Ellipsis involves a "variable" over properties (VP meanings) that occurs as argument of the auxiliary. Incidentally, all three of these cases are variables over meanings of type <e,t>, but many other kinds of free variables have been used in semantics. One example—a variable over numbers—will be discussed in section 16.3.2 in connection with the meaning of *many*. It is thus worth considering how these additional kinds of things which have gone under the rubric of variables would be handled in each of the accounts of pronouns developed in this chapter.

15.5.1. Free "variables" in the variable-ful account

Consider the meaning of *big* discussed in Chapter 8. There it was concluded that this means "big for an X" where X is something of type <e,t>, it remains free, and its value is set by the context. Putting this more formally, the value of *Dumbo is big* is a non-constant function from G to a proposition, and G must have in its domain not only the individual variables but variables of other types as well. Moreover, in the informal discussion we used just X, but this too must have an index and so there must be an infinite number of variables of this type available. Thus consider a sentence like (42) where the comparison class for *big* and the comparison class for *little* need not be the same (most likely they are not):

(42)   The big flea sat on the little elephant.

Were there just one variable of type <e,t> then the same comparison class would have to be supplied for both. And of course we could make a more complex S with more and more scalar adjectives, each getting a different comparison class. This means that *big* must come with an index in the lexicon, and $[[big_1]]$ would be "big for an X_1," and so forth.

Similarly, suppose that quantificational determiners (*every, some*, etc.) come with a domain restriction variable, such that [[every]] is $\lambda P[\lambda Q[P_S \cap X_S \subseteq Q_S]]$ where again X is of type <e,t>. (In section 10.6 the meaning for *every* was spelled out as above except that X_S was replaced with D—a variable over sets—the two are of course interchangeable.) Here too X actually must be indexed (so that there are items *every*$_1$, *every*$_2$, etc.) because one can have more than one quantifier in a sentence where the domains are interpreted differently; the reader is invited to construct relevant examples. Moreover, the <e,t> comparison class for *big* and the domain restriction for *every* in (43) have to be able to be distinct, indicating that the index of *every* and the index on *big* need not be the same:

(43)   Every elephant ate a big peanut.

The restriction on *every* might be the set of animals traveling with the circus troupe; the comparison class on *big* is most likely the set of peanuts.

What this means, then, is that the use of free variables as a way to model these meanings requires that the assignment functions are more complex than has been assumed so far. They are not simply functions from integers to individuals; ordinary integers will serve for the case of variables over individuals but the semantics (under this view) makes use of variables of other types. As one way to work out the technical details, the variables of type <e,t> can be ordered pairs of integers whose first member is any integer and second member is 1. (Thus the pair (3,1) is a formal way to think of what we have been calling X_3.) Other variables can be ordered tuples of other types. At the end of the day, then, a sentence like *He*$_5$ *has taken every*$_3$ *phonology course* has as its value a function from assignments to propositions, and the context will supply an assignment in which 5 is assigned to some individual, and (3,1) is assigned to some (characteristic function of a) set of individuals (e.g., the set of phonology courses offered at Brown).

15.5.2. Free "variables" in the variable-free theory

In the variable-free theory, these cases will be handled by assigning more complex types to the lexical items involved: they all are functions from something else to the type that was assigned in the original discussion. For example, [[big]] is not of type <e,t> but of type <<e,t>,<e,t>> with meaning (informally) $\lambda X[\text{big for an } X_S]$. (Since we are using X as a variable of type <e,t> rather than a variable over sets, read the inner brackets as "big for something in the set characterized by X".) Moreover, its category contains a superscript. The category of the superscript could, for example, be N, so the category of *big* would actually be AP^N. Similarly, [[every]]—if it does contain a domain restriction—is not just a relation between sets but has as its meaning a function from sets to such a relation. In particular, its meaning is $\lambda X[\lambda P[\lambda Q[P_S \cap X_S \subseteq Q_S]]]$. And the syntactic category of *every* would be revised to be $(L(NP))^N$, which in turn means that *every mouse* would be $L(NP)^N$.

In other words, what we have been informally calling free variables correspond to extra argument slots. These slots are passed up in the way a pronoun slot is, and so the meaning of a sentence like *Every elephant escaped* ends up being a function from <e,t> meanings to propositions. The listener applies this to some contextually salient set to get the domain restriction. Similarly, a sentence like *He has taken every phonology course* is a function of type <e,<<e,t>,t>>—it needs to have both the e-slot and the <e,t> slot filled and so will be applied to some contextually salient individual and a contextually salient set (again, perhaps, the set of phonology courses offered at Brown).

Both theories, then, posit more complex meanings for the lexical items. Other than that, though, nothing extra is needed in the variable-free theory for these. There is no change in the kinds of objects in the semantics; there just are fancier functions than would be needed if there were no cases of "free variables." The apparatus for passing up these slots is already in place. Incidentally, passing up the slots by use of **g-sup** and **l** makes for rather complex derivations, even though no new complexities are introduced in the rules or machinery. However, that too can be simplified by defining R-1 recursively; see the discussion in 15.3.3 and Exercise 15.12.

15.26. Given the meaning and category for *big* above, show the derivation (both the syntax and the semantics) in the variable-free framework for (i), using a combination of **g-sup** and **l** where needed.

(i) Dumbo is big.

*15.27. Having generalized R-1 to apply recursively as suggested in Exercise 15.12, show a shorter derivation of (i) than the one in Exercise 15.26 (unless you already used that generalized rule in your answer to 15.26).

15.6. The i-within-i effect revisited: A solution

And now we come full circle to consider a solution to the mystery with which this book opened: the i-within-i effect detailed in Chapter 1.4. Readers who skipped that section at the outset should read it now. The solution here is framed within variable-free terms, and also makes crucial use of the assumptions about the syntax/semantics interface taken in CG and which have been maintained throughout this book. It thus has three key ingredients: (i) binding is a matter of the merging of argument *slots*; (ii) the syntax and semantics closely parallel each other; (iii) nouns—while being of type <e,t>—do not have a syntactic subject slot, and, concomitantly, relational nouns are of type <e,<e,t>> but of category N/PP[OF] and hence have only one syntactic argument slot. Perhaps the punchline is obvious from just these observations. But if not, we provide elaboration.

   Recall first the basic puzzle, sketched only briefly here as it is amply detailed in Chapter 1. In the A-B-C party scenario—in which Betty and Bert were childhood sweethearts—I can describe my encounter with Betty using (44a) or (44b), but not (44c).

(44)   a. I enjoyed talking to the woman who married her childhood sweetheart.
   b. I enjoyed talking to the woman married to her childhood sweetheart.
   c. *I enjoyed talking to the wife of her childhood sweetheart.

Beginning with (44a), there is nothing surprising (on any theory) about this. For example, in the variable-free view, *marry* undergoes **z** and so its subject position binds the pronoun. (The lexical entry for *who*, given in Chapter 13, allows this to combine with the VP to give a relative clause.)

(44b) is also unproblematic, although it does have interesting consequences for the LF theory; see Exercise 15.28. We will assume that *married
to her childhood sweetheart* is an "AP" (should it turn out to be a slightly
different category nothing will change); but recall that "AP" is short for
S[A]/NP. In other words, "APs" combine in the syntax with subjects to give
fuller expressions (what are generally called *small clauses*). This claim is
motivated by examples like (45); see also the discussion in section 8.2 on
this point:

(45)   With Bill married to Calista, he'll travel the world.

This in turn means that *married* is (S[A]/NP)/PP[TO] and, of course, its
meaning is of type $<e,<e,t>>$. It can thus undergo **z**; *to her childhood
sweetheart* is a PP[TO]^{NP} and can thus occur as argument of **z**(married),
and the subject slot of *married* will bind the pronoun. This then maps to the
nominal modifier by R-2. Notice that there is no need to posit any silent
subject of *married* in these cases; the fact that it has a syntactic and semantic
subject *slot* is sufficient to allow for the binding of the pronoun.

15.28. Consider (44b) in the LF view. What does this view need to
assume in order to account for the binding of the pronoun here?

But now take (44c). Here *wife* is also of type $<e,<e,t>>$. Why then could
this not also input **z**? There would be nothing wrong with this semantically;
z(wife') is $\lambda f_{<e,e>}[\lambda x[\text{wife-of}'(f(x))(x)]]$ and *her childhood sweetheart* has a
meaning of type $<e,e>$. So **z**(wife-of')(her-childhood-sweetheart') is the set
of x's who are women and are married to x's childhood sweetheart; exactly
the reading that is asked for in (44c). The i-within-i mystery is that (44c)
lacks that reading, even though it seems like a perfectly sensible meaning.
And indeed, it is a sensible meaning. But the key lies in the syntax under the
assumption that the syntactic and semantic operations are tightly coupled.
The **z** rule (R-8) is formulated to apply only to items whose syntactic
category is (X/NP)/Y. The argument slot that binds the pronoun in the
semantics must also be present as a syntactic slot. And this formulation is
not a stipulation that is made up just for this case: it is just what would be
expected given the tight correspondence in CG between the syntactic and
semantic operations. But recall that—even though ordinary nouns are of
type $<e,t>$—they have no syntactic subject slot and relational nouns

similarly are just of category N/PP[OF], where "N" is not an abbreviation for a more complex category. This odd property of nouns was not stipulated for this case; it is independently motivated in view of the fact that nouns do not occur in small clauses:

(46)   *With Nora linguistics major, she'll learn lots of languages.
       *With Calista wife of Bill, he'll travel the world.

Hence relational nouns, while of the right semantic type to undergo **z**, are just not of the right syntactic category to do this. And so from these ingredients, the i-within-i effect follows.

Appendices to Parts I–III

The full fragment

Below is a summary of the full fragment developed to this point, along with some of the open questions and tentative suggestions. This is included before the final four chapters in Part IV (Further Topics) as we will not attempt to officially fold in the treatment of focus in Chapter 18. Chapter 19 proposes one revision to Rule-1 (**app**) to account for intensionality. Some other modifications are necessary in the rules to fully fold in intensionality, but this is straightforward, as will also be noted in Chapter 19. (Thus the interested reader can tackle this as an exercise.) Chapters 16 and 17 propose no changes to the basic rules, only some additional lexical items.

Appendix 1: The basic fragment

Foundational concepts

Semantic types: A *semantic type* means something which can be the value of a linguistic expression.

Basic types: The semantic types consist of the set e (individuals), t (truth values), w (worlds), and i (times); s is used to abbreviate world/time pairs.

Recursive definition of other types: If a is a type and b is a type, then any function from domain a to co-domain b is a type. The set of such functions is notated <a,b>.

Syntactic categories:

Basic categories: S, NP, PP, N, CP, along with a set of features on these categories. [A] and [V] are examples of features that can occur on S, so S[A] is an adjectival small clause, and we use S[V, TENSE] for an ordinary S. Other features are relevant for verbal morphology to give verbs in the progressive form (ending in -*ing*) or in the past participle, etc.; these are not spelled out here.

"VP" is an abbreviation for S[V]/NP and "AP" is an abbreviation for S[A]/NP.

Recursive definitions of other categories:
 (i) If A is a category and B is a category, $A/_R B$ is a category.
 (ii) If A is a category and B is a category, $A/_L B$ is a category.
 (iii) If A is a category and B is a category, A^B is a category.

Correspondence of categories and types: (ignoring intensions)

Any expression of category A/B or A^B has as its value a function in <b,a>.

All linguistic expressions are triples: <[sound], Category, [[meaning]]>.

The lexicon

For convenience, we distinguish between open- and closed-class items. The former (in general) have values which vary according to the world and time, and the latter in do not. The correlation is not perfect; names are obviously open-class items but we continue to follow Kripke (1980) in treating these as rigid designators (i.e., they have the same value for all worlds and times). However the fact that the correlation is not perfect is of no consequence, because the distinction between closed- and open-class items plays no actual role in the theory here and is largely just a convenient way to organize the presentation of the lexicon. (Chapter 19 does explore a possible view in which the distinction between those items taken here to have constant values across worlds and those which don't does play a role in the grammar; see section 19.2.) Note too that while numerical determiners (e.g., *three, three hundred and forty-eight*, etc.) might at first glance appear to be open class, they actually are not in that they are not basic lexical items. The basic items include only individually listed words or morphemes for numbers between 1 and 20 and the others are formed in predictable compositional fashion from these.

Because the open-class items generally have values that vary by world and time, we will not spell out the meanings; and so list these with syntactic category first, followed by their "phonology." The closed-class items are listed in the usual triple format, and are given extensionally.

Open-class items:

NP includes: *Mitka, Balto, Barack Obama, Porky, Farmer MacDonald,...*
S/NP includes: *walk, talk, grunt,...*
(S/NP)/NP includes: *kiss, likes, feeds,...*
(S/NP)/PP[TO] includes: *talk, speak,...*
(S/NP)/CP includes: *believe, think,...*
S[A]/NP includes: *honest, red, tall,...*

> *Possible revision* (in variable-free terms) to include comparison class argument, exemplified with *tall*:
> <[tall], (S[A]/NP)^N, $\lambda P_{<e,t>}$["tall" for a P_S]>

Most other adjectives also have a comparison class argument, though some may not.
(S[A]/NP)/PP[OF] includes: *fond*

> Might also need revision to include comparison class argument.

N includes: *table, dog, cat, pig,...*
N/PP[OF] includes: *mother, child, daughter, employer,...*

Closed-class items:

Definition of Π:
  i. Given two truth values a and b (i.e., members of {1,0})
      a Π b = a & b (i.e., Π = (1,1) → 1, (1,0) → 0, (0,1) → 0, and (0,0) → 0)
  ii. Given two functions f and g such that f Π g is defined, f Π g = $\lambda x[f(x)$ Π $g(x)]$.

Definition of Ц:
  i. Given two truth values a and b (i.e., members of {1,0})
      a Ц b = a v b (i.e., Ц = (1,1) → 1, (1,0) → 1, (0,1) → 1, and (0,0) → 0)
  ii. Given two functions f and g such that f Ц g is defined, f Ц g = $\lambda x[f(x)$ Ц $g(x)]$.

<[and], (X/X)/X, $\lambda A_x[\lambda B_x[A$ Π $B]]$> (for x the semantic type of expressions
  of category X)
<[or], (X/X)/X, $\lambda A_x[\lambda B_x[A$ Ц $B]]$>

Comment: an alternative possibility is to list *and* in the lexicon as being of category
  (S/S)/S with meaning $\lambda q[\lambda p[p\&q]]$, where all other occurrences of it from the
  generalization of **g-sl** given below. Similarly for *or*. See section 13.4.4.2.

<[didn't], X/X, $\lambda F_{<a,t>}[\lambda A_a[\sim F(A)]]$, where X is restricted to S/NP or S/(S/(S/NP))>

Comment: This is a placeholder. *did* is an auxiliary; English negation involves *not* or the clitic *n't* attached to an auxiliary. See Exercise 13.11.

<[to], PP[TO]/NP, $\lambda x_e[x]$>
<[of], PP[OF]/NP, $\lambda x_e[x]$>
<[that], CP/S, $\lambda p_t[p]$> (p is actually something of type <s,t> in a fully intensional fragment)
<[the], NP/N, $\lambda P_{<e,t>}[\iota x[P(x)]]$> (where here $\iota x[P(x)]$ means "the unique or most contextually salient x such that P(x) holds")

Comment: This might be revised as follows to include the domain restriction:
   <[the], (NP/N)^N, $\lambda Q_{<e,t>}[\lambda P_{<e,t>}[\iota x[P(x) \, \& \, Q(x)]]]$>

<[is], S[Tense]/(S[A]/NP, $\lambda P_{<e,t>}[P]$>
<[every], L_S(NP)/N, $\lambda P[\lambda Q[P_S \cap Q_S = P_S]]$>
<[some], L_S(NP)/N, $\lambda P[\lambda Q[P_S \cap Q_S \neq \emptyset]]$>

<[no], LS(NP)/N, $\lambda P[\lambda Q[PS \cap QS = \emptyset]]$>
<[three], LS(NP)/N, $\lambda P[\lambda Q[\, |PS \cap QS| \geq 3]]$>
<[most], LS(NP)/N, $\lambda P[\lambda Q[\, |PS \cap \underline{QS} > |PS| \,]]$>
$$2$$
Comments:
- All of the quantificational determiners above would have revised entries if it is correct that the domain restriction slot is part of their semantics.
- In the variable-free framework, the lexical entries for *every* and *some*—if they include a domain restriction—would be:
   <[every], L_S(NP)/N, $\lambda T[\lambda Q[\lambda P[Q_S \cap T_S \subseteq P_S \,]]]$>
   <[some], L_S(NP)/N, $\lambda T[\lambda Q[\lambda P[Q_S \cap T_S \cap P_S \neq \emptyset]]]$>

   <[which], RC/(S/$_R$NP) and RC/(S/$_L$NP), $\lambda P[P]$>
   <[who], RC/(S/$_R$NP) and RC/(S/$_L$NP), $\lambda P[P]$>

Comment: The lexical entries for *which* and *who* are almost certainly incorrect as they do not in any obvious way extend to pied-piping cases. See Jacobson (2008) for an alternative.

<[he], NP^{NP}, $\lambda x[x]$>
<[she], NP^{NP}, $\lambda x[x]$>

Comment: The contribution of gender should ultimately be folded in. One way is to treat these as partial functions. For example, the value of *he* is the identity function whose domain includes only male individuals.

Word order rules

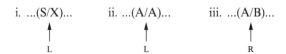

i. ...(S/X)...   ii. ...(A/A)...   iii. ...(A/B)...

where (i) and (ii) must apply before (iii)

Comment: Rules of this general sort can be used for case features; see (4) in section 6.4.

Unary and combinatory rules

R-1 (app):

Definition of functions corresponding to syntactic categories:

a. $F_{A/_R B}([a])([\beta]) = [a\text{-}\beta]$

b. $F_{A/_L B}([a])([\beta]) = [\beta\text{-}a]$

R-1.   If a is an expression of the form $<[a], A/B, [[a]]>$ and β is an expression of the form $<[\beta], B, [[\beta]]>$ then there is an expression γ of the form $<F_{CAT(a)}([a])([\beta])$, A, $[[a]]([[\beta]])>$ (where $CAT(a)$ means the category of a).

Comment: This might be given recursively. Formalizing the recursion is left as Exercise 15.12, but note that the result is that, for example, an expression of category $(A/_R B)^C$ can combine with an expression of category B (to its right) to give A^C. (The same result is possible by lifting B to $A/_L(A/_R B)$; then apply $\mathbf{g_c}$-**sup**, and applying that result to $(A/_R B)^C$. The suggestion above allows for a shorter derivation.)

R-2 (n-mod):

R-2.   Let a be an expression of the form $<[a]$, AP or RC, $[[a]]>$. Then there is an expression β of the form $<[a]$, N/N, $\lambda P_{<e,t>}[\lambda x_e[\, [[a]](x) \, \& \, P(x)]]>$.
        If $[a]$ consists of a single word then the result is $N/_R N$.

Comment: This should be defined recursively to apply also to, e.g., RC^{NP} and other input categories with superscripts. Hence we revise to R-2Rev.

Recursive definition of int:

a. Let f be a function of type $<x,t>$. Then $\mathbf{int}^0(f)$ is of type $<<x,t>,<x,t>>$ and is $\lambda g_{<x,t>}[f_S \cap g_S]$.

b. Let f be a function of type $<a,b>$ such that $\mathbf{int}^i$ is defined for b (for some i). Then $\mathbf{int}^n(f) = \lambda A_a[\mathbf{int}^{n-1}(b(A))]$.

Recursive definition of NMOD:

a. Let C be the category RC or AP (and perhaps some others). Then $\mathbf{NMOD}^0(C)$ is N/N.

b. Let C be any category X^Y such that $\mathbf{NMOD}^i$ (for some i) is defined for X. Then $\mathbf{NMOD}^n(C) = (\mathbf{NMOD}^{n-1}(X))^Y$.

R-2′:   Let a be an expression of the form $<[a], C, [[a]]$, for C any category for which $\mathbf{NMOD}$ is defined$>$. Then there is an expression β of the form $<[a]$, $\mathbf{NMOD}^n(C)$, $\mathbf{int}^n([[a]])>$.

R-3:

R-3.   Let a be an expression of the form $<[a]$, N/PP[OF], $[[a]]>$. Then there is an expression β of the form $<[\beta]$, NP/$_L$NP[GEN], $\lambda x_e[\iota y[a'(x)(y)]]>$.

R-4 (l):

Definition of l: For any x (of any type) in a set A and any set B, $L_{<A,B>}(x)$ is a function in $<<A,B>,B>$ such that for all f in $<<A,B>,B>$, $l(x)(f) = f(x)$.

Definition of **L:** For any category A, $L_B(A)$ is any category such that for all expressions x of category A and all expressions y and z such that $[x] = [z]$, $F_{L_B(A)}([y])([z]) = F_{CAT(z)}([z])([x])$.

R-4.   Let a be an expression of the form $<[a], A, [[a]]>$. Then there is an expression β of the form $<[a], L_B(A), \lambda f_{<a,b>}[f([[a]])]>$ (i.e., $l_{<a,b>}(a))>$.

Comment: This also should be recast as a recursive rule along the lines of the model above for **R-2**. Spelling this out is left as an exercise.

R-5 (g-sl):

Definition of g: For any function f of type $<a,b>$, there is a function $g_c(f)$ of type $<<c,a>,<c,b>>$ such that $g_c(f) = \lambda X_{<c,a>}[\lambda C_c[f(X(C))]]$.

R-5a.   Let a be an expression of the form $<[a], A/_R B, [[a]]>$. Then there is an expression β of the form $<[a], (A/_R C)/_R (B/_R C), g_c([[a]])>$ (for c the semantic type of expressions of category C).

R-5b.   Let a be an expression of the form $<[a], A/_L B, [[a]]>$. Then there is an expression β of the form $<[a], (A/_L C)/_L (B/_L C), g_c([[a]])>$ (for c the semantic type of expressions of category C).

Comments:
- R-5a and R-5b should ultimately be collapsed into one, and the directional features on the slashes would not be stipulated.
- The rule (or rules) might ultimately be generalized further to Generalized **g**.

  Example: Let f be a function of type $<a,<b,c>>$. Then **gen-g_d**(f) is of type $<<d,a>,<<d,b>,<d.c>>>$ such that:
$$gen\text{-}g_d (f) = \lambda X_{<d,a>}[\lambda Y_{<d,b>}[\lambda D_d[f(X(D))(Y(D))]]]$$
  The syntactic mapping would map, e.g., $(C/_R B)/_R A$ to $((C/_R D)/_R(B/_R D))/_R(A/_R D)$. This rule would allow *and* to be listed in the lexicon with the single category $(S/_R S)/_R S$ (and meaning of type $<<t,t>,t>$) where the other items are derived by recursive application(s) of **gen-g**. Note, however, that **gen-g** is not a "word-order-preserving" operation in the same way that **g** is; see Exercise 13.14.
- **g** should be given a recursive definition along the lines given for R-2. This is left as an exercise.

R-6 (argslot-l):

Definition:

Let f be any function of type $<K^\rightarrow,<e,<L^\rightarrow,t>>>$. Then **argslot$_{n+1}$-l**(f) is a function of type $<K^\rightarrow,<<e,t>,t>,<L^\rightarrow,t>>$ (where n = the number of slots in K) where $AS_{n+1}\text{-}L(f) = \lambda X_K^\rightarrow [\lambda P[\lambda X_L^\rightarrow [P(\lambda x_e[f(X_K^\rightarrow)(x)(X_L^\rightarrow)])]]]$.

R-6.   Let a be an expression of the form $<[a], ((S/A^\rightarrow)/NP)/B^\rightarrow, [[a]]>$ where A is of length n. Then there is an expression β of the form $<[a], ((s/A^\rightarrow)/GQ)/B^\rightarrow, argslot\text{-}l_{n+1}([[a]])>$.

R-7 (g-sup):

R-7.   Let a be an expression of the form $<[a], A/B, [[a]]>$. Then there is an expression β of the form $<[a], A^C/B^C, g_c[[a]]>$ (for c the type of expressions of category C).

Comment: **g-sup** should be given a recursive definition along the lines given for R-2. This is left. This is as an exercise for the reader.

Looking ahead (see section 17.3.2): This rule should be generalized to apply both to ordinary slash and to superscripts. The requisite generalization is as follows:

Notation: Let A|B be either A/B or A^B.

R-7   Generalized: Let a be an expression of the form $<[a]; A|B; [[a]]>$. Then there is an expression β of the form $<[a]; A^C|B^C; g_c[[a]]>$ (for c the type of expressions of category C). (The value of | is of course held constant from the input to the output.)

R-8 (z) (simplified):

Definition:

Let f be a function of type $<a,<e,b>>$. Then $z(f)$ is of type $<<e,a>,<e,b>>$, and is $\lambda Y_{<e,a>}[\lambda x_e[f(Y(x))(x)]]$.

R-8 (simplified):   Let a be an expression of the form $<[a], (A/NP)/B, [[a]]>$. Then there is an expression β of the form $<[a], (A/NP)/B^{NP}, z([[a]])>$.

Generalization of R-8:

Definition: Let f be a function of type $<b,<c^{\rightarrow n},<e,a>>>$ (where $c^{\rightarrow n}$ means n number of argument positions of any time, for $n \geq 0$). Then $z^a(f) = \lambda Y_{<e,b>}[\lambda Z^{\rightarrow n}[\lambda x_e[f(Y(x))(Z^{\rightarrow n})(x)]]]$.

R-8 Generalized: Let a be an expression of the form $<[a], ((A/NP)|C^{\rightarrow n})/B, [[a]]>$. Then there is an expression β of the form $<[a], ((A/NP)|C^{\rightarrow n})/B^{NP}, z^a([[a]])>$.

*Appendix 2: Possible extensions of the fragment for three-place verbs using Wrap

Assume each expression of the language is a string with an infixation point. We write this as [x|y] (but will suppress the infixation point when not relevant).

Add to the recursive definition of categories: If A is a category and B is a category, $A/_WB$ is a category and $A/_IB$ is a category.

The lexicon

Assume each lexical item in English is a string of the form [x|].

Add to lexicon:

((S/NP)/NP)/PP[TO] — give, donate, . . .

Word order rule

Add: ((S/NP)/NP)/X

W

Comment: X here ranges over any category. One could also allow it to range over any category including nothing; then ordinary transitive verbs would also be marked with a wrap slash. In that case the effect of Wrap is vacuous.

Revision of the definition of functions corresponding to categories of the form A/B

Let a be some expression whose string is [x|y]. Then

a. $F_{A/_R B}$ ([a])([β]) = [x|y-β]
b. $F_{A/_L B}$ ([a])([β]) = [β-x|y]

Define a function appropriate for $A/_W B$ as follows. Let a be some expression whose string is [x|y]. Then

$F_{A/_W B}$ ([a])([β]) = [x|βy]

Comment: These conventions ensure that the infixation point is inherited from the infixation point of the function.

Appendix 3: Informally discussed addition for VP Ellipsis

Phrased here in variable-free terms:

Lexicon   includes a set of auxiliary verbs (*did, will, might, be,* etc.) which are basically of category (S/NP)/(S/NP), but in each case specify a particular morphological feature on the complement. The class of auxiliaries is identifiable by the grammar, either in virtue of the selection property noted above, or perhaps because they themselves all also have a feature AUX.

Rule   maps all auxiliaries of category (S/NP)/(S/NP) into one of category $(S/NP)^{(S/NP)}$, with no change in meaning. These remain functions from VP meanings to VP meanings; the difference is in their syntax. The new items encode that they are pro-VPs and pass up the superscript feature, rather than expecting a complement in the syntax.

PART IV

Further Topics

The final part of this book consists of four chapters designed to show how the formal semantic tools developed here extend to give insightful treatments of an even larger and richer fragment than has been developed so far. This includes the distribution of so-called Negative Polarity Items, a number of further topics related to binding, the treatment of focus, and intensionality. The four chapters are logically independent and can be read in any order.

PART IV

Further Topics

16

Negative Polarity Items, semantic strength, and scalar implicature revisited

The central mission of this chapter is to understand the distribution of a group of items known as *Negative Polarity Items*. The beauty of this domain is that on the one hand, it shows an extremely interesting application of the tools developed so far (this requires only the tools through Chapter 10). On the other hand, there remain both open questions about the full distribution of these items and controversies as to the best characterization of this distribution, and so there is work yet to be done. Nonetheless, the history of research on this domain is a history of successes. Section 16.1 considers the relevant items, and 16.2 shows that the distribution is quite subtle and appears almost random. One can imagine ways to simply stipulate where these items occur with syntactic features, but a further look (in 16.3) reveals that the relevant environments all share a semantic property.[1] Clearly the

---

[1] The analysis of what these items have in common that is discussed in this book is accepted to be correct by the majority of researchers in this domain (it stems from

distribution should follow in some way from the meaning of these items combined with the property of these environments (and perhaps other principles), and indeed 16.4 discusses one influential account along these lines. Meanwhile, the tools elucidated here have another application: they allow for fine-grained predictions about just what scalar implicatures are found where, as is shown in 16.5.

16.1. The notion of Negative Polarity Items

16.1.1. any *and* ever

There are a number of items that have a very limited distribution. Consider, for example, the contrast in (1):

(1) a. Porky hasn't ever left the farm.
      b. *Porky has ever left the farm.

That the culprit in (1b) is the word *ever* is easily demonstrated by the fact that removing that word makes the sentence impeccable:

(2) Porky has left the farm.

And the only difference then between (1a) and (1b) is the presence of the negation in (1a). So, at first glance it looks like *ever* can occur only in negative sentences, and hence is commonly referred to as a *Negative Polarity Item* (NPI for short). We will continue to use this terminology even though it will be shown shortly that negation is just the tip of the iceberg.

Another NPI is *any*. Thus compare (3a) to (3b) and (3c); the contrast between (a) and (b) gives a minimal pair which differ only the presence of the negation, and the contrast between (b) and (c) gives a minimal pair differing only in the use of *any* vs *a*:

(3) a.   Tabby didn't catch any mouse.
      b. *Tabby caught any mouse.
      c.   Tabby caught a mouse.

work by Fauconnnier 1975 and Ladusaw 1979). Many of the controversies and open questions concern exactly why the generalization holds, and exactly from what aspect of grammar and/or pragmatics it follows. (See section 16.5.) But it should be noted that there are dissenting voices as to whether the basic analysis exposited here is correct; see especially Giannakidou (1997) and other works of Giannakidou's.

But a brief digression on the full distribution of *any* is in order before continuing. While often taken as the prime exemplar of the class of NPIs, *any* does have a wider distribution than *ever*. In addition to its use in (3a), there is a use of *any* exemplified in (4), which is generally referred to as "free-choice *any*." This free-choice reading emerges with modals such as *can, could, would*, and with also imperatives:[2]

(4)   a.   Any cat can catch Minnie (because she is such a slow mouse).
       b.   Calico can catch any mouse (because she is such a skillful hunter).
       c.   Calico would catch any mouse that dared to cross her path.
       d.   Pick any card.

Of course, the question arises as to whether there really are two distinct lexical items here: NPI *any* (as in (3)) and free-choice *any* (as in (4)). The wording above assumes that these are distinct items, but *a priori* we do not know that. Indeed, there is disagreement on just this point (for relevant discussion, see Horn 1972, Carlson 1981, Kadmon and Landman 1993, Lahiri 1998, and others). Still, it will simplify the discussion here to assume that free-choice *any* is a different lexical item, and we will rely on the readers' intuitions to be able to determine which *any* we are dealing with.[3] As one bit of evidence that the two are different (and as one way to help bring out the difference), note that the free-choice *any* can be replaced by *any old*, where *old* is not being used literally, whereas in the NPI usage in (6), *old* is good only on its literal meaning:[4]

(5)   a.   Any old cat can catch Minnie.
       b.   Calico can catch any old mouse.
       c.   Calico can catch any old mouse that dares to cross her path.

---

[2] Dayal (1995) points out that free-choice *any* can sometimes occur even in ordinary non-modal sentences if the common noun is modified by a relative clause:

(i)   Last year, Calico caught any mouse that dared to cross her path.

[3] While the two might be separate items, they clearly are related. Evidence for this comes from the fact that many languages use the same or closely related item to mean something quite similar to both free-choice *any* in English and also NPI *any* in English. See, e.g., Lahiri (1998) on Hindi.

[4] Some speakers might be able to force this into the free-choice reading, the idiomatic reading of *any-old* would require this. The NPI reading claims that she caught no old mouse (perhaps her mouse-catching abilities were restricted to young ones). The free-choice reading—to the extent one can force it at all—claims that it is not the case that any arbitrary mouse would become her supper.

(6)   (Last year), Calico didn't catch any old mouse.

---

*16.1. Another way to bring out the difference between NPI *any* and free-choice *any* is with certain verbs. Thus notice that (i) below is impossible even though imperatives generally allow for free-choice *any*:

(i) *Build any solar heated house.

(Compare this to *Don't build any solar heated house* which contains NPI *any*.)

   What are the verbs that block the free-choice reading, and why? What might you say about (ii) which is good, but only if *any* pie is interpreted as *any kind of pie*?

(ii) Bake any pie (you want). (Compare to *Eat any pie (you want)*.)

This exercise is intended to be open-ended; a completely precise or formal answer to the questions above is not expected.

Thus here we will treat free-choice *any* and NPI *any* as distinct lexical items, and will construct examples that make the free-choice reading difficult or impossible. Notice, incidentally, that there is no free-choice analogue to *ever* (compare (7a) to (7b)):

(7)   a. *Porky could ever leave the farm.
   b. Porky could leave the farm at any time.

16.1.2. Minimizers

In addition to *any* and *ever*, there is also a large class of NPIs known as *minimizers*—these are conventionalized or idiomatic expressions indicating a minimal amount, and are exemplified in (8)–(11):

(8)   a. Farmer MacDonald didn't lift a finger to clean out the sty.
   b. *Farmer MacDonald lifted a finger to clean out the sty.

(9)   a. Robin Hood didn't keep a red cent of what he stole.
   b. *Robin Hood kept a red cent of what he stole.

(10)   a. The disobedient pug didn't budge an inch when called.
    b. *The disobedient pug budged an inch when called.

Some of the (b) sentences here—such as (8b)—are good, but only on a very strange literal reading. The class of minimizers is quite large, and includes also very informal and/or idiomatic things like *give a hoot* (and other more colorful variants of *hoot*), *know* (and other verbs) *squat, drink a drop, spend a dime*, etc. For at least some speakers these seem to have a more limited distribution than *any* and *ever* do, and we will not provide detailed discussion of these. (See Krifka 1995 and Zwarts 1998 for discussion.)

16.2. The distribution of NPIs

NPIs are a rich domain for illustrating how formal semantic tools shed light on very commonplace and idiomatic facts about language. The relevant judgments are quite robust; the existence of NPIs (especially of the minimizer variety) is widespread cross-linguistically; and the feeling that these are quite "slangy" make it clear that facts about their distribution could never have been acquired as the end result of conscious instruction. But these turn out to have a rather subtle distribution, and it is to this that we now turn.

16.2.1. First pass

The very name *Negative Polarity Item* suggests that the occurrence of these items is limited to negative sentences (see, e.g., the good sentences above). But what exactly is a negative sentence? Note first that these occur within a VP whose subject is a GQ of the form *no N* whereas other GQs don't allow this:

(11)   a. No semantics student has ever climbed Mt Lafayette.
    b. *Some semantics student has ever climbed Mt Lafayette.
    c. *Every semantics student has ever climbed Mt Lafayette.

(12)   a. No student turned in any correct answer on the exam.
    b. *Some student turned in any correct answer on the exam.
    c. *Every student turned in any correct answer on the exam.

Perhaps this is not particularly surprising. While we have not given any actual definition of a negative sentence, it is not too difficult to imagine that one could be given that includes (11a) and (12a) and not the (b) and (c) cases. For example, let a "negative sentence" be one with *no, not, n't*, etc. and its variants; clearly these are all related both morphologically and semantically.

But this is not sufficient, for it says nothing about the contrasts in (13)–(16):

(13) a. Few semantics students have ever climbed Mt Lafayette.
     b. *Many semantics students have ever climbed Mt Lafayette.

(14) a. Few students turned in any correct answers on the exam.
     b. *Many students turned in any correct answers on the exam.

(15) a. At most five students have ever managed to climb Mt Lafayette.
     b. *At least five students have ever managed to climb Mt Lafayette.

(16) a. At most five students turned in any correct answers.
     b. *At least five students turned in any correct answers.

It is much less clear what it means to call *few* and especially *at most five* "negative." One might have the intuition that these all place an upper bound on the number of (in this case) students in question; that intuition would also capture the cases with *no*, for those too place an upper bound (zero). Indeed, this intuition is on the right track. But having moved away from the notion of a "negative" sentence to something else, it is then not so obvious how this extends the cases with simple negation, such as (1).

The notion of an upper bound (in the above sense) also does not account in any obvious way for the following contrasts:

(17) a. Michael doubts that Kolya will ever learn to howl on command.
     b. *Michael believes that Kolya will ever learn to howl on command.

(18) a. Michael doubts that any dog in the playgroup will turn out to be part wolf.
     b. *Michael believes that any dog in the playgroup will turn out to be part wolf.

(18b) may be marginal for some speakers but only on the free-choice reading (which easily emerges if *will* is changed to *could*). Note that NPIs are also allowed in the antecedent clause of a conditional (the clause introduced by *if*), but not in the consequent clause (the main clause); this also does not obviously fall under the "upper bound on a number" hypothesis:

(19) a. If Kolya ever learns to howl on command, he'll be able to appear in the dog show.
     b. *If Kolya learns to howl on command, he'll ever appear in the dog show.

(20) a. If any dog in the playgroup turns out to be part wolf, they'll close the dogpark.

    b. *If they open up a new playgroup, then any dog that goes will turn out to be part wolf.

16.2.2. Second pass

The discussion so far has considered only the distribution of NPIs within VPs. The plot thickens once one turns to their distribution within complex nouns that combine with quantificational determiners. (The discussion here assumes the analysis of the structure of NPs containing relative clauses that was discussed in section 13.2.1.) As detailed in Chapter 10, quantificational determiners like *some, no, every*, etc. denote Curry'ed relations between sets. We have already documented the distribution of NPIs within the VPs of sentences containing these determiners: *no, at most three*, and *few* all allow these; *some, many, at least three*, and *every* do not. Consider now what happens within the N portion of the relevant sentences. First, *no, at most three, no more than three*, and *few* all allow NPIs in that environment too:

(21) No student who has ever climbed Mt Lafayette found clear and sunny weather at the top.

(22) Few students who have ever climbed Mt Lafayette found clear and sunny weather at the top.

(23) At most three students who have ever climbed Mt Lafayette found clear and sunny weather at the top.

(24) No more than three students who have ever climbed Mt. Lafayette found clear and sunny weather at the top.

In view of this, it is rather unsurprising that *some, many*, and *at least three* also do not allow NPIs in the N portion, just as they do not allow them in the VP portion:

(25) *Some student who has ever climbed Mt Lafayette found clear and sunny weather at the top.

(26) *Many students who have ever climbed Mt Lafayette found clear and sunny weather at the top.

(27) *At least three students who have ever climbed Mt Lafayette found clear and sunny weather at the top.

(All of these facts can be repeated with *any*.) The discussion above seems a bit mundane: the determiners treat NPIs within the N portion exactly the same as within the VP portion.

But in fact not all determiners treat the N and the VP alike; *every* shows an asymmetry. While an NPI is not allowed in the VP, it is fine within the N, and similarly with *any*:

(28)   *Every semantics student has ever climbed Mt Lafayette.

(29)   Every student who has ever climbed Mt Lafayette said it was sleeting at the top.

(30)   *Every student turned in any correct answer on the exam.

(31)   Every student who turned in any correct answer on the exam passed the course.

16.3. The first breakthrough

16.3.1. Initial characterization of the environments

The first task, then, is to come up with a full characterization of the environments which allow NPIs (or, to use the common terminology, the environments which "license" NPIs). Early work on this within the history of generative grammar—which was done in a period in which there was little attention to semantics and more to syntax—assumed that the grammar contained some feature on "NPI licensors" which said that an NPI was allowed if the NPI was in a certain syntactic relation to the "licensor" (see, e.g., Klima 1964). Of course this leaves it as a purely accidental and stipulative property as to what items bear this feature (as well as what items are NPIs). Obviously there should be some explanation as to why some items allow NPIs and some don't, and clearly the best place to look would be some facts about meaning. In any case, the asymmetry with *every* (and, for that matter, with *if*) casts doubt on this solution; we need to ensure that *every* allows an NPI within the N that it combines with, but not within the VP. One might think that this is easily solved by taking the relevant syntactic relation to be c-command: *every* c-commands the material within the N but not within the VP. (For the definition of c-command, see Chapter 15, n. 4.) But then all other determiners such as *no* should also allow an NPI in the N and not in the VP, since the syntax is the same.

Indeed, the asymmetry with *every* gives an indication that the story is about meaning and not some arbitrary feature. For there is another relevant way in which the meaning of *every* differs from that of the other quantificational determiners discussed in the last section: the others are all symmetric (i.e., commutative) and *every* is not. To clarify, we temporarily remove *many* and *few* from the mix (they require further discussion, postponed until 16.3.2). Thus consider *some, no, at least three*, and *at most three*. These all denote Curry'ed relations between sets of individuals—relations which, in all cases, are symmetric. For any two sets A and B, if [[some]](A)(B) is true then [[some]](B)(A) is also true. One can convince oneself of this in two different ways. The first is to note that the two sentences *Some huskies howl* and *Some howlers are huskies* entail each other. But a note of caution: it can be dangerous to check out these sorts of semantic properties by considering actual sentences because two sentences with the same truth conditions can have different implicatures, which can make this method misleading. (In this case these sentences do in fact have different implicatures; the first implicates that there are also some non-howling huskies but has no implicature one way or the other about other possible howlers; the second implicates that there are other howlers but makes no implicature about non-howling huskies.) A better method is to simply consider the semantics of [[some]]; it applies to two sets A and B and returns true if there is a non-empty intersection. It of course then makes no difference as to what order these sets are taken. Similar facts hold for *no, at least three*, and *at most three*; these are all symmetric. [[every]], on the other hand, is quite obviously not symmetric: it is just the subset relation. The fact that it differs from the other determiners in just this way—and is also the only one which exhibits the asymmetry between the N argument and the VP argument—lends initial credence to the supposition that the distribution of NPIs has nothing to do with a syntactic restriction but follows in some way from the semantics.

The first major breakthrough on this came from insights in Fauconnier (1975) and Ladusaw (1979); the latter in turn drawing on work of Barwise and Cooper (1981). We initially give the insight informally, formalizing it in the next section.

(32)   Definition of *upward-entailing environment* (to be refined in 16.4.1):
       Take any sentence S containing an expression β which denotes a set B. Consider any expression γ whose denotation C is a superset of B, and consider a sentence S' in which β is replaced by γ. Then if S entails S', the environment in which β occurs is said to be an *upward-entailing* environment.

The definition here is awkward as it is phrased in terms of the substitution of linguistic expressions rather than being given purely in terms of semantic properties. In fact, as noted above, using linguistic expression substitution can be misleading since, in constructing sentences where one substitutes in one expression for another, one needs to be careful to sort out the implicatures and to make sure that these are not disguising the actual entailments. But we define it this way initially for expository convenience. The idea is that the environment is *upward-entailing* if substituting in a superset is destined to preserve truth. As one example, consider the VP in a simple sentence such as *Sally danced*. The set [[dance]] is a subset of the set [[move]], and *Sally danced* entails *Sally moved*. An ordinary VP then (one not containing negation) is an upward-entailing environment. We can check this in terms of the sentences themselves (as we just did) but we can also simply think about the semantics. The truth conditions for any sentence of the form [NP VP] are (in set terms) that [[NP]] is a member of the [[VP]] set. Obviously if this is true, that individual will also be a member of any superset of the original [[VP]].

Now consider sentences with quantified determiners such as *some N VP*. Such a sentence is true if and only if there is a non-empty intersection of [[N]]s and [[VP]]s. Clearly if that is the case, then expanding the N set to something bigger will preserve truth—if there was something in the intersection of the original sets, it will still be there when we expand the N set. The same of course is true of the VP set. So both the N and the VP positions are upward-entailing positions. This will also be true for all determiners that set a lower bound on the size of the intersection. So *at least three N VP* is also upward-entailing on both the N and the VP position by the same logic. The same is true for *three N VP* as we are assuming that *three* and *at least three* mean the same (and just have very different implicatures; see the discussion at the end of section 10.4).

16.2. The point was made above by consulting pairs of actual sentences to determine whether an environment is upward-entailing can be misleading because it is easy to imagine relevant contexts for sentences and to thus draw implicatures; if these are mistaken for the truth conditions the pattern can be obscured. Assuming that *three* really does mean "at least three," construct examples to show this point, explaining exactly why folding in the implicatures could lead one astray.

We can also define the reverse notion of a *downward-entailing environment*:

(33)   Definition of *downward-entailing environment* (to be refined in 16.4.1):
       Take any sentence S containing an expression β which denotes a set B. Consider
       any expression α whose denotation A is a subset of B, and consider a sentence S'
       in which β is replaced by α. Then if S entails S', the environment in which
       β occurs is said to be a *downward-entailing* environment.

The idea here is that when the substitution of a subset is guaranteed to
preserve truth, the environment is downward-entailing. Take then the case
of a sentence of the form *no N VP*. This is true if the intersection of the N set
and the VP set is empty. Obviously, then, shrinking either set to some subset
will not add anything more to the intersection (it can only remove material
from the intersection), and so substituting in a subset in either position will
preserve truth. Hence sentences of this form are downward-entailing on
both positions. The same holds true for determiners like *at most three*.
Again, if there are at most three things in the intersection of an N set and
a VP set, then shrinking either one will not change this fact. This too, then, is
downward-entailing on both the N position and the VP position. Notice
that an environment need not be either upward- or downward-entailing.
Consider *exactly three N V*. This says that the cardinality of the intersection
of the N set and the VP set is exactly three. Adding to the N set could change
this; if what the individual added happened also to be in the VP set then the
cardinality of the intersection is now greater than three. Subtracting something from the N set could have the same bad consequence; we could have
reduced the cardinality of the intersection. So the N position is neither
upward- nor downward-entailing. The exact same logic holds for the VP
position; it is neither.

16.3. Calculate whether the N position is upward-entailing, downward-
entailing, or neither in sentences of the form [most N VP]. Do the same
for the VP position. Once again it will be best to do this by thinking of the
meaning of *most* rather than constructing sentence pairs, to ensure that
no irrelevant factors are entering into the calculation of the truth conditions. The meaning of *most* was discussed in sections 10.1.3 and 10.2.3.

A clear pattern is emerging: it appears that NPIs are allowed in the downward-entailing positions—a proposal made originally in Ladusaw (1979). Thus *no* allows NPIs in both the N and the VP, as does *at most three*. *At least three, three,* and *some* all ban NPIs in both positions. A caveat: on the basis of just this data, the requirement could instead be that NPIs are allowed in non-upward-entailing positions. The difference concerns the predictions regarding sentences like *?Exactly three students who have ever climbed Mt Lafayette saw sun at the top*, and *?Exactly three students have ever climbed Mt Lafayette*. As noted by the ? at the beginning of these, the judgments actually seem to be intermediate; and speakers vary on these. We will bow here to the common wisdom in the literature that the relevant environments are downward-entailing environments rather than non-upward-entailing ones, and will leave the intermediate status of the sentences above as an unsolved problem. However, it will turn out that the solution to be discussed in section 16.4 can easily be modified if these sentences are basically good, where their slight degradation is a result of some other factor.

> **16.4.** Sentences with *most* are also relevant here. In light of your answer to (16.3) what are the different predictions with respect to *most* that are made by the two hypotheses: (a) NPIs are allowed only in downward-entailing positions, and (b) NPIs are allowed in non-upward-entailing positions? Construct the relevant sentences and see what the facts actually are (they might be unclear).

What about the case of *every*? The beauty of the above hypothesis regarding the distribution of NPIs is that the asymmetry with respect to *every* is completely unsurprising. For *every* is in fact downward-entailing on the N position and upward-entailing on the VP position. A sentence of the form *every N VP* is true if the N set is a subset of the VP set. Obviously any set B which a subset of the N set is still a subset of the VP set, so shrinking the N set to a subset is guaranteed to preserve truth. By the same logic, expanding the VP set to a superset is also guaranteed to preserve truth. And so the above hypothesis predicts that NPIs can occur within the N but not within the VP, and this is just what we find.

Of course, the point of departure in this chapter was the observation that NPIs occur in *negative sentences*—this is, after all, how they got their name. And so one might wonder whether that observation is also accounted for. The answer, happily, is yes. We have posited that [[didn't]] combines with a set to return its complement. Thus in a sentence of the form *NP didn't VP*, is the VP a downward-entailing environment? Indeed it is. Such a sentence is true if the individual denoted by the NP is in [[didn't VP]]$_S$ which in turn means that that individual is in the complement of [[VP]]$_S$ (equivalently, that individual is not in [[VP]]$_S$). If an individual is not in [[VP]]$_S$ then it is not in any subset of [[VP]]$_S$ either (put differently, i.e., that individual is in the complement of any subset of [[VP]]$_S$). So the ability of NPIs to occur in ordinary negated VPs is unsurprising. Recall that our treatment of negation, which involved taking *didn't* as an unanalyzed whole, is a placeholder for a more sophisticated treatment of *not* or *n't* as combining with auxiliaries, but the same point will hold with a more sophisticated treatment.[5]

The pattern with conditionals falls into place as well, although readers should be warned that there are aspects of the semantics of conditionals being oversimplified here (see, e.g., Kratzer 1986). But the oversimplified outline is nonetheless instructive. Hence consider any sentence of the form *if S₁ then S₂*. We can assume that a successful account of the semantics of the English conditional will predict the following. Let S_3 entail S_1. Then if a sentence such as *if S₁ then S₂* is true, a sentence of the form *if S₃ then S₂* is also true.[6] Let us recast this in set terms using the fact that the value of any S can be seen as a set of possible worlds. Then, if S_3 entails S_1, that means that the set of worlds in which S_3 is true is a subset of the set of worlds in which S_1 is true. Hence, substituting in a subset in the antecedent position of a conditional preserves truth; and so this is a downward-entailing environment.

---

[5] The discussion here surrounds only the case of NPIs within the VP. See Exercise 16.10 for discussion of NPIs in subject position.

[6] Truth be told, we are oversimplifying and glossing over a full set of interesting questions concerning the conditional in English. To give a flavor for this, note that *You struck a match and it was raining* certainly entails *You struck a match*. But, as discussed in Stalnaker (1968), the following entailment pattern does not hold:

(i) If you strike a match, it will light.
(ii) If you strike a match and it is raining, it will light.

(i) seems true and (ii) does not, and thus apparently (i) does not entail (ii). See Stalnaker (1968) and many since for proposed solutions.

16.5. Putting this in set terms as above, show that the consequent clause of a conditional (the *then* clause) is an upward-entailing environment.

16.6. Again, thinking of propositions as sets of worlds, show that (under a certain set of assumptions about belief states) the complement of *believe* (as in (17b)) is an upward-entailing position, while the complement of *doubt* (as in (17a)) is a downward-entailing position. What are the assumptions one needs to make about peoples' belief states in terms of the rationality of the believer?

*16.7. Consider the following:

(i) a. Herman denied that he committed any acts of harassment.
    b. Herman denied that he had ever harassed anyone.

Does the fact that NPIs occur here follow from the generalization regarding downward entailment? In what way does a fine-grained analysis of the meaning of *deny* bear on the answer?

16.8. Consider the following:

(i) Fewer than half of the bears have ever seen the other side of the mountain.

Is the ability of *ever* to occur here surprising or predicted? What about the occurrence of *ever* in (ii), where it seems (to this author at any rate) possible but not perfect:

(ii) ?Fewer than half of the undergraduates who ever took a formal semantics course went on graduate school in linguistics.

The story does not end here, of course. First, one would want to know *why* this pattern holds. Second, so far we have only a descriptive generalization; the question remains as to how to build something into the grammar from which this generalization follows. These questions are the subject of 16.4. Moreover, there are other places where NPIs occur; see the discussion in 16.5. But first we return to *many* and *few*, discussion of which was postponed earlier.

16.3.2. A note on many and few

At first glance, *many* and *few* appear to be neither upward- nor downward-entailing on the N position. Consider the pairs in (34) and (35):

(34) a. Many huskies dig holes in the snow to sleep.
     b. Many dogs dig holes in the snow to sleep.

(35) a. Few dogs like to pull sleds.
     b. Few huskies like to pull sleds.

A common intuition is that (34) does not entail (35); huskies do in fact like to dig holes in the snow to sleep, something which is probably not a general property of dogs. So (34) appears true and (35) false. This would mean that *many* is not upward-entailing on the N position (nor is it downward-entailing; *Many dogs like to play fetch* certainly does not entail *Many huskies like to play fetch*, for it could well be that all of the fetch-enjoyers are dogs of other breeds). Conversely, (35a) appears not to entail (35b); dogs in general are not sled pullers but huskies are, and so it would seem that (35a) is true and (35b) is not. By this reasoning, *few* is not downward-entailing on the N argument (nor is it upward-entailing, as the reader can easily verify). The reason why these appear to be neither upward- nor downward-entailing is clear on reflection: they *look like* proportional determiners (like *most, more than half*, etc.). That is, it appears that the number of individuals who dig holes in the snow to sleep is—in (34a)—dependent on the number of huskies, while in (34b) it is dependent on the number of dogs. But if it is true that *many* and *few* are proportional determiners, the distribution of NPIs is puzzling. For *few* happily allows these in the N position, while *many* does not:

(36) a. *Many students who have ever climbed Mt Lafayette stopped at the Greenleaf hut.
     b. Few students who have ever climbed Mt Lafayette stopped at the Greenleaf hut.

But if NPIs are restricted to downward-entailing environments, their ability to occur in (36b) seems surprising. If the restriction is actually non-upward-entailing environments then (36b) is unsurprising, but the (quite robust) badness of (36a) is unaccounted for.

Once again though, the fact that these are apparent counterexamples is due to the difficulty of sorting out the full set of truth conditions of a sentence from other factors that enter in. The question at issue is simple: are *many* and *few* truly proportional or is something else going on? As it turns out, the situation is similar to the situation with apparent non-intersective adjective modifiers discussed in section 8.4.4. Recall that the meaning of *big* seems to involve a "free variable" over sets of individuals, so that—in variable-ful terms—[[big]] means something like "big for a D_n," where the value of D_n is set by context. (In variable-free terms, [[big]] is λD[big for a D] where the open argument slot is passed up.) A reasonable hypothesis is that something similar is going on with *many*: what counts as "many" depends on setting some contextual parameter, and this is *often but not always* given by the size of the N set. In other words, the claim here is that *many* means (informally) "greater than n_n," where n_n is a "free variable" over numbers, and its value is determined by a variety of contextual factors. (Again the requisite translation of this into the variable-free setting is straightforward. We will continue to use the terminology of a "free variable" simply because this allows short cuts in the exposition.) If we hold n_n constant, then (34a) does in fact entail (34b) and similarly (35a) entails (35b). But the actual sentences are misleading, because the use of *dog* vs *husky* as the noun that *many* combines with pressures us to set a very different value for n in the two sentences. This is analogous to the pressure to take *big* quite differently in *big elephant* and *big flea*; there is a strong preference to use the head noun to set the value of D_n in "big for a D_n," but this is not required.

Is there independent evidence that this line of reasoning is correct? Indeed there is, and it comes from the following clever case discussed in Bennett (1974) and Partee (1989a) (although Partee's conclusion in that paper is actually somewhat different from that discussed here). The relevant context is a discussion of, for example, the dating habits of students at Brown (with respect to other Brown students), and someone says:

(37) (At Brown), many women date many men.

The interest in this example is that the cardinality of the women set of Brown students is roughly the same as the cardinality of the men set of Brown students. Yet what we take to be the number that would satisfy this for the women case is quite different than for the men case. Of course *many* is also vague—just exactly how to zero in on a precise value for n_n is unclear even once we fix the context. But this does not obscure the basic point here; one might have the intuition that, for example, (37) requires about 300 women to be multi-men daters. But surely, for each such woman, she does not need to date 300 men in order for the sentence to be true!

The conclusion, then, is that *many* is not really a proportional determiner (in the sense that, e.g., *most* is).[7] The size needed to count as *many* for the subject NP in (37) is different from that of the size needed for the object NP, and so its value can but need not be set at some proportion of the size of the N set. The value of n depends on a variety of contextual factors, one of which could happen to be the size of the N set. As noted above, once we keep n constant, then if (34a) is true, so is (34b). Or, put differently, in any world in which (38a) holds then so does (38b), holding n_n constant:

(38) a. | husky' ∩ digs-holes-in-snow'| > n_n
   b. | dog' ∩ digs-holes-in-snow'| > n_n

Surely if (a) is true, then any way to expand the husky set into a superset will still be true. Exactly the same logic holds in the *few* case. These, then, turn out to be perfectly well-behaved, and the downward-entailing generalization holds for *many* and *few*.

16.4. But why? And how?

Still, there are two unsatisfactory aspects with what has been accomplished so far. First, we have stated a descriptive generalization to the effect that NPIs are allowed only in downward-entailing environments, but have formulated no actual principle to ensure this. It is interesting to note that sometimes the descriptive generalization itself is treated as the actual

---

[7] The argument can be reproduced with *few*. But strictly speaking, the above shows only that *many* and *few* have a non-proportional (cardinal) reading but not that they don't also have proportional readings. It is possible that both are ambiguous (see Partee 1989a) but this does not affect the point here. As long as there is a cardinal reading for *few* it follows that NPIs will be licensed by *few*; and even if there is a proportional reading for *many*, then there will be no licensing of NPIs if NPIs exist only in downward-entailing environments.

principle in grammar: one often sees work that assumes (implicitly or explicitly) that the grammar contains a principle like the following:

(39) An NPI is allowed in a sentence only if c-commanded by a downward-entailing operator.

(See Chapter 15, n. 4 for the definition of c-command.) Notice that no constraint like this could be incorporated into the sort of Direct Compositional architecture assumed here. (39) is a filter on trees (i.e., on syntactic representations), and we have speculated that the grammar itself does not "see" trees and therefore cannot contain principles that refer to them. And even in a theory which does countenance filters of this sort, (39) is decidedly odd. For it mixes syntax and semantics: *downward-entailing* is a semantic notion, *c-command* is a syntactic notion. (39), then, is no ordinary filter: it is not simply a constraint on syntactic representations. Rather it refers also to the meaning of certain bits of the representation, and thus must be seen as a filter that blocks representation/meaning pairs. It is thus not only stipulative, but if fully fleshed out would be quite complex. And so the question remains as to how it is ensured that NPIs have the distribution they do.[8]

Second, even considering (39) (or something like it) to be a correct *descriptive* generalization, one asks why it should be so. For we have defined *downward-entailing* in terms of sets and subsets, and one might well wonder why these notions should have any relevance whatsoever for the distribution of some item. And what is the meaning of the NPIs? Ultimately one should hope that the constraint on their distribution follows from something about their meaning (possibly combined with other principles). The next task, then, is to recast the notion of downward-entailing in a more illuminating way. We then turn to the meaning of (some) NPIs, and explore one influential proposal that makes progress towards answering the question of why NPIs have the distribution that they do.

---

[8] An argument that is sometimes given for (39), which refers to the syntax, is the fact that NPIs (apparently) do not occur in subject position. As should be clear from Exercise 16.10, a purely semantic description of the licensing environments does not seem account for this fact. However, it is not entirely clear that NPIs really cannot appear in subject position, and there are theories that the badness of the simple cases (such as *Any mouse didn't chase Calico*) have a pragmatic explanation. See de Swart (1998) for such an account.

16.4.1. The insight from semantic strength

The key intuition (already in Fauconnier 1975) is that downward-entailing environments are environments where semantic strength is reversed. *Semantic strength* itself is a notion about the amount of information conveyed. Thus we begin by giving a recursive definition of the notion of semantic strength. The base step (40a) concerns the strength of propositions. Recall that a proposition is a set of worlds, and so a proposition p is at least as strong as a proposition q if p is a subset of q. The intuition is that a speaker uttering a proposition p is (assuming normal communication) telling a hearer that p is true in the actual world, thus narrowing the space of worlds we might be living in. A stronger proposition gives more information; it narrows the space of worlds more. Put differently, it is "harder" for a stronger proposition to be true. We thus give a recursive definition of strength in (40b) (for convenience, we give the definition of "at least as strong as" rather than "stronger than" although it could easily be done either way):

(40) a. A proposition p is at least as strong as a proposition q if $p \subseteq q$. (Thus p gives at least as much information.) We will notate this as $p \geq q$.
     b. For any two functions f and g (whose ultimate result is 1 or 0), $f \geq g$ iff for all x, $f(x) \geq g(x)$.

Note then that [[dances]] is at least as strong as [[moves]]. In set terms, for any world w, $[[dances]]^w_s$ is a subset of $[[moves]]^w_s$. Or, to put this in terms of the functions: $[[dances]] \geq [[moves]]$ because for all x, $[[dances]](x) \geq [[moves]](x)$, and the latter holds because for all w, $[[dances]](x)(w) \geq [[moves]](x)(w)$. (From now on we will generally omit the world argument, as has been done throughout most of this text.) The intuition can again be recast in terms of information. If one VP characterizes a subset of another, the first is "harder" to be true of an individual, and so to know that, for example, Sabrina dances is to know more than to know that Sabrina moves.

From here, we can give a general definition of an *upward monotone* or *downward monotone* function (the informal definition of downward- and upward-entailing earlier are just special cases of this).

(41) Consider any function F whose ultimate result is t, and which takes as argument a function (of any type whose ultimate result is t).
     a. F is upward monotone iff for all f and g, if $f \geq g$ then $F(f) \geq F(g)$.
     b. F is downward monotone iff for all f and g, if $f \geq g$ then $F(g) \geq F(f)$.

(Note that both F above and the functions which are its argument must ultimately have a truth value as their ultimate result; this is because $\geq$ is defined only for such functions.)

We illustrate with *every*, which was the interesting case. In the earlier informal discussion we spoke about the downward entailingness of the VP position in a sentence of the form *every N VP*. Technically, though, it makes no sense to talk about the VP "argument" of *every*; in a sentence like *every ballerina danced*, the VP is actually an argument of *every ballerina*. (Recall that [[every]] is the Curry'ed relation between sets, and is of type $<<e,t>,<<e,t>,t>>$.) So now consider [[every ballerina]]. The definition in terms of sets and supersets showed that this is upward-entailing (if some set S is in [[every ballerina]] then so is any superset of S). But the intuition can also be phrased in terms of semantic strength. As shown above, [[dance]] is stronger than [[moves]]. And in fact, it is "harder" for *every ballerina danced* to be true than for *every ballerina moved* to be true. So [[every N]] (for any N) is upward monotone; it preserves the strength direction. But *every* itself reverses the strength direction (this is what it means to say that it is downward monotone on its N argument). [[husky]] is stronger than [[dog]], but [[every dog]] is stronger than [[every husky]]. It is easy to see this: for any set S, it is "harder" for S to be in [[every dog]] than to be in [[every husky]]. To show this more formally using the recursive definition: [[every]] is downward monotone because for any two functions f such that f $\leq$ g, [[every(g)]] $\leq$ [[every(f)]]. This follows from the recursive definition of $\leq$. Given two f and g such that f $\leq$ g, [[every]](g) $\leq$ [[every]](f) because for all functions h (of type $<e,t>$), [[every]](g)(h) $\leq$ [[every]](f)(h).

16.9. (i) Show that for any N, [[some N]] is upward monotone. Show that [[some]] is upward monotone.

(ii) Show that for any N, [[no N]] is downward monotone. Show that [[no]] is downward monotone.

(iii) We took the lexical meaning of *honest* to be a function of type $<e,t>$, and we will use honest$'_1$ as a notation for that function. However, the lexical item *honest* can also shift to the prenominal version, of category N/$_R$N and with meaning $\lambda P_{<e,t>}[\lambda x[P(x)$ & honest$_1$'(x)]]. Call this meaning [[honest$_2$]]. Is [[honest$_2$]] upward monotone, downward monotone, or neither? Show exactly how you arrive at the conclusion you arrive at. (Ignore the possibility that *honest*—like *big*—might be relativized to some contextually salient comparison class.)

---

*16.10. There is a complex set of questions surrounding the ability of *any* within a subject that combines with a negated VP. Common wisdom is that they don't; cases like (ia) are bad (compared to (ib)):

(i) a. *Any mouse didn't chase Calico.
     b. Calico didn't chase any mouse.

We have yet to give any semantics for expressions of the form *any N* (this will be done in 16.4.2.2) but assume for the purposes of this exercise that these are indeed GQs. That is, in the CG syntax they are of category S/(S/NP) with meanings of type $<e,<e,t>>$.

   One might then think at first glance that the badness of (ia) follows because these are not strictly speaking in downward monotone environments. For the VP is an argument of the subject, not vice versa, thus the definition above does not include the subject. Unfortunately, this line of reasoning is not sufficient to explain why (ia) is bad. Why not?

   Incidentally, the oft-cited generalization that NPIs do not occur in subject position is not really correct; there are well-known good cases like (ii) where the NPI is embedded within the subject.

(ii) A book with any torn pages will not be found in this library.

See de Swart (1998) for a pragmatic explanation for the contrast between (ia) and (ii).

It is now reasonable to speculate that what is important about downward-entailing or downward monotone environments is that they reverse semantic strength (or informativeness). Perhaps, then, there is something about the meaning of NPIs which makes them odd or nonsensical in environments where the strength is not reversed.

16.4.2. The second breakthrough: Kadmon and Landman on any

And indeed this hypothesis is explored both in Kadmon and Landman (1993) and in Krifka (1995). The two accounts differ, but both aim to derive the distribution from the strength reversal generalization combined with the meanings of NPIs (and with possibly other pragmatic principles). Here we explore only the former proposal; the interested reader will be able to consult Krifka (1995) on their own after reading Chapter 18. Although we will not follow Kadmon and Landman in all details, the discussion below is based on their general idea.

Recall the discussion in section 10.6 regarding the possibility that determiners come with a slot for a domain restriction. (Readers who initially skipped that section should consult it now.) This forms the background for the Kadmon and Landman proposal. They suggest that *any* actually has almost the same meaning as *some*, but contains as part of its meaning the notion that it is a *domain widener*. That is, its meaning ensures that the relevant individual can be drawn from a domain wider than the normal contextually salient domain. While Kadmon and Landman do not actually formally write out the meaning for *any* and do not discuss the issues surrounding domain restriction, one conceivable way to formalize their proposal is to suppose that the meaning of *some* is as in (42a) (in variable-ful terms) or (42a') (in variable-free terms) and *any* is as in (42b or b'), where D is a variable over sets of individuals:

(42) a. [[some]] = $\lambda Q[\lambda P[Q_S \cap D \cap P_S \neq \emptyset]]$ (using a free variable)
     a'. [[some]] = $\lambda D[\lambda Q[\lambda P[Q_S \cap D \cap P_S \neq \emptyset]]]$ (in variable-free terms)

     b. [[any]] = $\lambda Q[\lambda P[\exists D'[D \subset D' \& Q_S \cap D' \cap P_S \neq \emptyset]]]$ (using a free variable)
     b'. [[any]] = $\lambda D[\lambda Q[\lambda P[\exists D'[D \subset D' \& Q_S \cap D' \cap P_S \neq \emptyset]]]]$ (in variable-free terms)

Thus (42b) gives *any* a meaning such that *any student*, for example, is ultimately interpreted with respect to some contextually salient domain (exactly as is the case for *some student*). But *any* says more: it says that the student in question which ultimately satisfies the three-way intersection can be drawn from a wider domain than the obvious one. It is also necessary to assume that the contextually salient domain (the one which is widened) is never set to the widest possible domain.[9]

Now consider the meaning of *any pig* vs the meaning of *some pig*. To illustrate take the following two sentences, whose truth conditions are given below each sentence (we give these using the free variable D rather than in

---

[9] This is because of the way we have formalized the meaning. If we assume that D can be the widest possible domain, then a sentence using *any* could be false simply because there is no way to widen D. This result is not intended as part of the Kadmon and Landman proposal.

variable-free terms simply because this is easier to read and is fine for informal exposition):

(43) a. Some pig ate this morning.
      a'. pig's ∩ D ∩ ate-this-morning' ≠ Ø

      b. *Any pig ate this morning.
      b' ∃D'[D ⊂ D' & pig's ∩ D' ∩ ate-this-morning' ≠ Ø]

(43b) is of course bad, but—assuming that [[any]] is as given above—we know that it should have the meaning shown in b'. This says that there is a D' wider than the normal D such that a pig drawn from D' ate. Crucially, this is a weaker statement than (43b). The claim that one can find a wider domain than the contextually salient one is trivially true (given the assumption made above that D is never the widest possible domain) and so this part has no effect on the truth conditions. But (43b) also says that there's a pig drawn from this wider domain who ate. Thus if (43b) is true then (43a) is true, and so (b) is a weaker statement than (a).

When would widening the domain strengthen a statement? In just those environments where the strength directions are reversed: i.e., in monotone decreasing environments. Let us check this with a couple of examples. Consider the pair in (44):

(44) a. Every farmer who fed some pig decided not to then eat bacon for breakfast.
      b. Every farmer who fed any pig decided not to then eat bacon for breakfast.

As discussed in Chapter 13, relative clauses denote sets; [[who fed some/any pig]] is the set of feeders of a (domain-restricted) pig. Given the semantics of relative clauses and of GQs in object position, [[who fed some pig]] is the set of individuals x such that there is a pig out of some domain D that x fed. By the same token, [[who fed any pig]] is the set of individuals x such that there is a pig out of a wider domain D' that x fed. In both cases this intersects with the set of farmers, giving the following (informally shown) meanings to the two complex Ns at issue:

(45) a. [[farmer who fed some pig]]_S = {x| x fed a pig in D}
      b. [[farmer who fed any pig]]_S = {x| x fed a pig in D', where D' is wider than the contextually salient D}

Note that it is "easier" to be in the (b) set than in the (a) set; (a) is thus stronger than (b). But *every* reverses strength direction, and so (44b) is a stronger statement than (44a). Put differently, [[every farmer who fed any pig]] is a stronger function than [[every farmer who fed some pig]]. If, however, we

were to take *farmer who fed some/any pig* as the N argument of *some*, we can
see that the version with *any* is weaker than the version with *some*.

16.11. Show that [[no farmer who fed some pig]] is weaker than [[no
farmer who fed any pig]].

And so this brings us to the second key part of the Kadmon and Landman
proposal, which is that there is some principle as follows: *any* is allowed only
if it strengthens a statement. This is simply a stipulation here: what remains
to be explained is both why this should be true and from what this requirement follows. But before elaborating on these points, we turn to *ever* to
show that the basic proposal can be generalized.

16.4.3. ever

Although Kadmon and Landman did not deal with *ever*, the proposal
extends rather naturally to *ever*. In fact, while some authors have had the
intuition that domain widening is not quite the correct analysis for *any* (see,
e.g., Krifka 1995), the parallel story with *ever* seems very plausible. To
consider the semantics of *ever*, something needs to be said about the semantics of tense in English. As a first pass, past-tense sentences seem to existen-
tially quantify over points in time. Thus, (46) means something that can be
represented as (47), where t is a variable over moments in time, "now" is of
course the speech time, and < means "earlier than":

(46)   Strawbuilder went to market.

(47) $\exists t[t < now$ & Strawbuilder go to market at t].

But in general the understanding of sentences is restricted to some contextually salient window of times. This once again is illustrated by an
example due to Partee (1984) (although Partee actually used this example
for a somewhat different point). Suppose my husband and I are in the car
beginning a four-day vacation, and I turn to him and say (48):

(48)   Uh oh. I didn't turn off the stove.

Here there is a past tense (which we are assuming involves existential quantification over times in the past) and a negation. The question thus arises as to

whether the meaning is appropriately represented in (49a) (with the negation scoping over tense) or (49b) in which the scopes are reversed (note that we are not concerned here with how the compositional semantics puts things together, so these formulas are just intended as a way to notate the final meaning):

(49)   a. ~∃t[t < now & I turn off the stove at t]
       b. ∃t [t < now & ~[I turn off the stove at t]]

Clearly (49b) is not correct. Of course there is some time at which I didn't turn off the stove, but this is hardly the point of the comment in (48). (49a) is closer: it's saying there is no time at which I turned off the stove. But that can't quite be right either; I could have turned off the stove many times in the past. We care only about the fact that within some relevant interval, there is no time at which I turned off the stove. So (49a) is fine, provided that the domain of quantification over times is domain-restricted to some salient set of adjacent times (i.e., some interval). Thus, as with quantifiers in general, quantification over times is arguably domain-restricted.

What is the meaning of *ever*? It seems fairly clear that *ever* broadens the interval of times at which the truth of a sentence is being evaluated. Consider, for example, the contrast in (50):

(50)   a. I haven't climbed Mt Chocorua.
       b. I haven't ever climbed Mt Chocorua.

(50) is interpreted with respect to a much narrower interval. We could be discussing my hiking activity this summer, and I say (50a) where it is clearly understood as my not having climbed Mt Chocorua during this last hiking season. But (50b) broadens that to a much greater temporal window (in fact one might argue that *ever* broadens to the widest domain possible; we leave it open as to whether or not that is correct).

The Kadmon and Landman account of *any* thus does extend naturally to *ever*: *ever* widens the temporal domain at which a sentence is evaluated and we can assume that there is some restriction here too that widening is not allowed unless it also strengthens. As with the case of *any*, the domain-widened interval results in a stronger sentence exactly in those environments in which the general strength is reversed—i.e., in downward monotone environments.

16.12. Show that (ia) is stronger than (ib), and that (iia) is weaker than (iib). (Note that of course (iia) is bad, but assuming that it were good and that *ever* only widens the temporal domain, one can show the point.) Do the same with the pairs in (iii) and (iv) (this is relatively straightforward). To show this for (i) and (ii) it is best to construct contexts in which the sentences without *ever* have a clear restriction to some temporal interval, as was done in the text with respect to (50).

i. a. Everyone who has ever climbed Mt Chocorua enjoyed the view.
    b. Everyone who has climbed Mt Chocorua enjoyed the view.
ii. a. *Someone who has ever climbed Mt Chocorua enjoyed the view.
    b. Someone who has climbed Mt Chocorua enjoyed the view.
iii. a. I have not ever climbed Mt Chocorua.
     b. I have not climbed Mt Chocorua.
iv. a. *I have ever climbed Mt Chocorua.
    b. I have climbed Mt Chocorua.

16.5. Open questions and further discussion

While this account goes quite far, there are many details left incomplete in the Kadmon and Landman proposal, and which will also be left incomplete here. It is still an open question as to just what the strengthening requirement on *any* and *ever* follow from, or how to even exactly state this requirement. Is it encoded into the lexical entry for *any*? Kadmon and Landman propose that indeed it is, but they do not spell out just what the lexical entry actually looks like so as to enforce this requirement.[10] Note that

---

[10] Notice that the requirement would have to be encoded in such a way that it can be satisfied not directly when *any* combines with its sister, but much later in the combinatorics (or, to use representational terms to make the point, "higher in the tree"). In other words, consider a sentence like (i):

(i) Every farmer who fed any pig decided not to eat bacon.

Here the requirement of downward monotonicity is satisfied in virtue of the complex N *farmer who fed any pig* occurring as argument of *every*. But *any* does not "know" when it combines with *pig* that it will ultimately end up in such an environment. Thus if this ultimately is encoded into the meaning of *any*, it has to stay "active" so that it projects to larger expressions—in this case to the expression *farmer who fed any pig*.

the meaning spelled out in (42b–b′) gives widening, but says nothing about strengthening. Does this requirement follow from some pragmatic principle governing competing utterances? One might think that the latter is quite reasonable—one can imagine a principle to the effect that a speaker should not make a weaker statement when a stronger statement is possible. But this is not obviously correct: it could well be that the weaker statement is the only one that the listener is sure of. In other words, it is not obvious that a pure pragmatic principle will explain the anomaly of *Any pig ate this morning*. If I am sure that some pig ate, but am not sure that that pig comes from the obvious contextually salient domain (say, our farm), I might be able to say nothing more than the sentence above. Yet it is still unacceptable.[11]

So let us recap the story told in this chapter. It was pointed out that early accounts of the distribution of NPIs do nothing more than posit a syntactic feature on some items with a stipulation that NPIs must occur in some syntactic relationship to items with this feature. This was discarded for a semantic characterization of the environments. We briefly entertained the possibility that the grammar instead contains a stipulation like (39), and this too was discarded in favor of an analysis that relies in part on the meanings of *any* and *ever*. Yet there remains a final (and unformalized) stipulation to the effect that *any* and *ever* are allowed only if they strengthen the utterance. One might, then, argue that we have simply cashed in one stipulation for another. But in the opinion of at least this author this is not really true, for each step along the way seems to be zeroing in on the full solution.

Before leaving this, though, we should also note that there is a vast amount of literature on this domain and even plenty of controversy, and we have just scratched the surface. Even within the broad picture here, we have had nothing to say about the full distribution of NPIs. They are allowed in questions (both *yes/no* questions and *wh*-questions) which are obviously beyond the scope here. There are, moreover, a number of environments discussed as early as Klima (1964) which have not been covered

---

[11] Kadmon and Landman (1993) also question the viability of a pragmatic account by claiming that such sentences are "ungrammatical" rather than simply odd. However, we do not really have *a priori* intuitions about what sorts of anomalies are due to the grammar (rendering something "ungrammatical") rather than due to other factors, and so this objection does not seem valid. It is, however, true that the oddness cannot be cancelled, suggesting that something more is at work than a pure pragmatic principle.

here. NPIs also interact interestingly with presupposition; for discussion, see von Fintel (1999) which should be reasonably accessible at this point. Moreover, it is well known that NPIs can be licensed by implicatures (see Linebarger 1987 and much subsequent discussion) and see Giannakidou (1997) for an alternative to the strength reversal generalization presented in this chapter.

16.6. Semantic strength and scalar implicatures

The fact that semantic strength is reversed in certain environments is also relevant to the distribution of scalar implicatures. And not surprisingly. After all, the Gricean program discussed in section 10.4 posits that scalar implicatures result from competition between a potentially stronger statement and a weaker one. Should a speaker utter a weaker statement where a stronger statement directly competes with the weaker one, then the hearer will conclude that the speaker did not have grounds to utter the stronger one. This—combined with the assumption that the speaker is in a position to know the truth or falsity of the stronger statement (the "knowledgeability assumption")—leads to the conclusion that the stronger statement is false. Obviously, then, when strength is reversed one should see a different behavior. A sentence with *some* should not implicate that the corresponding sentence with *all* is false in those cases where the former is actually stronger than the latter. And in fact this is exactly the pattern that we find.

Thus recall the discussion in section 10.4, where it was shown that *some* cannot have *not all* as part of its meaning, because the *not all* suggestion disappears in certain contexts. Among these was the linguistics department prerequisites scenario: the department manual reads *Everyone who has taken some Phonetics course is allowed to enroll in Phonology I, and no one else is.* As discussed there, an instructor is not entitled (at least not by just what the manual says) to ban a student who has taken all of the Phonetics courses. (27) in section 10.4 showed that the exclusive *or* implicature disappears in the similar sentence *Everyone who has taken (either) Phonetics I or Phonology I is allowed to enroll in Phon/Phon II (and no one else is).* These implicatures also disappear in the antecedent of a conditional, as in (51):

(51) If you have taken some Phonetics course you may enroll in Phonology I.

This carries with it no implicature that the student who has taken all of the Phonetics courses is not covered under (51). Similar facts can be constructed with *or*.

So exactly where does the *some* to *not all* implicature disappear? In downward monotone environments![12] But this is exactly what we would expect. Consider the pairs in (52):

(52) a. Every student who handed in some of the homework assignments got a B or better.
b. Everyone who handed in all of the homework assignments got a B or better.

(52a) is a stronger statement than (52b); it entails (52b) which is a reversal of the usual situation with respect to *some* and *all*. For in normal (non-downward monotone) environments a sentence with *all* entails the corresponding sentence with *some*. But because this is a strength-reversing environment, the entailment direction reverses. It is thus not surprising that (52a) does not implicate that (52b) is not true. (Indeed, (52a) entails that (52b) is in fact true.)

It gets even more interesting. For in fact the implicature direction reverses; a sentence containing *all* (in a downward-entailing environment) implicates that the speaker is not in a position to say the corresponding sentence with *some*. Add to this the speaker knowledgeability assumption, and it follows that a sentence *all* implicates that the corresponding sentence with *some* is false. (The observation that the normal implicatures disappear in downward monotone environments is discussed in Horn 1989; the extended observation that the implicatures in fact reverse in these environments can be found in Levinson 2000; see also Horn 1972.)[13] Thus the general Gricean view predicts that on hearing (52b), a listener will conclude (assuming speaker knowledgeability) that (52a) is false. That in turn means that there is at least one student who handed in some of the homework assignments who did not get a B or better. Of course the falsity of (52a) by itself is compatible with someone who handed in all of the homework assignments not getting a B (since *some* does include *all*). But the listener assumes that (52b) is true, and so the truth of (52b) (the assertion) combined

---

[12] This is not the only place they disappear, nor would one expect it to be since implicatures arise from a complex interaction of factors.

[13] The interaction of implicatures and downward-entailing environments is also discussed in detail in Chierchia (2004) (and other more recent works by Chierchia on this subject), although the conclusion that he draws from this fact is somewhat different from that drawn here.

with the falsity of (52a) (the implicature) leads the listener to conclude that there is at least one student who handed in some but not all of the homework assignments who didn't get a B or better. (The discussion here assumes that (52b) presupposes that there are students who handed in all of the homework assignments.) And indeed this is exactly the inference that (in a normal conversational setting) a listener will draw on hearing (52b); i.e., that a B was not guaranteed if a student handed in only some but not all of the homeworks.

Consider also the following:

(53)   Not every student likes formal semantics.

As noted as early as Horn (1972), this implicates that there is some student who likes formal semantics. That *not every student* does not entail *some student* can be shown by our usual embedding this itself in (another) downward monotone context:

(54)   If not every student in the school passes the statewide exam, the school will lose its funding. (Otherwise, the funding will be guaranteed to continue.)

Surely the principal at the school hoping to receive continued funding—and knowing that some students will fail—will not then tell all students that they should fail. But if *not every student* was literally the same as "not every student but at least one student," then it would be quite a rational move on the part of the principal to make sure that no student passes—for then the school would be guaranteed funding. Once again, then, the *not every* to *some* inference disappears, showing that this is an implicature, not part of the meaning of *not every*.

The reason for the implicature in (53) is exactly parallel to the discussion surrounding (52). (55) is stronger than (53) and presumably competes with it; a listener hearing (53) will thus conclude that the speaker was not in a position to utter (55) and combining this with the knowledgeability assumption we arrive at the conclusion that (55) is false:

(55)   No student likes formal semantics.

This is part of the more general phenomenon of implicature reversal in downward monotone environments. To simplify the discussion, think of *not* here as "scoping over" the whole sentence, and so we recast this as (56):

(56)   It is not the case that every student likes formal semantics.

(This move is made simply to avoid giving a semantics for the version of *not* that directly combines with a determiner like *every*. To do so is straightforward, as the interested reader can verify, but it involves expository space and details that are irrelevant to the point at hand.) *It is not the case that* is ordinary propositional negation (thus of type $<<s,t>,<s,t>>$) and so of course it is a downward monotone function. Thus we would expect that (56) would implicate that the corresponding sentence in (57) is false (note that (57) is equivalent to (55)):

(57)   It is not the case that some student likes formal semantics.

And for this to be false, there must be at least one student who does like formal semantics, exactly the implicature that we find here.

16.13. Consider the following:

(i) No student read every book on the reading list.

This implicates (given the usual caveats about speaker knowledgeability) that at least one student did read at least one of the books on the reading list. Work through exactly why this implicature arises.

17

More binding phenomena

This chapter explores several (related) domains that involve "binding" phenomena although not in the obvious sense, for many of them involve cases where what is being bound is not an overt pronoun but rather what is sometimes thought of as a hidden variable. An especially interesting aspect of these cases is that they provide striking support for the variable-free view, as their analysis is quite effortless under that view. But independent of the issues surrounding variables, these domains form a rich set of (interrelated) phenomena which are quite interesting in their own right.

17.1. Functional questions

17.1.1. The phenomenon

The first observation of interest centers on a surprising interpretation of *wh*-questions (and their possible answers). Some preliminary remarks are in order concerning ordinary *wh*-questions (and answers) as in (1):

(1)   Q. Who does Romeo admire (the most)?
      A. Mercutio.

A serious account of the semantics of questions is beyond the scope of this book (see Hamblin 1973, Karttunen 1977, and Groenendijk and Stokhof

1984 for seminal proposals which have formed the basis of most subsequent work). Here two points will suffice. The first is that the question asks for the identity of an individual; one can paraphrase this as "what is the x_e such that Romeo loves x (the most)"? This is not meant as an actual analysis of the semantics, for this simply uses one question to paraphrase another. But the paraphrase is meant to stress the fact that the question is about the identity of an individual; hence *Mercutio* is an appropriate answer.

Second, some rudimentary account of the compositional semantics is needed. As is well known, the interior portion of questions (e.g., *Romeo admire* in (1)) has much in common with the interior of a relative clause. For example, in the LF theory with movement it is assumed that *who* has raised from the object position of *love*, leaving a trace and yielding (roughly) the structure in (2) which is also the LF:

(2)   Who [$_{\Lambda_8}$ [$_S$Romeo admire t_8 (the most)]]

We restrict the discussion here just to the composition of the node labeled Λ_8; this is exactly the same as the composition of the corresponding material in the relative clause (8) in Chapter 13. Hence, [$_{\Lambda_8}$ *Romeo admire t_8*] is (on any g) that function of type <e,t> which characterizes the set of individuals that Romeo loves. We will not develop the rest of the composition of (2) as it requires a full theory of the meaning of questions, and will simply assume [[Λ_8]] combines with the meaning of *who* to give the full question. Note incidentally that although the *who* is homophonous with the relative pronoun *who* they are not the same lexical item; question words and relative pronouns are a distinct set. (For example, *what* is only a question word.) In the Direct Compositional and variable-free approach sketched in section 13.4, the meaning of *Romeo admire (the most)* is similar, but is done without use of traces or LF. Recall that here *Romeo* lifts, undergoes **g-sl**, and takes *admire* as argument. (For short, lifted *Romeo* function composes with *admire*). No use of variables and assignments was needed for this, and so *Romeo admire* is the characteristic function of the set of individuals that Romeo admires. Again assume that this combines with [[who]].

Now consider (3):

(3)   Who does every man admire (the most)?

This too can be a run-of-the-mill question asking for the identity of some individual—here an appropriate answer might be *Hillary Clinton*. But it has another interpretation, brought out by embedding this in the discourse in (4):

(4)   Q. Who does every man$_i$ admire (the most)?
    A. His$_i$ mother.

How is it that the question here can have a reading in which *his mother* is an appropriate answer? The initial temptation is to think of this as basically a question about an individual, but where *every man* "scopes over" the question. In other words, one can try to paraphrase this informally as "for every man y, what is the identity of the individual x such that y admires x (the most)"? This assumes that there is some way to combine the meaning of a question with the meaning of a GQ, which depends in part on just what is the type of meaning for questions. But even if those two can combine, the scope solution breaks down when one switches to a GQ like *no man*, as was noted in Groenendijk and Stokhof (1984):

(5)   Q. Who would no man$_i$ invite (to his wedding)?
    A. His$_i$ ex-wife.

Clearly it makes no sense to try to paraphrase this as "for no man y, what is the identity of the x such that y loves x?" (See also Engdahl 1986 for detailed discussion of problems with the scope strategy.)

17.1.2. An analysis with complex traces

In light of this, Groenendijk and Stokhof (1984) and Engdahl (1986) analyzed these as *functional questions*. They ask not for the identity of an individual but rather for the identity of a function from individuals to individuals. (5-Q) can be informally paraphrased as: "what is the identity of the function f of type <e,e> such that for no man, x, x invited f(x)?" By way of elaboration, we first embed the basic idea into the LF theory using traces.[1] The idea is that the movement of *who* can leave a *complex* trace: one which corresponds to a variable over functions of type <e,e> applied to a variable of type e. Mechanically this can be accomplished by giving the trace two indices (see, e.g., Groenendijk and Stokhof 1984 and Chierchia 1991). As the two indices need to be kept distinct we notate the trace as $t_{f\text{-}8/x\text{-}7}$. The assignments have as their domain not only variables over individuals (for

---

[1] The actual mechanics in Engdahl (1986) are slightly different as she was not using traces but a different device, and Groenendijk and Stokhof (1984) also used a slightly different notation. But these differences are inconsequential.

which we have been using the positive integers) but also an infinite number of variables over functions of type <e,e>. (Indeed, as discussed in section 15.5, the assignments have as their domain variables over all sorts of objects.) Call f_8 the 8th variable of type <e,e>, and x_7 the 7th variable of type e. Then the interpretation of $t_{f-8/x-7}$ on any g is $g(f_8)(g(x_7))$. The relevant portion of the meaning of the question is put together by assuming an LF as follows, where *who* has left a complex trace and where *no man* has undergone QR and so the individual argument of the complex trace is bound in the normal way that binding takes place:

(6)

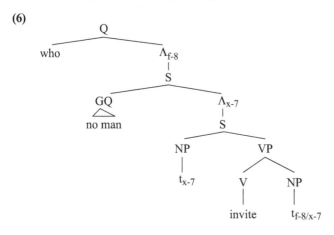

The value of the lowest S-node on any g is the proposition that $g(x_7)$ invited $g(f_8)(g(x_7))$. The interpretation of Λ_{x-7} closes off the individual variable, and so the value of this node differs only on assignments which differ on the value of f_8 (since that is the only open variable here). Thus on any g, $[[\Lambda_{x-7}]]$ is the set of individuals who invited the value of $g(f_8)$ applied to themselves. This is then taken as argument of [[no man]] (on g); so the value of the next S up the tree is—on any g—the proposition that the intersection of the set just named and the man set is empty. Then f_8 is closed off by the λ-abstraction step which is used to interpret Λ_{f-8}. The result of that step is that the value of Λ_{f-8} is (on any g) a function of type <<e,e>,t>. It characterizes the set of functions f which are such that no man invited the value of f applied to self. Put differently, it characterizes the set of functions f such that the set of individuals x who invited f(x) has an empty intersection with the man set. And this then presumably combines with the meaning of the question word *who* (note that *who* would need to have a generalized meaning as it can combine with functions of type <e,t> or—in this case—functions of type <<e,e>,t>). Notice, incidentally, that each node labeled Λ needs a full index such as f-7 or x-8. For example, it is not sufficient to label the higher Λ-node with just the index 7, because the semantic interpretation of this node needs to be sensitive to whether or not abstraction is happening over the function variable f-7 or the individual variable x-7.

The analysis succeeds in giving the right meaning to a sentence which at first glance appears rather intractable to paraphrase. But this particular implementation of the basic analysis has costs (aside from the fact that here we are abandoning Direct Compositionality). For there is no reason to expect the existence of the functional reading for questions: this comes as quite a surprise. This phenomenon is accounted for only by the hypothesis that traces can be complex in the requisite way, but nothing in the theory of variables and traces so far predicts that there should be complex as well as simple traces. In fact, Engdahl pointed out that the traces need to be of arbitrary complexity; there are similar questions asking for the identity of functions of type <e,<e,e>>. So, for example, consider (7) in the context of a linguistics department with all male phonology students, all female semantics professors, and a wonderful curriculum in which the phonology students are required to take courses each year from every semantics professor:

(7) Q. Which assignment does every phonology$_i$ student (every year) hope that every semantics professor$_j$ will ignore?
     A. The first one that he$_i$ hands in to her$_j$.

This requires the trace (after *ignore*) to be of the form $t_{R\text{-}8/x\text{-}7/x\text{-}9}$ for R the 8th variable of type <e,<e,e>> (where this is applied to two individual variables).

17.1.3. A variable-free analysis

Strikingly, the functional meaning for questions comes for free in the variable-free account sketched in section 15.3. It does not require positing extra structure in the "gap" position, and the existence of the functional reading follows automatically from the mechanisms for binding in general.[2]

---

[2] There is a potential caveat: the meaning of *who* must be such that it takes as argument both functions of type <e,t> (as in the ordinary individual reading of questions) and one of type <<e,e>,t> for the functional questions. Whether a single item can be listed with the more complex meanings derived from this is something we leave open, as it cannot be answered without a more detailed account of the

For the sake of discussion, we collapse the two steps of **g-sl** plus application into function composition, which is a harmless expository simplification. The functional reading for (4) is just a consequence of the fact that *invite* can undergo **z**; if *no man* composes with z(*invite*) the result is exactly the meaning of the lambda node in the LF in (6). It is the set of functions f of type <e,e> such that no-man z-invites f. In other words, it is the set of functions f (of type <e,e>) such that the intersection of the man set with the set of individuals who **z**-love f is empty. That set in turn is the set of individuals x who love f(x). And so ultimately the question asks for the identity of that function. Of course, **z** does not have to apply; when it doesn't the result is the ordinary individual reading for (4). So the existence of functional readings for questions is simply a consequence of the mechanisms for bound pronouns in general.

17.1. Show the details of the syntactic and semantic composition of the functional reading for *no man invite* in the variable-free view. (Note that the syntactic category of this expression is different from that of the same string on the individual reading.)

Engdahl's observation that these can be asking for the identity of functions of type <e,<e,e>>—or even more complex ones—follows as well, since there can be various applications of **z** and **g**. Readers who worked through the details of Exercise 15.23 should be able to see how to get the relevant reading for (7); those who did not can content themselves with the intuition that the apparatus for multiple binders and multiple pronouns extends automatically to multiply complex functional questions.

Finally, we note that functional readings interact with WCO in just the ways one would expect (under either the complex trace analysis or the variable-free analysis). The relevant facts were first observed in May (1985) (although he did not hook these into the analysis of functional questions). Thus (8a) has a functional reading but (8b) does not:

meaning of question words. However, we can note that the variable-ful account of functional questions also needs a way to predict these extra meanings for question words.

(8)   a. Which woman would no man invite (to his wedding)? His ex-wife.
     b. *Which woman would invite no man (to her wedding)? His ex-wife.

The fact that this contrast reduces to WCO was noted in Engdahl (1988) and in Chierchia (1991). The point here is neutral between the LF-with-traces view and the view here. In the LF view, the only way (9b) could have the functional reading is for there to be a complex trace in subject position of *invite* (where *which woman* moves, even though the movement here does not affect the word order), of the general form $t_{f-n/x-m}$, where *no man* is indexed m and hence raises and leaves a trace indexed m in object position. While the WCO filter (9) in Chapter 15 does not literally block this (as the interested reader can verify), it can easily be revised to do so. (The term "pronoun" in that formulation would have to be expanded to include both pronouns and the individual index portion of a complex trace. That some revision is needed here may well be just an artifact of the particular formulation that was chosen.) In the Direct Compositional and variable-free view, the only way to arrive at the functional reading would be by application of *s* on *invite*, which is impossible.

17.2. Binding and coordination (in variable-free semantics)

A persistent theme throughout this book has been that the Direct Compositional tools allow for simple treatments of cases of coordination without having to maintain some version of a conjunction reduction analysis. Chapter 5 motivated Curry'ing transitive verbs in part to give a smooth account of sentences with VP coordination; Chapters 10 and 11 showed how VP coordination interacts with the analysis of GQs to give the appropriate readings of sentences containing both; Chapter 14 showed some interesting interactions of coordination of Ss with GQs in object position, and Chapter 13 showed that the adoption of the **g-sl** (or function composition) allows for a simple analysis of sentences like (10) (the basic point originally from Dowty 1988):

(9)   Calista loves and Samantha hates model-theoretic semantics.

In light of these results, consider (10) in which one pronoun is apparently bound by two different subject positions:

(10)   a. Every man$_i$ loves but no man$_i$ wants to marry his$_i$ mother.
  b. Every third grade boy$_i$ loves and every fourth grade boy$_i$ hates his$_i$ math teacher.
  c. Every man$_i$ loves and no man$_i$ marries his$_i$ mother.

We won't dwell on how these may or may not be handled in the LF theory since the issues are somewhat complex; for discussion see von Stechow (1990) and Jacobson (1999). Suffice it to point out here that these are unproblematic, given the variable-free fragment developed so far. (10c) will be used to illustrate. *Every man loves* is put together as shown above in the discussion of functional questions: the *every man* function composes with **z**-*love* to give an expression of category S/$_R$NP^{NP}; this expression denotes the characteristic function of the set of functions f such that every man z-loves f. *no man marries* is similar and is {f|f such that no man z-marries f}. These two sets intersect (by the generalized definition for *and*), and the expression *every man loves and no man marries* denotes (in set terms) the set of functions f (of type <e,e>) such that every man z-loves f and no man z-marries f. The analysis of *his mother* is also straightforward. It denotes the-mother-of function and is of category NP^{NP}. Both its syntax and semantics are thus right to be the argument of *every man loves and no man marries*; and the truth conditions thus require that the-mother-of function is in the set of functions described above. (Note too that the fact that *his mother* is an appropriate answer to a functional question follows in the same way: it denotes a function of type <e,e> which is what the question asks for.)[3]

17.3. "Paycheck" pronouns (and "donkey" pronouns?)

17.3.1. Paychecks

Both theories of pronouns developed in Chapter 15 handle both free and bound pronouns. But there is another use of pronouns which does not fall under these categories, at least not in the obvious sense. These are called

---

[3] The fact that *his mother* is an appropriate answer to a functional question is not, however, necessarily problematic for the variable-ful approach. For many proponents of this approach would also argue that answers themselves are elliptical for full sentences, and so this answer would be taken to hiddenly be the full sentence *Every man$_8$ loves his$_8$ mother (the most)*, where *his$_8$* is bound in the normal way.

paycheck pronouns, so-named because of their introduction into the literature in Karttunen (1969) whose example was along the lines of (11) (modified from Karttunen's actual example):

(11)   The woman who put her paycheck in the bank was far wiser than the one who
put it in the Brown University Employees Credit Union.

A more manageable example for the purposes of discussion is (12):

(12)   Every third grade boy$_i$ loves his$_i$ mother. But every fourth grade boy hates her.

Of interest here is the reading where *her* can be paraphrased as "his mother"
(and where *his* in the paraphrase is bound by the subject position of *hates*).
On this reading, *her* is neither a free nor a bound pronoun in the usual sense.
Clearly it is not free: in the reading of interest there is no single individual
that it picks up. But neither is it bound: the only thing it could be bound by is
no fourth grade boy and obviously this is not the reading we are after (and in
any case has a gender clash).

   Broadly speaking, there are two main analyses of paycheck pronouns.
One assumes the pronoun is—at some level of representation—represented
as fuller material; this is much like the ellipsis account of VP Ellipsis. Call
this the *full NP analysis*. This was suggested (for a related case) in Geach
(1962) under the rubric *pronouns of laziness*. The full NP analysis was
argued for (for cases of this sort) explicitly in Karttunen (1969, 1971),
Partee (1975b), Jacobson (1977), and for a slightly different but related
group of cases in Evans (1980). It is revived in more recent literature such
as Heim (1990) and most notably Elbourne (2005) (who takes the view—
also espoused in much traditional transformational work—that *all* pronouns are short for full linguistic material). If paycheck pronouns are
represented as full definite NPs at some level, there is no problem getting
the appropriate reading. At the level relevant for interpretation (LF, perhaps) *her* in (12) *is* actually *his mother*, where *his* is bound by the subject
position of *hates* in the way that the binding of any ordinary pronoun takes
place (one can take one's pick of theories for that part). This removes the
mystery of how it is that the paycheck reading is available. But it comes at a
cost: some device is needed to effect the mapping between the fuller representation and the simple pronoun (perhaps a rule deleting linguistic material
as in most of the accounts above). Incidentally, one will often see these kinds
of pronouns (and some other cases) discussed under the rubric of *e-type
pronouns*, a terminology from Evans (1980). Along with this goes a common

slogan that "e-type pronouns go proxy for definite descriptions." Presumably this is meant to claim that such pronouns are actually full definite NPs
at the level that inputs the semantics. Here, however, we will continue to use
the term paycheck pronouns rather than e-type pronouns, both because the
general points (and analysis) predate Evans's analysis, and because the term
e-type pronouns is used by different authors in slightly different ways.
(Moreover, since the term e-type pronouns is also frequently coupled with
the above slogan, those using this term are often making a commitment to
the full NP analysis. The term paycheck pronouns is intended here in an
analysis-neutral way.)

The second broad tradition begins with seminal work of Cooper (1979),
subsequently slightly modified in Engdahl (1986), who observes an interesting commonality between functional questions and paycheck pronouns. We
exposit this initially under the LF view. Like the trace of a functional
question, Engdahl posits (following Cooper) that a pronoun can correspond
not just to a simple variable over individuals, but also a complex variable,
i.e., a variable over functions of type <e,e> applied to an individual variable.[4] Thus in (12b) the pronoun *her* can be indexed as $her_{f-8/x-7}$, where—just
like the corresponding trace $[[her_{f-8/x-7}]]$—on any g is $g(f_8)(g(x_7))$. The rest of
the composition is unsurprising: the individual variable is bound in the way
that binding of ordinary pronouns happens in general. For example, in the
LF theory, *no fourth grade boy* is, on the reading of relevance, indexed 7 and
undergoes QR, leaving t_{x-7} in subject position, and the composition proceeds in the familiar way.

Key to the analysis is the fact that f_8 is never bound, so the second
sentence in (12) contains a free variable over functions of type <e,e>. For
any g, it asserts that the set of lovers of the value of $g(f_8)$ applied to self has
an empty intersection with the set of fourth grade boys. The final assignment-dependent proposition is applied by the listener to some contextually
salient assignment. Although we have left it open as to how an assignment
becomes contextually salient, we assume that there is a salient assignment in
which f_8 is mapped to the-mother-of function; (which in turn is a salient
function in view of the meaning of the first sentence). Thus, using the

---

[4] If traces are taken to be simply unpronounced pronouns, then this commonality
is not surprising. But it is not clear that it makes sense to consider traces as a species
of pronouns, as it is not obvious that traces should be listed in the lexicon with an
index. After all, the index is inherited from that of the moved expression.

informal terminology that we have often used in this text, the free variable f_8 picks up the contextually salient mother-of function.

Engdahl further points out that—just like the case of functional traces— pronouns can have meanings that are indefinitely complex. Consider (13):

(13)   The woman$_i$ who told Sears$_j$ that the bill she$_i$ owed them$_j$ was in the mail was wiser than the woman who told Filenes that it had not yet been mailed.

Here *it* is, in this account, a function of type <e,<e,e>> applied to two individual variables; in the end it picks up the function that maps people and stores to the bill that the former owes the latter.

17.3.2. A variable-free analysis of paycheck pronouns

While again quite elegant in some respects, the Cooper/Engdahl theory— like the full NP theory—comes at a cost. For one must posit additional pronouns in the lexicon. Not only are there (an infinite number of) pronouns with simple indices, but there are also pronouns with complex indices, where the indices themselves can be arbitrarily complex. But it turns out that if the basic insight in this analysis is translated directly into the variable-free view here, the existence of paycheck readings on pronouns is completely unsurprising, and requires no extra lexical entries for pronouns. With only one small (and quite natural) modification to the system above, these readings come as an automatic consequence of the system.

To show this, we translate the Cooper/Engdahl account into the variable-free system in three steps. For the first step, we temporarily pretend that there are variables and retain the free function variable from the Cooper/Engdahl proposal. The individual variable, however, can immediately be eliminated. The relevant reading is obtained just like the functional question case in (4) and (5); *hates* in the second clause undergoes **z**. In other words, the meaning of the second sentence can be represented as [[no fourth grade boy]](z([[loves]])(f)).

Of course, this is cheating since it makes use of a free function variable f. So the second step is to eliminate this and treat the paycheck reading of *her* in a way analogous to any other free pronoun. Let the actual meaning of paycheck *her* be not only the identity function over individuals, but also the identity function over functions of type <e,e>. Thus it can have the meaning $\lambda f_{<e,e>}[f]$, which is of type <<e,e>,<e,e>>. The category for this pronoun is (unsurprisingly) $(NP^{NP})^{(NP^{NP})}$. This category looks complex but its existence follows from the recursive definition of categories. The superscript feature NP^{NP} passes all the way up by the normal **g** rules. So the second clause is composed as shown in (14) which is a schematic representation of both the syntax and the semantics:

(14) $g_{<e,e>}$(no-fourth-grade-boy) ($g_{<e,e>}$(z (hates)) (paycheck-her))

Recasting this in perhaps somewhat more transparent notation, the final meaning is $\lambda f_{<e,e>}$[no-fourth-grade-boy(z-hates f)], or, equivalently, $\lambda f_{<e,e>}$ [no-fourth-grade-boy(λx[x hates f(x)])].

---

*17.2. Show the full syntactic and semantic computation which is sketched above, using the lambda notation to show that this does indeed mean what is claimed above.

But there still remains one unsatisfying aspect, for the analysis so far relies on the assumption that *her* has two meanings: the identity function on individuals and the identity function on functions of type <e,e>. This has little advantage over the variable-ful analogue if these two meanings need to be listed in the lexicon. It would be an accident that pronouns are homophonous in this way (and here too would be needed an infinite number of pronoun meanings as they can be indefinitely complex). But the final step relies on the observation that the paycheck meaning of *her* is nothing more than the **g** operation applied to the ordinary meaning of *her*.[5] To predict the existence of this (and all the other extra meanings), we simply need to generalize the **g-sup** operation to apply not only to ordinary slashes but also superscripts: let an expression of category A^B map to one of category $(A^C)^{B^C}$ with the normal **g** semantics. This generalization was anticipated in the final fragment given at the end of Part III, so readers can consult the **g-sup** rule (R-7) given there to see this formalized. (15) shows that g applied to the ordinary meaning:

(15) $g_{<e,e>}(\lambda f[f]) = \lambda h_{<e,e>}[\lambda y_e[\lambda f[f](h(y))]] = \lambda h_{<e,e>}[\lambda y_e[h(y)]] = \lambda h_{<e,e>}[h]$

All more complex paycheck meanings are just further applications of the **g-sup** rule. Finally, Jacobson (1977) and (2000) detail that paycheck pronouns

---

[5] I owe this important observation to Mark Hepple.

also show WCO effects in just the way that one would expect under either the full NP theory or any variant of the Cooper/Engdahl theory (including the variable-free variant above).

17.3.3. Donkeys

No discussion of pronouns would be complete without at least a brief mention of another unexpected reading for pronouns: the so called *donkey pronouns* as in (16) (Geach 1962):

(16)   Every farmer who owns a donkey beats it.

The actual scope of what goes under the rubric of donkey pronouns varies in different works; here we use the term to refer to cases where the apparent antecedent or binder is indefinite, is in a position which normally cannot bind the relevant pronoun, and where the interpretation of the pronoun co-varies with something else (in this case, with the farmers). Notice that these cannot (in an obvious way) be analyzed as a case where *a donkey* "scopes out" and binds *it* because this gives the wrong meaning. In other words, this cannot be paraphrased as *There exists a donkey such that every farmer who owns it beats it.*

Many authors have argued that these are just another instance of pay-check pronouns. Take, for example, the Cooper/Engdahl analysis sketched above. Indeed Cooper's (1979) proposal was originally designed specifically for the case of donkey pronouns. Thus, using Engdahl's modification of this, the idea is that here too *it* is simply a complex variable such as *f-8 (x-7)* where the individual variable x-7 is bound in the normal way by the subject slot, and the f variable remains free and picks up the contextually salient function mapping each farmer to the donkey that he owns. The translation into the variable-free setting is obvious and proceeds exactly as for the case of any other paycheck pronoun, so for the sake of saving space we will not make that translation here. And the same idea has an obvious analogue under the full NP view; here *it* would simply be short for *the donkey that he owns.*

The well-known difficulty with assimilating donkey pronouns to pay-check pronouns is that there need not be a *unique* donkey owned by each farmer. (16) is (according to many speakers) felicitous in a context where Farmer MacDonald is a mule breeder and hence owns eight donkeys. If *it* is analyzed as *the donkey that he owns*, then (where *he* is understood MacDonald) this should be infelicitous, but many speakers find this fine. And note that while uniqueness with *the* is generally relativized to context (possibly by a domain restriction as part of the meaning of *the*), this fact is not of any help. For (16) can (for many speakers) be felicitously uttered in a context in which no one particular donkey of the mule breeder is salient. An analysis based on the Cooper/Engdahl tradition (whether in variable-free or variable-ful terms) has the same problem. A function, by definition, maps each member of its domain to a unique member of the co-domain, so analyzing this as involving a free function variable or argument slot runs into the same problem: the mapping between farmers and donkeys in (16) need not be function. And for those speakers (including the present author) who actually do find (16) very odd in the above scenario (where a farmer may own multiple donkeys), the problem persists, since other examples make the same point. Thus Heim (1982) constructs an example which illustrates the basic problem but seems impeccable:

(17)   Everyone who bought a sage plant bought nine others to go along with it.

The literature abounds with possible solutions; a number of authors have argued that if one relativizes the interpretation of these sentences to small enough situations, one can indeed maintain that donkey pronouns reduce to paycheck pronouns by finding a unique donkey in (16) and sage plant in (17). (See Heim 1990, Elbourne 2005, and others.) On the other hand, a very different kind of analysis of donkey sentences is found in the related traditions of Discourse Representation Theory (Kamp and Reyle 1993), File Change Semantics (Heim 1982), and Dynamic Semantics (Groenendijk and Stokhof 1991 and many since), all of which enrich the semantics to give an account of the way in which sentences change the context as the discourse proceeds. (See also Barker and Shan 2008 for a different recent account.) And it should be noted that there are a number of other well-known questions with respect to the interpretation of donkey pronouns. For example, in (16) most speakers have the intuition that our mule breeder MacDonald must be a mass donkey abuser and beat every one of his eight donkeys (thus this is making some claim about every farmer–donkey own-ing pair). Yet clearly this requirement is not always there, as shown by the fact that (18) (from Schubert and Pelletier 1989) surely does not have the analogous requirement:

(18)   Everyone who had a quarter put it in the parking meter.

For more discussion, see among others, Kadmon (1987) and Kanazawa (1994). In any case we will leave it open here as to the best analysis of donkey pronouns, noting that the hope would be—with Cooper (1979), Heim (1990), Elbourne (2005), and others—that these can reduce to paycheck pronouns.

17.4. "Hidden variables"

17.4.1. Hidden variables can always be complex

There are many lexical items that have been argued to contain hidden variables as part of their meaning. (Initially we phrase this in variable-ful terms as this once again is expositorily convenient.) This has come up in various places throughout this book: the domain restriction variable with respect to quantificational determiners, the comparison class variable found in adjectives like *tall*, and the numerical standard variable n in the meaning of *many*. There is a striking (although perhaps not entirely surprising) generalization that emerges about these: these can always have the kind of complex readings that we have seen for pronouns and functional gaps. Call this the *paycheck generalization*.

Thus, sticking again for the moment to the terminology of a theory with variables, all of these hidden variables can not only be simple, but can also be variables over functions of some sort applied to an individual variable. Thus call them *paycheck variables*: a paycheck variable consists of an indexed variable F_i of type $<e,z>$ (where z is any type) applied to an indexed individual variable. Then the generalization that appears to emerge is that any time there is a variable of type z as part of the meaning of some expression, it can also be a paycheck variable of the form $F_i(x_j)$. (One might suspect that it can actually be even more complex—this suspicion seems to be correct and will be discussed below.)

Consider first the case of quantifier domain restrictions. Recall from section 10.6 that there are two conceivable explanations for the fact that a GQ like *every student* is interpreted with respect to a given domain. One is that it contains "free variable" of type $<e,t>$ as part of its meaning: [[every student]] is $\lambda P[\text{student'} \cap D_S \subseteq P_S]$. (Recall that, as detailed in section 15.5.1, there must also be some index on each of the free variables, but for the sake of exposition we will consistently suppress the index in the discussion here.) An alternative explanation (see, e.g., Kratzer 2004) rests on the observation that sentences are generally interpreted not with respect to full worlds but smaller situations, and the domain restriction might just be a consequence of this.

While the latter is undoubtedly true, there is an interesting argument that the domain restriction is in any case a part of the meaning of the GQ. (This argument is originally due to von Fintel 1994 and is further discussed in Stanley and Szabo 2000.) This is that the domain restriction can be complex, in the sense discussed above. Consider, for example, (20) in the context set up in (19):[6]

(19) It is well known that the ceramics courses at Brown are quite difficult. One requirement for a student to pass is that she/he must be able to crack a pot with only a nutcracker. And this requirement turns out to be the downfall of many a student. This can be especially worrisome for seniors who might be in danger of not meeting the graduation requirement if they don't pass the class. The Dean of the College always sends a note to all faculty during the year, asking if they have any worries about the (hopefully) graduating seniors in their class. And this year it is a complete mess, for it turns out that:

(20) Every ceramics professor is pretty sure that no senior will successfully complete the pot-cracking requirement.

How is *no senior* interpreted in this context? It of course is not "no senior in the world." Nor is it "no senior at Brown." It is not even "no senior who is taking a ceramics class." For suppose that Tina (a senior) is in Professor Carberry's ceramics class, and another senior Zorro is in Professor Glazie's ceramic class. Professor Carberry might be quite sure that Tina will fail at pot-cracking, but (20) does not require him to have any opinion about how Zorro will do. (Of course, in the scenario at hand, Professor Glazie must feel that Zorro will be incapable of completing the requirement, but Glazie need not have shared this information with Carberry.) Rather, this is interpreted as "no senior in the course of x," where x is bound by *every ceramics professor*. Thus we can represent the meaning of *no senior* as

---

[6] Notice incidentally that positing a "free" variable in these cases would lead us to expect to find cases where it is also bound; it is however difficult to construct convincing cases along these lines probably because there happens not to be the right convergence of properties to find "binding" of something of type <e,t>.

$\lambda P[senior's \cap F_{<e,<e,t>>}(x_e)_S \subseteq P_S]$. As is similar to the case of paycheck pronouns on the Cooper/Engdahl analysis, x ultimately is bound in the normal way that binding happens by the position occupied by *every ceramics professor*, F remains free and picks up the contextually salient function mapping each professor into the set of students in her/his course.

Similar facts can be constructed with *the*. In section 8.3 it was posited that the meaning of *the* is a function of type <<e,t>,e>, but where an NP like *the psychologist* is also interpreted with respect to some domain. Hence the meaning of *the* might be fleshed out as a function from P (of type <e,t>) to the unique (or most salient) member of $P_S \cap D_S$, where D is a free variable of type <e,t> whose value is fixed by context. Interestingly, here too the restriction can be complex and hence best represented as a paycheck variable. Suppose we are at an interdisciplinary conference of linguists and psychologists, with equal numbers of each. In order to achieve maximal cross-talk between the two groups the organizers pair each linguist with a psychologist to talk together at dinner. But it was not successful, for I report this as:

(21) Unfortunately, no linguist felt that the psychologist knew much about language.

Here the meaning of *the psychologist* can be represented as $\iota x[x \in psychologist's \cap R_{<e,<e,t>>}(y)_S]$ where y is bound by *no linguist*, and R remains free and picks up the salient relation of being paired with.

Following some observations of Breheny (2003) (although he was arguing for a different point), one can show that these paycheck domain variables can be even more complex. Let's expand our scenario to a multidisciplinary conference of linguists, philosophers, and psychologists, with an equal number of participants from each field. To maximize interaction among the participants, each linguist is assigned to pour a drink for one and only one philosopher at the party, and also one and only one psychologist. And each philosopher will pour a drink to their assigned linguist and to their assigned psychologist, and similarly for the psychologists. It turns out to be a particularly bad year for jobs for recent PhDs in philosophy. And so the philosophers at the conference—all being philosophers of language—hatch a plot: they decide kill off the linguists, thereby creating some new openings. And so each philosopher serves a poisoned drink to her/his appointed linguist (a foolproof plot, for they can always blame the psychologists for the mass die-off of linguists). But the plot failed: the linguistics figured it out, and alas:

(22) No philosopher managed to get any linguist to actually accept the drink.

What is the domain restriction on *the drink*? Obviously it is not unique in the world, nor the unique drink at the party. Nor can it even be the unique drink relative to each philosopher, for the philosopher also served a drink to a psychologist. Nor can it be the unique drink relative to the linguist, for she also gets a drink from a psychologist (after all, this is what the philosophers are banking on to put the blame on the psychologists). So it must be the drink unique to the pairing of the philosopher and his/her assigned linguist. In other words, the semantics of *the drink* can be represented as $\iota x[x \in \text{drink's} \cap Q_{<e,<e,<e,t>>>}(y)(z)_S]$. z is bound by the subject of *accept*; y is bound by the subject of *manage*; and Q remains free and picks up the salient relation between three individuals and drinks such that for all x,y,z, Q(y)(z)(x) holds if z serves x to y. (The order of placement of these variables in the prose description is arbitrary.)

---

*17.3. Construct a case using a quantificational determiner like *every* or *no* to show that there can be a domain restriction which is complex in the same way as the domain restriction on *the drink* above (i.e., where the domain restriction must be a domain in $<e,<e,<e,t>>>$).

The point can also be made with other cases of "hidden" variables. Take the comparison class for adjectives like *tall*. As noted originally in Kennedy (1997), this too can be complex where it is bound into by the subject slot, as in (23):

(23) All of John's children are tall.

What is the comparison class for *tall* (on the obvious interpretation)? It cannot be everyone in the world, of course. But neither is it all children. Rather it is, for each child, the set of children approximately their own age. Hence in the simple cases we can think of *tall* as meaning "tall for a P_i" (for P_i the ith variable of type $<e,t>$), but it can also mean "tall for a $F_i(x_j)$" for F the ith variable of type $<e,<e,t>>$. In (23), the individual variable x is bound by the subject position in the way binding normally takes place, while the F variable remains free, and picks up the contextually salient function mapping any child to the set of individuals of the same age.

17.4. Construct a case that the "hidden" variable n as part of the meaning of *many* can also be a complex variable of the form $N_i(x_j)$ where N is the ith variable that is a function from individuals to numbers. (We leave it open as to the status of numbers in the theory; we have not formally introduced these as part of the model-theoretic apparatus.)

17.4.2. Translating into variable-free

Strikingly, the paycheck generalization follows immediately once the notion of a hidden variable is translated into the variable-free setting. First as discussed in section 15.5.2, the notion of a "hidden variable" is recast as an argument slot. Take, for example, the case of domain restriction. If it is correct that the meaning of *every* senior encodes the expectation that this will be limited to some domain, this means that [[every senior]] contains an extra argument slot; it is $\lambda Q_{<e,t>}[\lambda P_{<e,t>}[\text{senior's} \cap Q_S \subseteq P_S]]$. Hence, [[every senior]] is of type $<<e,t>,<<e,t>,t>>$ (a function into GQ meanings rather than a pure GQ). And that slot will of course be passed throughout the combinatorics by the normal **g** process. In the end, a sentence like *every senior will fail* is a function from domains to propositions, and the listener supplies this to a contextually salient domain. One additional aspect that must be resolved here concerns the syntax: what is the appropriate super-script feature on the category of *every senior*? Unlike the case of slots that come from the meaning of pronouns, this is less straightforward, since we have no overt pro-form of the appropriate type. For convenience, assume that it is N, so *every senior* actually has category $(S/(S/NP))^N$. (We assume that ultimately the argument slot comes from the meaning of *every* as was shown in section 15.5.2.)

17.5. Show the details of the syntactic and semantic composition of a simple case like *Every student failed* in the context where the domain is understood as something simple, such as the set of students at Brown.

As noted above, the paycheck generalization is automatic, for this slot can be made more complex by application of **g-sup** and can be "bound into" by **z**. (Recall that **g-sup** was generalized in the fragment at the end of Part III to apply to superscript argument positions as well as slash argument positions.) Consider, for example, a slightly trimmed-down version of (20) *Every ceramics professor thinks that no senior will complete the requirement* in the Seniors-Fail-Ceramics scenario. As was worked out (for a parallel case) in Exercise 17.5, *no senior will complete the requirement* is of category S^N with meaning of type $<<e,t>,t>$—it is waiting to find a domain to give a proposition. But it can also map to a fancier meaning and category by **g-sup**. The relevant mapping yields an expression category $(S^{NP})^{(N^{NP})}$. Semantically, this wants a function of type $<e,<e,t>>$ (a two-place relation) to give something that is a function of type $<e,t>$. (Computing the actual meaning is left for the exercise below.) Now consider *think*. Its lexical category is (S/NP)/S, but it can map by **z** to $(S/NP)/S^{NP}$. This is the run-of-the-mill binding rule. But in the case at hand it does not combine with just an S^{NP} but with the more complex category above. This is unproblematic: application of **g-sup** maps this to $(S/NP)^{(N^{NP})}/(S^{NP})^{(N^{NP})}$ and so can take *no senior will complete the requirement* as argument. Lest this seem a mysterious mechanical exercise, the intuition can be summarized as follow. Normally *no senior will complete the requirement* has a domain restriction argument slot (the analogue of a free variable in a variable-ful theory), and this passes all the way up, never being bound, and so in the end is a free slot. But in the scenario at hand, more happens. This maps by **g-sup** to the more complex slot of type $<e,<e,t>>$. The e-position created in that step is ultimately bound by **z** on *think*, and the two-place relation slot just continues to pass up by **g-sup**. So this is quite analogous to the variable-ful treatment where the complex variable has a part which remains free and a part which is bound by the normal binding process. The only difference is that here the complex meaning of the domain restriction is unsurprising, for it follows that it can be made more complex by application of **g-sup**. Fancier examples such as (22) (the philosophers-kill-linguists scenario) are also automatic and simply involve additional applications of the rules.

---

*17.6. Show the full details of the above derivation.

*17.7. Show the syntactic and semantic composition of (46) (in the case where *tall* is restricted to a contextually salient function of type $<e,<e,t>>$). Since expressions like *all of John's children* are not in the fragment, recast this as *every child of John*.

One final case that was treated earlier as a case of a free variable encoded as part of the meaning of an item was the analysis of VPE. Recall that it was posited in section 14.4.2 that an auxiliary like *will* of category VP/VP and of type <<e,t>,<e,t>> could map to a second item which is just a VP and has a meaning *will'(P)*. In the variable-free view this can't be quite right, since it contains crucial use of a free variable. But the necessary revision is obvious; the category of the "ellipsis" *will* is actually VP^{VP} with meaning λP[will'(P)]. Does the paycheck generalization extend to this argument slot as well? Indeed it does: a relevant example is a case like (24):[7]

(24)   Every fourth grade boy$_i$ hopes that the principal won't call his$_i$ mother; but every third grade boy hopes that the principal will.

This is analogous to the sloppy identity cases discussed in section 15.4.1.3, except that here the missing VP is embedded further down. So here we have the elliptical version of *will*, but (as in the case of ACD) it picks up not a function of type <e,t> but rather the two-place relation [[call his mother]] of type <e,<e,t>>. (That [[call his mother]] is of this type follows in the variable-free view because it contains a pronoun; it is the two-place relation λx[λy[y call the mother of x]]. Thus ellipsis-*will* maps to something of category (VP^{NP})$^{(VP^{NP})}$ which is of type <<e,<e,t>>,<e,<e,t>>>. The VP^{NP} superscript passes all the way up by **g-sup**; it is "bound into" by **z** on *hopes*. The reader can fill in the full details.

---

[7] Actually examples of this general sort were discussed in Sag (1976) who thought they were bad, but it has since been shown that the particular examples used by Sag had other problems (see Evans 1988 for discussion).

18

Additional semantic dimensions: The semantics of focus

It is easy to get the idea that the enterprise of formal compositional semantics has little to say about the many subtle nuances expressed linguistically in actual conversational contexts. The propositional content of a sentence—i.e., its truth conditions—is one dimension and certainly a central one. For it is the proposition expressed by a sentence that adds to our understanding of the facts of the world. But speakers use linguistic forms to express many additional aspects of meaning (broadly construed). For example, a speaker can express her attitude towards the proposition (as in *Oh shoot, the puppy just chewed up my students' exams!*) (items like *"oh shoot"* are sometimes called expressives). Another non-truth-conditional kind of meaning is exemplified by a sentence like: *He is a phonologist but he loves model-theoretic semantics*. This suggests that phonologists generally don't love model-theoretic semantics. But is not a matter of truth conditions, for if it turns out that all phonologists love model-theoretic semantics this sentence could still be true. Or, in the case that will be under consideration in this chapter, a sentence like *LARRY loves eels* (with heavy stress on *LARRY*) conveys that there is something at issue as to whether other people love eels. Incidentally, while all three of the examples above involve inferences that are not part of the truth conditions, they also are not conversational implicatures. For here it is the particular linguistic forms—*oh shoot*, *but*, and special stress on *LARRY*—that give rise to the inferences. Hence the role of these forms is part of English speakers' knowledge, and not something that follows just from principles of cooperative conversation. Gricean conversational implicatures, on the other hand, refer to those inferences that follow from general principles of reasoning and/or principles governing cooperative conversation (combined, of course, with the literal meaning of a sentence) and hence not generally taken to be part of the grammatical knowledge of a speaker.[1] The inferences here are crucially tied in to the form, and are sometimes referred to under the rubric of *conventional implicature*: something which is conventionalized but not literally part of the truth conditions.

What this shows is that indeed sentences have more than one dimension as part of their meaning (using "meaning" in a broad sense here). But for at least some of these dimensions, the basic compositional tools developed for the truth-conditional dimension can help elucidate the compositional contribution of the relevant linguistic forms. The contribution of "focal" or "contrastive" stress is the poster child for this point, and so it is to this that we now turn. The discussion will necessarily be brief and incomplete, but hopefully sufficient as to give a flavor of the enterprise.

18.1. Computing alternatives compositionally

The analysis here is based on the seminal work of Rooth (1985), although it departs from Rooth in some detail. Rooth's contribution often goes under the rubric of *alternative semantics*. This does not mean an alternative to the usual view of semantics. Rather, Rooth showed that the role of focal stress is to conjure up a set of alternatives, and he provided a way for these to be computed compositionally.

---

[1] But, as discussed in Chapter 10, n. 4, there are recent works that claim that conversational implicatures are also part of the grammatical computation. See that footnote for references, as well as references to defenses of the Gricean view.

As noted above, focal stress in certain cases contributes nothing to the actual truth conditions of a sentence, yet it does create this additional dimension of meaning. Thus while (1a) and (1b) have the same truth conditions, they are appropriate in different contexts:

(1)   a. COYOTES eat chipmunks.
   b. Coyotes eat CHIPMUNKS.

(In these sentences, *coyotes* and *chipmunks* are not plural common nouns, but are what is known as bare plural NPs; see Carlson 1980.) (1a) is most likely uttered in a context where what is at issue is the question of what sort of animals are chipmunk-eaters; (1b) is more appropriate in a context where what is at issue is the feeding habits of coyotes.

Especially interesting is the fact that focus actually *does* contribute to the truth conditions in some cases. This emerges when sentences like these are embedded in constructions involving so-called *focus-sensitive* words like *only*. Thus take the pairs in (2) and (3) ((3) is considerably less natural but its analysis is simpler and so we will often use this kind of frame in this chapter):

(2)   a. I only believe that COYOTES eat chipmunks.
   b. I only believe that coyotes eat CHIPMUNKS.

(3)   a. It is only the case that COYOTES eat chipmunks.
   b. It is only the case that coyotes eat CHIPMUNKS.

(3a) denies that other relevant animals eat chipmunks while (3b) is entirely neutral on that point. Take, for example, the case of an environmentalist charged with figuring out what is responsible for the declining population of chipmunks in her region. A group of overly zealous homeowners who all love the local chipmunks are thinking that the solution is to thin out the population of wolves and mountain lions. "Not so," says the environmentalist, "It's only the case that COYOTES eat chipmunks." (Of course she probably utters a more colloquial version of (3a).) And so here (3a) entails that the wolves and mountain lions are not preying on the chipmunks. But (3b) has no such entailment. It might instead be uttered by a coyote defender (concerned with the fact that humans seem to feel that the coyote population needs to be thinned) in a context where chipmunks are quite plentiful. The coyote defender can argue against thinning the coyote population by uttering (3b)—here she is committed to the fact that coyotes are not bothering any other species. Thus the meaning of *only* (or, *it is only the case*) is such that it is sensitive to the role of stress. In general, then, the role of this kind of stress is to conjure up a set of alternatives (an intuition which is reflected by the common use of the term *contrastive stress*). Moreover, when embedded under a focus-sensitive word like *only*, those alternatives become relevant to the truth conditions.

In light of this, Rooth (1985) proposed that the meaning of expressions has a second dimension of meaning. In addition to what is known as its *regular semantic value*, it has a *focus value* which is also compositionally computed. From now on, when we wish to distinguish the focus value of a from its regular value, we will use the notation $[[a]]^{REG}$ vs $[[a]]^{FOC}$; we also continue to use $[[a]]$ (and, for that matter, a') interchangeably with $[[a]]^{REG}$ whenever there is no need to distinguish this from the focus value. The focus value of an expression is a set of things of the same kind as the regular value of the expression (and the context will restrict this to relevant alternatives). For a full sentence like *COYOTES eat chipmunks* it is therefore a set of alternative propositions. That the focus value must be compositionally computed is obvious from the fact that the location of the stress is on a single word, but what is at issue is alternative propositions.

Hence, let every linguistic expression (even those containing no focal stress) have these two values. In the case of items with no focal stress, the focus value is simply the singleton set of its regular value. (Having all items have a focus value allows for a smooth compositional computation.) Focused items, on the other hand, have as their value a set of alternatives, where the actual members of the set of alternatives is determined by context. Moreover, one member of the set of alternatives which comprise the focus value will be the regular value of the expression (this is a technical move to make the compositional computation simpler).

Consider then a simple case like (4):

(4)   a. Sally SWIMS.
     b. SALLY swam.

In (4a), the regular value for *Sally* is s, and the focus value is {s}. The regular value for *SWIMS* is swim' and the focus value is a set such as {swim', run', walk', jog'}. (Imagine a context in which what is at issue is how Sally gets her exercise.) In (4b) the regular value of *SALLY* is again s, but here the focus value is {s,b,r, ... }, while $[[swim]]^{REG}$ is swim', but $[[swim]]^{FOC}$ is just {swim'}.

The above gives just the regular and focus values of the lexical items; the interesting step is in how the compositional computation of focus values works. This is quite straightforward: the computation of the focus value always parallels that of the regular value. Take (4a). In the computation of the regular value, $[[SWIM]]^{REG}$ applies to $[[Sally]]^{REG}$. For the focus computation, each member of the focus value of the function applies (one by one) to each member of the focus value of the argument. Thus R-1 can be expanded to include the focus computation as follows (we again use bold-faced curly brackets to indicate the ordered pair of regular and focus values):

R-1-amended: Let α be an expression of the form $<[\alpha], A/B, \{[[\alpha]]^{REG}, [[\alpha]]^{FOC}\}>$ and β be an expression of the form $<[\beta], B, \{[[\beta]]^{REG}, [[\beta]]^{FOC}\}>$. Then there is an expression γ of the form $<[F_{CAT(\alpha)} ([\alpha])([\beta]), A, \{[[\alpha]]^{REG}([[\beta]]^{REG}), \{X| \exists f [f \in [[\alpha]]^{FOC} \& \exists y [y \in [[\beta]]^{FOC} \& X = f(y)]\}\}>$.

Notice that there can be more than one item in a sentence with focal stress. Take for example (5) a context where Farmer MacDonald asks which of his animals will manage to find which of the edible plants in his field:

(5)   PORKY will find the TRUFFLES.

Here the main value is find'(the truffles')(porky') and the focus value is a more complex set of alternative propositions which differ both on the subject and object position. For example, let our relevant set of individuals be {p, el, ey} (Porky the pig, Elsie the cow, and Eeyore the donkey), and our relevant set of edible plants be {t, c, a} (truffles, clover, and arugula). Then the focus value of (5) has nine propositions: {find'(t)(p), find'(t),(el), find'(t),(ey), find'(c)(p), etc.}.[2]

> **18.1.** Show in detail the compositional computation of the focus value for (5) (using the focus value for **PORKY** and for **TRUFFLES** as given above). As usual, ignore *will*.

---

[2] Actually, (5) is ambiguous between a reading in which the effect of the focal stress is to give alternatives to *truffles* and a reading (called broad focus) in which the alternatives are alternatives to the entire VP; thus the focus value of the VP would be something like (using informal prose): {find the truffles, roll in the mud, grunt, ...}. This is discussed in section 18.4.

18.2. The meaning of *only*

What happens with this combines with a focus-sensitive word like *only*? The lexical meaning of *only* is such that it accesses not just the regular value but also the focus value—and so the truth conditions for something like *It is only the case that Sally SWIMS* makes crucial reference to the alternatives. To flesh this out, there are some issues regarding both the syntax and the semantics of *only* that need to be (briefly) dealt with. First, its syntax is complex. *Only* can combine directly with the focused material itself, as in (6):

(6)   a. Only SALLY swims.
      b. Tom saw only SALLY.

But it need not, it can also combine with a VP which contains focused material within it, as in (7):

(7)   a. I only believe that Sally SWIMS.
      b. Coyotes only eat CHIPMUNKS.

The end result of the contribution of *only* in, say, (7b) is (among other things) to assert that none of the alternative propositions are true (i.e., it entails that coyotes don't eat mice or cats or rabbits). This means that its contribution is, in some sense, a sentence-level contribution. The same is true in (6): (6a) denies that Martha swims and that Tom swims. Yet *only* in the syntax does not combine directly with sentences.

By now the Direct Compositional techniques for handling this apparent mismatch should be quite familiar; one can simply "fancy up" the packaging of the meaning of *only* to respect its syntax. But to save space, we will not do this here. Rather, we will take the expositorily convenient tack of pretending that we are dealing with a single word "it is only the case that" which attaches itself to a sentence. (This is analogous to the move made for negation in section 3.4.) Hence we recast (7b) as (3b) given above.

The second point concerns the semantics. Does (3b) (and (7b)) assert that coyotes eat chipmunks, or do these sentences just presuppose this? There is debate in the literature about this, but nothing in the remarks here hinge on the outcome of this debate. The discussion is simplest if we assume that this is part of the assertion rather than a presupposition, but the meaning given below could be revised. In light of this, we now somewhat informally give a "lexical entry" for *it is only the case*:

(8)   *it is only the case*, S/$_R$S, [[it is only the case]] takes both the regular and the focus value of the S that it combines with, and returns true (at a world w and time t) iff [[S]]^{REG} = 1, and $\forall$p[p ϵ [[S]]^{FOC} and p $\neq$ [[S]]^{REG} [p is false (at w and t)]].

Thus prefixing this to a sentence with meaning p (for some proposition) has the effect of asserting that p is true and that all propositions in the focus value which are not p itself are false.[3] Note that (8) is incomplete as it leaves open what is the focus value of a sentence like (3b). Assume here that *it is only the case* also "swallows up" the alternatives, so that the resulting focus value is—as in the case for material with no focused constituents within it— just the singleton set containing the regular value.

Thus the focus value for (1b) *coyotes eat CHIPMUNKS* is the set of propositions of the form (stating these propositions in ordinary English) {coyotes eat chipmunks, coyotes eat beavers, coyotes eat deer, etc.} and the environmentalist asserting (3b) is saying that the first of those propositions is true, but none of the others are.

---

*18.2. Take the occurrence of *only* in (6a). Assume that *only* combines here with *SALLY*, and so is of category GQ/$_R$NP. Give it a meaning such that (6a) is synonymous with *It is only the case that SALLY swims* (under the meaning given for the latter above). In other words, the task is to "fancy up" the meaning of *it is only the case* shown in (8) to allow this to combine directly with the NP, even though its contribution is ultimately to say something about alternative propositions.

Consider now the case of a sentence with more than one focused item, as in (5). As noted above, the alternatives are the set of propositions varying on the set of contextually salient animals (in this case Elsie, Eeyore, and Porky) and contextually salient edible plants (clover, arugula, and truffles).

---

[3] This is a slight oversimplification. A better approximation of the meaning of *only* is such that it negates not all members of the focus value distinct from the main proposition, but rather all members that are not entailed by the main proposition. For example, if it is correct that *four* entails *three* (as would follow if *three* means "at least 3") then we surely don't want to say that *It's only the case that he has taken FOUR linguistics courses* entails that he has not taken three linguistics courses.

Suppose that Farmer MacDonald is concerned about the resourcefulness of his animals: would they be able to survive on their own should he die? He knows that there are good edible plants on his farm, and so to test their survival ability he lets them loose to see what they find. We report the sad outcome of this test:

(9)   Unfortunately, it is only the case that PORKY found the TRUFFLES.

This negates all of the alternative propositions in the focus value of (5), indicating to our altruistic farmer that only Porky will survive and then only if the land is filled with enough[4] truffles.

---

*18.3. Consider (i) in the same scenario:

(i) Unfortunately, only PORKY found TRUFFLES.

This can (at least for some speakers) have the same value as (9), and can be used to report that no other animal found any of the other edible plants. Does this follow from your answer to Exercise 18.2? If not, revise that so that it does follow.[4] You may want to try to do this informally.

18.3. Additional focus-sensitive words

Only is not the only lexical item sensitive to the focus value of the expression with which it combines. Among the other focus-sensitive words are *also* (and its variants such as *too*) and *even*. Consider the pair in (10):

(10)   a. It's also the case that DENISE snowboards.
      b. It's also the case that Denise SNOWBOARDS.

(10a) presupposes that someone else snowboards. If presupposition failure is a matter of a sentence having no truth value, then the "lexical entry" for *it is also the case* can be written informally as follows:

---

[4] This judgment was disputed by an anonymous referee, but has been checked with many speakers so perhaps there is some speaker variation here. Another instance of this with a different scenario can be found in Jacobson (2012).

(11)   it is also the case that, $S/_R S$,

$[[\text{it-is-also-the-case-that-S}]]$ = 1 if $[[S]]^{\text{REG}}$ =1 and $\exists p[p \neq [[S]]^{\text{REG}}$ & $p \in [[S]]^{\text{FOC}}$;

$[[\text{it-is-also-the-case-that-S}]]$ = 0 if $[[S]]^{\text{REG}}$ = 0 and $\exists p[p \neq [[S]]^{\text{REG}}$ & $p \in [[S]]^{\text{FOC}}$;

$[[\text{it-is-also-the-case-that-s}]]$ is undefined otherwise.

(Of course a different treatment of presupposition would require modifying (11) in the appropriate way.)

Even is even more interesting (pun intended). A sentence like *It's even the case that BALTIMORE beat the Red Sox* requires some way to rank the alternative propositions in the focus value of *BALTIMORE beat the Red Sox* on a scale—perhaps a scale of likelihood. Moreover, it presupposes or at least implies that all of the propositions which are lower-ranked are true, and it asserts that the ordinary value of *BALTIMORE beat the Red Sox* is true. The exact nature of the types of scales required by *even* has been the subject of considerable research; see, e.g., Kay (1990) for interesting work on this.

18.4. Further compositional issues

There are two further issues about the compositional semantics of focus values that we mention here without solution, as the goal is just to whet the reader's appetite to pursue this further. First, the computation of the alternatives in the focus value need not start with the actual item that is stressed. In a context in which I am at my vacation house in New Hampshire after a snowstorm and someone asks me what I did this morning I can answer (12):

(12)   I spent the morning shoveling SNOW.

Most likely in this context what is at issue is surely not alternative substances that I might have been shoveling. Rather, the focus value in the relevant context is a set like {I spent the morning writing my textbook; I spent the morning cross-country skiing; I spent the morning shoveling snow}. In other words, the focus is really on the entire VP *shoveling snow*, but the rules of English prosody are such that the actual stress needs to land on one word, and so it lands on *snow*. This is called *broad focus*. The set-up in this chapter does not account for the broad-focus interpretation and so additional principles effecting a mapping between the actual prosody and the computation of alternatives are needed. For some discussion, see Selkirk (1984), but note that this is not embedded in a kind of Direct Compositional architecture and allows the grammar to crucially refer to trees. Thus a detailed account of the mapping between the prosody and the contribution of focus is an interesting project for the Direct Compositional program.

The second issue concerns what is known as *second occurrence focus*. (5) (the Porky/truffle case) is a case where more than one item has focal stress, and (9) shows what can happen when such a sentence combines with *it is only the case*. Here we set up the Concerned Farmer MacDonald scenario, which supported a reading in which the effect of *it is only the case* was to negate all of the alternatives. But *only* (or its more verbose counterpart *it is only the case that*) can also "swallow up" just one of the items in focus, while the other remains active and is thus available for additional focus-sensitive items. The sentences and scenarios are sufficiently complex that using the circumlocutious *it is only/also the case* only makes things worse, so we illustrate with the more natural uses of *only* and *also*. Thus let us return to Farmer MacDonald. This time his concern is that all of the edible plants except the arugula on his farm will be killed in a severe drought brought on by global warming. As a result, he is training all of his animals to get used to eating only arugula. Then we can say:

(13) a. Farmer MacDonald has begun to feed only ARUGULA to Elsie.
  b. He's also begun to feed only ARUGULA to EEYORE.

ARUGULA in (13b) is in small capital letters to indicate that it does not receive the same phonological prominence as *EEYORE*, but it does receive some (see Rooth 1996 for discussion of the actual acoustics here).

Note first that ARUGULA is what gives rise to the alternatives that *only* in (13b) is sensitive to. Assume that *also* has scope over *only* (as both the semantics and the word order would suggest). Then here *only* "swallows up" the alternative propositions that are introduced by the prosodic focus on *ARUGULA* but it cannot have the effect of saying that the only plant-fed-to-animal pair is arugula to Eeyore. After all, (13a) asserts (or presupposes) that MacDonald feeds arugula to Elsie as well. (And (13b) itself presupposes that MacDonald feeds arugula to some other animal.) Hence here the compositional contribution of *only* is to negate alternatives such as {Mac-Donald feeds truffles to Eeyore, MacDonald feeds clover to Eeyore, ... }, saying nothing about the other animals. Then role of *also* is to introduce the presupposition (satisfied in virtue of (13a)) that indeed there is a true proposition of the form "Mac feeds only arugula to x" for some x besides Eeyore. The key point, then, is that the alternatives stemming from focal stress on *EEYORE* have to still be active after *only* has made its contribution, and these are then relevant to the contribution of *also*.

Another example to bring this out can be constructed with *even*. Here we add the fact that donkeys are well known to be quite adverse to arugula. We can then follow (13a) with (13c), where the role of *even* is parallel to that discussed above for *also*:

(13) c. He has even begun to feed only ARUGULA to EEYORE.

This means that the compositional computation of a sentence with two foci must sometimes make a kind of nested focus where one focus-sensitive word operates on one set of alternatives, and another on the alternatives to those alternatives. We leave it open here as to how to accomplish this. Incidentally, the same remarks hold if we replace *also*, *even*, and *only* with their more verbose counterparts *it is only/also/even the case that*. This means that the phenomenon demonstrated is not tied to the fact that *only* in (13b) and (13c) forms a constituent with *ARUGULA*; the reader can construct the relevant examples.

18.5. Focus and binding

Section 15.4.1 showed that the pronoun in (14) can have the understanding shown there either by being a free pronoun or a bound pronoun.

(14)   Jack$_i$ called his$_i$ mother.

One piece of evidence for this was the existence of both the strict and the sloppy reading with VP Ellipsis, as in (15) (see the discussion in section 15.4.1.3):

(15)   Jack$_i$ called his$_i$ mother and Bill did too.

Similar facts emerge with focus.[5] Thus note that focal stress on *JACK* in (16) conjures up two different kinds of alternative sets:

(16)   JACK$_i$ called his$_i$ mother.

One possibility is that what is at issue is what other boys called their own mothers (call this the bound, sloppy, or co-varying reading). This emerges

---

[5] It is well known that there are a number of similarities between ellipsis and focus; see Rooth (1992) for some relevant discussion.

naturally in the Mothers' Day Scenario of section 15.4.1.3. The other is the "free" reading—i.e., what is at issue is who else called Jack's mother; this emerges in the Hospitalized Mother scenario. As one might expect, one can even more clearly bring out the two readings by embedding (16) *it is only the case that*, where the two readings are truth-conditionally distinct:

(17)   It is only the case that JACK$_i$ called his$_i$ mother.

It is worth considering how the accounts of binding given in Chapter 15 can be folded in with the account of focus to explicitly predict this. We will work this through in the variable-free account, leaving it as an exercise for the reader (in 18.4) to work through the details in the LF account.

   Before considering the bound or co-varying reading, a word is necessary about the focus values of expressions containing free pronouns in the variable-free setting. In other words, consider first a simple case like (18) where *him* is simply a free pronoun:

(18)   NORA called him.

The details of the compositional computation are beyond the scope of this work, but a reasonable guess is that the focus value of (18) will be a function from individuals to alternative propositions. In other words, the focus value of (18) is a function of the form $\lambda x[\{$nora called x, sally called x, macdonald called x, ... $\}]$. Like with the regular value of an expression with a free pronoun, this will be applied by the listener to some contextually salient individual which ultimately gives the set of alternative propositions of relevance. Thus if the pronoun in (16) is not bound, the focus value of (16) is the set of alternatives $\lambda x[\{$Jack Sprat called x's mother, Billy called x's mother, Tom Thumb called x's mother ... $\}]$. Applying this to the contextually salient Jack gives the relevant free reading.[6]

   The bound reading is also straightforward (under any theory of binding), as long as we continue to assume that the computation of the focus value of any sentence always parallels the computation of its regular value. Thus one way to arrive at the relevant understanding (of the regular value) of (16) is via application of **z** to *call*. The result of this is that **z**-*call his mother* is the set of self-mother-callers, which then takes [[Jack]] as argument. The focus

---

[6]   More needs to be said as something is needed to ensure that the individual taken as argument of the regular value is the same as the one taken as argument of the focus value. See Jacobson (2012) for details.

value of the lexical item *call* is just {call'}. But since the focus computation exactly parallels the regular computation, this means that when this maps to $z(call')$ in the computation of the regular value, exactly the same will happen in the focus value. *his mother* is the mother-of function; and so the focus value of *call his mother* will be {$z(call')(the-mother-of')$}, still a singleton set. But because $[[JACK]]^{FOC}$ is a set like {j, b, s, ...}, the focus value of *JACK called his mother* will be the set {j z-called the-mother-of, b z-called the-mother-of, s z-called the-mother-of, ...}. And this is just what we want for the bound or co-varying reading of (16). (17) is straightforward; *it is only the case* combines with this, and hence the regular value of (17) asserts that Jack is a self's mother-caller, and says that none of the other propositions in the focus value of (16) is true.

18.4. Work through the analysis of (16) on the bound reading using the LF theory of pronominal binding (section 15.2), while still maintaining the basic set-up for focus computation given here. (Note that that set-up is neutral with respect to the issue of how to do binding.)

18.6. More generally: Multidimensional semantics

The computation of alternatives and the way in which they interact with focus-sensitive words like *only* is, as noted earlier, the poster child for the notion that the compositional rules can compute more than one dimension simultaneously. But the focus value is not the only dimension that has been explored in this regard. In a classic paper, Karttunen and Peters (1979) proposed that presuppositions and what are known as conventional implicatures can also be computed compositionally in parallel with the "main semantic" value of a sentence. (A conventional implicature is an inference that is tied to linguistic form—such as the implicatures associated with *but*—and hence not derived by Gricean principles, but which does not appear to be part of the truth conditions.) For some discussion of multidimensional semantics, see Potts (2005).

19

Intensionality and the syntax/semantics interface

A chapter on intensionality could either be very long or very short. The long chapter (which should really be at least a book) would include a rich discussion both of lexical semantics and of issues about how natural languages carve up the dimensions of times and the space of possible worlds. For the lexical meanings of words which crucially combine with *intensions* give us a window into the latter domain. For example, a sentence like *It must be raining* appears to involve some sort of universal quantification over worlds, but surely it is not saying that it is raining in all possible worlds (that would make it a logical necessity that it is raining). Rather it says that it is raining in all worlds in some subset of worlds—perhaps all those compatible with the speakers' beliefs. Other modal auxiliaries access other sets of worlds. (One can think about this for any of the following cases: *She can lift 150 pounds*; *It can sometimes snow in May*; *He should take five courses this semester*, etc. See Kratzer 2012 for rich discussion of the semantics of some modal auxiliaries.) Other words that make crucial reference to some set of worlds as part of their meaning are those verbs known as *propositional attitude* verbs. As the name implies, these indicate the subject's attitude towards some proposition and include *think, believe, hope*, etc. As noted in Exercise 4.2, even such ordinary words as *bachelor* arguably encode a modal dimension (i.e., refer to other possible worlds), and as pointed out in section 2.3.4 ordinary grammatical devices as the progressive construction also make reference to possible worlds. And there are many words and morphemes whose meanings crucially combine with items of type $<i,x>$ for some x—i.e. words whose meanings include something about times. The past-tense morpheme is one such obvious example.

But this will be a short chapter. We give just a few examples of words which crucially are sensitive to the intension of expressions with which they combine, and then comment on the ways in which the fragment needs revision to take this into account.

19.1. Intensionality-sensitive words

First consider a verb like *think*, as in (1):

(1)   Sarah thinks that the world's largest bell weighs 800 pounds.

For convenience, we have been treating *think'* as of type $<t,<e,t>>$ (with frequent reminders that this is oversimplified). The reason that *think'* cannot really be just of type $<t,<e,t>>$ is that this would make it a function from {1,0} to (the characteristic function of) a set of individuals. But Sarah is not having some thought about 1 or 0, but rather a proposition. So in reality, *think'* is (ignoring times) of type $<<w,t>,<e,t>>$. To assert (1) is to assert that the set of worlds consistent with Sarah's beliefs is a subset of the worlds in which the proposition "the world's largest bell weighs 800 pounds" is true. Note incidentally that this particular way of putting it assumes that Sarah need not have a single world in her belief state. Presumably there are many propositions about which she has no opinion and so the object of someone's beliefs is a set of possible worlds. Thus *think'* combines with a proposition p (a set of worlds), and returns the set of individuals x such that for each x, the set of worlds in their belief state is a subset of p. That the set of worlds compatible with the relevant individuals' beliefs is only a subset of p is easy to see, for p includes, for example, worlds in which the bell sentence is true and Porky found Farmer MacDonald's arugula as well as other worlds in which the bell sentence is true and Porky failed the arugula test. Sarah might believe that Porky failed and that the bell sentence is true, and thus her belief worlds are only a subset of those where the bell sentence is true.

What this means is that the fragment must be revised, for the full **app** rule (R-1) was formulated to have the function combine with the *extension* of the expression that it takes as argument. Before making the necessary revision, let's give the meaning of a few other words that are sensitive to intensions. First, take one which is sensitive to times—a classic example is *former* (as in *former senator*). This is of category N/$_R$N. Notice thought that (unlike ordinary adjectives such as *tall* and *red*) it has no predicative counterpart:

(2)   *That senator is former.

This is hardly surprising; the semantics for predicative adjectives in section 8.1 takes the individual denoted by the subject and says it is in the set characterized by the adjective. But it makes no sense to speak of the set of *former* things; one is former only with respect to some other set. For this reason, the prenominal version is obviously not intersective in the sense that *red* or even *tall* is (recall the semantics of R-2 (**mod**) which is responsible for the prenominal versions of *tall* and *red*, and recall the discussion in section 8.4 justifying the claim that *tall* is intersective. To show that *former* is not intersective, we can note not only that there is no set of things that are "former," but also that a *former senator* is not a senator (unlike a *tall senator*). Hence prenominal *former* is not derived by R-2 from a predicative version; it is just listed in the lexicon as N/N.

> ***19.1.** This fact actually introduces a wrinkle into the fragment so far. Single-word nominal modifiers are exceptional in their directional feature, and this was handled by a clause regarding the output of R-2 (**mod**) which treats single-word outputs in an exceptional way. Comment on why the behavior of *former* creates a problem for this account, and on a possible way or ways to solve this.

What about the meaning of *former*? As it combines with a time-dependent set to give a time-dependent set, its meaning is as follows:

(3) $[[former]] = \lambda P_{<i,<e,t>>}[\lambda i[\lambda x[\exists i'[i' < i \;\&\; P(x)(i') \;\&\; \sim P(x)(i)]]]]$

In prose: this takes a time-dependent set P and returns a function that maps an individual x to true at a time i if there is an earlier time i' at which x was in P and x is no longer in P.

19.2. If one describes Tim as now being *a former former senator*, it must be the case that Tim is now a senator. Show exactly why this inference follows, given the definition in (3).

Former is sensitive to intensions in the sense of combining with time-dependent sets. Other prenominal modifiers of this sort include *future* (*a future astronaut*), perhaps *past* (though the range of nouns that *past* can combine with seems rather limited), and a few others whose meaning is more complex and arguably contains a hidden variable or argument slot as part of their meaning; see the following exercise.

*19.3. Thus note the following sentence, and comment on its implications for the analysis of the meaning of *previous* (and for the issues discussed in section 17.4).

(i) Every class begins with a review of the previous class.

There are also a few prenominal adjectives sensitive not necessarily to times but to worlds. A nice example is the word *wannabe* which might be unfamiliar to some readers as it is a reasonably recent coinage (1980s according to some online sources) and may be best-known in American English. (But to a reader unfamiliar with this word, do not worry, for we will actually define it.) Examples are in (4):

(4)   a. The wannabe drill sergeant spent hours and hours in the gym doing pushups.
   b. Every syntactician is a wannabe semanticist.

While there might be some additional implicatures associated with this word at least a rough approximation to its meaning is in (5) (we ignore the temporal parameter here):

(5) $\lambda P_{<w,<e,t>>}[\lambda w[\lambda x[\forall w'$ [w' in set of want-worlds of x in w, $P(w')(x)]]]]$

Not surprisingly, *wannabe* cannot be used predicatively:

(6)   *The semanticist/drill sergeant is wannabe.

(Although *wannabe* has by now also shifted to a noun such that *a wannabe* is now a predicative noun, with perhaps an understood noun argument slot as in "You've become a wannabe," from <http://www.copyblogger.com/are-you-a-wannabe/>).

---

*19.4. Most of the clearly non-intersective adjectives (such as *former*, *future*, *wannabe*, etc.) do not have predicative forms, as we would expect. But there is at least one whose behavior is puzzling. Thus a *fake gun* is necessarily not an actual gun, yet (i) is perfectly fine:

(i) That gun is fake.

But notice also the existence of expressions like *toy gun*, *water gun*, and—most interestingly—*real gun* (along with *That gun is real*). While the first two are noun compounds and might have frozen meanings, it is still the case that these—and in particular *real gun*—suggests that part of the solution might lie in there being an extended meaning of *gun*. (Note that this is not limited to *gun*; cf. *fake Christmas tree*.) Elaborate on this, and suggest a possible meaning for *fake* if this is correct. Most interestingly, discuss the semantic composition of (ii) (recalling relevant discussion from Chapter 17):

(ii) Everything in that store is fake.

This question is meant to be entirely open-ended and is an invitation to speculation; don't expect to necessarily find a tidy answer.

19.5. Write out a meaning for the auxiliary *will*, as in (i):

(i) The Red Sox will beat the Yankees.

The task here is to think of this purely as a "future operator" (there might well be additional aspects to the meaning of *will* brought out in other contexts, but these can be ignored here). Note though that one does need some notion of the structure of time. Assume that time is a set of discrete points ordered by a relation < (earlier than).

19.2. Revising the fragment: Type-sensitive rules

Once intensionality is folded in, the combinatory and unary rules given in Appendices to Parts I–III are in need of some revision. Before delving into this, we will for simplicity fold the worlds and times in together as has been done in various sections in this book, and continue to use s for the set of world/time pairs. Now consider the **app** rule. Most of the cases considered in this book involved the application of a function to the *extension* of its argument. Hence recall that R-1—the **app** rule—was formulated for this. In the fragment as spelled out in the Appendices it is given extensionally, but the full version that is needed for most of the material up until this chapter would be INT-R-1 as follows:

INT-R-1. If a is an expression of the form $<[a], A/B, a'>$ and β is an expression of the form $<[\beta], B, \beta'>$ then there is an expression γ of the form $<F_{CAT(a)}([a])([\beta]), A, \lambda w[a'(w)(\beta'(w))]>$.

This is a perfectly straightforward revision. The problem is that it is not always correct—for all of the cases considered above involve cases where a function applies to the *intension* and not the *extension* of the expression with which it combines. The syntax looks exactly the same either way. Thus *former* and the prenominal modifier *tall* are both of category $N/_R N$, but the first applies to the intension of *senator* in *former senator* and the latter to the extension (in *tall senator*). So the semantic composition is not always a transparent reflection of the syntactic composition.

There are (at least) two conceivable solutions. The first is the one taken in Montague (1973) which a reader who has carefully followed the various Montagovian solutions mentioned throughout might be able to guess. Keep the semantic composition uniform and simple, and put the complexity in the lexical entries. In other words, this strategy is to revise R-1 so that a function *always* applies to an intension. But those words that "really" want only extensions do so by building this fact into their lexical meaning. Take, for example, *grunt*, whose meaning we have been assuming is of type $<s<e,t>>$. Montague's suggestion to keep the combinatorics completely uniform is to revise this so that its meaning is of type $<s,<<s,e>,t>>$. Call *grunt*' the "ordinary" grunt function—i.e., the function that maps all grunters to 1 and non-grunters to 0. Then one can recast [[grunt]] as what we will call *grunt'-*$_{MONT}$ as follows: $\lambda s[\lambda X_{<s,e>}[grunt*'(s)(X(s))]]$. This can then apply to the intension of *the truffle-loving pig* and the lexical meaning ensures that ultimately the actual grunt function is applied to the extension of that NP at the world in question.

This is a possible strategy, and it will mean that all of the other rules in our fragment need only minor modification. But it is a trade-off: while keeping the rules simple and elegant it seems (to many modern researchers) to be a rather heavy-handed approach to lexical meaning. The second solution, which is more in keeping with the more "modern" thinking on such things, is to keep the lexical meanings simpler but simply make R-1 slightly more complex. Indeed, the strategy is simply to use a version of the notion of type-driven interpretation. Recall (see the discussion in section 6.5) that this was originally proposed in Klein and Sag as a means of allowing the semantic side of the syntactic combinatory rules to be predictable from the semantic types of the combining expressions. For the most part this was not needed in the CG fragment here because the rules themselves are stated extremely generally. Later this idea was imported into non-Direct Compositional frameworks as a way of predicting just what semantic operation will interpret a mother node in a tree on the basis of the types of its daughter(s). (See especially Heim and Kratzer 1998.) But here we will reintroduce this notion as a way to predict when intensions are crucial. The basic idea is simple and obvious: if a function asks for an extension, it gets an extension; if it asks for an intension, it gets an intension. To make this precise, we simply define the semantic operation *app* as follows:

(7)   Type-sensitive *app*:
   i. If a' is of type $<s,<a,b>>$ (for a $\neq$ $<s,x>$ for some x), and β' is of type $<s,a>$, then $app(a'(\beta')) = \lambda s[a'(s)(\beta'(s))]$.
   ii If a' is of type $<s,<<s,a>,b>>$ and β' is of type $<s,a>$, then $app(a'(\beta')) = \lambda s[a'(s)(\beta')]$.

This, however, is not quite enough, as we need to revise some of the other rules to also take into account intensions and operate in a type-driven way. Note first that all of the rules need minor "tweaking" in that they apply to expressions whose actual values are always intensional objects; i.e., their values are of type $<s,a>$ (for some a), while the rules were formulated purely extensionally. For the most part these revisions are straightforward and the reader can supply the details. (The strategy is quite similar to the strategy seen earlier of having rules ignore argument positions in the semantics that correspond to superscript positions in the syntax.) But some of the rules also need to be stated in a type-sensitive way, as they will need to be sensitive to the distinction between extensions and intensions. We give just one example, which is the lift rule (*l*). If *senator* is lifted from its basic meaning to combine with a modifier like *former* it must do so in a different way than when it combines with *tall*. Hence we restate *l* as follows:

(8) Type-sensitive *l*:
  i. Take any expression a of type <s,a>. Then **ext-l**(a') is a function of type <s,<a,b>,b> such that **ext-l**(a') = $\lambda s[\lambda f_{<a,b>}[f(a'(s))]]$.
  ii Take any expression a of type <s,a>. Then **int-l**(a') is a function of type <s,<<s,a>,b>,b> such that **int-l**(a') = $\lambda s[\lambda f_{<a,b>}[f(a')]]$.

Either version of *l* can apply to *senator*, but only the intensional lift in (ii) will yield an output that can take *former* as argument.

   Ultimately one would hope to avoid separate statements for each of the rules that need to be recast and to have very general statements governing the intensional versions of all the rules, but this will not be attempted here. We will, however, note one other possible way to revise the earlier fragment. Recall that the strategy of having the closed-class items denote constant functions was motivated by giving a uniform type and combinatorics for everything. The Montagovian strategy noted just above of course takes this to the extreme. But if it is correct to depart in any case from that strategy, one might rethink this treatment of the closed-class items, and have them merely have extensions. One might, then, add a further type-sensitive version of **app** as follows:

   iii. If a' is of type <a,b> (for a $\neq$ s), and β' is of type <s,a>, then **app**(a'(β')) = $\lambda s[a'(\beta'(s))]$.

So, for example, a case-marking preposition like *of* can be taken to be just the identity function over individuals (i.e., of type <e,e> and not of type <s,<e,e>>); if it combines with *the fastest skier* (of type <s,e>) it does so by (iii) above (the result is that *of the fastest skier* will have the same meaning as *the fastest skier*). Of course if this strategy is correct, additional principles will be needed to fill out the full system. In the end, the trade-off between simplifying the lexical entries and potentially complicating the various rules will depend on just exactly how the latter are stated and how generally this can be done.

This will not be attempted here. We leave this as a project for any interested reader, along with many of the other suggestions and open questions that have emerged throughout this text. And of course there are vast areas of natural language semantics (including cross-linguistic work) not even touched in this book. But we hope to have given the reader the background, tools, and—most importantly—the appetite to delve into this endlessly rich territory.

References

AJDUKIEWICZ, KAZIMERZ. 1935. Die syntaktische Konnexität. *Studia Philosophica* 1: 1–27.

ANDERSON, ALAN. 1951. A note on subjunctive and counterfactual conditionals. *Analysis* 12: 35–8.

BACH, EMMON. 1968. Nouns and noun phrases. In E. Bach and R. Harms (eds), *Universals in Linguistic Theory*. New York: Holt, Rinehart and Winston, 90–122.

BACH, EMMON. 1979. Control in Montague grammar. *Linguistic Inquiry* 10: 515–31.

BACH, EMMON. 1980. In defense of passive. *Linguistics and Philosophy* 3: 297–341.

BACH, EMMON and ROBIN COOPER. 1978. The NP-S analysis of relative clauses and compositional semantics. *Linguistics and Philosophy* 2: 145–50.

BACH, EMMON, ELOISE JELINEK, ANGELIKA KRATZER, and BARBARA PARTEE (eds). 1995. *Quantification in Natural Languages*. Dordrecht: Kluwer.

BARKER, CHRIS. 1995. *Possessive Descriptions*. Stanford: CSLI.

BARKER, CHRIS. 2001. Introducing continuations. In R. Hastings, B. Jackson, and Z. Zvolenszky (eds), *SALT XI: Proceedings of the Eleventh Conference on Semantics and Linguistic Theory*. Ithaca: CLC, 20–35.

BARKER, CHRIS and CHUNG-CHIEH SHAN. 2008. Donkey anaphora is in-scope binding. *Semantics and Pragmatics* 1: 1–42.

BARSS, ANDREW and HOWARD LASNIK. 1986. A note on anaphora and double objects. *Linguistic Inquiry* 17: 347–54.

BARWISE, JON and ROBIN COOPER. 1981. Generalized quantifiers and natural language. *Linguistics and Philosophy* 4: 159–219.

BAYER, SAMUEL. 1996. The coordination of unlike categories. *Language* 72: 579–616.

BENNETT, MICHAEL. 1974. *Some extensions of a Montague fragment of English*. PhD dissertation, UCLA.

BOLINGER, DWIGHT. 1967. Adjectives in English: Attribution and predication. *Lingua* 18: 1–34.

BOUTON, LAWRENCE. 1970. Antecedent-contained pro-forms. In M. Campbell, J. Lindholm, A. Davison, W. Fisher, L. Furbee, J. Lovins, E. Maxwell, J. Reighard, and S. Straight (eds), *Papers from the Sixth Regional Meeting of the Chicago Linguistic Society*. Chicago: Chicago Linguistic Society, 154–67.

BREHENY, RICHARD. 2003. A lexical account of implicit (bound) contextual dependence. In R. Young and Y. Zhou (eds), *SALT XIII: Proceedings of the Thirteenth Conference on Semantics and Linguistic Theory*. Ithaca: CLC, 37–54.

BRESNAN, JOAN and JANE GRIMSHAW. 1978. The syntax of free relatives in English. *Linguistic Inquiry* 9: 331–91.

CARLSON, GREGORY. 1980. *Reference to Kinds in English*. New York: Garland.

CARLSON, GREGORY. 1981. The distribution of free-choice *any*. In R. Hendrick, C. Masek, and M. Miller (eds), *Papers from the Seventeenth Regional Meeting of the Chicago Linguistic Society*. Chicago: Chicago Linguistic Society, 8–23.

CARPENTER, BOB. 1998. *Type-Logical Semantics*. Cambridge, MA: MIT Press.

CHIERCHIA, GENNARO. 1991. Functional WH and weak crossover. In D. Bates (ed.), *Proceedings of the Tenth West Coast Conference on Formal Linguistics*. Stanford: CSLI, 75–90.

CHIERCHIA, GENNARO. 2004. Scalar implicatures, polarity phenomena, and the syntax/ pragmatics interface. In A. Belletti (ed.), *Structures and Beyond, Volume 3: The Cartography of Syntactic Structures*. Oxford: Oxford University Press, 39–103.

CHIERCHIA, GENNARO, DANNY FOX, and BENJAMIN SPECTOR. 2012. The grammatical view of scalar implicatures and the relationship between semantics and pragmatics. In P. Portner, C. Malenborn, and K. von Heusinger (eds), *Semantics: An International Handbook of Natural Language Meaning, Volume 3*. Berlin: Mouton de Gruyter, 2297–332.

CHIERCHIA, GENNARO and SALLY MCCONNELL-GINET. 1990. *Meaning and Grammar: An Introduction to Semantics*. Cambridge, MA: MIT Press.

CHOMSKY, NOAM. 1957. *Syntactic Structures*. The Hague: Mouton.

CHOMSKY, NOAM. 1965. *Aspects of the Theory of Syntax*. Cambridge, MA: MIT Press.

CHOMSKY, NOAM. 1970. Deep structure, surface structure and semantic interpretation. In D. Steinberg and L. Jakobovits (eds), *Semantics*. Cambridge: Cambridge University Press, 183–214.

CHOMSKY, NOAM. 1976. Conditions on rules of grammar. *Linguistic Analysis* 2: 303–51.

CHOMSKY, NOAM. 1977. On wh-movement. In P. W. Culicover, T. Wasow, and A. Akmajian (eds), *Formal Syntax*. New York: Academic Press, 71–132.

CHOMSKY, NOAM. 1981. *Lectures on Government and Binding*. Holland: Foris Publications.

COOPER, ROBIN. 1979. The interpretation of pronouns. In F. Heny and H. Schnelle (eds), *Syntax and Semantics, Volume 10: Selections from the Third Groningen Round Table*. New York: Academic Press, 61–92.

CORMACK, ANNABEL. 1984. VP anaphora: Variables and scope. In F. Landman and F. Veltman (eds), *Varieties of Formal Semantics*. Dordrecht: Foris Publications, 81–102.

CURRY, HASKELL AND ROBERT FEYS. 1958. *Combinatory Logic, Volume 1*. Amsterdam: North Holland.

DAYAL, VENEETA. 1995. Licensing any in non-negative/non-modal context. In M. Simons and T. Galloway (eds), *SALT V: Proceedings of the Fifth Conference on Semantics and Linguistic Theory*. Ithaca: CLC, 72–93.

DOWNING, PAMELA. 1977. On the creation and use of English compound nouns. *Language* 53: 810–42.

DOWTY, DAVID. 1979. *Word Meaning and Montague Grammar*. Dordrecht: Kluwer.

DOWTY, DAVID. 1982. Grammatical relations and Montague grammar. In P. Jacobson and G. Pullum (eds), *The Nature of Syntactic Representation*. Dordrecht: Reidel, 79–130.

DOWTY, DAVID. 1988. Type-raising, functional composition, and non-constituent coordination. In R. Oehrle, E. Bach, and D. Wheeler (eds), *Categorial Grammars and Natural Language Structures*. Dordrecht: Kluwer, 153–98.

DOWTY, DAVID. 1992. Variable-free syntax, variable-binding syntax, the natural deduction Lambek calculus, and the crossover constraint. In J. Mead (ed.), *Proceedings of the Eleventh West Coast Conference on Formal Linguistics*. Stanford: CSLI, 161–76.

DOWTY, DAVID, ROBERT WALL, and STANLEY PETERS. 1981. *Introduction to Montague Semantics*. Dordrecht: D. Reidel.

ELBOURNE, PAUL. 2005. *Situations and Individuals*. Cambridge, MA: MIT Press.

EMONDS, JOSEPH. 1976. *A Transformational Approach to Syntax: Root, Structure-Preserving, and Local Transformations*. New York: Academic Press.

ENGDAHL, ELISABET. 1986. *Constituent Questions: The Syntax and Semantics of Questions with Special Reference to Swedish*. Dordrecht: Reidel.

ENGDAHL, ELISABET. 1988. Relational interpretation. In R. Kempson (ed.), *Mental Representations: The Interface between Language and Reality*. Cambridge: Cambridge University Press, 63–82.

EVANS, FREDERIC. 1988. Binding into anaphoric verb phrases. In J. Powers and K. de Jong (eds), *Proceedings of the Fifth Annual Eastern States Conference on Linguistics*. Columbus: Ohio State University, 122–9.

EVANS, GARETH. 1980. Pronouns and variables. *Linguistic Inquiry* 11: 337–62.

FAUCONNIER, GILLES. 1975. Pragmatic scales and logical structure. *Linguistic Inquiry* 6: 353–75.

VON FINTEL, KAI. 1994. *Restrictions on quantifier domains*. PhD dissertation, University of Massachusetts.

VON FINTEL, KAI. 1999. NPI licensing, Strawson entailment, and context dependency. *Journal of Semantics* 16: 97–148.

FOX, DANNY. 2002. Antecedent-contained deletion and the copy theory of movement. *Linguistic Inquiry* 33: 63–96.

FOX, DANNY. 2003. On logical form. In R. Hendrick (ed.), *Minimalist Syntax*. Oxford: Blackwell, 82–123.

FOX, DANNY. 2007. Free choice disjunction and the theory of scalar implicatures. In U. Sauerland and P. Stateva (eds), *Presupposition and Implicature in Compositional Semantics*. New York: Palgrave Macmillan, 71–120.

FOX, DANNY and JON NISSENBAUM. 1999. Extraposition and scope: A case for overt qr. In S. Bird, A. Carnie, J. Haugen, and P. Norquest (eds), *Proceedings of the*

Eighteenth West Coast Conference on Formal Linguistics. Somerville, MA: Cascadilla Press, 132–44.

FRAZIER, LYN. 1978. *On comprehending sentences: Syntactic parsing strategies*. PhD dissertation, University of Connecticut.

GAZDAR, GERALD. 1982. Phrase structure grammar. In P. Jacobson and G. Pullum (eds), *The Nature of Syntactic Representation*. Dordrecht: Kluwer, 131–86.

GAZDAR, GERALD, EWAN KLEIN, GEOFFREY PULLUM, and IVAN SAG. 1985. *Generalized Phrase Structure Grammar*. Oxford: Blackwell and Cambridge, MA: Harvard University Press.

GAZDAR, GERALD and IVAN SAG. 1981. Passive and reflexives in phrase structure grammar. In J. Groenendijk, T. Janssen, and M. Stokhof (eds), *Formal Methods in the Study of Language*. Amsterdam: Mathematical Centre Tracts, 131–52.

GEACH, PETER T. 1962. *Reference and Generality: An Examination of Some Medieval and Modern Theories*. Ithaca: Cornell University Press.

GEACH, PETER T. 1970. A program for syntax. *Synthese* 22: 3–17.

GEURTS, BART. 2009. Scalar implicature and local pragmatics. *Mind and Language* 24: 51–79.

GIANNAKIDOU, ANASTASIA. 1997. *The landscape of polarity items*. PhD dissertation, University of Groningen.

GRICE, H. PAUL. 1975. Logic and conversation. In P. Cole and J. Morgan (eds), *Syntax and Semantics, Volume 3: Speech Acts*. New York: Academic Press, 41–58.

GRIMSHAW, JANE. 1982. Subcategorization and grammatical relations. In A. Zaenen (ed.), *Subjects and Other Subjects*. Bloomington, IN: Indiana University Linguistics Club, 35–55.

GROENENDIJK, JEROEN and MARTIN STOKHOF. 1984. *Studies on the semantics of questions and the pragmatics of answers*. PhD dissertation, University of Amsterdam.

GROENENDIJK, JEROEN and MARTIN STOKHOF. 1991. Dynamic predicate logic. *Linguistics and Philosophy*, 14: 39–100.

HAMBLIN, C. L. 1973. Questions in Montague English. *Foundations of Language* 10: 41–53.

HANKAMER, JORGE and IVAN SAG. 1984. Toward a theory of anaphoric processing. *Linguistics and Philosophy* 7: 325–45.

HAYES, BRUCE and MAY ABAD. 1989. Reduplication and syllabification in Ilokano. *Lingua* 30: 331–74.

HEIM, IRENE. 1982. *The semantics of definite and indefinite noun phrases*. PhD dissertation, University of Massachusetts.

HEIM, IRENE. 1990. E-type pronouns and donkey anaphora. *Linguistics and Philosophy* 13: 137–77.

HEIM, IRENE and ANGELIKA KRATZER. 1998. *Semantics in Generative Grammar*. Oxford: Blackwell.

HENDRIKS, HERMAN. 1993. *Studied flexibility: Categories and types in syntax and semantics.* PhD dissertation, University of Amsterdam.

HEPPLE, MARK. 1990. *The grammar and processing of order and dependency: A categorial approach.* PhD dissertation, University of Edinburgh.

HORN, LAURENCE. 1972. *On the semantic properties of logical operators in English.* PhD dissertation, UCLA.

HORN, LAURENCE. 1989. *A Natural History of Negation.* Chicago: University of Chicago Press.

HORN, LAURENCE. 2004. Implicature. In L. Horn and G. Ward (eds), *The Handbook of Pragmatics.* Oxford: Blackwell, 3–28.

HUYBREGTS, RINY. 1976. Overlapping dependencies in Dutch. *Utrecht Working Papers in Linguistics* 1: 24–65.

JACKENDOFF, RAY. 1972. *Semantic Interpretation in Generative Grammar.* Cambridge, MA: MIT Press.

JACOBS, RODERICK and PETER ROSENBAUM. 1968. *English Transformational Grammar.* Waltham, MA: Xerox College Publishing.

JACOBSON, PAULINE. 1977. *The syntax of crossing coreference sentences.* PhD dissertation, University of California at Berkeley (published by Garland Press, New York, 1980).

JACOBSON, PAULINE. 1983. *On the Syntax and Semantics of Multiple Relatives in English.* Bloomington, IN: Indiana University Linguistics Club.

JACOBSON, PAULINE. 1987. Phrase structure, grammatical relations, and discontinuous constituents. In A. Ojeda and G. Huck (eds), *Syntax and Semantics, Volume 20: Discontinuous Constituency.* New York: Academic Press, 27–69.

JACOBSON, PAULINE. 1992. Antecedent contained deletion in a variable-free semantics. In C. Barker and D. Dowty (eds), *SALT II: Proceedings of the Second Conference on Semantics and Linguistic Theory.* Columbus: Ohio State University, 193–213.

JACOBSON, PAULINE. 1993. i-within-i effects in a variable-free semantics and a categorial syntax. In P. Dekker and M. Stokhof (eds), *Proceedings of the Ninth Amsterdam Colloquium.* Amsterdam: ILLC, University of Amsterdam, 349–68.

JACOBSON, PAULINE. 1998. Antecedent-contained deletion and pied-piping: Evidence for a variable-free semantics. In D. Strolovitch and A. Lawson (eds), *SALT VIII: Proceedings of the Eighth Conference on Semantics and Linguistic Theory.* Ithaca: CLC, 74–91.

JACOBSON, PAULINE. 1999. Towards a variable-free semantics. *Linguistics and Philosophy* 22: 117–85.

JACOBSON, PAULINE. 2000. Paycheck pronouns, Bach-Peters sentences, and variable-free semantics. *Natural Language Semantics* 8: 77–155.

JACOBSON, PAULINE. 2003. Binding without pronouns (and pronouns without binding). In G. J. Kruiff and R. Oehrle (eds), *Binding and Resource Sensitivity.* Dordrecht: Kluwer, 57–96.

JACOBSON, PAULINE. 2007. Direct compositionality and variable-free semantics: The case of "Principle B" effects. In P. Jacobson and C. Barker (eds), *Direct Compositionality*. Oxford: Oxford University Press, 191–236.

JACOBSON, PAULINE. 2008. Direct compositionality and variable-free semantics: The case of antecedent-contained deletion. In K. Johnson (ed.), *Topics in Ellipsis*. Cambridge: Cambridge University Press, 30–68.

JACOBSON, PAULINE. 2012. Direct compositionality and "uninterpretability": The case of (sometimes) "uninterpretable" features on pronouns. *Journal of Semantics* 29: 305–43.

JÄGER, GERHARD. 1996. *Topics in Dynamic Semantics*. PhD dissertation, Humboldt University.

KADMON, NIRIT. 1987. *On unique and non-unique reference and asymmetric quantification*. PhD dissertation, University of Massachusetts. (Published by Garland Press, New York, 1993.)

KADMON, NIRIT and FRED LANDMAN. 1993. Any. *Linguistics and Philosophy* 16: 353–422.

KAMP, HANS and UWE REYLE. 1993. *From Discourse to Logic: Introduction to Model-Theoretic Semantics of Natural Language, Formal Logic and Discourse Representation Theory*. Dordrecht: Kluwer.

KANAZAWA, MAKOTO. 1994. Weak vs. strong readings of donkey sentences and monotonicity inferences in a dynamic setting. *Linguistics and Philosophy* 17: 109–58.

KARTTUNEN, LAURI. 1969. Pronouns and variables. In R. Binnick, A. Davison, G. Green, and J. Morgan (eds), *Proceedings of the Fifth Regional Meeting of the Chicago Linguistic Society*. Chicago: Chicago Linguistic Society, 108–16.

KARTTUNEN, LAURI. 1971. Definite descriptions with crossing coreference. *Foundations of Language* 7: 157–82.

KARTTUNEN, LAURI. 1977. Syntax and semantics of questions. *Linguistics and Philosophy* 1: 3–44.

KARTTUNEN, LAURI and STANLEY PETERS. 1979. Conventional implicature. In C.-K. Oh and D. A. Dinneen (eds), *Syntax and Semantics 11: Presupposition*. New York: Academic Press, 1–56.

KATZ, JERROLD and JERRY FODOR. 1963. The structure of a semantic theory. *Language* 39: 170–210.

KAY, PAUL. 1990. Even. *Linguistics and Philosophy* 13: 59–111.

KAYNE, RICHARD. 1984. *Connectedness and Binary Branching*. Dordrecht: Foris Publications.

KEENAN, EDWARD. 1971. Names, quantifiers, and a solution to the sloppy identity problem. *Papers in Linguistics* 4: 1–22.

KEENAN, EDWARD and LEONARD FALTZ. 1985. *Boolean Semantics for Natural Language*. Dordrecht: Reidel.

KEENAN, EDWARD and JONATHAN STAVI. 1986. A semantic characterization of natural language determiners. *Linguistics and Philosophy* 9: 253–326.

KENNEDY, CHRISTOPHER. 1997. *Projecting the adjective: The syntax and semantics of gradability and comparison*. PhD dissertation, University of California at Santa Cruz. (Published by Garland Press, New York, 1999.)

KENNEDY, CHRISTOPHER. 2007. Vagueness and grammar: The semantics of relative and absolute gradable adjectives. *Linguistics and Philosophy* 30: 1–45.

KLEIN, EWAN and IVAN SAG. 1985. Type-driven translation. *Linguistics and Philosophy* 8: 163–201.

KLIMA, EDWARD. 1964. Negation in English. In J. FODOR and J. KATZ (eds), *The Structure of Language*. Englewood Cliffs, NJ: Prentice Hall, 246–323.

KLUENDER, ROBERT. 1998. On the distinction between strong and weak islands: A processing perspective. In P. Culicover and L. McNally (eds), *Syntax and Semantics, Volume 29: The Limits of Syntax*. New York: Academic Press, 241–80.

KRATZER, ANGELIKA. 1986. Conditionals. In A. Farley, P. Farley, and K. McCollough (eds), *Papers from the Parasession on Pragmatics and Grammatical Theory*. Chicago: Chicago Linguistic Society, 115–35.

KRATZER, ANGELIKA. 1998. More structural analogies between pronouns and tenses. In D. Strolovitch and A. Lawson (eds), *SALT VIII: Proceedings of the Eighth Conference on Semantics and Linguistic Theory*. Ithaca: CLC, 92–109.

KRATZER, ANGELIKA. 2004. Covert quantifier restrictions in natural language. Presentation accessible at: <semanticsarchive.net/Archive/mIzMGUyZ/Covert%20Quantifier%20Domain%20Restrictions.pdf>.

KRATZER, ANGELIKA. 2012. *Modals and Conditionals*. Oxford: Oxford University Press.

KRIFKA, MANFRED. 1995. The semantics and pragmatics of polarity items. *Linguistic Analysis* 25: 209–57.

KRIPKE, SAUL. 1980. *Naming and Necessity*. Cambridge, MA: Harvard University Press.

KUNO, SUSUMU. 1975. Three perspectives in the functional approach to syntax. In R. Grossman, L. J. San, and T. Vance (eds), *Papers from the Parasession on Functionalism*. Chicago: Chicago Linguistic Society, 276–336.

LADUSAW, WILLIAM. 1979. *Polarity sensitivity as inherent scope relations*. PhD dissertation, University of Texas, Austin.

LAHIRI, UTPAL. 1998. Focus and negative polarity in Hindi. *Natural Language Semantics* 6: 57–123.

LAKOFF, GEORGE. 1971. On generative semantics. In D. Steinberg and L. Jakobovits (eds), *Semantics*. Cambridge: Cambridge University Press, 232–96.

LAKOFF, GEORGE and STANLEY PETERS. 1969. Phrasal conjunction and symmetric predicates. In D. Reibel and S. Schane (eds), *Modern Studies in English: Readings in Transformational Grammar*. Englewood Cliffs, NJ: Prentice-Hall, 113–42.

LAMBEK, JOACHIM. 1958. The mathematics of sentence structure. *The American Mathematical Monthly* 65: 154–70.

LANGACKER, RONALD. 1969. On pronominalization and the chain of command. In D. Reibel and S. Schane (eds), *Modern Studies in English*. Englewood Cliffs, NJ: Prentice-Hall, 160–86.

LARSON, RICHARD. 1988. On the double object construction. *Linguistic Inquiry* 19: 335–91.

LASNIK, HOWARD. 1976. Remarks on coreference. *Linguistic Analysis* 2: 1–22.

LEVINSON, STEPHEN. 1983. *Pragmatics*. Cambridge: Cambridge University Press.

LEVINSON, STEPHEN. 2000. *Presumptive Meanings: The Theory of Generalized Conversational Implicature*. Cambridge, MA: MIT Press.

LEWIS, DAVID. 1970. General semantics. *Synthese* 22: 18–67.

LINEBARGER, MARCIA. 1987. Negative polarity and grammatical representation. *Linguistics and Philosophy* 10: 325–87.

LINK, GODEHARD. 1983. The logical analysis of plurals and mass terms: A lattice-theoretical approach. In R. Bauerle, C. Schwartze, and A. von Stechow (eds), *Meaning, Use, and the Interpretation of Language*. Berlin: de Gruyter, 302–23.

MAY, ROBERT. 1977. *The grammar of quantification*. PhD dissertation, MIT.

MAY, ROBERT. 1985. *Logical Form: Its Structure and Derivation*. Cambridge, MA: MIT Press.

McCAWLEY, JAMES. 1971. Where do noun phrases come from? In D. Steinberg and L. Jakobovits (eds), *Semantics*. Cambridge: Cambridge University Press, 217–31.

McCAWLEY, JAMES. 1987. Some additional evidence for discontinuity. In G. Huck and A. Ojeda (eds), *Syntax and Semantics, Volume 20: Discontinuous Constituency*. New York: Academic Press, 185–200.

MERCHANT, JASON. 2001. *The Syntax of Silence: Sluicing, Islands, and the Theory of Ellipsis*. Oxford: Oxford University Press.

MITCHELL, JONATHAN. 1986. *The formal semantics of point of view*. PhD dissertation, University of Massachusetts.

MONTAGUE, RICHARD. 1970. English as a formal language. In B. Visentini et al. (eds), *Linguaggi Nella Societá e Nella Tecnica*. Milan: Edizioni di Communita, 188–221.

MONTAGUE, RICHARD. 1973. The proper treatment of quantification in ordinary English. In K. J. J. Hintikka, J. M. E. Moravcsik, and P. Suppes (eds), *Approaches to Natural Language: Proceedings of the 1970 Stanford Workshop on Grammar and Semantics*. Dordrecht: Reidel, 221–42.

MOORTGAT, MICHAEL. 1997. Categorial type logics. In J. van Benthem and A. ter Meulen (eds), *Handbook of Logic and Language*. Amsterdam: Elsevier, 95–179.

MORRILL, GLYN. 1994. *Type-Logical Grammar: Categorial Logic of Signs*. Dordrecht: Kluwer Academic.

MUNN, ALAN. 1993. *Topics in the syntax and semantics of coordinate structures*. PhD dissertation, University of Maryland.

OEHRLE, RICHARD. 1976. *The grammatical status of the English dative alternation.* PhD dissertation, MIT.

OEHRLE, RICHARD. 1990. Categorial frameworks, coordination, and extraction. In A. Halpern (ed.), *Proceedings of the Ninth West Coast Conference on Formal Linguistics.* Stanford: CSLI, 411–25.

PARSONS, TERENCE. 1990. *Events in the Semantics of English.* Cambridge, MA: MIT Press.

PARTEE, BARBARA. 1973. Some transformational extensions of Montague grammar. *Journal of Philosophical Logic* 2: 509–34.

PARTEE, BARBARA. 1975a. Montague grammar and transformational grammar. *Linguistic Inquiry* 6: 203–300.

PARTEE, BARBARA. 1975b. Deletion and variable binding. In E. Keenan (ed.), *Formal Semantics of Natural Languages.* Cambridge: Cambridge University Press, 16–34.

PARTEE, BARBARA. 1984. Nominal and temporal anaphora. *Linguistics and Philosophy* 7: 243–86.

PARTEE, BARBARA. 1989a. Many quantifiers. In J. Powers and K. De Jong (eds), *Proceedings of the Fifth Eastern States Conference on Linguistics.* Columbus: Ohio State University, 383–402.

PARTEE, BARBARA. 1989b. Binding implicit variables in quantified contexts. In C. Wiltshire, R. Graczyk, and B. Music (eds), *Proceedings of the Twenty-Fifth Regional Meeting of the Chicago Linguistic Society.* Chicago: Chicago Linguistic Society, 342–65.

PARTEE, BARBARA. forthcoming. *A History of Formal Semantics.* Oxford: Oxford University Press.

PARTEE, BARBARA and VLADIMIR BORSCHEV. 2003. Genitives, relational nouns, and argument-modifier ambiguity. In E. Lang, C. Maienborn, and C. Fabricius-Hansen (eds), *Modifying Adjuncts.* Berlin: de Gruyter, 67–112.

PARTEE, BARBARA and MATS ROOTH. 1983. Generalized conjunction and type ambiguity. In R. Bäuerle, C. Schwarze, and A. von Stechow (eds), *Meaning, Use and Interpretation of Language.* Berlin: Walter de Gruyter, 361–83.

POLLARD, CARL. 1984. *Generalized phrase structure grammars, head grammars, and natural language.* PhD dissertation, Stanford University.

POLLARD, CARL and IVAN SAG. 1994. *Head-Driven Phrase Structure Grammar.* Chicago: University of Chicago Press.

POPE, EMILY. 1971. Answers to yes–no questions. *Linguistic Inquiry* 2: 69–82.

POSTAL, PAUL. 1966. On so-called "pronouns" in English. In F. Dinneen (ed.), *Report of the Seventeenth Annual Round Table Meeting on Linguistics and Language Studies.* Washington, DC: Georgetown University Press, 177–206.

POSTAL, PAUL. 1970. On coreferential complement subject deletion. *Linguistic Inquiry* 1: 439–500.

POSTAL, PAUL. 1971. *Cross-over Phenomena.* New York: Holt, Rinehart and Winston.

POSTAL, PAUL. 1974. On certain ambiguities. *Linguistic Inquiry* 5: 367–424.

POTTS, CHRISTOPHER. 2005. *The Logic of Conventional Implicature*. Oxford: Oxford University Press.

QUINE, WILLARD. 1960. Variables explained away. *Proceedings of the American Philosophical Society* 104: 343–7.

REINHART, TANYA. 1983. *Anaphora and Semantic Interpretation*. London: Croom Helm.

ROOTH, MATS. 1985. *Association with focus*. PhD dissertation, University of Massachusetts.

ROOTH, MATS. 1992. Ellipsis redundancy and reduction redundancy. In S. Berman and A. Hestik (eds), *Proceedings of the Stuttgart Ellipsis Workshop*. Stuttgart: University of Stuttgart, 1–26.

ROOTH, MATS. 1996. On the interface principles for intonational focus. In T. Galloway and J. Spence (eds), *SALT VI: Proceedings of Sixth Conference on Semantics and Linguistic Theory*. Ithaca: CLC, 202–26.

ROSS, JOHN. 1967. Constraints on variables in syntax. Cambridge, MA: MIT Press.

ROSS, JOHN. 1969. On the cyclic nature of English pronominalization. In D. Reibel and S. Schane (eds), *Modern Studies in English*. Englewood Cliffs, NJ: Prentice-Hall, 187–200.

RUSSELL, BENJAMIN. 2006. Against grammatical computation of scalar implicatures. *Journal of Semantics* 23: 361–82.

RUSSELL, BERTRAND. 1905. On denoting. *Mind* 14: 479–93.

SAG, IVAN. 1976. *Deletion and logical form*. PhD dissertation, MIT.

SCHÖNFINKEL, MOSES. 1924. Über die bausteine der mathematischen logik. *Mathematische Annalen* 92: 305–16.

SCHUBERT, LENHART and FRANCIS JEFFRY PELLETIER. 1989. Generically speaking, or using discourse representation theory to interpret generics. In G. Chierchia, B. Partee, and R. Turner (eds), *Properties, Types, and Meaning, Volume II: Semantic Issues*. Dordrecht: Kluwer, 193–268.

SELKIRK, ELISABETH. 1984. *Phonology and Syntax: The Relation between Sound and Structure*. Cambridge: MIT Press.

SHAN, CHUNG-CHIEH and CHRIS BARKER. 2006. Explaining crossover and superiority as left-to-right evaluation. *Linguistics and Philosophy* 29: 91–134.

SHARVIT, YAEL. 1998. Possessive wh-expressions and reconstruction. In P. Tamanji and K. Kusumoto (eds), *Proceedings of the Twenty-Eighth Meeting of the North Eastern Linguistic Society*. Amherst: GLSA, 409–23.

SHIEBER, STUART. 1985. Evidence against the context-freeness of natural language. *Linguistics and Philosophy* 8: 333–43.

SMITH, CARLOTA. 1969. Ambiguous sentences with "and." In D. Reibel and S. Schane (eds), *Modern Studies in English: Readings in Transformational Grammar*. Englewood Cliffs, NJ: Prentice Hall, 75–9.

STALNAKER, ROBERT. 1968. A theory of conditionals. In N. Rescher (ed.), *Studies in Logical Theory*. Oxford: Oxford University Press, 98–112.

STALNAKER, ROBERT and RICHMOND THOMASON. 1973. A semantic theory of adverbs. *Linguistic Inquiry* 4: 195–220.

STANLEY, JASON and ZOLTAN SZABO. 2000. On quantifier domain restriction. *Mind and Language* 15: 219–61.

VON STECHOW, ARNIM. 1990. Layered traces. Paper presented at the 40th Conference on Language and Logic. Revfülöp, Hungary.

STEEDMAN, MARK. 1987. Combinatory grammars and parasitic gaps. *Natural Language and Linguistic Theory* 5: 403–39.

STEEDMAN, MARK. 1996. *Surface Structure and Interpretation*. Cambridge, MA: MIT Press.

STOCKWELL, ROBERT, PAUL SCHACHTER, and BARBARA PARTEE. 1972. *The Major Syntactic Structures of English*. New York: Holt, Rinehart, and Winston.

STORTO, GIANLUCA. 2000. On the structure of indefinite possessives. In B. Jackson and T. Matthews (eds), *SALT X: Proceedings of the Tenth Conference on Semantics and Linguistic Theory*. Ithaca: CLC, 203–20.

STOWELL, TIM. 1981. *Origins of phrase structure*. PhD dissertation, MIT.

STOWELL, TIM. 1983. Subjects across categories. *The Linguistic Review* 2: 258–312.

STRAWSON, PETER F. 1950. On referring. *Mind* 59: 320–44.

DE SWART, HENRIETTE. 1998. Licensing of negative polarity items under inverse scope. *Lingua* 105: 175–200.

SZABOLCSI, ANNA. 1987. Bound variables in syntax: Are there any? In J. Groenendijk et al. (eds), *Proceedings of the Sixth Amsterdam Colloquium*. Amsterdam: ITLI, University of Amsterdam, 331–53.

SZABOLCSI, ANNA. 1992. Combinatory categorial grammar and projection from the lexicon. In I. Sag and A. Szabolcsi (eds), *Lexical Matters*. Stanford: CSLI, 241–68.

WASOW, THOMAS. 1972. *Anaphoric relations in English*. PhD dissertation, MIT.

WILLIAMS, EDWIN. 1978. Across-the-board rule application. *Linguistic Inquiry* 9: 31–43.

WINTER, YOAD. 1995. Syncategorematic conjunction and structured meanings. In M. Simons and T. Galloway (eds), *SALT V: Proceedings of the Fifth Conference on Semantics and Linguistic Theory*. Ithaca: CLC, 387–404.

ZWARTS, FRANS. 1998. Three types of polarity. In F. Hamm and E. Hinrichs (eds), *Plural Quantification*. Dordrecht: Kluwer, 177–238.

Index